Traumatic Encounters in Italian Film

Locating the Cinematic Unconscious

By Fabio Vighi

Traumatic Encounters in Italian Film
Locating the Cinematic Unconscious

By Fabio Vighi

intellect
Bristol, UK
Portland, OR, USA

First Published in the UK in 2006 by
Intellect Books, PO Box 862, Bristol BS99 1DE, UK

First published in the USA in 2006 by
Intellect Books, ISBS, 920 NE 58th Ave. Suite 300, Portland, Oregon
97213-3786, USA

A catalogue record for this book is available from the British Library

Cover Design: Gabriel Solomons
Copy Editor: Holly Spradling
Typesetting: Mac Style, Nafferton, E. Yorkshire

ISBN 1-84150-140-9

Printed and bound in Great Britain by 4edge Ltd.

CONTENTS

Acknowledgements

First I wish to express my gratitude to the *Arts and Humanities Research Council* (AHRC), as without their support I would never have been able to complete this monograph as expeditiously as I did. I am also indebted to Geoffrey Nowell-Smith for his precious words of advice, to May of *Intellect* for her assistance, and to Mat for his contribution as copy-editor. I would also like to thank Antonis (Gus), César (Boludo) and Andrés (Fafà) for always distracting me from my writing at the right time, and especially Heiko, whose intellectual energy and contagious enthusiasm I enjoy in the Lacanian sense of the term! I must also acknowledge those students who in recent years have taken my courses on cinema at Cardiff University, for they have often acted, unconsciously perhaps, as a "silent cause" of my fascination with film. Finally, a special thanks to Alice, for all those reasons one should never even try to understand.

Acknowledgement is here made to Rai Cinema, British Film Institute and Centro Studi "Archivio Pier Paolo Pasolini", as well as to the distributors of the films whose images have been used in this book.

Previous versions of some materials of this volume have appeared as the following publications: 'Lacan for cinema today: the uncanny *pouvoir de la vérité*' (*Psychoanalysis, Culture and Society*, vol. 10 n. 1, 2005); 'Encounters in the real: subjectivity and its excess in Roberto Rossellini' (Studies in European Cinema, vol. 1, n. 3, 2004); 'Pasolini and Exclusion: Žižek, Agamben and the Modern Sub-Proletariat' (*Theory, Culture and Society*, vol. 5, n. 20, 2003); Unravelling Moretti's (political) unconscious: the abyss of the subject in *La stanza del figlio* (*Journal of Romance Studies*, vol. 3, n. 2.)

INTRODUCTION

In the last sequence of Bernardo Bertolucci's cerebral puzzle *La strategia del ragno* (The Spider's Stratagem, 1970), Athos Magnani Jr (Giulio Brogi), the film's protagonist, is at the train station preparing to leave Tara, his hometown. He had arrived at that same train station a few days earlier, determined to discover the truth about his father's mysterious assassination, more than 30 years before. An anti-fascist fighter, Athos Magnani Sr (also played by Giulio Brogi) had allegedly been killed by an unidentified fascist sniper in the town's opera house during a performance of Verdi's *Rigoletto*, and had since been celebrated as a legendary and unsurpassed hero by the inhabitants of Tara. However, by the time he decides to leave, the son has been exposed to a devastating truth: his father was not murdered by the enemy but had instead consciously *staged* his own assassination after betraying a plot to kill Benito Mussolini, so that he would be idealised as an anti-fascist martyr. His comrades, not the fascists, had killed him... Alone in the sun-beaten station, pale and forlorn, Athos hears from the loudspeaker that his train is ten minutes late. The delay increases to twenty minutes, then half an hour, and so on, until he decides to set off on foot along the railway line. As he walks away the camera closes in on the tracks showing them covered in long grass, a clear signal that no train could have passed through Tara for weeks, or perhaps even longer.

This final image of the grass eclipsing the railway tracks functions as a cinematic figuration of the explosive character of the Lacanian unconscious – the central topic in this book – for it is an image that retroactively erases the narrative framework within which we attempt to decipher the meaning of the film. The symbolic search for the father comes to a stalemate that first bewilders the son and then brings him to the verge of madness, whilst simultaneously causing the narrative to implode. More to the point: if no train has passed through Tara for weeks, then the initial return of the son is recast as an event that *could not have happened*, or could only have happened in a radically changed temporal dimension. And is not this impossibility the real target of Bertolucci's narrative? The very fact that the father is eventually portrayed as an impostor is a logical consequence of this narrative deadlock, in as much as Magnani Sr comes to embody the failure of his symbolic role, a notion here clearly suspended on the abyss of its own cause. To paraphrase the film's title, by the end of the journey the father's stratagem is fully exposed, its web of fictions blatantly revealed. The brave son accomplishes his mission precisely by deconstructing the meaning of paternal authority into its incongruous conflation of heroism and cowardice, fiction and void.

Strategia del ragno

The son's approach to the enigmatic cause of the father's death – the kernel where the truth about the father is situated – slowly reveals that the film is less a chronologically coherent narrative than an attempt to visualise the surreal spectacle of the unconscious. Bertolucci's strategy comes to full fruition with the conclusive scene at the deserted railway station, as we realise that Tara was always a fantasmatic place disconnected from our perception of space and time, providing an ideal figurative backdrop to the director's endeavour to project the unconscious onto the silver screen.[1] This final close-up on the grass engulfing the railway, therefore, signals the definitive failure of interpretation, the limit dimension where truth and void overlap. However, Lacanian psychoanalysis tells us that it is precisely through these failures that interpretation paradoxically succeeds, since the target of the analysis is the kernel of non-sense that demarcates the unconscious: 'The fact that I have said that the effect of interpretation is to isolate in the subject a kernel, a *kern*, to use Freud's own term, of *non-sense*, does not mean that interpretation is in itself nonsense' (Lacan, 1998a, p. 250). Thus, it would seem that in *La strategia del ragno* Bertolucci successfully establishes a figurative link with the unconscious.

Yet, as I shall further develop in the final pages of the present study, this conclusion is far from satisfactory. Founded as it is upon the awareness of Bertolucci's manipulation of the viewer's expectations through a deliberate deployment of psychoanalytic theory, the above reading misses the most profound structural function played by what in this book, drawing on Jacques Lacan and Slavoj Žižek,[2] I theorise as the cinematic unconscious. For if in Lacanian terms the unconscious of film can only be defined as a paradoxical *knowledge that does not know itself*, this knowledge will be completely detached from the symbolic signification(s) that a film might wish to attain or with which it is critically authorised. Ultimately, this is why the unconscious of film can only come about as a traumatic encounter with the disavowed core of cinematic representation.

Mario Monicelli's classic comedy caper *I soliti ignoti* (Persons Unknown, 1958) presents us with a charming demonstration of the logic that sustains the rapport between film and its displaced underside. The narrative is structured around a pawnbroker's safe, which functions as the proverbial object of desire for a small gang of amateur thieves from Rome's periphery. One fateful night, after a number of hilarious escapades leading up to the big hit, everything seems to be ready for the plan to be executed. Thanks to an ingenious ploy the improbable gang manage to penetrate the living room of the flat adjacent to the pawnshop. Unfortunately, however, as a result of a crucial topological miscalculation they set about drilling the wrong wall, which means that instead of reaching the pawnshop they find themselves in that very flat's kitchen. The allure of this moment of truth is encapsulated in the shot of the wall as it is finally broken through: instead of the anxiously awaited treasure (the safe), the hole in the wall reveals to the mystified thieves the bedraggled figure of Capannelle (Carlo Pisacane), the eldest member of the gang, who in the meantime had meandered into the kitchen looking for a glass of water. In psychoanalytic terms the brilliantly disguised shot of the other side of the wall tells us that the true object of desire belongs in the unconscious, for the latter is *the place where we already are* but which nevertheless *cannot fail to appear as an utterly foreign location*. In Lacan, desire is always sustained by a secret liaison with void, whose unexpected manifestation is coterminous with what we might call a "truth-effect". What is true in the climactic sequence of the drilling of the wall is the shocking encounter with the empty kernel of the thieves' desire: instead of the empirical "thing" (the safe with the loot) they get *the form* of the object itself, i.e. the reference to void that had set in motion and nourished their desire up until that moment.

The following scene is emblematic of the way in which the traumatised subject attempts to regain a minimum of symbolic balance. Languishing in a condition of utter dejection, the unfortunate thieves come across some *pasta e ceci* (pasta and chick-peas, a traditional Italian dish), which unwittingly offers them a chance to salvage the situation. They warm up the food, sit down at the kitchen table, and start eating as if they had just met for an informal meal, even discussing the single merits of the dish (too much oil, slightly overcooked, etc.). Apart from the comical emphasis on the way in which trauma is overcome, what needs to be underlined here is the resurfacing of the central and constantly disavowed element of the narrative: hunger as absence (of food), and as such the real object of desire. In a way, therefore, the thieves do get to the core of their desire. When we say that the true object of desire belongs in the unconscious this also means that it cannot be reached directly – that we hit the target only by missing what we are consciously aiming for.

As these two brief critical samples demonstrate, this study is structured around the assumption that a film does not attest to the power of teleology, that is to say, of a given (conscious) message to achieve its goal and fulfil its purpose. One of its alternative subtitles could well have been the Lacanian motto "a letter always arrives at its destination". As Žižek (2001b, pp. 9–23) has convincingly argued, this multi-faceted motto essentially means that the true message of any linguistic act is to be sought in the displaced and often imperceptible materialisations of senseless enjoyment (*jouissance*) which parasitise the communicative field, bearing witness to the fact that our very symbolic existence (the way we engage with the world and relate to others) is irredeemably stained by an excess of desire, the traumatic substance that Lacan calls the Real. This book is indeed full of letters that uncannily arrive at their destination, carrying the unbearable weight of an unconscious message: the letter that Lidia reads to Giovanni at the end of Antonioni's *La notte* (The Night, 1961); the letter ripped apart and never delivered by Mario, the dreamer, in Visconti's *Le notti bianche* (White Nights, 1957); the secret letters exchanged by Andrea and Arianna in Moretti's *La stanza del figlio* (The Son's Room, 2001) – to mention but a few. Ultimately, the object of my investigation is the *jouissance* secreted by film, which implies that cinematic communication is always skewed and tainted, always the effect of some kind of misunderstanding. The lack of faith in *telos* related to the very presence of unconscious *jouissance* does not, however, lead me to embrace a sceptical (deconstructionist) attitude towards the authority of fictions, and even less to the rejection of fixed referential meanings. What qualifies my methodology is not a relativistic (empiricist, cognitivist) approach to the cinematic language, but a reflection on its fundamental *duplicity*: filmmaking here is regarded as the effect of a dialectical relationship with its unconscious underside, which is produced by filmmaking itself as it struggles to attain a degree of symbolic consistency. Precisely because there is no film without the invisible unconscious excess it constantly generates, the cinematic unconscious is film at its purest, the disavowed matrix of the moving image. But how do we get to this elusive core of film?

Let us proceed by developing the argument in the crudest Lacanian terms possible, i.e. by positing the existence of a transferential relationship between the critic and the film. As is well known, transference represents the starting point of the psychoanalytic situation, insofar as the analysand transfers his expectations for knowledge onto the analyst, the Lacanian "subject supposed to know" (about the analysand's desire). If we replace *analysand* with *film* and *analyst* with *critic*, we can imagine that in the course of the transferential relationship the analysand/film might complain to the analyst/critic about not knowing what he/it wants (to say), perhaps even challenging him to find the proverbial true message. The critic, in turn, draws his insight from the privileged position he occupies in the eyes of the film, as he stands for the knowledge embodied by the Lacanian big Other (the universe of language and law, the symbolic network that allows the subject to mediate its relationship with other subjects). Thus, the film/analysand expects the critic to unravel the enigma of its desire ("what do I actually want to say?"), since it considers this enigma to be a temporary epistemological impasse whose solution is already inscribed in the cognitive field of the critic. In Lacan, however, transference is nothing but a necessary masquerade that sooner or later dissolves itself. What happens at the end of the analysis, with the termination of transference, is the crucial passage from (in philosophical terms) "epistemology" to "ontology", which in our hypothesis would imply that film realises that what it had perceived as a momentary deadlock determined by specific circumstances is actually an abyssal lack affecting and indeed defining also the field of the critic. This mutual ontological lack is what marks the domain of the unconscious.

If applied to film studies, then, Lacanian psychoanalysis teaches us that the desire (to speak, to communicate) articulated by a film is groundless and unfathomable. The critic does not have the answer because his own perspective is always-already vitiated by the same structural inconsistency. To avoid the trap of relativism, however, two main points must be introduced. Firstly, we need to acknowledge that the groundlessness of desire is a form of (unconscious) knowledge. This is demonstrated by the fact that the end of the analysis, the point at which film would be "cured", is signalled by the realisation (knowledge) that desire is authorised only in itself. Why? Because desire is literally beyond ourselves: it is always the other's desire, always the reflection of our traumatic encounter with the desiring other (the child, for example, desires through the indecipherable desire of the mother who caresses him: "what does she want from me?", "why does she enjoy caressing me?"). Secondly, it is particularly important for our approach that we recognise how the strictly speaking unattainable cause of cinematic desire is locatable through the traces it leaves on the film narrative, for these traces function as the exact equivalent of Lacanian symptoms. What we need to clarify here is that from the start of the 1960s Lacan progressively moves away from his early idea that the symptom, like the unconscious, is structured like a language (see Lacan, 1989, p. 65). From its status as a linguistic or ciphered message, "symptom" slowly evolves into "sinthome", an opaque residue of *jouissance*, a hard kernel of enjoyment that can only be posited in its relationship with the traumatic dimension of the Real, remaining beyond analysis and signification.[3] The essential purpose of this study is therefore to locate the Lacanian symptoms (*sinthomes*) of film, in the awareness that circumscribing their ambiguous presence/absence amounts to accomplishing the task of film analysis.

As the title of each part of the book indicates, the enigmatic and volatile Real of Lacanian theory (the substance of unconscious enjoyment) works as the catalyst for a series of reflections on Italian cinema that bring into contention a range of films by prominent Italian directors. To understand the rationale behind my choice of films and directors it is necessary to appreciate that with this book I intend to move beyond the standard critical presupposition of the autonomy of film as a self-entrenched, specialised academic discipline. This goes a long way to explain the unpredictable nature and irregular pattern of my filmic references: film here is used more as a privileged means to unravel the dialectics of knowledge and desire than as an end in itself. The object of my investigation is less the history of Italian cinema with its celebrated masterpieces (whatever methodological approach one might have to their study) than the traumatic encounters I try to isolate as non-specific and yet fundamental forms of cinematic knowledge. The films referred to in this volume – by no means representative of an anthological survey of Italian cinema – seem to me particularly pertinent for a critique that replaces epistemological questions concerning the medium with a method of evaluation aimed at unearthing the disavowed ontological core of the medium itself. In Lacanian psychoanalysis, the ontological core of any symbolic structure is the Real, the excessive dimension where signification overlaps with its own intrinsic distortion; consequently, the aim of this book is to identify ways of reaching the cinematic Real, with the persuasion that what counts in a critical study of film is the demarcation of the territory occupied by its hidden ontological presuppositions. My selection of films is thereby based on what I perceive as these films' distinctive propensity to expose cinema's structuring liaison with the Real.

From this angle the question of nationality, whilst far from decisive, can help me shed some light on the nature of the chosen approach. If post-war Italian cinema is generally regarded as stylistically innovative, thematically subversive or defiant and driven by a strong political agenda, my claim is that these specific qualities should be read in close relation to Italian cinema's penchant for *radical self-reflexivity*, i.e. for its wilful desire to test and exceed the intrinsic limits of filmic representation. As two patently dissimilar but equally suggestive examples of this tension (both of which are dealt with in the course of the book), one could safely mention the Neorealist movement (1945–55), with its overwhelming trans-fictional thrust, and Pasolini's attempt to write a heretical semiology of cinema (mid to late 1960s). What comes to the fore in both cases is the elusive "object" that Theodor Adorno (2001, p. 180), in an effort to define Antonioni's style, aptly called the 'uncinematic' core of (his) cinema, the secret and impenetrable presupposition ('the emptiness of time') upon which the cinematic invention is constructed.

The central place granted to the Lacanian Real is what allows for the connection between psychoanalysis, film and politics. It is a choice borne out of the awareness that psychoanalytic film theory has so far privileged exclusively the Lacanian categories of the Imaginary and the Symbolic. Despite their pioneering role in generating the right conditions for a long-term joint effort between psychoanalysis and cinema, the 1970s and 1980s appropriations of Lacan by film studies were intrinsically reductive, as they resulted in the promotion of a discursive practice that concerns itself primarily with the effects of cinematic production on the viewer (spectatorship theory). In so doing, these studies glaringly overlooked the order of the Real. More recently, it would appear that the potential for a fertile crossbreeding between psychoanalysis and cinema has either been absorbed by the suspect appeal of cultural studies, or reconsidered and eventually discarded by both cognitive-historicist approaches and conventional film theory. Žižek is the only theorist today who advocates the convergence of psychoanalysis and film as part of a project for the radical repoliticisation of culture. It is within such a project that this study finds its scope. Contrary to how it has been so far for film studies, psychoanalytic theory is not employed here as yet another theoretical framework for the understanding and discussion of film. The point is rather that focusing on the Real as the cinematic unconscious allows me to turn the standard interpretative logic ("from theory to film") on its head, and suggest that film can only realise its potential by "becoming theory".

Of all the directors I discuss, Michelangelo Antonioni and Pier Paolo Pasolini are indeed invoked as central and constant references, as their respective productions testify precisely to a subversive (if unconscious) desire to push cinema beyond its representational status, into an uncanny realm where representation itself conflates with the explosive potentialities of the Real. In this respect, Lacan's notion of gaze and his musings on feminine sexuality are employed as the most useful theoretical tools to unpack the politically relevant underpinnings of Antonioni's formalism, while Pasolini's emphatic realism is primarily assessed through the classic psychoanalytic concept of death-drive, which was brought to fruition by Pasolini himself in his vastly underrated ruminations on editing. Desire, fantasy, violence, masochism, law, subversion and virtuality feature amongst the main topics treated throughout the book, in strict correlation with the attempt to demarcate the symptomal breaking point of a number of key Italian films. The sections in part 1 are the most theoretically dense, although they aim at clarity and simplicity, assuming no previous knowledge of Lacanian psychoanalysis – or, where appropriate, Hegelian dialectics. Parts 2 and 3 build on the foundations laid in part 1 to engage more directly with a wide range of film narratives, some of which are discussed in full while others are briefly sketched with the purpose of clarifying more general theoretical arguments. With specific regard to these quick references, footnotes play a crucial symptomatic role in this book, since their dislocation (given my take on the unconscious) grants them a strategically central position within the text. If my critical method allows me to disregard questions of historical progression, part 4 nonetheless suggests that a chronological shift of emphasis may be perceived in contemporary Italian cinema, where the emergence of the explosive Real would seem to be the unavoidable upshot of the typically postmodern injunction to depoliticise film. Each of the four parts of the book is fairly self-contained, hence my decision not to add a conclusion, which would have resulted in a series of unnecessary repetitions.

Finally, when quoting from written sources I have generally referred to English editions, although in some cases I have had to translate directly from Italian and occasionally from French. Film titles are given in the original Italian, with the English or American title in brackets when the film is first mentioned, or if it is discussed a second time in a different part of the book.

NOTES

1 One should note the explicit quotation here, as Tara (originally the ancient seat of the mythical kings of Ireland) is the name of the beautiful Georgian plantation in Victor Fleming's *Gone with the Wind* (1939), the land where Scarlett O'Hara (Vivian Leigh), the film's heroine, meets her destiny and finds her true identity. It is not a coincidence that in Fleming's classic film Tara is associated with paternal authority: when Scarlett laments that life at Tara is boring, her Irish father, the owner of the plantation, cautions her that 'land is the only thing worth living for, worth dying for, it is the only thing that lasts'. From then on Tara becomes Scarlett's only concern, the true object of her desire. If on the one hand Bertolucci aims to subvert the theme of the sacredness of the land (which in *Gone with the Wind* had strong ideological implications, at a time when the mounting political unrest in Europe was beginning to be perceived as a serious threat in the United States), on the other hand one can see that by associating the land with the unconscious, the idea of its sacredness is also uncannily confirmed. The same, as I will develop at the end of part 4, can be said about the notion of the father.

2 Here it is enough to mention Terry Eagleton's oft-cited statement that Žižek is 'the most formidably brilliant exponent of psychoanalysis, indeed of cultural theory in general, to have emerged from Europe in some decades' (Eagleton, 2003, p. 200). Žižek's writings have almost single-handedly resurrected Lacanian psychoanalytic theory as a vital instrument for understanding ideology critique and agency in post-Marxism, especially by emphasising the normally undervalued link between Lacan and German philosophy – mainly post-Kantian Idealism (Hegel and Schelling) – as well as by building on psychoanalysis' potential for application to popular culture (cinema in particular).

3 "Le sinthome" is also the title of the unpublished 1975–76 seminar. Here Lacan develops an enthusiastic reading of James Joyce aimed at describing the relationship between writing and the writer's private *jouissance*, which comes to the fore through impenetrable "sinthomes". The term itself was meant to render some typical Lacanian puns such as *synth-homme* (artificial being) or *saint homme* (saint).

1

FIGURATIONS OF THE REAL: LOCATING THE UNCONSCIOUS

1.1 EDITING AS REAL, OR DEATH-DRIVE IN FILM THEORY

In Pasolini's *La ricotta* (1963) Orson Welles plays an intellectually lucid but supercilious leftist director; when asked what he thinks of death, his answer is: 'As a Marxist, it is a fact I do not take into consideration'. Although the Welles character is meant to voice many of Pasolini's own controversial views on modernity and religion, his categorical "ban on death" is exactly what the film sets out to refute, as by the end, after the tragicomic demise of the film's sub-proletarian hero Stracci (Mario Cipriani), the Welles character is forced to acknowledge: 'Poor Stracci, he had to die to show us that he was alive!' The idea of the constant interpenetration of life and death is perhaps the founding theme of Pasolini's cinema.

In 1967 Pasolini wrote a series of short essays in which he argued that a finished film is comparable to a finished life insofar as both are constituted by a series of significant facts retroactively selected by editing and death respectively. Only after editing and death, that is, can film and life be submitted to critical analysis and interpretation, for only then are they withdrawn from the contingency of time and arranged into a past that cannot be modified any further.[1] The paradoxical point is that the encounter with meaning is correlative to the death of the subject and the editing of the film:

It is therefore absolutely necessary to die, *for while we are alive we lack sense*, and the language of our life (with which we express ourselves, and which we hold in the utmost importance) is untranslatable: a chaos of possibilities, an endless search for relations and meanings. *Death accomplishes an instantaneous montage of our life*: that is, it chooses its truly significant moments (not modifiable anymore by other potentially contrary or incoherent moments), and puts them in succession, turning our infinite, unstable, uncertain (and thus linguistically undescribable) present, into a clear, stable, certain (and thus linguistically well describable) past [...]. *Only through death does our life help us to express ourselves*. Editing, therefore, does to the filmic material [...] what death does to life (Pasolini, 1995, p. 241).

Pasolini's fascination with death was certainly not as morbid as many critics have hastily intimated. As the above parallel with editing suggests, it should rather be taken with a degree of theoretical flexibility. My working hypothesis is that to fully appreciate the significance of Pasolini's argument we need to read it through a Lacanian lens: as an attempt to dialecticise the relationship between what we generally assume to be visible and teeming with meaning (film/life), and the dimension which, on the contrary, alludes by definition to an abyssal (non-)place outside space and time (editing/death) – if we think, that is, of editing as a series of spatio-temporal gaps between shots, and simultaneously if we perceive death, as Pasolini did (1995, p. 252), from a lay, completely immanent, perspective.[2] The specific Lacanian issue at stake is that the opening of the space of meaning depends on a radically displaced kernel of absolute negativity, whose inaccessibility is guaranteed precisely by the editing procedure and, on an existential level, by the event of death. Slavoj Žižek makes this point forcefully apropos of any symbolic constellation:

> One of the lessons of Lacanian psychoanalysis – and at the same time the point at which Lacan rejoins Hegel – is the radical discontinuity between the organic immediacy of "life" and the symbolic universe: the "symbolization of reality" implies the passage through the zero point of the "night of the world". What we forget, when we pursue our daily life, is that our human universe is nothing but an embodiment of the radically inhuman "abstract negativity", of the abyss we experience when we face the "night of the world" (Žižek, 2001b, p. 53).

In this section I intend to show that Pasolini's incursions into film theory were neither theoretically naive nor, as Joan Copjec (2002, pp. 200–01) has recently insinuated, incomprehensible. Instead, they intuitively anticipated what was to become (and still is, since its potential has not been fully exhausted) the debate on the most stimulating contributions that Lacanian psychoanalysis has made to film studies, namely the theories of suture and, indirectly, of the gaze, which will be discussed in the following sections of the book. More specifically, I shall argue that the notions of suture and gaze, once extremely popular theoretical references for film studies, both share with Pasolini's understanding of editing a decisive connection with what Lacan termed the Real, the traumatic domain inaccessible to meaning and yet inescapably related to it.

I begin by reading Pasolini's argument through the key psychoanalytic notion of the unconscious. The claim that what guarantees the consistency of film is the operation of editing *qua* death (i.e. *qua* inscription of the abyssal void of death) should indeed be taken as a Lacanian paradox, insofar as the Lacanian subject is, strictly speaking, a void (in the form of unconscious desires) that gives body to a being: 'Once the subject himself comes into being, he owes it to a certain nonbeing upon which he raises up his being' (Lacan, 1988, p. 192); 'everything exists only on a supposed background of absence. Nothing exists except insofar as it doesn't exist' (Lacan, 1966, p. 392).[3] Put differently, Lacanian psychoanalysis, in its theoretical and analytic capacity, always deals with a subject that constitutes itself against the backdrop of the impossible relationship between conscious and unconscious self: between the ego as a place of fictional misrecognition generated by the interplay of fantasy and desires, and the "acephalous" (impossible to assume or subjectivise) unconscious.

Such radical division can perhaps be grasped more comfortably by considering the three orders of Lacanian theory, the Imaginary, the Symbolic and the Real. Since his famous 1949 paper on the *Stade du miroir* (mirror stage), Lacan (1989, pp. 1–8) granted the Imaginary and the Symbolic dimensions a central role in the formation of subjectivity. If the Imaginary implies that the subject has a first insight into self-consciousness through narcissistic identification with the other, the formation of subjectivity proper can only be secured in the Symbolic, the realm of language and meaning, which we access through the Oedipus complex. The bottom line, which leads Lacan (1989, p. 1) to state that psychoanalysis opposes 'any philosophy directly issuing from the *Cogito*' (i.e. from a self-transparent and autonomous understanding of subjectivity), is that entrance in the Symbolic is ontologically equivalent to the incision of a radical cut in the subject (which he calls *fente* or *refente* in French, and often *Spaltung* from Freud), a wound that the subject will never be able to heal. As soon as we say "I", in other words, there intervenes a division between the subject of the enunciated (the subject of consciousness), and the subject of the enunciation (the subject of the unconscious enunciation). This break (*Ichspaltung*, the splitting of the I) corresponds to the formation of the unconscious, just as much as it is the necessary precondition for the emergence of self-consciousness.[4] This is why Lacan (1966, p. 830) can say that '(t)he unconscious is a concept forged on the trace of what operates to constitute the subject'.

Thus, if on the one hand the unconscious appears inextricably entwined with the Symbolic, on the other hand it is also connected with the Real, the inaccessible domain of what resists symbolisation absolutely. This is why it would be misleading to think the unconscious as a latent narrative waiting to be rescued to signification, temporarily occupying the place of what is repressed. Its peculiarity is that it remains radically other, in as much as the thinking self can only establish with it a negative relationship, a rapport based on non-recognition. Precisely as the 'censored chapter' of the history of the subject (Lacan, 1989, p. 55), and at the same time that which is 'structured like a language' (Lacan, 1993, p. 167), the unconscious takes the form of an uncanny message in which the conscious subject does not and cannot recognise himself or herself.[5] As Žižek often suggests, David Lynch is one of the directors who best exemplifies the paradox of the Lacanian unconscious, for most of his films are structured around an enigmatic phrase (for example, "Dick Laurent is dead" in *Lost Highway*, or "The owls are not what they seem" in the *Twin Peaks* series) that can only be subjectivised at the price of the hero's death, or symbolic destitution (see Žižek, 2000, p. 299). As we will see later, in the final years of his teaching Lacan abandons his early idea of the linguistic constitution of the unconscious to propose the latter's substantial coincidence with the Real, which in turn is firmly associated with the notion of *jouissance*, the obscure realm of enjoyment.

At this stage, however, we should emphasise that the paradox of the unconscious is supplemented, in Lacan, by another paradox, which this time concerns ethics. Despite the impossibility of bringing the content of the unconscious under the jurisdiction of the conscious self, the subject is nevertheless requested to assume responsibility for its dislodged underside, as it is there that its destiny is played out. Lacan's rereading of Freud's famous *Wo Es war, soll Ich werden* contains a clear ethical stance which ultimately coincides with the very aim of the analytic treatment: the self must come to be where the unconscious is, it must attempt to disturb the fantasmatic kernel of fundamentally disavowed enjoyment that an unconscious desire always-already is,[6] for that is the only way to accede to the truth of the subject. What does this task, if taken seriously, imply for film studies today? Let us propose, for the time being, that the aim of our approach to film is to assess if, how and to what extent a given film allows us to locate and describe the dialectical relationship between its narrative structure and what "ex-sists" therein, i.e., those elements which antagonise radically that structure despite being integral to its significance, functional to its symbolic economy. The basic assumption in place is that the reason why the meaning of a given film can only be endlessly discussed and rediscussed, written, rewritten and, in a sense, recreated (as our postmodern wisdom has it), is that, precisely as symbolically constituted, a film "never succeeds", it always-already gives way to its own unconscious destabilising desire, which seeps through the narrative and stains it profoundly. And the Lacanian point is that it is only by learning to read these traces of unconscious desire, these cinematic signifiers that speak the film's "discourse of the Other", that we can attempt to accede to the truth of film. Needless to say, only certain films will demonstrate the potential to express, in one way or another, the deep-seated logic that governs their own representational status.

By focusing on the foundational ambiguity of cinema, Pasolini's intervention on editing takes us to the heart of the above question, allowing us to explore further Lacan's notion of the Real. Following Pasolini, we have suggested that editing actively participates in the production of the cinematic unconscious, as it introduces the paradox of a structuring cut that anchors film in the Symbolic and, simultaneously, dislodges some of its content to an unconscious foundation. In doing so, therefore, editing also intervenes in the Real, since the cinematic Real can be thought of as a nucleus of traumatic fantasy that operates at the level of the unconscious; or, put differently, as an impenetrable hard core of enjoyment that signals the presence of an unconscious desire. We should be absolutely precise in defining the status of the Real in Lacan. As Žižek has repeatedly claimed, the Real is not simply a domain beyond the remit of language and symbolisation (as the early Lacan seems to imply), 'the terrifying primordial abyss that swallows everything', but instead it emerges as a traumatic formation produced by language itself, a troubling surplus of sense which inevitably "bends" our vision and understanding of reality: the Real is 'that invisible obstacle, that distorting screen, which always "falsifies" our access to external reality, that "bone in the throat" which gives a pathological twist to every symbolisation, that is to say, on account of which every symbolisation misses its object' (Žižek, 2003, p. 67). If therefore any symbolic configuration is intrinsically dependent on its hidden relationship with the Real, filmmaking is nothing but the distortion it shapes itself into whilst trying to achieve meaning. Or, to put it in a slightly different way, it coincides with the effect of the "gravitational pull" it suffers from the self-generated Real.

For Pasolini, this crucial pull that gives body to the signifying cinematic chain originates in the editing procedure: editing is Real since it functions as the receptacle of an inherently disruptive fantasmatic excess, whose displacement situates film within a linguistically consistent and yet anamorphically distorted dimension. And if the key point for our approach is 'to assume fully the impossible task of symbolising the real, inclusive of its necessary failure' (Žižek, 1993, pp. 199–200), can we not argue that, by pairing editing and death, Pasolini was pointing us precisely towards such a titanic task – a task hinging on the Lacanian paradox that everything exists only against a background of absence? It is this kind of investment in the Real *qua* structuring "motor" of film which lends Pasolini's theory a strong psychoanalytic bias, prompting us also to call into question, after the unconscious and the Real, a third key notion, which complements and brings to fruition the first two: that of death-drive. For what is the typically Pasolinian (decadent) *topos* of the 'symbiosis of sex and death' (as he put it in a famous poem on Antonio Gramsci, of all people!, see Pasolini, 1993, p. 226), which cuts across and problematises his entire oeuvre, if not the libidinal persistence of that very reference to Nothingness which qualifies the death-drive? The Freudian death-drive designates precisely 'the paradox of "wanting unhappiness", of finding excessive pleasure in suffering itself' (Žižek, 2003, p. 23). In another essay on cinema ('Il cinema impopolare', The unpopular cinema), published in 1970, this persistence of drive becomes apparent:

> '"Freedom". After giving it considerable thought, I have realised that this mysterious word only means, after all, in its deepest connotation… "freedom to choose death". This no doubt is a scandal, because to live is a duty: on this point both Catholics (life is sacred as it is a gift of God) and Communists (one must live as it is a duty towards society) agree. Nature also agrees: and, to help us be lovingly attached to life, it provides us with the "conservation instinct". However, differently from Catholics and Communists, nature is ambiguous: and to prove its ambiguity it also provides us with the opposite instinct, the death-drive. This conflict, which is not contradictory – as our rational and dialectic mind would like it to be – but oppositional and as such non-progressive, unable to perform an optimistic synthesis, takes place in the depths of our soul: in the unfathomable depths, as we all know. But "authors" have the responsibility to render this conflict explicit and manifest. They are tactless and inopportune enough to reveal, somehow, that they "want to die", or else that they want to disobey the conservation instinct: or, more simply, disobey conservation as such. Freedom is, therefore, a self-damaging attack on conservation. Freedom can only be expressed through martyrdom, either an insignificant or a substantial one. And each martyr martyrs himself through the reactionary executioner' (Pasolini, 1995, p. 269).

Pasolini's 'freedom to choose death' represents a stubborn endorsement of the constitutive surplus of sense, and as such it demands to be read alongside the theorisation of the death-like quality of editing. His notion of death essentially coincides with Lacan's death-drive, 'the dimension of the "undead", of a spectral life which insists beyond (biological) death […] the excess of life itself' (Žižek, 2003, p. 94). And, again, editing is Real precisely because it entails the *insistence* of the death-drive in its reference to a hard kernel of fantasy that remains utterly non-symbolisable. Hence, the invisible spatial and temporal gaps between cinematic images function as a paradigmatic, *ante litteram* receptacle for all the unconscious desire whose disavowal allows filmmaking to become film. As Freud and Lacan would have put it, "the cinematic letter kills",[7] and Pasolini's aim is precisely to show how the many "cuts" of film correspond to its many necessary "deaths", implying that film is a symbolic structure whose coherence is negotiated, *strico sensu*, through its relationship with its own foundational void.

1.2 PASOLINI AS A READER OF HEGEL

But let us reconsider the core of Pasolini's argument: the truth-content of a film is connected with the constitutively ambiguous experience of the subject, insofar as the subject needs to die to achieve meaning. How should we read this attempt at connecting subjectivity and objectivity? The properly dialectical point is that the intimate contradiction characterising the subject, the paradox of "meaning after death", is externalised into the underlying split (editing) of film *qua* external reality. In other words, external reality is not simply given in advance irrespective of the psychic apparatus, but rather *it is posited by the subject through the displacement of its own (the subject's) inherent deadlock.* What we regard as the objective world "out there" is inevitably a by-product, a secondary ontology, as it constitutes itself through a kind of evacuation of that immanent and original antagonism situated at the heart of the human psyche – which Freud, in *Beyond the Pleasure Principle,* branded the death-drive. This is how we should read Hegel's well-known insistence on the speculative identity of Substance and Subject (see Hegel, 1977, p. 10): the split of substance, the impossibility of the Absolute to fully coincide with itself, is correlative to the self-divided and finite nature of the subject. Read from Pasolini's viewpoint, and despite Pasolini's own hasty dismissal of Hegel,[8] this amounts to saying that editing gives body to that very fundamental inconsistency which belongs, originally, to the subject, and which, precisely as an excessive, disturbing feature, *needs to be externalised if the subject is to enter into some kind of relationship with the outside world.* The antagonism in our relationship with reality, the opposition between the pleasure principle (our demands) and the reality principle (the demands of the external world), is thus nothing but the effect of the displacement of the founding negativity of the subject. And the final result of this movement of externalisation, in Hegel, is the awareness that the negativity of substance overlaps with the negativity of subject: the displaced element returns and demands to be fully assumed by the self as its founding kernel.

Once perceived against this dialectical background, editing appears as an objective concretion of the traumatic impasse at the very heart of the subject. Consequently, Pasolini's attempt to wrest theoretical consequence from editing,[9] via its affinity with death, entails the full endorsement of the gap that structures the human experience. Editing is nothing but the self-fracture of film *qua* fiction, and as such *it is essential,* the site of an infinite virtuality that is glued to the making of cinematic sense. The fact that for sense to emerge this virtual kernel has to be compressed within the imperceptible intersticial breaks between shots, only attests to editing's fundamental role, while the force of its presence can be measured through the specific "torsion" taken by the narrative. Editing thus discloses the binary logic of filmmaking: film is not just a field antagonised by a multitude of contents relating to a transcendental and constitutively lost Truth. It is, first and foremost, a field antagonised by its own self-generated impediment, the very structuring fracture separating its fictional status from the negative underside dissimulated by the editing process. The Hegelian (and Lacanian) significance of Pasolini's claim rests on the intuition that the ultimate truth of film has to be looked for in film's relation with the negativity from which it raises its meaning, a negativity that is inscribed in the cinematic field as its dialectical other, its intrinsic self-division.[10]

Another way of rendering the Hegelian core of Pasolini's argument is by mapping it against the relation between contingency and necessity articulated by Hegel in the *Science of Logic.* From this standpoint, Pasolini's theory implies the intervention of an utterly external formal gesture (the cutting and pasting of the filmed images *qua* synthetic activity of the subject) as the precondition for the emergence of a necessary content (the film). Let us consider Žižek's claim that the reality into which we intervene is always-already the product of our intervention: 'Before we intervene in reality by means of a *particular* act, we must accomplish the *purely formal* act of converting reality as something which is objectively given into reality as "effectivity", as something produced, "posited" by the subject'. In Hegel, positing implies precisely this formal gesture of retroactively setting up the framework for our particular intervention:

> in his particular-empirical activity, the subject of course presupposes the "world", the objectivity on which he performs his activity, as something given in advance, as a positive condition of his activity; but his positive-empirical activity is possible only if he structures his perception of the world in advance in a way that opens the space for his intervention – in other words, only if he retroactively posits the presuppositions of his activity, of his "positing". This "act before the act" [...] is a purely formal "conversion" transforming reality into something perceived, assumed as a result of our activity (Žižek, 1992, pp. 217–18).

Dialectically speaking, this implies that the subject comes to terms with the openness of contingency only by retroactively impressing upon it the mark of necessity. It is precisely the act of "naming reality" that transforms the openness of contingency into necessity, concurrently designating the space of freedom: 'the passage of contingency into necessity is an act of purely formal conversion, [...] so that the very act by means of which the subject recognizes (and thus constitutes) necessity is the supreme act of freedom and as such the self-suppression of necessity' (Žižek, 1993, p. 150). What is crucial for our argument is to insist on the Hegelian paradox of the coincidence of necessity and freedom: by "positing the presuppositions" of his/her activity, the subject effectively steps into uncharted territory where the emergence of meaning coincides with its radical withdrawal/contraction. More precisely, the formal feature that transforms the chaos of contingency into "reality as we know it" is Hegel's version of Kant's Transcendental Idea, that is, the persuasion that 'the Suprasensible is *appearance qua appearance*' (Hegel, 1977, p. 89), the experience of *Schein* in the midst of our everyday life – a pure semblance devoid of substantial support, a metonymy of radical negativity functioning as the invisible structuring "prop" of the phenomenal world. Ultimately, Pasolini's couple editing/death coincides with this Hegelian gap within immanence, which necessarily, and retroactively, generates the possibility of experiencing film/reality. In philosophical terms the fundamental question to ask is: what does the act of editing actually conceal? The only plausible answer is that it conceals nothing, i.e., the foundational negativity whose displacement allows for the emergence of a meaningful representation of reality. Editing can thus be read alongside freedom, as it always taps into the very lack which turns contingency into necessity. No wonder Pasolini stringently defines freedom as 'freedom to choose death', as a 'self-damaging attack on conservation': it is the choice of the negative, the emptying gesture of the subject who thereby overidentifies with the gaps inherent in the texture of the external world, which opens up the space for the resignification of reality.

Again, it is worth underlining that, from a theoretical perspective, Pasolini's argument confirms the main accomplishment of Hegel's speculative idealism, as it undermines the common supposition that reality is an a priori given that simply exists before the intervention of knowledge. On the contrary, it asserts that reality is produced by the very process of knowledge. It is important to stress, however, that far from affirming the ultimate freedom and autonomy of the subject as the mediating agent who "creates the world" (far from concluding that the dialectical process implies the triumph of absolute Form/Spirit over content/materiality), Hegelian dialectics fully endorse the deadlock constitutive of the process of knowledge, *insofar as this deadlock is constitutive of the object of knowledge too*: at the end of the dialectical process, when the contingent openness of reality is fully mediated into necessity by the subject, the subject itself is thrown back into the fundamental undecidability which characterises its position within the newly established reality.

Back to cinema. In somewhat overstated terms, we could say that by editing a film the director assumes upon himself/herself the weight of the world, the world's fundamental inconsistency. The equivalence of editing and death then holds: editing is homologous to the act which, in Hegel, demarcates the emergence of man, i.e. the symbolic assumption of death through the funeral rite (see Hegel, 1977, pp. 270–71). As a case in point illustration of the Hegelian tarrying with the negative, editing is the formal gesture that suddenly turns contingency into necessity, reality into life, cinema into film.[11]

1.3 THE MINIMAL GAP BETWEEN OTHELLO'S TWO HEADS

The paradox implied in the shift from contingency to necessity finds an exemplary validation in one of Pasolini's most accomplished and generally overlooked cinematic works, *Che cosa sono le nuvole?* (What are the Clouds?, 1968), a short film released at a time when the director was attempting to theorise the consubstantiality of death and editing. Like the previous *La Ricotta* (1962), *Che cosa sono le nuvole?* displays an explicitly self-referential intention, as is clear from the opening sequence. It begins in the backstage of a theatre where a black marionette (Othello) is being fabricated. As soon as the head is screwed into the body, the character (Ninetto Davoli) is lined up against the wall, alongside other marionettes waiting to be brought on scene to act out Shakespeare's *Othello*. The curious thing is that once they have been assembled, these marionettes also, somewhat miraculously, come alive: 'Why am I so happy?' asks Othello as he joins his fellow puppets; 'Because you have been born!', replies Iago (Totò), next to him. So the first hint of meta-narrativity can be found in the fact that the actors/puppets have emerged from dead matter to a relatively autonomous life. As we later discover, their being attached to strings and controlled by the puppeteer (Francesco Leonetti) does not prevent them from either reciting their lines or, more importantly, discussing their fictional roles behind the scenes. In the tracking shot that follows Othello's birth, there is a second, decisive albeit more complex allusion to meta-narrativity: the camera pans over a wall with four posters, the last of which is a reproduction of Velazquez's painting *Las Meninas*, announcing Pier Paolo Pasolini's *Che cosa sono le nuvole?* as the day's show. The juxtaposition of the film's title with a painting that famously problematises the question of representation by way of generating an intriguing short-circuit between the author and his work (or between seer and seen, outside and inside), substantiates the perception that this will be a film about filmmaking. Two observations spring to mind apropos of this parallel: firstly, Velazquez's painting is implicitly cinematic, in that it reproduces the double movement of shot/reverse shot in a condensed format, including the establishing

Las Meninas

shot (from the point of view of the sovereigns) into the reverse shot (what they are looking at); secondly, as Michel Foucault knew very well, *Las Meninas* is not only about representation but more specifically about the dynamics of power, not least because the two sovereigns seem to be reduced to an ephemeral mirror image.

In the opening chapter of *The Order of Things*, Foucault draws on Velazquez's painting in order to surmise 'the necessary disappearance of that which is its foundation' (Foucault, 2003, p. 18): the centre of the image (the place of power) is demarcated as essentially empty. This is because the mirror image of King Philip IV and Queen Mariana is displaced and ultimately dissolved by the painting's focus on a number of foregrounding features, first and foremost the young Infanta, situated at the intersection of the main compositional axes, flanked by the meninas and bathed in golden light. Here Foucault comes very close to the Lacanian definition of the gaze as visual unconscious (a concept that will be discussed in the following sections), as when he claims that 'the profound invisibility of what one sees is inseparable from the invisibility of the person seeing' (Foucault, 2003, p. 17). However (as the rest of his seminal book and his thinking in general confirm) he is more interested in assessing the way in which this painting of the Classical age attempts to construct its own interrelated systems of representation, its own power-related discourses, while at the same time failing to provide us with that unified representation of man which will only become available, according to Foucault, in modernity: 'it is not possible for the pure felicity of the image ever to present in a full light both the master who is representing and the sovereign who is being represented' (Foucault, 2003, p. 17). My point, however, is that it is Foucault himself who fails to make the most of his own insight into the symptomal role played by the "missing painting in the painting", which in fact is nothing but the unseen portrait that is being painted by Velazquez, whose presence is nevertheless detectable from the edge of the canvas on the left of the picture. Is this detail not *the part of the content that frames the frame itself*, that is to say, the point where the supposedly invisible/impossible frame that limits our historically mediated vision materialises into an almost unnoticeable detail?

What *Las Meninas* evokes is thus the uncanny absence/presence of its own formal framework, the fact that, ultimately, representation relies on its strict correlation with an intangible object. The centrifugal effect of power disintegration, in other words, should alert us to the fact that the meaning of this painting hinges on its self-referential negativity, which materialises as the little piece of wood in the left corner. From this angle, Foucault's reference to the void of the image proves to be crucial if we are to understand how power works: power always-already relies on the dissimulation of its founding illegitimacy, of the fact that the place it occupies is originally empty. The disavowed focus of Velazquez's painting is its objectal remainder, a dislocated concretion of the missing kernel of the image. The very fact that, as many commentators have noted, we cannot even be certain that the reflected image in the mirror is that of the sovereigns outside the picture (the laws of perspective suggest, rather, that it is a reflection of the actual painting), simply reinforces the uncanny impression that the structuring gaze is missing!

In light of these considerations, how can *Las Meninas* contribute to our understanding of *Che cosa sono le nuvole?* It seems to me that Pasolini's emphasis on self-referentiality should be read alongside the notion of self-fracture as elaborated apropos of Velazquez's work: what is redoubled and reflected in his short film is, essentially, the self-relating negativity of the symbolic field. In a clear attempt to put his film theory into practice, Pasolini shows us that visual art, just as much as whatever manages to attain a certain degree of symbolic complexity, is suspended on the abyss of its own radical formal inconsistency, whose dislocation is functional to the very process of symbolisation.

One of the key details is to be found in the double life of the characters, who are presented as radically split between their roles in Shakespeare's drama, and what we could call a kind of backstage conscience, which allows them to express a moral judgment on their performance. At one point, for example, Othello reproaches Iago behind the scenes for not being the good friend he thought he was (adding that he is also disappointed with himself). The charm of Pasolini's reading lies in the disproportion between the characters' profound self-awareness and the fictional rigidity to which they are confined. However, self-awareness is not complemented by moral knowledge here: despite being able to identify their weaknesses and lament the limitations of their roles, these characters are nevertheless incapable of finding their real selves, for what lies beneath their staged personae is nothing but the redoubling of appearance. When Othello asks 'why are we so different from what we think we are?', Iago calls the unconscious into question: 'we are in a dream within a dream', i.e., the truth about ourselves is hidden in a knowledge that does not know itself. Put differently, the deeper order of truth behind fictions can only be defined in negative terms as a more profound form of fictionality. In a second exchange, Othello returns to his question by asking Iago if the truth is 'what *he* thinks, what *people* think, or what *that guy up there* [the director] thinks'. Iago's reply is even more revealing than the previous one: 'What do you feel? Concentrate!' After a short while, Othello triumphantly exclaims: 'Yes, I feel something!', at which point Iago brings a finger to his lips and intimates 'Shhh! Don't say anything, for as soon as you name it, it vanishes'.

Arguably, what comes to the fore here is the typically Pasolinian correlation of truth and body, a risky equivalence that lends itself to be classified under reactionary banners such as irrationalism, vitalism, aestheticism, and so on. In fact, the two "metaphysical" dialogues between Othello and Iago could be seen as combining the psychoanalytic subject's frustrating inability to "meet itself" (which could also be conceived as a modernist melancholia) with an allusion to an intuitive, somewhat supernatural realm of physical authenticity which would certainly resolve the first impasse, although not without smacking of decadent, dangerously unproblematic irrationalism.

Despite its apparent legitimacy, I would suggest that the above reading does not do justice to Pasolini's intentions. A more pertinent appreciation of Iago's reference to the incompatibility of truth and verbal/spoken language may arise from a focused analysis of Pasolini's much castigated contention that the language of cinema is the written language of reality (see Pasolini, 1995, pp. 198–226), i.e., that there is no difference between a fictional character and a real person, since their truth is located in an unnamable real that can be visualised (it pertains to the body) but cannot be expressed in words. Let us recall that Pasolini expounded his theory of cinema in a series of semiological essays written between 1965 and 1971, and collected in the third section of the volume *Empirismo eretico* (Heretical Empiricism), first published in 1972. Despite the generally sceptical response to these essays,[12] I believe few other Pasolinian writings would enable one to grasp the philosophical force that underpins his cinema. Challenging the structuralist approach to film that was very much *en vogue* at the time, Pasolini argued that 'the smallest units of cinematic language are the various real objects that compose a shot' (Pasolini, 1995, p. 202). In its seemingly paradoxical character, such a claim invites us to reflect on the axiomatic belief upon which the whole edifice of Pasolini's theory stands: that amongst all languages, cinema is the most likely medium to evoke absence of mediation, that is, in the director's characteristically cryptic expression, reality itself: 'When I make a film […] there is no symbolic or conventional filter between me and reality as there is in literature' (in Stack, 1969, p. 29).

Despite lacking philosophical rigour, Pasolini's stance deserves further consideration. After all, he was fully aware of Christian Metz's contribution to the semiological research on cinema, and expressly of his original sintagmatic model exposed in 1966 at the second edition of the Pesaro Film Festival.[13] Metz had claimed that the smallest cinematic unit was the shot, adding that it retained much more symbolic complexity than the smallest unit of verbal language. Hence, a shot could not correspond to a word, as the latter was deemed unable to garner the magmatic complexity of the former. From these considerations Metz went on to conceive a structural grammar of cinema that provided a modern model of textual analysis, igniting a series of fertile theoretical debates. Pasolini, an assiduous contributor to the Pesaro Film Festival, was one of the first to evaluate and reply to Metz's ideas. Despite repeatedly acknowledging that reality is a coded system of culturally determined signs, he maintained that the only way to validate intellectual knowledge is by conceding that something in the object itself (extant reality) ultimately defies mediation. The main point of his heretical semiotics is that the cultural medium needs to find a way to reflect this "surplus of sense" attached to our perception of the external world. As my previous reference to Hegel testifies, Pasolini's strategy implies that the other can only be reached via a detour through the self – which is why, as I will demonstrate later through a reading of his debut feature *Accattone* (1961), his Marxism and strenuous defence of the sub-proletariat cannot be disconnected from this crucial reference to subjectivity.

If we take literary language as a point in case, Pasolini claimed that free indirect speech allows the writer to create the effect of absence of mediation, thus facilitating a more authentic approach to reality in its non-symbolic dimension. The importance of this method, also articulated in cinematic terms (see Pasolini, 1995, pp. 167–87), cannot be underestimated. By using free indirect speech the narrator relinquishes his or her vantage point of control over the narrative in order to whole-heartedly adopt the psychological and linguistic point of view of one (or more) of the characters, so as to be able to see and represent the world through that character's eyes. Translated in psychoanalytic terms, this operation implies a kind of "symbolic suicide" on the part of the narrator, the emptying of his or her subject position. In what way, then, is this emptying to be linked to the avoidance of mediation and the connection with the non-symbolic dimension of reality? The only way to answer this question is by going back to the Hegelian coincidence of substance and subject: what allows us to truly connect with external reality is the acknowledgment that the split of substance is always-already in us – it is also the split that defines the self. For that reason, the gap at the heart of the subject, which opens the way for symbolic suicide, is what connects the subject with the "surplus of sense" in external reality – and, as such, it should be regarded as the fundamental presupposition of Pasolini's cinema.

Going back to *Che cosa sono le nuvole?*, we can now appreciate the consequences of its focus on self-referentiality. The characters' ability to recognise the "untruth" of their fictional roles causes a radical split at the level of their subjectivity, which is then transposed to the level of external reality through one of Pasolini's preferred topics: death. Significantly the audience – a rather unlikely crowd of humble peasants and workers – starts to play a key role at this stage. What happens is that Iago's vindictive plan to ruin Othello's marriage with Desdemona (Laura Betti) is brought to a sudden end by the "revolutionary" intervention of these sub-proletarian spectators who, outraged by the injustice perpetrated before their eyes, climb on stage and proceed to kill both Iago and Othello. Having now been returned to their original status of lifeless puppets, Iago and Othello (still played by Totò and Ninetto Davoli) are taken away by the garbage collector (the then popular Italian singer Domenico Modugno) who, whilst performing the song (written by Pasolini himself) that gives the film its title, drives them to the middle of the countryside, and eventually dumps them on top of a pile of refuse. Here, the third miracle of the film takes place, as the pair of dead marionettes covered in refuse start to speak again. Facing the open sky for the first time in their lives, they ecstatically acknowledge, in Iago's final words, 'the torturous, incredibly marvellous beauty of creation'.

The structural role of these miracles should not be underestimated: first, the birth of life/consciousness out of lifeless matter; then, the revolutionary intervention of the sub-proletarian audience; and finally, the typically Rossellinian theme of the subject's mysterious connection with the sacred "humus of reality". These miracles are crucial insofar as they display the potential to turn the narrative on its head: they permit Pasolini to demonstrate that there is a Real/unconscious substratum of the narrative that film has a chance to evoke. The puppets' final reconciliation with the sacredness of the world is reminiscent of the predicament faced by Karin (Ingrid Bergman) at the end of Rossellini's *Stromboli, terra di Dio* (Stromboli, 1949) when, once the dreadful eruption of the volcano is over, she invokes God and pays homage 'to the magnificent stillness all around her'. In both cases the epiphanic moment of reconciliation functions as a portentous reminder that the power of the symbolic field can be radically suspended.[14]

The political implications in *Che cosa sono le nuvole?* are fairly obvious. The traumatic event of the puppets' "symbolic death" – their sudden withdrawal from their symbolic roles – is achieved through the revolutionary insurgence of the sub-proletariat, the excluded social subjects.[15] The decisive point is that the distance between fiction and truth suddenly collapses, as the insurgent sub-proletariat take the order of fictions absolutely seriously. However, we are not dealing with ignorance or naivety. Instead, the storming of the stage reveals the false consciousness that nourishes the workings of ideology (its fundamental hypocrisy), for it is precisely through such commonplaces as "things are not what they seem" that the ideological machine functions. Bypassing such hypocrisy, the sub-proletarian audience refuses to consider that there may be a different and more profound truth behind what they see. What determines their revolutionary intervention is the fact that their condition of exclusion allows them to circumvent the ironic distance that remains silently operative in any hegemonic situation.

The revolutionary zeal of the sub-proletariat leads to a magical *tuché* and the sudden opening up of a new perspective, which is splendidly captured by Pasolini's use of the soundtrack (Modugno's song), the Chaplinesque use of the fast-forward, and an almost imperceptible fairytale sound-effect, kicking in the moment the two dead puppets are loaded onto the lorry. The next shot is even more decisive. Once on the lorry, submerged by rubbish, Othello and Iago come to occupy the impossible limit-position of "awareness in death": they are dead, but also strangely aware of the fact that they are leaving their bodies. Although reduced to their original wooden rigidity, they can still rotate their eyes to see what goes on around them. They try to shout but even with their mouths wide-open, as if in a nightmarish animation of Edward Munch's *Scream*, they cannot produce a sound. Despite the overall comical register of the film, for a few seconds Pasolini manages to reproduce in a moving and truly effective manner the terrifying encounter with the Real of death: a withdrawal of life substance that entails a collapse of the self into the empty frame of the body.

Then, as if by magic, this traumatic experience suddenly turns into epiphany, an ecstatic instance of renewal characterised by what Lacan calls *separation*, the overlapping of two lacks: the lack in the subject (the otherness implied by death, but also the otherness of the wretched, "excremental" condition to which the characters are reduced) comes to overlap with the lack in the object (the sacredness of nature, its unnatural, meaningless, virtual core). It is at this stage that the two stranded characters experience freedom, as it becomes apparent that beyond false appearances (fiction) there is *the form of appearance itself*, appearance deprived of its illusory paraphernalia, the very negativity which upholds the symbolic order of fiction. From a psychoanalytic angle we could say that the characters' unconscious is thoroughly exposed here, literally *à ciel ouvert*. Pasolini has accomplished for his characters what they had refused to do themselves: he has forced them to confront the truth that cannot be spoken — and the secret aim of the film, one needs to add, is precisely to disprove Iago's ban on speaking the truth. Meanwhile, the *nuvole* (clouds) of the title hint at a radically new, transformed landscape outside the theatre, outside the frame of the characters' symbolic universe, just like Velazquez's *Las Meninas* reflects on that invisible/impossible "frame within the frame" that evokes the absent centre of the image. In both cases what counts is the passage through the "zero point of symbolisation", the visualisation of a movement of disconnection that opens up the space for a new beginning.

Again, what we should remark upon is Pasolini's fundamentally Hegelian perception of subjectivity: the cinematic image carries the potential to push thought beyond self-consciousness, towards a traumatic encounter with the "object in the subject" which first alienates the subject from itself, then goes on to project such alienation onto the external world so as to allow for a certain contact with it. First the subject is conceived as profoundly split, traversed by a fundamental inconsistency (the double life of the characters), then this intimate antagonism is externalised into the social field (the revolutionary intervention of the audience), and finally, it is resolved in the Hegelian tarrying with the negative, the perception of the Real through the vantage point of symbolic destitution.

Such a reading, then, calls for a final observation, which concerns the critical question of film's relationship with its own narrative/cinematic unconscious. It would seem that, amongst the many twists of *Che cosa sono le nuvole?*, its central feature is to be discerned in the first miracle, the most displaced and yet essential one: the birth of life from matter.[16] The first observation to make is that this incident confirms the Lacanian notion that the subject is nothing but the result of a certain encounter with an objective surplus that cannot be symbolised (the unfathomable "desire of the Other"). On a strictly meta-narrative level, however, this almost imperceptible detail not only sets up the fairytale framework of the film (in a way that remains vastly unacknowledged), but it also presents itself as *a miraculous event that can only be edited in the film*, i.e., that can only take place through the intervention of a cut that conceals/reveals its impossibility. What happens is that Pasolini's camera cuts from Othello's "fake" wooden head, as it is screwed onto its wooden body, to Ninetto Davoli's "real" smiling face, and ultimately the miracle of filmmaking, the birth of cinema, is all condensed in this dialectical relationship between the image and its concealed underside (the gap between Othello's two heads). Put differently, the space between the two heads represents cinema at its purest, the cardinal operation of disavowal which signals the origin of film, the explosive power of imagination – and, for that matter, what is Ninetto's glowing smile if not Pasolini's favourite proof that the language of cinema is the language of reality?

This short but sophisticated narrative can thereby legitimately be regarded as a practical application of Pasolini's heretical semiotics, as it strives to show how the structuralist assumption that reality is a closed system of symbolic signs falls short of a decisive consideration: what grounds reality as a symbolic structure is a dimension beyond symbolisation, which is analogous to the Lacanian Real. As Pasolini himself put it, this dimension (the *nuvole* of his film, but also the miraculous birth of Ninetto's smile) can be equated to what he called the Ur-code of reality (see Pasolini, 1995, pp. 277–84), a kind of elusive and yet fundamental placeholder for the network of cultural associations that constitute our universe of meaning. Let us remind ourselves of the other subtext of this short film, its own "narrative within the narrative". What is normally missed is that beneath Shakespeare's *Othello* there lies a concealed and yet extremely significant reference: Aristophanes' classic comedy *The Clouds*, where Socrates, who features as one of the characters, compares the clouds of the title to divinities (Goddesses), sovereign celestial powers that defy language while also functioning as the founding principle of all living things. Despite Aristophanes' mocking of Socrates, and the overall comical mood of the play, the analogy seems evident, for Pasolini's clouds, which fill the last shot of the film, are also symbols of the sacred bedrock of reality. And as Pasolini objected to Umberto Eco, semiotics inconveniently operates as a typically bourgeois science, since it fails to acknowledge that beneath the symbolic order of reality there exists, as he put it, 'un burrone', an abyss, in other words that essentially non-symbolic (Real) dimension whose legitimacy cinema has the potential to restore (see Pasolini, 1995, p. 279).

1.4 SUTURING VOID

In combining Godardian experimentalism with the visionary/revolutionary impetus of Antonin Artaud's theatre aesthetics, Bernardo Bertolucci's *Partner* (1968) is generally regarded as a highly representative cinematic product of 1968 utopianism. Freely adapted from Dostoevsky's novel *The Double* (1846), it chronicles the strange encounter between Giacobbe (Pierre Clementi), a frustrated drama lecturer, and his revolutionary double (also called Giacobbe and played by the same actor). The central idea developed by Bertolucci is that the double starts masquerading as Giacobbe in order to accomplish some of his unconscious desires, such as killing his vain girlfriend Clara (Stefania Sandrelli) and teaching his students how to assemble a Molotov cocktail. As the narrative progresses, Giacobbe grows more and more intimate with his double, and starts sharing some of his revolutionary views. However, in the last shot of the film, after their miserable failure at staging a public revolt, we see the double step out onto a windowsill and walk along the building's ridge until, out of frame, he leaps out into the void. A bold attempt at providing a "figurative mapping" for the enigmatic effulgence of the unconscious, Bertolucci's early film strikes one as an endearing experimental effort, especially if seen from today's unadventurous cinematic times.

That said, the emphasis placed on the merging of the two characters represents a classic example of what we might call misplaced figurative emphasis, for the unconscious of Bertolucci's film does not seem to be related to the treatment of the theme of the double, but rather to the extraordinary visual energy produced by the film.[17] There is one particular shot that alerts us to the formal character of the film's unconscious. Half way through the film, the two Giacobbes come face to face within the same medium shot. The character on the left of the frame signals to his double to come closer. Whilst walking towards him, the latter suddenly fades in the invisible split that evidently (since the same actor plays both characters) cuts through the image. Then the remaining Giacobbe puts his jacket on, moves towards the other side of the shot as if to exit the room and, similarly to his double, vanishes in the same indiscernible cleavage of the shot. Explicitly drawing attention to its own formal magnitude, this technical detail points us towards the exact location of the film's unconscious, the strictly speaking non-figurative kernel of the image whose unacknowledged role is to buttress the relative narrative consistency of a surreal and inchoate story about schizophrenia. With this shot Bertolucci manages to suture the properly repressed core of his film, to the extent that the conclusive image of the empty frame of the widow, which allusively registers the disappearance of the two Giacobbes, should be read as tantamount to the reappearance of the film's disavowed ground.[18]

Apropos of this stitching up of the cinematic other, Stephen Heath has recently noted that, in the context of psychoanalytic film theory, '[s]uture is no longer doing too well [...]; as for real and symptoms, they have come up strong indeed' (Heath, 1999, p. 33). Despite the objective truthfulness of this statement, my immediate concern is that there is something fundamentally wrong if suture is dropped for the Real. What gets lost in this critical assumption is the capacity to understand that *the Real operates at the level of suture* (and vice versa), i.e., that excluding suture from film theory also implies doing away with the subversive dimension of the Real. On the contrary the crucial psychoanalytic insight resides in the obverse operation of *bringing the Real at the level of suture*, showing that the Real is operative precisely in the field from which it is supposedly excluded.

Let us start by addressing the question of the Lacanian origin of the term under scrutiny. In Lacan, the medical term suture (literally, stitching a wound) denotes the 'conjunction of the imaginary and the symbolic' (Lacan, 1998a, p. 118), the stitching together of the two representational registers at the expenses of the Real, which is thus closed off, or foreclosed. When, in the late 1970s, *Screen* translated and published a 1966 intervention by Jacques-Alain Miller on suture in Lacan (see Miller, 1977), followed by a 1969 article by Jean-Pierre Oudart (see Oudart, 1977), Stephen Heath, one of the journal's main theorists, was quick to recognise the political potential of those interventions. Thus, the debate on suture, film and semiotics flourished, marking one of the most intense decades in British film theory. In the meantime French semiologist Christian Metz had published his controversial and highly influential *The Imaginary Signifier. Psychoanalysis and the Cinema* (French original in 1975, English translation in 1977), which further inflamed the cause of the *Screen* critics. In this seminal text, Metz uses Lacan to demonstrate the imaginary status of film as mirror, which in turn leads to investigating questions of spectatorship. Metz sees the spectator as inevitably caught up in the repressive logic of imaginary identification. He regards the act of looking as essentially aggressive and narcissistic, driven by the will to control the cinematic image despite the latter being, by definition, ineffable. However influenced by Lacan's dialectics of desire, and therefore verging on the question of the Real, Metz's approach remains fundamentally indebted to structuralism, and as such it draws its political potential from the critique of the manipulative power of the film-structure over the spectator.

Between the 1970s and the 1980s, suture was thus employed as a symptomatic piece of evidence in a comprehensive effort to think cinema in conjunction with a re-politicised critical appraisal of culture. To put it simply, French film theory was offering two corners (semiology and psychoanalysis) of a conceptual triangle which critics like Heath, Teresa de Lauretis and others (particularly those writing for *Screen*) were striving to complete with Althusserian Marxist theories of ideology. My specific point is that in this attempt to bring together formalism and materialism, or rather psychoanalysis, Marxism and semiotics, *the victim was Lacan himself*, insofar as what was overlooked was the most destabilising feature of his theoretical edifice, namely the Real. I would suggest that Metz's "mirror", together with Laura Mulvey's "gaze" (undoubtedly the two theories that formed the dominant paradigm for the psycho-semiotics of film and media in the 1980s) were constructed around an insightful and yet limited recourse to Lacan, for the simple reason that they tended to concern themselves solely with the imaginary-symbolic level. The same line of argument can be applied to suture. In the heyday of structuralism, the debate on suture developed as a critique of the ways in which the filmic image resolves its foundational instability by anchoring it to a signifying structure, an operation which guarantees the consistency of film as "discourse of the Master", suturing the point of view of the spectator. As in the classic case of the shot/reverse-shot technique, the radical imbalance caused by the establishing shot and the apparent lack of its point of enunciation is immediately corrected by the reverse shot, which aligns the absent point of view to a character within the diegetic space, thereby neutralising the fracture between enunciated content and point of enunciation. The achievement of suture is that 'the difference between image and its absence/void is mapped onto the intra-pictural difference between the two shots' (Žižek, 2001a, p. 33), contributing to erasing traces of external disturbance, and consequently guaranteeing a sense of seamless continuity.

However, the weakness of this standard take on suture is not only that it reduces 'the spectator/film relation to one of pure specularity' (Heath, 1999, p. 33), but also, more crucially, that it fails to consider the relation between the cinematic image and its own unacknowledged excess. Apart from manipulating our perception, the cinematic image is always-already destabilised by its own secret liaison with the Real, since the Real (and this is the Lacanian crux of the matter) not only *sustains*, but also *stains*, what we see. Against the classic structuralist thesis that the spectator, trapped in imaginary identification, misrecognises the signifying mechanisms that effectively "run the ideological show" behind his or her back, Lacan claims that the ultimate illusion lies precisely in such a belief in the overwhelming consistency of the big Other (*qua* film).[19] From this angle it becomes apparent that, while Lacan's *Seminars* of the 1960s and 1970s were moving more and more decidedly towards the drives and the Real, the psycho-semiotic film studies of the 1970s and 1980s were still digesting the very first Lacan of imaginary/symbolic identification. While *Screen* theorists were elaborating the notion of fantasy as a repressive weapon (still at the heart of Metz's book), Lacanian theory was beginning to develop a more radical critical perspective, one involving precisely the "traversing of the fantasy", i.e. the endorsement of the fundamental inconsistency that cuts across the protective/repressive screen of fantasies. In this context, Lacan's *objet petit a*, the elusive object-cause of desire, is less a function of imaginary identification than the distorting feature responsible for what we see – the point being that it extends into the Real. Similarly, suture should not only be read alongside closure, identification and enforced meaning, but also as a reference to a Real which, far from simply deconstructing any stable representation of reality, *insists* in cinematic representation, sticking to it as the very deadlock that determines its specifically distorted outcome. The main question, therefore, seems to concern the nature and positioning of the unconscious *qua* lack: while Metz and other film semiologists had already identified the paradoxical function of a lack that organises our perception, they had not thought of it as Real, that is to say, as always-already there, on the surface, in the form of a contingent encounters invested by a wealth of unacknowledged fantasies whose parasitical insistence and pressure ultimately testify to film's failure as a system of symbolic signs.[20]

From a philosophical angle, what is at stake in this reading of the function of suture is the Hegelian notion of concrete universality, which refers to the presence of a particular element working as the generative matrix for all the others, allowing for the emergence of a symbolically consistent representation of reality. The fact that, as Žižek suggests (2001a, p. 33), this universally concrete element is 'very rarely encountered in its purity', only attests to its fundamentally displaced and enigmatic nature. Such a view can be measured against contemporary tendencies in film studies to dismiss over-arching theoretical paradigms. To cognitivist and new historicist Post-Theory claims that film analysis should be conducted through the examination of the multiple and relatively independent dimensions involved in the filmmaking process (the ideological bias of the narrative, the contingent economic determinants, the stylistic approach employed, etc.), Žižek replies that all of these dimensions ultimately coalesce around their own shared short-circuit, the place where they encounter an inherent impossibility common to all of them. This ground of "discursive derailment" is locatable through suture, the point where the external limitations/differences which relativise the film narrative (the different sets of analytic levels with their partial truths and epistemological gaps) become visible as *the internal impossibility for the film to fully become itself*. Ultimately, 'suture means that [...] the excluded externality always leaves its traces within' (Žižek, 2001a, p. 58). And precisely in the form of "internalised impossibility" (an excessive formation that defies integration) the Real of suture can be conceptualised as a traumatic encounter within the cinematic space, a filmic rendering of the Lacanian *tuché*: 'the encounter in so far as it may be missed, in so far as it is essentially the missed encounter' (Lacan, 1998a, p. 55). The passage is decisive, for it allows us to propound a theory of film which does not rely on the resigned and melancholic acknowledgement of the inevitability of phenomenal and epistemological limitations of film (the coexistence of a number of relatively independent fields such as style, narrative, ideology, etc.). By contrast, suture testifies to the fact that the theoretical basis for film analysis is to be sought in the fundamental internal inconsistency that structures the narrative content:

> We only attain the level of true Theory when, in a unique short-circuit, we conceive of a certain formal procedure not as expressing a certain aspect of the (narrative) content, but as marking/signalling the part of the content that is excluded from the explicit narrative line, so that – therein resides the proper theoretical point – *if we want to reconstruct "all" of the narrative content, we must reach beyond the explicit narrative as such, and include some formal features which act as the stand-in for the "repressed" aspect of the content* (Žižek, 2001a, p. 58).

With respect to film studies, the proper wager of Lacanian psychoanalysis pertains neither to the imaginary compulsion to identify with the narrative, nor to the typically postmodern melancholy of the inevitable inherent limitation of fictional representations. Rather, to put it bluntly, what matters on a theoretical level is that we have a chance to accede to truth. In 'la Chose Freudienne' Lacan speaks deliberately about the *pouvoir de la vérité*, the power of truth:

> And the meaning of what Freud said may be conveyed to anyone because, addressed as it is to all, it concerns each individual: to make this clear, one has only to remember that Freud's discovery puts truth into question, and there is no one who is not personally concerned by the truth. It must seem rather odd that I should be flinging this word in your faces – a word almost of ill repute, a word banished from polite society. Yet is it not inscribed at the very heart of our analytic practice, since this practice is constantly re-making the discovery of the power of the truth in ourselves, in our very flesh? In what could the unconscious be better recognized, in fact, than in the defences that are set up against it, with such success that they appear no less real? I am not reviving here the shoddy Nietzschean notion of the lie of life, nor am I astonished that one should believe oneself capable of belief, nor do I accept that it is enough to wish for something sufficiently to will it. But I am asking where the peace that follows the recognition of an unconscious tendency comes from if it is not more true than that which constrains it in the conflict? (Lacan, 1989, p. 130).

The paradox of truth as a Real that makes its presence felt through the unconscious is here fully articulated. The aim of Lacanian analytic treatment is that the analysand must strive to develop a relationship with the truth-thing inside, that symptomatic blot which forever remains a foreign body and nevertheless "speaks to us through us", fashioning our symbolic existence. From this awareness we can perhaps risk formulating what I would be tempted to call a "therapy of cinema". Its goal would be to locate and read the enigmatic traces left by the Real on the narrative plane of a film (or of a series of films), and recognise them in their direct relation to the narrative content, *insofar as the latter is nothing but the idiosyncratic swerve through which the Real makes its presence felt*. By saying that the aim of a Lacanian approach to film is to disturb the cinematic unconscious, we therefore imply that this unconscious can be tapped into by locating the disavowed and excessive cinematic features that are sutured in the narrative space of film so as to sustain the effect of self-enclosure. It is there, in the gaps between meaning and its hidden core, that one can come across the cinematic unconscious – just like, in Freud, the unconscious desire of a dream does not manifest itself through allegory or symbolism, but inhabits the psychotic gaps between the dream-text and the latent dream-thought.[21] In either case, the question of the unconscious does not concern meaning as such, but the dynamics that determine the emergence of meaning.

1.5 *BLOW-UP*: ABOUT NOTHING, WITH PRECISION

Another useful way to approach the cinematic unconscious is by focusing on Lacan's highly debated theory of the gaze, together with its corollary notions of the eye and the scopic drive. Owing to the exaggerated privilege accorded to the imaginary order, film critics who claim to draw on Lacan generally deploy a much abridged if not plainly misperceived understanding of the gaze (see Copjec, 1994, pp. 15–38; Jay, 1993). To rectify this approach one should first and foremost observe that Lacan posits the gaze as something ontological ('I have my own ontology – why not – like everyone else', Lacan, 1998a, p. 72), which does not coincide with the act of looking (which he calls "the eye"), but rather with the missing partial object of the scopic drive, the blot in the visual field that the eye cannot see and that, at the same time, always-already looks back at the subject: 'I see only from one point, but in my existence I am looked at from all sides' (Lacan, 1998a, p. 72). Bearing in mind that Lacan developed his theory of the gaze around 1964, in strict conjunction with his notion of *objet petit a*, it is vital to stress that the gaze assumes the specific connotation of object-cause of desire. As such the gaze is on the side of the object, a radically elusive formation which persists beyond visual representation, in as much as it does not directly emanate from the subject but it constitutes itself as a remainder of the act of looking: 'In our relation to things, insofar as this relation is constituted by the way of vision, and ordered in the figures of representation, something slips, passes, is transmitted, from stage to stage, and is always to some degree eluded in it – that is what we call the gaze' (Lacan, 1998a, p. 73).

Because of its distinctly elusive nature as object-cause of the visual drive, the gaze should be accorded a key strategic role in psychoanalytic film theory. To start with, it allows us to confer a new meaning to the notion of reflexivity. If we take the standard postmodern view of reflexivity as the quality of a work that more or less ostensibly displays a reflection on (the irreducibly inauthentic nature of) its own form, would it not be much more productive to radicalise the point and claim for it a foundational role, on the ground that cinema owes its representational status to the way in which it relates to the gaze *qua* radically decentred object? Could we not claim, to put it bluntly, that the necessary precondition for the emergence of cinema is cinema's own dialectical relationship with what it does not see? Paraphrasing Lacan, the camera sees and records the external world, and yet something constantly slips away from the visual field; rather than just disappearing, however, this kind of "excremental remainder" insists within the field, giving body to what Lacan calls 'the ambiguity that affects anything that is inscribed in the register of the scopic drive' (Lacan, 1998a, p. 83). It is against the backdrop of such ambiguity that we ought to read Lacan's claim that 'the gaze *qua objet a* [...] leaves the subject in ignorance as to what there is beyond appearance' (Lacan, 1998a, p. 77). The gaze is always-already attached to the visual field, its fundamental elusiveness transpires in what we see, to the extent that, ultimately, it determines the inherent distortion of the image (anamorphosis).

My wager is that cinema's own reflexive/self-referential nature offers us a unique chance to investigate the correlation between what we see and permeate with meaning and the displaced element that governs it most secretly. If, as Lacan indicates, in a state of consciousness the gaze is inevitably elided, the potential of cinema as the reflexive art *par excellence* is that of recasting this elision as 'the underside of consciousness' (Lacan, 1998a, p. 83), illuminating the way in which what is excluded remains 'operative in what is seen': 'what counts is not what is there to be seen but the insistence through it of unconscious desire, which indeed is decisively operative in what is seen' (Heath, 1999, p. 30). The crux of the matter, the quandary that convinced Freud of the impossibility of any productive interconnection between psychoanalysis and cinema, is the thorny issue of the figurative/non-figurative nature of the unconscious (see Heath, 1999, pp. 30–1). To Freud, the obstacle between the two disciplines is insurmountable because of the inescapably plastic dimension of cinema, which relies too much on the assertiveness of images, and is thus ill equipped to render the "invisible presence" of the unconscious. Lacan, however, allows us to solve the problem by completely turning around its presuppositions, that is, by claiming that what we see is always-already an effect of the invisible Real, insofar as reality itself is a field which holds up 'only by the extraction of the *objet a*, which, however, gives it its frame' (Lacan, 1989, p. 247). Shifting the emphasis on the legibility of the unconscious and on the visibility of the Real (with the proviso that the unconscious and the Real can be located through the analysis of the effects they have on the visual field), Lacanian theory bridges the Freudian gap between the non-figurative and the figurative, suggesting that it is precisely in the "too-visual" of cinema, in the redundancy of the image, that one should seek its unacknowledged structuring kernel.

In Italian cinema, Michelangelo Antonioni's *Blow-Up* (1967) provides an ideal terrain to access the Lacanian dialectics of eye (the act of looking) and gaze, whilst indirectly confirming Pasolini's views on editing. Rather than a self-referential meditation on the impossible relationship between cinema (art) and reality, as the standard interpretation has it, Antonioni's film obfuscates the dividing line between the two. It does so by focusing on what I am tempted to call its own fundamental fantasy (its deepest fantasmatic kernel), as it targets and unpacks the normally repressed dialectics of representation – which incidentally should be understood as relating not only to cinema, but to the visual field *tout court*.

The plot revolves around Thomas (David Hemmings), a young London fashion photographer obsessed with (and increasingly frustrated by) his job, which involves, essentially, the act of looking (as well as working in the fashion industry, he is also preparing a book of art photographs about life in London). From the start, the audience is compelled to partake in Thomas's visual universe, which is less organised around his desire to see than around what I would be tempted to call a desire turned scopic drive. In rigorous correlation with the Lacanian gaze, this drive manifests itself as a compulsion to look and miss, an indomitable, exasperating urge to chase the elusive object in the visual field. The sheer persistence of Thomas's will to see, however, soon provokes a turn of events, a kind of epiphany: the missing object (the gaze) suddenly materialises. After developing the photographs of two lovers secretly taken in a London park, Thomas notices that in one of the pictures the woman (played by Vanessa Redgrave) turns her head away from her lover, directing her eyes apprehensively at something else. Through successive enlargements and an ingenious editing operation (whereby the pictures are pinned against the wall one after the other in strict chronological order) the photographer discovers that the woman was looking at the blurred contour of a man hidden behind bushes, holding a gun. Despite being convinced of having saved somebody's life, as he tells his friend Ron on the phone, Thomas is still somewhat unhappy with his discovery; later, in fact, he goes back to enlarging and matching more pictures related to the incident, until he encounters a further piece of evidence. What the enlargements allow him to see is what seems to be the head of the dead lover protruding from behind the bottom of a tree. More blowups confirm this first impression, although the zoomed-in point in the photograph that attracts Thomas's eye eventually comes to resemble an uncannily derealised blot resembling an abstract painting. In a desperate attempt to verify the truthfulness of the image, he rushes to the park, sees the dead body, even touches it, and then returns to his studio. There he finds out that all his evidence, film and prints (apart from the abstract image of the dead man), have been stolen (presumably by the Redgrave character, who had previously paid a visit to Thomas and unsuccessfully attempted to gain possession of the film). After much hesitation, Thomas resolves to return to the park, but only to discover that even the dead body has now vanished. In the final sequence, an utterly dejected and disoriented Thomas watches a group of mimes (the same ones we saw at the start of the film) playing a fake tennis match in the park, with no rackets nor ball. In the very last shot, Antonioni's camera zooms out and Thomas himself disappears from the frame.[22]

The central question upon which Thomas's destiny depends could be formulated as follows: what is the exact status of the blurred image of the dead man that emerges on the background of the blown-up photograph? The first point to make is that this ambiguous image relates less to the homicide in the actual narrative than to the question of the ontological status of

Blow-up

reality as such. Indeed, this unclear detail functions like the crucial piece of evidence in a detective story, although instead of throwing light on the murder it uncovers the dialectics of the eye and the gaze, the visual field and its unacknowledged kernel. More precisely, the film suggests that reality relies on the abyssal elusiveness of what, in normal conditions, remains unseen by the subject. Almost paraphrasing Lacan's reference to expressionism as a corrective exception to the 'taming of the gaze' generally perpetrated by painting,[23] Antonioni commented that Thomas 'wants to see things more closely. But he discovers that, in enlarging too much, the object itself decomposes and disappears. Thus there is an instant in which reality comes forth, but then immediately thereafter it vanishes' (quoted in Chatman, 1985, p. 141). This reality that comes forth and vanishes, this nucleus of *jouissance* provided by the gaze, however, is not the proverbial "unattainable beyond" that condemns us to the painful relativity of knowledge; rather, it corresponds to the Lacanian *objet a*, whose elusiveness sets up the subject's fictional perception of reality. With reference to Thomas's relationship to *objet a*, what we should insist on is that his desire to see turns into death-drive, that is, he is overwhelmed by a compulsion to over-identify with the blind spot responsible for his subjective perception of the world. The key point is therefore that Thomas's confrontation with the radical ambiguity of the blurred image is eventually what determines the collapse of his sense of selfhood (literally, Thomas collapses into *objet a*), as he is thrown into a kind of Hitchcockian estrangement, a condition of radical alienation (which Lacan calls symbolic death) that literally makes him a stranger to himself.

After seeing the dead body, and after the shock of the disappearance of all the evidence, Thomas goes through a series of circumstances whose function is precisely to highlight his sense of estrangement, the fact that he has "died to himself". First he thinks he sees the accomplice of the Redgrave character, tries to follow him but ends up in an underground concert which ends with the band smashing the equipment and throwing a broken guitar to the audience, who start fighting for it. Thomas manages to get hold of the object, runs away but eventually drops it as if he had suddenly grown totally indifferent to it (the piece of guitar clearly functioning as a fetish, an ultimately insignificant surrogate of *objet a*). Then he goes looking for his friend Ron at a party where everyone is taking drugs, including Ron. Very agitated, he tries to convey to his friend the gravity of what he has witnessed, but eventually, when Ron asks him 'So, what did you see in that park?', his answer is 'Nothing' (which of course, metaphorically speaking, is exactly what he saw).

The devastating impact that the showing of gaze has on the main character is perfectly captured the first time Thomas witnesses the existence of the dead body in the park: seconds after he has touched this body, we hear an uncanny, unlocatable background noise that seems to emanate from the rustling of the trees in the wind, and yet resembles the clicking of a camera or, possibly, a gun. The scene is reminiscent of the famous passage in Sartre's *Being and Nothingness*, commented upon by Lacan and functional to his theory of the gaze, where the existence of others is deduced from the surprising and shaming intervention of an unseen gaze, introduced precisely by such noises as the rustling of foliage. However, Lacan points out that the problem with Sartre's gaze is that it is 'not a seen gaze, but a gaze imagined by me in the field of the Other'. For Lacan, by contrast, the gaze does not depend on what we hear (rustling of leaves, footsteps, etc.) but it pertains to the organ of sight; as such, it is something that the subject *can* encounter in the visual field, precisely insofar as we posit the subject of the visual field as 'sustaining himself in a function of desire'. The encounter with the gaze thereby signals a traumatic event for the subject who wants to see, a short-circuit that radically undermines the allegiance between desire and the visual field: 'Is it not precisely because desire is established here in the domain of seeing that we can make it vanish?' (Lacan, 1998a, pp. 44–5). This vanishing of desire, correlative to the showing of the gaze, implies nothing less than *aphanisis* (see Lacan, 1998a, pp. 216–29), the collapse of the subject's symbolic efficiency, which is exactly what Thomas experiences at the end of his brave investigations.

Going back to the background noise, we can clarify its significance through Lacan, rather than Sartre, not only because the gaze shows, but also because its showing coincides with a traumatic moment of truth for the subject. More precisely, when the gaze finally appears as a figuration of lack (the dead man) bravely acknowledged by Thomas (who, like a modern Saint Thomas, needs to touch it to believe it), the photographer himself, for the first time without his camera, literally *falls into the picture*, i.e. is "photographed" (hence the clicking noise), reduced to the very empty kernel of his subjectivity finally overlapping with the empty kernel in the visual field. The dead man is thus the metonymical manifestation of the elusiveness of the gaze ('the blind spot in the field of the visible from which the picture itself photographs the spectator', Žižek, 2001b, p. 201),[24] where the truth about Thomas emerges. This is why it is possible to rethink Thomas's existential trajectory in relation to Lacan's ethics of the unconscious: the subject (Thomas) comes to be in the very gap that structures external reality.

With specific reference to the ontological status of reality, the standard critical view that to Antonioni appearances matter *in themselves*, and not for their relation to a more authentic dimension, should be clarified. On the evidence of *Blow-up*, it seems that what lies behind the fictitious layer of reality is always-already another appearance, which, however, qualifies itself through its relationship to void. The very question of the gap between appearance and reality, therefore, should not deceive us: what is at stake here is not the postmodern commonplace of the limits of representation, nor the equally worn out notion that reality 'does not have any *inherent*, immutable, fixed meaning', as its significance 'is always socially (and therefore historically) determined' (Brunette, 1998, p. 117). Rather, the great merit of Antonioni's filmmaking is to be sought in its insistence on absolute immanence: in the fact that it thoroughly rejects the opposition between the notion of an 'immutable, fixed meaning' of reality (the "impossible beyond") and appearances. Instead, it focuses, with unparalleled precision, on the foundational gap between a pervasively fictional domain and its disavowed, excessive, non-symbolisable underside. With specific reference to this gap, *Blow-up* demonstrates that if we get rid of appearances we get rid of reality *tout court*: what we encounter once we strive to purify reality of its frustratingly incomplete, phenomenal dimension, once we try to reach the very core of what is real, is nothing but a fundamental lack, the trace of void of the gaze, whose "showing" leaves the subject, literally, in ignorance as to what there is beyond appearance (insofar as, 'if beyond appearance there is nothing in itself, there is the gaze', Lacan, 1998a, p. 103).

The fact that this utterly enigmatic gaze coincides with a dead body should not prevent us from drawing the crucial conclusion: it is not that, as argued by Ropars-Wuilleumier (in Cuccu,

1988, p. 208), death cannot be seized and written by the film; even less is Antonioni warning the artist (himself) that 'the search for visual truth can be dangerous' as 'the artist risks disorientation, a kind of madness and even death' (Chatman, 1985, p. 142). On the contrary *Blow-up* shows that cinema has the potential to establish a relationship with that non-representational kernel which, far from simply indicating the presence of death, announces the traumatic/impossible dimension of the Real as the final stage in the journey of desire turned drive. As Žižek (2001b, p. 202) remarks *apropos* of Hitchcock, we go from 'the impossibility to see the object' to 'an object that gives body to this very impossibility'. Consequently, the conclusion elicited by *Blow-up* is that as soon as the gaze reveals the abyssal emptiness concealed behind its fantasmatic status, the subject fascinated by this gaze (Hemmings) "loses the ground from under his feet". Put differently, and emphasising the traumatic/liberating dimension at play in such a predicament, it is obvious that the hero of the film accomplishes the Lacanian *traversée du fantasme*, the traversing of the fantasy (see Lacan, 1998a, p. 273), which is the very aim of the analytic treatment: he discovers that his fantasy scenario (the representation of reality), and consequently his own consistency as a desiring subject, was sustained by an empty signifier.

When Antonioni told painter and personal friend Mark Rothko that his paintings were, like his own films, 'about nothing, with precision' (quoted in Chatman, 1985, p. 54), he hit the right cord: his cinema obsessively encroaches upon the question of representation, as its ultimate aim is that of showing how representation hinges on a decentring short-circuit, the unbridgeable fracture between what we see and what we do not see, what we see and what is always-already looking back at us. Or how else are we to explain the unmistakably static, frustratingly open ended, uncannily enigmatic quality of his films? What we should not forego is the crucial insight into self-reflexivity: Antonioni's films appear non-cinematic, in the sense that they tend to defy the basic rules of narrativisation, because they are driven by an unstoppable attraction to the gaze, the blind spot whose proximity undermines any form of symbolic/narrative stability.

1.6 A THEOREM ON THE NON-EXISTENCE OF TERENCE STAMP

A similar mechanism is at work in Pier Paolo Pasolini's *Teorema* (Theorem, 1968), which was released a year after *Blow-up*, and shares with Antonioni's film an obvious concern with the rebellious spirit of the late 1960s. The standard interpretation of *Teorema* draws upon a basic assumption, by and large confirmed by Pasolini himself (see Stack, 1969, pp. 155–62): that the film's central theme is to be found in the rigid opposition between the authenticity of the nameless Terence Stamp character (the "stranger", the mysterious guest of a bourgeois Milanese household who seduces each member of the family and then leaves them to mourn his sudden departure) and the hypocrisy of the bourgeois milieu in which he intervenes. This reading seems corroborated by the coupling of two powerful motifs: the magnetic sexual attraction exercised by the stranger and the classic Pasolinian topic of the "sacredness of the sub-proletariat" (represented by the maid Emilia first,[25] and, secondly, by the literary reference to the character of Gerasim[26] in Tolstoy's *The Death of Ivan Ilych*). Both these motifs are clearly aimed at ruthlessly exposing the vacuity of the bourgeois universe, the existential void behind its luxuriously hypocritical façade. However, precisely such a reference to the sacred nature of the stranger demands a certain awareness of the film's presuppositions: what is the exact meaning and impact of the notion of authenticity in this film (and, by extension, in Pasolini's oeuvre)? To answer this question we need to refine the standard critical approach to the film's ideological concern: rather than embodying anthropological authenticity (that is, in Pasolini's terms, a human being who has managed to remain uncorrupted by bourgeois values) the stranger should be perceived as a sublime and fantasmatic incarnation of a lack, if only because, given his role as object-cause of desire, he conforms to the Lacanian view that desire is always set in motion by a trace of void. In other words, it is only by accomplishing the step from "anthropological substance" to "pure form" that we can grasp the subversive content of the film, as well as how it relates to Pasolini's film theory of the 1960s. Pasolini's own definition of the Stamp character as a kind of divinity, a historical materialisation of some unfathomable super-sensible content, conveys precisely the idea of a formalised life-substance enmeshed with its particular context while simultaneously eluding it (see Stack, 1969, pp. 155–62).

Furthermore, this reference to form allows us to rectify two divergent critical commonplaces about Pasolini's cinema: firstly, the idea that it is characterised by a quasi-naturalistic endeavour to document the existence of anthropologically authentic and vastly unaccredited realities; secondly, that it is driven by a beguiling attachment to such notions as "the sacred" and "myth", or, more generally, to an aestheticising vision of the world. Against these persuasions, I would argue that Pasolini's cinema is neither phenomenological nor particularly poetic, but rather intellectualistic. From this angle *Teorema* is perhaps one of Pasolini's trademarks precisely because of its extreme rationalism, mainly conveyed by its abstract and geometric rigour, which translates into a somewhat delirious attempt to capture the essence of reality through a latent self-referential loop. In this respect Pasolini's theoretical reflections, despite their amateurish appearance, are inseparable from his film practice.

Given its heavy reliance on semiotics, *Teorema* demands to be read as a crystalline demonstration of how the Real is always-already entangled in the structure, i.e. in the operative framework that in the 1960s circumscribed the space for cultural and political intervention. Despite his affinity to the sub-proletariat or, as has been suggested, his potential closeness to the student movement, I argue that the Stamp character is a sign to be deciphered as an anthropomorphic figuration of *objet a*. As such, he embodies the hidden/repressed formal condition for the possibility of narration itself.

This logic is uncovered right at the start of the film. After each family member is briefly sketched in sepia colours, with diegetic sound eerily replaced by an angst-ridden musical comment, we witness an abrupt and unexpected cut to another cinematic dimension (a structural jump) which signals the arrival of the stranger/visitor, as images are suddenly filled with colours and diegetic sound. What does this cut imply? According to the standard interpretation, Pasolini intended to portray middle-class life as grey, meaningless and nightmarish, whilst the arrival of the stranger would bring vitality and desire. This view, however, should be submitted to a significant revision: what if the materialisation of the foreign body is simply aimed at re-establishing a sense of "normality as we know it", a normality accompanied and authenticated by a proper narrative, familiar and bearable enough for us to identify with? As is well known, Lacan claims that the perception of our universe as symbolically stable depends on the distance we keep, through fantasy, from the object-cause of desire. Contrary to what we tend to believe, the main function of desire is not to destabilise, but to help us achieve stability, insofar as it inscribes a safety distance between ourselves and the "impossible" object-cause of desire. So what we get at the beginning of the film is the passage from a strange "reality without desire", to a normalised "reality with desire", which emerges when *objet a* falls into the picture, setting in motion a desire that assembles the narrative and automatically restores the credibility of the image. In a nutshell, "we see" (our world is symbolically meaningful) precisely because "we fantasise" (fantasy is what sustains our field of vision).

However, this explanation is not entirely convincing, for we could legitimately argue that fantasy and desire must have already been at work in the opening scene (where the characters appear fully immersed in their everyday lives, and yet their depiction is oddly out of focus), which, therefore, has no reason to be visually distorted. Decisive to our argument is the acknowledgement of the structural significance held by the disturbingly derealised images that open the narrative. Far from simply designating the grey humus of the bourgeois universe, these images indicate that the dimension of the Real is foundational, that is to say, it is always-already at work as the underlying premise of any narrative. The establishing shots of the film appear oddly warped because they connote a displacement of visual perspective: what we see is less reality without desire than *reality looked at from the point of view of the decentred, free-floating gaze*, from the impossible angle of the Thing, whose elision instantly sets up the symbolic world of the characters. To put it in Lacan's own words, what matters in this passage 'is the pre-existence of a gaze – I see only from one point, but in my existence I am looked at from all sides' (Lacan, 1998a, p. 72): while the family members carry on with their normal lives, the stranger *qua* gaze is looking at them all the time from all sides, and what happens in the opening scene is effectively an attempt (inevitably destined to fail, and yet successful all the same) to align our point of view with that of the impossible Thing.[27]

Herein lies the hidden theoretical key to unlock Pasolini's narrative: the stranger intervenes in a situation in which he is always-already operative, as it is the radical otherness/externality of his gaze that secures the framework of the visible. Nevertheless, it is only when he enters this framework in the guise of an enigmatic human being (*objet a*) that, for us, the normal perspective is restored. This movement from outside to inside accomplishes the shift of *our* visual perspective from the impossible point of view of the gaze (the stranger before appearing) to that of the characters (the eye) who manage to focus on *objet a*. This is how the film reflects upon the inner functioning of the scopic field: we see not because everything is visible, but because something always defies the eye, persisting beyond the remit of mere representation. This *something*, which Pasolini endeavours to situate at the heart of filmmaking, is precisely 'that which always escapes from the grasp of that form of vision that is satisfied with itself in imagining itself as consciousness' (Lacan, 1998a, p. 74).

Pasolini understands that only by cutting from the external to the internal (from the point of view of the Thing to our own) it is possible, visually speaking, to do the logic of desire full justice, as the object-cause of desire occupies a radically displaced dimension, the very self-fracture of the visible. The extraordinary cut which kick-starts *Teorema* represents therefore a vertiginous cinematic act, revealing to us the meaning of Pasolini's "passion for the Real". What is ultimately sutured is none other than the gap between the Universal (the impossible, free-floating gaze) and the Particular (the eye), a gap which is filled out by the stranger in his function of *objet a*. Such an ingenious displacement of perspectives corresponds to the miraculous passage from the impossible to the possible, from "the appearance of truth" to "the truth of appearance". The inherently subversive dimension of this act is discernible in the fact that the formal co-ordinates of the entire narrative situation (colour and sound) are profoundly transformed. No wonder the film is ridden with biblical references and religious undertones: the stranger is effectively a Christ-like figure who mediates between his own impossible nature (God *qua* gaze) and the world of humans immersed in the field of the visible (the eye), oblivious to what lies beyond it (the Ur-code of reality).

The implicitly Lacanian ambition displayed in this shift of perspectives is touched upon by Pasolini in his famous 1967 essay 'Observations on the long-take', where he focuses on the discrepancy between the famous 16 mm. long-take film of Kennedy's death by Abraham Zapruder, and the ideal film that would vouchsafe the truth on the assassination by garnering 'all the remaining visual angles: from Kennedy's visual angle, to that of Jacqueline, of the killer as he was shooting, of his accomplices, of the better-placed witnesses, of the bodyguards, etc.' (Pasolini, 1995, p. 237). Despite being fully aware of how constitutively unconceivable it is to bring together in one long-take a sum of concomitant visual perspectives, Pasolini nevertheless holds that these perspectives can be organised diachronically through editing. The cutting and selection of the hypothetical long-takes of Kennedy's death would convert the impossibility of the truth/gaze (say, the impossible point of view of God) into the possibility of its technical reconstruction. Nonetheless, this passage from impossible to possible (from invisible to visible) can only be attained through a kind of visual trick, a "deception through displacement" whereby the abyssal fracture separating the (objective) gaze from the (subjective) single shot (or long-take) is redoubled in the shot itself, since the fundamental and necessary presupposition of the cutting and pasting of cinematic images is, according to Pasolini, the mediation of the negativity of death. In view of this, we can see how the cut that introduces the Stamp character in *Teorema* effectively lays bare the fundamental logic of editing: it makes the invisible visible through the sheer displacement of the negative.

At this stage it is worth returning to the specific nature of Pasolini's *objet a*. The stranger's visibility is clearly informed by strong socio-political connotations, in line with most of Pasolini's films and theoretical interventions on cinema: to acquire visibility, the underlying Ur-code of reality (the Real) has to assume the precise anthropological content of that social body which represents, either directly or metaphorically, the point of exclusion of a given hegemonic context. As anticipated, due to *Teorema*'s abstract and lapidary quality, the point of exclusion is not merely associated with the sub-proletariat but becomes perceivable in its purely formal function of mediator between the Universal and the Particular. This is crucial, for it allows us to appreciate the Lacanian underpinnings of Pasolini's cinema. If we remind ourselves that one of the definitions of *objet petit a* is that of a thing whose appearance coincides with its withdrawal, or a figuration of lack, it is easy to see that Pasolini's audacity resides in his attempt to represent what is by definition beyond representation. So what matters here is less the stranger in its historical capacity than what he evokes, that is, the emptiness conjured up by his mesmeric presence on screen (a "void-effect" which is conveyed particularly well by the recurrent long held close-ups of his indifferent facial expressions). That is why any attempt to pin him down as a direct socio-political signifier does not work.[28] Perhaps it would be more productive to probe his (unconscious) significance through one of the many meta-narrative references of the film, such as the allusion to the English expressionist painter Francis Bacon (1909–1992). Do we not find in this brief passage (when Pietro shows the stranger an album of paintings by Bacon) the condensed nucleus of explosive libido that structures the narrative? Does not Bacon, a homosexual artist whose work thrived on his propensity for sado-masochism, represent an almost perfect pendant to the subversive core of Pasolini's (cinematic) desire?

On the other hand, it may be useful to consider Pasolini's own definition of the stranger: 'This character has come out ambiguous, half-way between the angelic and the demonic. The visitor is good-looking, and good, but there is something vulgar about him as well (since he, too, is a member of the bourgeoisie). [...] So there is this element of vulgarity in him, which he has accepted to descend among these bourgeois people, so he is ambiguous' (in Stack, 1969, p. 158). What counts here is that the divine has, as it were, accepted to metamorph into a bourgeois human being *in order to make himself visible*. The implication is that the fracture between transcendence (the divine) and immanence (the bourgeois universe of fictional appearances) is inherent to immanence itself, i.e., it can only manifest itself as the minimal difference between the appearance of our everyday world and the appearance of the residual object (*objet a*) that comes to occupy the place of the empty Thing, thus assuming upon itself all the weight of the inaccessible beyond. This transcendental beyond, therefore, can only be conceived as a gap in our world of appearances. As such, the inconsistency of the phenomenal world corresponds to both the Hegelian appearance *qua* appearance, and the Lacanian *doublure* (the redoubling of the gap between transcendence and immanence into immanence itself):

> What the object is masking, dissimulating, by its massive, fascinating presence, is not some other positivity but its own place, the void, the lack that it is filling in by its presence – the lack in the Other. And what Lacan calls "going-through the fantasy" consists precisely in the experience of such an inversion apropos of the fantasy-object: the subject must undergo the experience of how the ever-lacking object-cause of desire is in itself nothing but an objectification, an embodiment of a certain lack; of how its fascinating presence is here just to mask the emptiness of the place it occupies, the emptiness which is exactly the lack in the Other – which makes the big Other (the symbolic order) perforated, inconsistent (Žižek, 1992, p. 195).

It is in this specific theoretical context that Pasolini's appraisal of Christianity should be understood. As one can deduce from his entire cinematic oeuvre, and particularly from *Il vangelo secondo Matteo* (The Gospel according to St. Matthew, 1964), Christianity for him represents a unique narrative capable of projecting essence (the sacred) onto the field of actuality, insofar as it turns the externality/transcendence of essence (God) into the minimal difference that cuts across the surface of things. And the Stamp character occupies a position correlative to this gap within immanence, for what shines through him is the evanescent and yet traumatic light of another dimension that radically antagonises the finite field of phenomena. This also means that with his fundamental elusiveness the Christ-like stranger effectively makes visible, in a literal sense, the non-existence of God, i.e. the fact that God coincides with an abyss of negativity. To say it with Robert Musil, he is a man without qualities: he represents the very gap between the human and the divine which designates the divine dimension in man.

Precisely as a profoundly Christian figure, the Stamp character should be appreciated as a metonymy of lack: ultimately, its significance derives from that prodigious cut at the start of the film, that brutal interference of editing through which he makes his appearance. This cut that allows the visitor to materialise is the exact equivalent of the cut between the two shots of Othello's head in *Che cosa sono le nuvole?* In both cases what is sutured is the void from which the cinematic image emerges. And in the late 1960s, in the glory days of structuralism, the question at the heart of Pasolini's film theory and practice was precisely how to posit and represent the fundamental lack that sustains film as a symbolic texture. *Teorema* is perhaps Pasolini's clearest attempt at answering that question: a lucid parable, a geometrically consistent allegory that shamelessly reveals its empty core.

The very fact that the stranger comes from nowhere and disappears back into the same narrative hole can be reformulated in strictly self-reflexive terms, i.e. as evidence that he belongs to the intersticial fissures of editing. That is what he is: an impossible signifier whose miraculous appearance is ultimately aimed at exposing the liminal presence of the cinematic unconscious, the dimension of filmmaking which has to be barred if film is to occur. We are now in the position to put forward the decisive claim that the Stamp character is nothing but the Lacanian analyst, the 'subject supposed to know' (see Lacan, 1998a, pp. 230–43), a Master Signifier whose imposture (as he occupies the place of the impossible Thing) aims at bringing the analysand (the bourgeoisie) face to face with their traumatic fundamental fantasy.[29] What the second part of the film successfully demonstrates is not only that the fascination with the object-cause of desire is fundamentally an illusion, but, more crucially, that this illusion can only be experienced as a traumatic encounter:

> To "unmask the illusion" does not mean that "there is nothing to see behind it": what we must be able to see is precisely this *nothing as such* – beyond the phenomena, there is nothing *but this nothing itself, "nothing" which is the subject*. To conceive the appearance as "mere appearance" the subject has effectively to go beyond it, to "pass over" it, but what he finds there is his own act of passage. [...] the subject is the void, the hole in the Other, and the object the inert content filling up this void; the subject's entire "being" thus consists in the fantasy-object filling out this void (Žižek, 1992, pp. 195–96).

To put it differently, we could say that after the stranger's departure the bourgeois characters realise that they have accomplished the Lacanian "going though the fantasy", which has brought them to occupy the Hegelian place behind the 'curtain of appearance' (Hegel, 1977, p. 103), where they experience the void constitutive of the subject.

Strictly speaking, therefore, Pasolini's conceptualisation of editing in its specific correlation with death should be seen as an act of violence. Each editing cut that contributes to the creation of film is tantamount to a deadly wound: as Lacan would have put it, the construction of film-sense can only take place if underscored by a succession of imperceptible crimes, and the more these crimes are repressed and displaced, the more film will strengthen its fictional meaning, what we might dub its cinematic ego. Pasolini, it appears, was well aware of this dialectical logic, if from the moment he decided to re-invent himself as a film theorist he never stopped trying to formulate the seemingly eccentric notion that film as a cultural medium had to do with death. His declared faith in editing, and therefore in a cinema that tells stories (see Pasolini, 1995, pp. 245–47), also entails a belief in the implicitly destructive power of filmmaking. His very conviction that there is no substantial difference between cinema and reality, since both are anchored in the same ineffable Ur-code, amounts to an endorsement of the foundational sway of the negative. Ultimately, each of Pasolini's many objects of desire, from the Roman sub-proletariat to the African peasants, are nothing but as many emblematic manifestations of his Hegelian determination to "tarry with the negative": in each of them we can read what Cesare Garboli (1969, p. 15), coining a very apt oxymoron, called Pasolini's 'deadly vitality'. From this angle, *Teorema* works as a purified demonstration of its author's deep-seated faith in the power of the negative.

It is quite a paradox that those who speak about Pasolini's cinema as essentially "uncinematic", i.e. as relying more on the autonomy of the shot than on narrative consistency, should completely misperceive the impact of his theorisation of editing.[30] What is normally missed is that Pasolini's films appear to privilege the unity of single shots *precisely because, in them, editing draws attention to itself*. Let us repeat the main argument: Pasolini's idea of editing as *the* formal feature responsible for the emergence of cinematic meaning only makes sense if read alongside the parallel between editing and death, as editing stands for the intangible negativity of death, its profoundly disruptive potential. No wonder, then, that Pasolini's films seem fragmented and lacking in narrative continuity! What should be emphasised is not just the primacy of the shot, but the relationship between the shot and its underpinning negativity. Pasolini's typically long-held, frontal close-ups, his stylistic cipher *par excellence*, are nothing but ephemeral figurations of the Real, so many "masks of death" giving form to the central void around which his narratives are woven. The auratic character of these frontal shots relates to the very void of editing from which they emerge. Thus, these films are indeed fully-blown narratives that *appear* disjointed due to the emphasis they confer on the ambiguous, deeply antagonistic function of editing. It is the intrusiveness of the editing procedure that shackles narrative continuity.

So, again, the critical discussion should centre on the rift opened up by Pasolini's cinema, the split between its conscious content and its unconscious/negative underside. In *Teorema*, as we have seen, this rift is locatable as a vertiginous shifting of visual perspectives, from that of the impossible signifier to that of the family members. We start on the side of an external gaze, we move inside the picture and change point of view as the gaze enters the universe of the characters by becoming an unnamed visitor, and finally we remain inside the picture to witness the vanishing of this elusive figure and the consequential reappearance of the gaze in all its lacerating negativity. The crisis of the "bourgeois signs" is therefore determined by the presence of a ghost: *the presence of absence*, the awareness that the characters have been left with an unbearably empty gaze weighing upon them. And the point is that this gaze, as Pasolini himself put it in a 1967 interview, is inextricably enmeshed with life, i.e. it is Real: 'Cinema is identical to life, because each one of us has a virtual and invisible camera which follows us from when we are born to when we die' (Pasolini, 1967, p. 609).

The significance of this insistence on the gaze *qua* Real is perhaps best explained by the biblical quotation that opens the film: 'Thou hast seduced me, oh God, and I have left myself be seduced; thou hast violated me and thou hast prevailed. I am in derision daily, every one mocketh me', from the Book of Jeremiah. The Christological visitor causes a violent subjective shattering that brings the characters, literally, through the desert of the Real, face to face with the inconsistency of their fundamental fantasy – which is, of course, none other than *capital* itself. Each of them realises that their subjective positions coincides with their socio-historical roles, which in turn are moored in capital. As we have seen, the violence of this act of divine penetration is formally subsumed in the initial shift of perspectives. The following content-related penetrations (the real sexual acts between the Stamp character and the members of the Milanese family) are more easily detectable filiations of this primary formal shift.

1.7 THE DESERT AND THE PARK

If the Terence Stamp character is a ghost, a metonymy of lack, there is in *Teorema* another feature subtly situated between the narrative and the non-narrative, that deliberately discloses the film's secret dynamics: the desert. *Teorema* is punctuated by a number of apparently immaterial and redundant shots of sand dunes (in actual fact, shots of mount Etna). With respect to this bizarre diegetic intruder, the first thought goes again to editing. Despite the fact that, as the narrative develops, the image of the desert acquires well-defined symbolic connotations, I would argue that precisely as a spectral mediator between different narrative situations the desert in *Teorema* offers itself as a figurative illustration of the symptomatic function of editing. In brief, the structuring negativity underpinning the editing procedure is reflected onto the narrative through recurrent shots of an empty desert. In fact, one could say that the "formal desert" (related to editing) eventually overlaps with the "symbolically meaningful desert". Owing to such a convergence of form and content, this feature seems to epitomise the very function of the Lacanian Real. It is in his book *Teorema*, published in 1968 at the same time of the film's release, that Pasolini reveals his intention to deploy the image of the desert as a symbol of the Real, particularly when he defines it a 'reality / stripped of everything except its own essence' (Pasolini, 1968, p. 197).

What we find in this unique book, conceived as something between a script of the film and a literary work (mixing prose and poetry) in its own right, is a series of references describing the encounter with what Žižek, quoting a famous line from the Wachowski brothers' film *The Matrix* (1999), calls 'the desert of the Real' (see particularly Žižek, 2002a). In sections 25 and 26 of the first part of the book, Pasolini describes the sexual encounter between the stranger and Paolo, the father, as we see it unfold in the film: the two go for a drive on a country road, stop by a river and disappear together in the nearby vegetation. At this stage in the film we have the usual cutting to/through the image of the desert, which is matched, in the book, by a six-page section allusively entitled 'The Jews made their way...', and explicitly focused on the image of the desert. The book expands on what the film had only briefly mentioned at the beginning, when a slow pan of the desert was accompanied by an off-screen voice commenting 'And God forced the people through the desert'. This biblical reference is clarified in section 27 of the book, when the fictional character Paolo is smoothly transubstantiated into the biblical Paul. Pasolini does not elaborate on Paul's conversion,[31] he simply tells of his shattering experience in the desert, defining the latter as an overwhelming and totalising presence: 'It was born out of itself, it continued in itself and it finished in itself'. The desert is One, the very 'idea of One-ness [Unicità]': 'The One-ness of the desert was like a dream that does not let you sleep and from which you cannot awake' (Pasolini, 1968, p. 88). The homology with the Lacanian Real is reasserted when the desert takes on the typical connotation of the gaze: 'the desert was looking at him [Paul] from every point of its infinitely open horizon. Nothing could protect Paul from that gaze: wherever he was – that is, always in the same place – [...] that gaze reached him without difficulty: with the very peace, spontaneity and violence typical of the sun, unchangeable' (Pasolini, 1968, p. 91).

Let us now consider the end of *Teorema*, when Paolo – the rich industrialist who as a consequence of his encounter with the stranger donates his factory to the workers – ends up like Paul on the way to Damascus, alone in the desert (of the Real). His scream of pure despair that ends and yet does not end the film, since it continues after the last shot, can be regarded as a symptom of his final intrusion into the Real. And could we not argue that *Teorema*, with its circular narrative mapped against the metonymical image of the desert, is precisely a parable on the Real as gaze, the virtual eye of an invisible camera that follows us around everywhere we go, whatever we do? If the arrival of the stranger signifies the materialisation of the gaze in its function of *objet a*, his departure does not imply its vanishing, but rather its persistence in the symbolic universe of the characters. Hence the profoundly distressing effect this departure has on the four members of the family, all of whom suddenly find themselves in a state of crisis: Odetta turns psychotic and eventually catatonic, Pietro leaves home to become a neurotic, deeply dissatisfied bohemian artist, Lucia tries obsessively, but in vain, to recapture the experience with the stranger by sleeping with different men, and Paolo, as we have seen, undergoes what we might well call a symbolic suicide. All in all we are left with two cases of neurosis (Pietro and Lucia) and two of psychosis (Paolo and Odetta), a limit-situation that allows us to suggest the parallel with *Blow-up*, where Thomas also ends up on the brink of a complete breakdown.

The point is that *Teorema* and *Blow-up* manifest an essentially self-reflexive intention by focusing on the void that structures the cinematic image, in other words on the ontological presence of a fantasmatic gaze whose insistence in the visual field, if identified and endorsed, causes the collapse of what we see in terms of the consciousness we derive from it. With Antonioni, the gaze is generally evoked as a purely spatial dimension, i.e. through an insistent and pervasive framing of spaces that appear empty even though they are not necessarily so. Antonioni perfected this dramatisation of frames filled with a kind of metaphysical emptiness in his films of the early 1960s (*L'avventura*, *La notte* and *L'eclisse*), regarding which the question of aestheticism has often been raised. *Blow-up* does not forsake this stylistic cipher; on the contrary, it refines its use, as Antonioni seems to realise that his fascination with void needs to acquire a more strategic role: rather than overpowering the narrative, it ought to reveal its inner functioning. This is why in *Blow-up* the reliance upon open and vacant spaces is condensed in the crucial shots of the vast expanse of Maryon Park, whereas most of the narrative, by contrast, focuses on the hectic London lifestyle of the "swinging sixties". Like the desert in *Teorema*, Maryon Park functions as another objective correlative for that reference to void that appeals to Antonioni's vision whilst bolstering his narrative. As noted by Jameson, more than the corpse it is the background that matters here, the peripheral presence of the park with its imposing trees 'shaken with wind as though by a kind of permanent violence, day or night never at rest' (Jameson, 1992, p. 196). Much like Mulholland Drive, the Los Angeles location in David Lynch's film of the same title (*Mulholland Drive*, 2001), Maryon Park is another desert of the Real, a really existing and yet unreal place of ghostly apparitions and shattering encounters which comes to overlap with the void of the subject.

As Sandro Bernardi (2002, pp. 189–99) has remarked, the "mystery of the park" is a recurrent theme in Antonioni, particularly noticeable in *I vinti* (The Vanquished, 1953), *La notte* (The Night, 1960), and *Blow-up*.[32] In sharp contrast to the Romantic project of the English garden as *locus amoenus*, as a place of idyllic communion with nature away from the corrupting influence of modern civilisation (as for instance in Rousseau's *Les rêverie du promeneur solitaire*, 1782), Antonioni chooses the image of the park to reflect on the enigma of the image itself – and, more extensively, of reality *tout court*. In Antonioni's parks the Romantic idyll becomes a nightmare, for what the characters meet there is the inconsistency of their own desires.[33]

One of Antonioni's main achievements lies precisely in this ability to evoke an enigmatic correspondence between the landscape and the subjective universe of the character. Both components of this mirroring correspondence are pervaded by an instance of radical detachment, whereby we realise not so much that the world is not real, but rather that it is *as unreal as the subject*. The question is thus less an epistemological one (concerning the exploration of the subject's relationship with the outside world) than an ontological one, for what counts is the relationship between subjective and objective inconsistency. And Antonioni's cinema is at its most subversive when it manages to capture this "overlapping of gaps".

For the time being let us recall the few shots of *Deserto rosso* (Red Desert, 1964) in which, after the sexual *frissons* inside the red shack, Giuliana (Monica Vitti), the neurotic protagonist, is suddenly seized by a fit of anxiety at the sight of her husband Ugo and their friends standing still in front of her, transmuted by the thick fog into nightmarish silhouettes bearing a closer resemblance to zombies than to human beings.[34] Or even more explicitly the famous episode of Anna's disappearance in *L'avventura* (1959), which was insightfully defined by Pascal

Deserto rosso

Bonitzer as 'the disappearance of the disappearance of Anna' (quoted in Brunette, 1998, p. 31): the outcome of this extraordinary event (Anna disappears whilst visiting a deserted island with a group of friends, and the film simply does provide any explanations) is precisely the insertion of an abyssal fracture in the very heart of the narrative, a void-effect that Antonioni then proceeds to fill out with elusive figurations of lack, objects that incarnate the impossible Thing. Whilst searching for Anna's body, the characters, as in the aforementioned passage from *Deserto rosso*, are slowly reduced to a bunch of automata mapped out against the equally formalised backcloth of the island – as if to suggest that Anna's absence has become *their absence to themselves*. Halfway through the lengthy search there come a few uncannily non-cinematic moments when we feel that there is simply no difference between what these human beings are and the breathtakingly barren landscape of the island, with its rocks and vertiginous gorges. As they search for the lost one, *they lose themselves*, flattened against the landscape, deprived of their narrative depth. Antonioni visualises the void opened up by Anna's absence through the strange correspondence between his other characters and that very landscape that mysteriously swallowed Anna. Such figurations of lack are strictly related to what I call the cinematic unconscious, insofar as they remain utterly extraneous to narrative symbolisation, and yet they are at the very pulsating heart of the film. Along these lines, Anna's unexplained disappearance and Thomas's erasure from the final shot of *Blow-up* can be regarded as one and the same thing. This is also why Antonioni's cinema cannot be understood in terms of content-related binary oppositions such as culture vs. nature, masculine vs. feminine, appearance vs. reality, for ultimately what fascinates the director is the ontological rift that cuts across the field of these binary oppositions, affecting all its elements.[35]

The affinity between the Antonionian park and the Lacanian gaze, particularly evident in *Blow-up*, becomes even more intriguing if we consider the shift of perspectives implied by the director's framing of the park, which is to be linked to the shift of visual angles at the start of *Teorema*. The point is that we pass from the forced, artificial and implicitly impossible objectivity of the gaze (in the bird's-eye shots of the open common traversed by a miniaturised Thomas) to subjective shots of Thomas's investigation in the park, and it is through this drastic change in point of view that the director manages to inscribe the subversive instance of the gaze into the fabric of film. In *Teorema* and *Blow-up*, both produced and released around 1968, the focus on the radical antagonism pertaining to the visual field can paradoxically be read along the lines of the students' motto "Soyons realistes, demandons l'impossible" (let's be realistic, let's demand the impossible). When Lacan states that '*[y]ou never look at me from the place from which I see you*' (Lacan, 1998a, p. 103), thus asserting the intractability of the gaze, he is in fact opening up the space for a reappropriation of the utopian urge implicit in the tarrying with the explosive negativity that cuts across the visual field.[36]

Again, we should insist on the apparently incongruous fact that what is at stake in this utopian urge is the Freudian notion of death-drive. At one point, in both *Teorema* and *Blow-up* desire turns into drive, a compulsion to traverse the fantasy and confront its (desire's) constitutional lack. In the first part of *Teorema*, for instance, the sexual dimension is presented as inextricably entwined with drive, as each character is unable to escape their lethal fascination with the void opened up by the stranger's departure. The reactions to this departure are exemplary of the functioning of the death-drive. As Pasolini knew very well, the sexual domain is deeply antagonistic: 'From Freud onwards, all tendencies of psychoanalysis have agreed in identifying in the erotic dimension an element that is always the same and the contrary of what it is (i.e., antagonistic)... Freud calls it Thanatos, the death-drive [...] Eros retains a power that cannot satisfy itself' (in Duflot, 1993, pp. 73–4). In *Blow-up*, as Fredric Jameson has noted, Thomas' obsessive looking is repeatedly connoted as a sexual yearning, which fittingly culminates in an orgy with two young aspiring models: 'The matter of sex is important, because the physical encounter with the two girls punctuates the development and "blowing up" of the images. Before that episode, the protagonist thinks he has prevented a murder; after satiety, the well-known link between sex and death causes him to look more closely, and to discover the traces of the corpse' (Jameson, 1992, p. 194).

It should not come as a surprise that, a few years before shooting *Teorema*, Pasolini had fervently defended *Deserto rosso*, praising it against the formalism of Antonioni's previous trilogy (see Pasolini, 1996, pp. 78–81). However, what he liked about *Deserto rosso* was the fact that Antonioni's gaze had finally freed itself from pretextual sociological preoccupations, thus becoming *rigorously formalistic* and revealing 'the absolute pre-eminence of the world as aesthetic spectacle over plot and characters' (Pasolini, 1996, p. 80). In line with his film theory, Pasolini claims that through his formalism Antonioni is able to evoke the ineffable objectivity of the world by 1) reducing the movements of the camera and even repeating the same shot from slightly different angles or with different lenses,[37] and 2) by bringing his point of view in line with that of Giuliana (free indirect subjective shot), the neurotic protagonist of the film. In short, Pasolini admires the psychotic method that informs *Deserto rosso*, the way in which the film openly embraces a split vision of the world.

Fully endorsing Pasolini's analysis, I would argue that *Deserto rosso* provides a lucid illustration of the duplicity of the cinematic image, of the fact that what operates in it is always a visual distortion between the fictional representation of the narrative and the invisible Real. To be more precise, it is because the fictional world we perceive on screen is explicitly connoted as Giuliana's profoundly neurotic vision that we can "feel" the effect of the Real. For example, the fact that during Giuliana's crises the colours of certain objects around her actually change, regardless of whether the camera is in line with her viewpoint or not, implies that we are forced to look at the world from her pathological perspective. The upshot of this is, as Pasolini noted, the inscription of a gap between the camera and the object, a certain detachment which inevitably triggers the crucial question: if it is clear that we are watching the film from a distorted point of view, where is it that we can find the true, "healthy", or at least neutral perspective? Here the similarity with *Teorema* becomes patent, as Antonioni's film also introduces what one would be tempted to call a "psychotic" perspectival shift.

More or less halfway through the film, Giuliana tells her son an enigmatic parable about a little girl on a beautiful deserted island. What this narrative diversion achieves is the supplementation of the main plot with "another scene", whereby the coldly observed story of Giuliana's vicissitudes in a modern industrial environment cuts abruptly to a lyrical tale of seemingly utopian harmony between man and nature. What kind of dialectical relationship is there between this isolated sequence and the main narrative? Are we supposed to infer that the originally distorted point of view has been straightened, and that we are now given a chance to see things directly? If it were simply so, there would be something idealistically false about Antonioni's depiction of a utopian niche outside the modern world. From a Lacanian standpoint this visualisation of utopia certainly does not correspond to the showing of the gaze – and even less, therefore, to the unfolding of the cinematic unconscious. However, a more attentive reading of the scene suggests an alternative interpretation. The point is that this "narrative within the narrative" has its own structuring core in the mysterious materialization of an unmanned ship that first approaches the beach, and then suddenly turns around and moves away. As we watch the advancing of the vessel through the young girl's eyes, we should be able to realise that *a certain gaze*, in the Lacanian sense, makes a furtive and somewhat distressing appearance on screen, an intrusion emphasised (as Pasolini, again, noticed) by Antonioni's change of lenses. Rather than underline the rapport between modern alienation and natural or holistic harmony,[38] the scene allows Antonioni to bring about the kernel of his filmmaking, that is, the gaze as object-cause of desire in the scopic field. The narrative creates a zooming-in or blowing-up effect through an initial instance of displacement (from industrial alienation to nature), which is then properly radicalised by the decisive addition of the empty vessel exposing us to the presence of the gaze; only then do we realise that our looking at the world is always-already the effect of the elision of the Lacanian gaze. The theoretical point to make is that such a procedure bears a close formal homology with what, according to Žižek, defines a true revolutionary intervention, as the latter always relies on a first movement of detachment from a given context whose aim is to prepare the ground for a second, more radical and disturbing move.[39]

An analogous procedure, although with opposite results, can be observed in the surreal orgy sequence of *Zabriskie Point* (1970), the film where Antonioni more openly tackles the issue of late-1960s counter-culture. Having reached and explored Zabriskie Valley (a typically Antonionian non-place or limit-dimension) Mark and Daria, the two young protagonists on the run from their respective environments, smoke cannabis and then make love. Gradually, as the musical theme begins ('Love scene' by Jerry Garcia), they are joined by numerous other couples (actually, members of Joe Chaikin's "Open Theatre") who, in a surreal fantasy of therapeutic collective sex, perform an erotic show on the dunes of the desert. What is untypical of Antonioni in this otherwise visually stunning scene, is precisely the liberating potential accorded to the sexual act, the gentrification of the utopian potential of libido, which is exactly the reason why the passage does not work. The overall feeling of unproblematic sexual harmony that the love-in evokes (despite a trace of melancholy) is essentially false, for it bypasses the central question of the disruptive potential of eroticism. Differently to what happens in the aforementioned sequence of *Deserto rosso*, here the first movement of displacement, which coincides with the characters' arrival at Zabriskie Point and the encounter with the death-like

silence and emptiness of the desert, is not followed up by the showing of the gaze; instead, the narrative break is recomposed by this stereotypically counter-cultural reference to cosmic unity in sex.

The question of the relationship between gaze and desert is then revisited at the beginning of Antonioni's next work, *Professione: reporter*

Professione: reporter

(The Passenger, 1975), and particularly in its opening sequence where David Locke (Jack Nicholson), a British television reporter, finds himself stranded in mid desert whilst searching for a group of African rebels he intends to interview. As he is looking around, a man on a camel fully clad in white suddenly appears in front of him. Locke waves his hand, but the man simply looks at him and moves away. The landscape, in other words, produces an object that returns to the subject an empty look, thus transforming the subject itself into an object, into the target of a non-specified gaze.

In the next few shots Locke's subjective point of view continues to be alternately excluded and included. First we have a panoramic shot which we immediately identify as Locke's own point of view; however, it immediately becomes evident that somebody else must be watching, as in the next shot Locke appears as a minute figure on the background, standing next to his car. An African man emerging from a hovel on top of a mountain soon appropriates this external gaze. In the next shot, the subjective point of view of this mysterious man is also objectified, as a small movement of the camera, seemingly placed in the same position on the mountain, shows him guiding Locke uphill. Then, after a line of soldiers appears in the distance, the guide vanishes, and Locke finds himself alone in the empty desert once again, surrounded by the absence of a gaze that has now fully manifested itself through these displacing movements of inclusion and exclusion. In a few shots Antonioni tells us how the externality of a field (an out-of-frame point of view) can be successfully inscribed in the field *whilst remaining what it was*, a reference to a lack, a missing link.

1.8 INFINITE REPETITIONS OF THE SAME THING

The metaphorical deployment of the desert in its affinity with the Lacanian Real is a recurrent feature of Pasolini's entire filmic production of the late 1960s, and particularly of the so-called "mythical films" (*Edipo Re*, *Porcile*, *Medea*). For example, the second of the two intertwining narratives of *Porcile* (Pigsty, 1969) uses the image of the desert as an ideal backdrop for the unravelling of unconscious desires. The opening parallel montage sequence of the film immediately suggests that Julian Klotz (Jean-Pierre Leaud), the bourgeois protagonist of the first story, is nothing but the conscious half of the nameless savage (Pierre Clementi) of the second story, who is introduced as he wanders aimlessly through a desert landscape (Mount Etna), eating butterflies and snakes. Essentially, *Porcile* suggests that history is cut across by myth in the form of a non-symbolisable event that cinema, however, has a chance to resuscitate. If *Teorema* shows how the socio-symbolic order always-already relies on what it excludes, *Porcile* propounds the same concept by interlinking a similar bourgeois macrocosm with figurations of a disruptive unconscious dynamism that must be repressed. On a more formal level, the fact that the two narratives are intertwined to clockwork perfection is aimed at reaffirming Pasolini's belief in the key role of editing, for each story effectively "accomplishes the editing of the other", suturing the part that needs to be excluded if meaning is to emerge.

The question of exclusion, however, is developed well beyond the reference to editing, for what we gradually realise as the film progresses is that the two narratives are not mutually exclusive. Rather, the conflict between historical consciousness and the unconscious desire (or, in Pasolini's own terms, between the profane and the sacred) establishes itself as the very subject matter of both stories. In the main narrative, set in contemporary Germany, the unconscious is instantly evoked by the opening shots of a modern pigsty, whose enigmatic (in)significance subtends the entire narrative, finding its putative resolution in Julian's absurd death. In the second narrative, set approximately in XV century Italy, we are fully immersed in the "desert of the Real" from the very beginning, as the repulsive acts performed by the Pierre Clementi character – the nameless cannibal who enjoys a wild freedom outside the law – express a desire that refuses to be caged in symbolic meaning, and that can be summed up by the only words spoken by the character during the entire narrative: 'I killed my father, I ate human flesh, and I quiver with joy' (repeated four times).

Porcile's primary concern seems to be that of reflecting on the relationship between oppressive power structures and unconscious potentialities for resistance or rebellion. If it is fairly clear that both protagonists personify the same attitude of defiance, the content of this defiance is much more problematic to define. Perhaps the most precise way of describing it is by calling into question the persistence of the death-drive, which manifests itself through a double movement. Firstly, the two characters are introduced in the film as hysterical subjects, in the sense that it is impossible to establish what they actually want – thus, they tell us that desire is rooted in the unconscious;[40] secondly, this hysterical trait is turned into a self-obliterating act of disattachment, whereby the characters overcome the enigma of their desire by fully assuming the negativity embedded at its heart. It is important to underline the paradoxical passivity that accompanies this act of over-identification with the unconscious: Julian, who entertains a perverted/fetishistic relationship with pigs, eventually lets himself be devoured by them; similarly, the Clementi character does not oppose any resistance to his arrest, he simply takes off his clothes and consigns himself to the authorities without a fight (whereas his partner in crime, played by Franco Citti, displays a more openly militant attitude by engaging in physical struggle).

This attitude of passive self-contraction is rendered in a particularly accomplished way in the first narrative, which unfolds in and around the cold, claustrophobic Renaissance palace owned by Julian's father, symbolic of the all-pervasive dominance of modern capitalism.[41] Confronted by his girlfriend Ida (Anne Wiazemski) who is impatient with his protracted indolence, Julian falters, alludes to 'a distant grunt' (thus immediately establishing an obscure connection with pigs) and finally proclaims: 'If you could only see me for what I really am, you would call an ambulance!'. Of course, the point is that we *can* see him for what he truly is, as the second narrative, set in a seemingly meta-historical desert, works as the first narrative's "other scene", a relentless endeavour to represent Julian's unconscious. However, to confirm that the two episodes ought not be read as mutually exclusive but rather as traversed by the same deadlock, we need to acknowledge that the structural imbalance introduced by

Porcile

the image of the desert is already included in the first narrative. Firstly, Julian's enigmatic confession that he desires 'the infinite repetition of the same thing' is a clear allusion to his death-drive, the compulsion to repeat endlessly the encounter with the Thing – as it is confirmed by his collapsing into a catatonic state, half way through the film. Secondly, the cinematography itself suggests the overwhelming presence of the deadlock of the Real, denoting precisely a somewhat inane emphasis on repetition: the camera is locked into a frozen compulsion to endlessly repeat the same shot; space is organised around the same compulsion to arrange objects symmetrically; the estranged characters always occupy the centre of the frame whilst reciting their lines mechanically, "á la Brecht". If therefore the true core of the German episode lies in its excluded subtext (in its unconscious other scene) this also means that, in a typically Hegelian gesture of turning "reflexive determination" into "determinate reflection", this disavowed truth is reflected back into the first story: the Real is already there, represented precisely by such signifiers as Julian's enigmatic half-sentences alluding to the pigs. The German episode thus confirms that the Real is not a meta-historical, a priori given, but that it is instead an uncanny impasse that can only reveal itself in historically concrete contexts.

This understanding of the Real allows us to unearth the driving force behind Pasolini's critique of late capitalism, which comes to fruition in the second part of *Porcile*, when Mr Klotz, representative of old-style, monopoly capitalism, strikes a business alliance with his rival Mr Herdhitze (Ugo Tognazzi), who symbolises late capitalism. It is this alliance, alluding prophetically to the advent of a new mode of global capitalist domination, which eventually disables the subversive potential of the unconscious. Through an effective, if intricate, use of montage, Pasolini tells us that Julian's recovery from his catatonic condition and consequent re-integration in the socio-symbolic order coincides with the arrest of the Clementi character. This event, in turn, stands for the crucial neutralisation of the unconscious, and is immediately linked to Herdhitze's disclosure of Julian's secret passion (his copulation with pigs). What follows is Herdhitze's (again, very prophetic) declaration of tolerance towards sexually deviant subjects ('poor Julian, God knows how much he must have suffered'). In the early 1970s, Pasolini will go to great lengths to argue that, within the new ideological consensus imposed by the consumer society, tolerance is nothing but the other side of repression, as its function is purely that of regimenting people to the needs of capital. By the same token, *Porcile* seems to suggest that all forms of resistance and transgression are inevitably co-opted by capitalist ideology in its universalising function.

So if the film takes stock of the overwhelming force displayed by contemporary capitalism, which defuses even the most profound and explosive encrustations of the unconscious – let alone other forms of conscious antagonistic practice such as the student movement, here embodied by Ida – does it simply abandon itself to the resignation implicit in the critical analysis? As anticipated, my belief is that Pasolini's cinema is structured around a kind of obsessive-compulsive disorder: the obligation to represent the baleful and yet life-enhancing contradiction inherent in the death-drive. It is this disorder that takes centre stage in *Porcile*, well beyond typically Foucauldian argumentations on how power and resistance to power are locked in a deadly mutual embrace. From this angle, one could even argue that the subversive impact of Julian and his anarchic double lies in their withdrawing from the compulsion to act, from the urge to participate in some kind of principled activity. Instead, they remain open to a potential revolutionary/subversive break by opting out of history and insisting on the "endless repetition of the same thing", which implies a confrontation with the traumatic Real of desire. Despite the feeling of hopelessness voiced by the film – which significantly ends with Herdhitze's "totalitarian" injunction to erase any possible trace of Julian's death – the rebellious core of *Porcile*, as with most of Pasolini's films, is firmly situated in the self-destructive nature of its split protagonist, in the overwhelming and scandalous emphasis accorded to his death-drive.

After recovering from catatonia, Julian tells Ida about a dream he had, which is ostensibly modelled on a notorious hallucination of the Wolf-Man (one of Freud's most famous patients) thus revealing the extent to which *Porcile* explicitly relies on psychoanalysis (see Viano, 1993, pp. 231–32). In Julian's dream, a little pig bites off four fingers from his right hand: 'The fingers, however, remain attached and do not bleed, as if made of rubber. So I wander with my fingers hanging loose, distraught by that bite. A bid for martyrdom? Who knows what the truth of dreams is, in addition to their making us anxious for the truth'. The whole point of this allusion to the Wolf-Man is to confirm Julian's faithfulness to the Real core of desire. Just as his nameless double had remained loyal to such practices as parricide and cannibalism, which designate the very object of the psychoanalytic discourse (the Real of *jouissance*, of pleasure in displeasure), Julian's fidelity is the fidelity to the fantasmatic object of a desire turned drive: an endless repetition of the same movement around the empty sexualised object (symbolised by the penis-like fingers). And as Žižek often reminds us, the death-drive, at least in its Lacanian specification, paradoxically designates the place of immortality, of the "undead" substance invested by *jouissance* which persists beyond biological death.[42] Incidentally, it is in this context that Pasolini's reliance on editing should be conceived: what editing ultimately sutures is not just a series of symbolic correspondences, but crucially, the non-symbolisable object of drive.

Porcile also prefigures the main accomplishment of Pasolini's *Salò, o le 120 giornate di Sodoma* (Salò, or the 120 Days of Sodom, 1975) by starting to shift the focus onto the inconsistency of power itself. Mr Herdhitze's intervention, for example, does not only cause the collapse of Julian's unconscious resistance, but it also alludes to the fundamental contradiction inherent in capital. By the same token the visual association of Herdhitze's arrival with the capture of the Clementi character and his gang of outlaws is not just emblematic of the "colonisation" of the unconscious, but it also suggests the uncanny redoubling of the Real of drive that will explode in *Salò*: the antagonistic core of Julian's unconscious is transposed onto the symbolic configuration that absorbs it. In this respect, the Herdhitze character, played by a convincingly chameleonic Ugo Tognazzi, bears all the symptoms of the intense libidinal instability that will be displayed in all its self-destructive force by the four libertines of *Salò*. Similarly to Iago in *Che cosa sono le nuvole?*, Herdhitze's final injunction to keep quiet over the scandalous death of Julian (which, however hard we try to resist the analogy, cannot but remind one of Pasolini's own death) achieves the opposite aim: to recast the traumatic truth of the unconscious as the explosive Real of capital.

1.9 ON NEOREALISM: EXCURSUS 1

The problematisation of the act of looking, which achieves powerful dramatic results in films like *Blow-up* and, on a less explicit level, *Teorema*, is undoubtedly one of the defining features of Italian cinema (see Bernardi, 2002, pp. 37–84). With regard to this feature, it is worth us broadening our critical horizon by taking into account three crucial stages of cinematic development. Firstly, in primitive cinema, the camera was completely engrossed in its act of looking at the world; then, with classical narrative cinema, it learned to detach itself from this awestruck compulsion to look, inscribing a distance between itself and the external world, thus starting to constrain the latter into a narrative. Later, particularly with Italian neorealism, the camera rediscovers the freshness of an unimpaired and unmediated rapport with the outside world. However, instead of simply abandoning themselves to a hypnotic look, filmmakers start exploring the relationship between the strict dynamics of narrativisation inherited from classical cinema and the somewhat mythical or mythicised act of looking pure and simple. The result of this hybridisation is explosive, since for the first time cinema is forced to reflect upon its own complexity as an act of looking – on the fact that the cinematic eye is always-already included in a problematically polymorphous universe. Narrativity is suddenly shaken by questions regarding the very function of a gaze that refuses to be explained in plot-related terms. This is the meta-narrative friction at the heart of neorealism, which determines the crisis of the so-called action-film: the constant shifting from traditional narrative constraints to a kind of delirious documentarism that is never content with simply looking but seeks to include the impossible point of view *from which things look back at the camera* – those spectral figurations of the Real whose displaced persistence in the scopic field grounds representation itself.

The devastating novelty of Visconti's *Ossessione* (Obsession, 1943), well before his more overtly neorealistic *La terra trema* (The Earth Trembles, 1948), is thus to be found in its use of long takes and *temps morts*. This original, if risky, approach to editing was used by Visconti despite strong discouragement from prominent director Alessandro Blasetti, who went so far as to try and impose a version of the film that he himself had re-edited in a more conventional way (see Rondolino, 1981, p. 115–16). Beyond the film's oft-noted debt to the poetic realism of French directors such as Jean Renoir and Marcel Carné, especially as far as characterisation is concerned, Visconti's idiosyncratic method is already noticeable here. In *Ossessione* the camera discovers a world (the Po valley with its bleached and dusty roads extending into an invisible horizon, beaten by the August sun) but does not proceed to explain it, rather contemplating it as if beguiled by its implacable, ontological "being-there".[43] The detachment of Visconti's camera seems therefore to be the result of the encounter with a world that retains a strong semblance of mythical impenetrability. It is a camera that lingers on a carefully composed and yet aseptic mise-en-scène, or otherwise on a landscape that, in its blunt and impassive self-assertiveness, simply returns to us the detachment of the cinematic eye.

What is above all neorealistic about *Ossessione*, however, is its profound visual ambiguity, which is not merely the result of technical manipulation,

Ossessione

but rather of its naturalistic ambition, its deep-seated determination to represent reality as it is. That is why the innovative value of the film does not belong to its narrative content (an adaptation from *The Postman Always Rings Twice*, 1934, a hard-boiled novel by James Cain), but instead to its many non-narrative pauses, to the overwhelming sense of apathy that transpires from most scenes and forces the spectator into a confrontation with the very vacuum of the image.[44] If there is something both brazen and scandalous in these images, this is less due to the subject matter *per se* than to their willingness to encompass their own non-narrative limit. *Ossessione* is one of the first Italian films to be subtended by the awareness that to look also means to expose oneself to the gaze, to the enigma of the image, to the precariousness of the seen. Visconti's camera takes a risk and exposes itself to the blind spot in the field of the Other, and it is in this risk that we should recognise the impact of neorealism, as well as its profound influence on post-war Italian (and world) cinema.

The exposure to the gaze is not only apparent in the film's relation with landscape. If undoubtedly there is something spectral about the God-forsaken trattoria on the endless sandy road of the Po valley, it is also the camerawork and the often praised unconventionality of the editing style that speak for Visconti's originality. Let us take the famous scene of the first encounter between Gino (Massimo Girotti) and Giovanna (Clara Calamai). Gino walks into the trattoria kitchen, exchanges a couple of sexually loaded looks with Giovanna, and then moves towards the stove, where some food is being prepared. As he picks up bits of food from the saucepan the camera is positioned right in front of him, on the other side of the stove; however, in the following reverse-shot we realise that the camera could never have been placed there, since the stove is now shown as attached directly to the wall. What we have here is the inclusion of an impossible point of view, which implies that the angle from which we are looking cannot be subjectivised. *Ossessione*'s conscious avoidance of subjective shots contributes to evoking an unspecified and fundamentally empty point of view.

If we go back to the film's use of landscape, we should acknowledge that it is precisely the opening up of objective and yet non-subjectivisable space that matters here. The scene of the reconciliation between Gino and Giovanna towards the end of the film, for example, is shot on the vast sandy delta of the river Po, which resembles a desert, thus creating a strange feeling of absence and paranoia by successfully exposing the forlorn couple to an unseen gaze. Significantly, this uncanny presence of a gap in the field of the visible is confirmed at the end of the scene, when the two lovers awaken to the realisation that *they have been watched by the police* all the time. Previously, Visconti's camera had followed Gino and his unnamed friend nicknamed "lo spagnolo" (the Spaniard) as they walked through the streets of Ancona, to end up sitting on a wall facing the Adriatic Sea. After a quick shot/reverse-shot there is a cut to a long shot from behind the two characters which breaks the unity of space and shifts the focus on the openness of the sea in front of them. Unexpectedly, the traditional relationship between characters and landscape (whereby the latter was used to define the former) is turned around, for here the characters become a function of the landscape. It is this new focus on landscape as an overwhelming and unfathomable dimension of the visible that will influence generations of neorealist and post neorealist directors: 'Rossellini's and Antonioni's films are more a discovery of space than a discovery of man. With the growing importance of space inside the shot, telling stories becomes increasingly difficult, and a new character makes its appearance on screen with no intention of leaving: the void, the landscape' (Bernardi, 2002, p. 81).

This tension towards the void of the image, towards its Real nucleus, in as much as this nucleus configures itself as the enigmatic presence of an indiscernible gaze, features in most neorealist films. We find it in the cityscapes of *Roma, città aperta* (Rome, Open City, 1945), *Germania anno zero* (Germany Year Zero, 1947), *Ladri di biciclette* (Bicycle Thieves, 1948) and *Umberto D* (1951), where the narrative is constantly breached by the camera's stupefied discovery of squalid or half-destroyed urban space. We also find it in the increasingly dominant focus on open scenery displayed not only by *Ossessione*, but also by films like *Paisà* (Paisan, 1946), *La terra trema* (1948) and *Riso amaro* (Bitter Rice, 1949), where landscape often contradicts its traditional symbolic or aesthetic function, acquiring a certain formal autonomy that stains the cinematic image and unsettles the narrative pace.

With neorealism, then, the cinematic unconscious for the first time assumes a consistent figurative role, its visual emergence coinciding with a new way of relating to what sustains narrative action. As a result, neorealistic landscapes should not be merely perceived as realistic, but rather as Real in the Lacanian meaning of the term. In Bernardi's words, landscape becomes a 'negative interlocutor' that determines 'a true revolution in the way we see' (Bernardi, 2002, p. 107). Most neorealist directors start looking at the world in such a way that the world seems to return the look, silently introducing a minimal gap in the very process of cinematic signification. All of a sudden we are exposed to what Deleuze (1989, p. 2) calls 'a pure *optical situation*' (a certain unexpected delay, a suspension or fragmentation of the narrative, an unnecessarily idle shot of an apparently insignificant or negligible aspect of reality) whose ultimate function, however, is less that of establishing 'a principle of indeterminability, or indiscernibility', whereby 'the distinction between subjective and objective [...] loses its importance' (Deleuze, 1989, p. 7), than that of unveiling the surreptitious connection between the narrative and its negative underside. If for Deleuze neorealism represents the first step towards a cinema conceived as an impersonal agglomeration of multiple virtualities disengaged from a fixed subject-position, this notion of the "virtual beyond subject and object" ought perhaps to be given a psychoanalytic twist and resignified as the unconscious gap that structures both subjectivity and the external world.

If there is a certain triteness in the notion that neorealism discovered 'a dispersive and lacunary reality' which expresses itself through 'a series of fragmentary, chopped up encounters' (Deleuze, 1986, p. 212), we need to add that this new emphasis on the elliptical signals the return of what had been repressed by classical narrative cinema. Bazin was right when he contended that neorealism should be defined firstly by its formal criteria, and only secondly by its socio-political content. At its heart is the strange connection between the figurative and the non-figurative, insofar as the cinematic unconscious, always at work in film, is given a chance to appear as Real, as the non-symbolisable core of reality. From this angle, Deleuze's well-received observation that the reasons why neorealism emerged in Italy (and not elsewhere) are to be found outside cinema, in the combination of a solid cinematographic tradition and the shattering devastation of a war that humiliated Italy – not only in material terms but also at the level of symbolic and imaginary identification – strikes a cord: neorealism was essentially an attempt to translate the encounter with the non-symbolisable Real of war and destruction in cinematic terms. As Pasolini would have put it, the fragmentation of the cinematic image reflects the fragmentation of the image of reality *tout court*, the impossible confrontation with that "zero level" where the Real happens.

NOTES

1. I am referring to the essays 'Osservazioni sul piano sequenza' (Observations on the long take), 'Essere è naturale?' (Is being natural?) and 'I segni vivi e i poeti morti' (Living signs and dead poets), (see Pasolini, 1995, pp. 237–55).

2. Of course, as a number of film theorists such as Metz, Oudart and Dayan had already pointed out, it is possible to identify other cinematic features that introduce a threatening lack in perception, such as, for example, the presence/absence of off-screen space, which inevitably accompanies each frame like a shadowy double. However, I would claim that Pasolini's reference to editing intended as the invisible gaps between individual shots, represents the clearest illustration of the function of lack in film, and as such it allows us to develop our Lacanian thesis to its full potential.

3. It is precisely by relating Pasolini's concept of death to the inaccessible kernel of the Lacanian subject – which is *not*, as Žižek points out, 'the *Lebensphilosophie* "unconscious" of deep "irrational" instincts' (Žižek, 2004a, p. 137) – that we can attempt to explain its overwhelming presence in both his literary and cinematic work.

4. Lacan (1966, p. 843; 1998b, p. 214) indicates that to "separate" is correlative to "se parare", which in Latin means "to generate oneself".

5. Lacan sums up the divisive topology of the unconscious as that of 'an entrance at which one only arrives at closing time (it will never be a touristic location)' (Lacan, 1966, p. 838).

6. Žižek argues that the unconscious should not simply be described as an 'objective mechanism that regulates my phenomenal experience', but, more accurately, as the very *fundamental fantasy* of the subject, a place occupied by 'an excessive, nonsignifiable, erotic fascination and attachment' which, through its inaccessibility, deprives the subject of its most intimate self-experience (Žižek, 2004a, pp. 96–7). The key Lacanian notion of fundamental fantasy (see Lacan, 2001a, p. 127), to which I will return time and again in the course of the book, designates precisely the deepest albeit unconscious kernel of subjective attachment.

7. The metaphorically "lethal" character of the unconscious and its traces had already been highlighted by Freud: 'Almost everywhere noticeable gaps, disturbing repetitions and obvious contradictions have come about – indications which reveal things to us which [the dream] was not intended to communicate. In its implications the distortions of a [manifest dream] text resemble murder: the difficulty is not in penetrating the deed but in getting rid of its traces. We might well lend the word distortion the double meaning to which it has a claim, but of which today it makes no use. It should mean not only "to change the appearance of something" but also "to put something in another place, to displace". Accordingly, in many instances of textual distortion, we may nevertheless count upon finding what has been suppressed and disavowed hidden away somewhere else, though changed and torn from its context. Only it will not always be easy to recognize it' (Freud, 1964, p. 43).

8. As many a critic has emphasised, Pasolini lacked authentic philosophical preparation. For example, he typically oversimplified Hegel's dialectical thought by compressing it into an unsophisticated reading of the legendary triad Thesis-Antithesis-Synthesis: 'I am against Hegel [...]. Thesis? Antithesis? Synthesis? I think it is too easy. My dialectics are now binary, not ternary. There are only irreconcilable oppositions' (in Magrelli, 1977, p. 99). As this very quotation suggests, intuitively Pasolini was much closer to Hegel than he might have wanted to be, since I would argue that the very panlogicist reading of Hegel does not do justice to his thought.

9. Which, incidentally, could also be seen as a radicalisation of Eisenstein's famous defence of montage as *the* fundamental feature of cinema, as it is through editing alone that a film 'gives rise to an idea' (Eisenstein, 1988, p. 144).

10. The Hegel I am referring to is of course less the champion of teleological thought than a philosopher of negativity, immanence and contingency. As Žižek has consistently argued, the fundamental difference between Kant and Hegel lies in the changed apperception of the transcendental Idea (the noumenal Thing-in-itself): from being located beyond phenomenality (Kant), the unattainable Thing falls into immanence (Hegel), coinciding with the experience of radical negativity which underscores any positive given. Hegel's key point lies in conceiving radical negativity as the foundational break between phenomena and the impossible Thing-in-itself:

precisely as the constitutional gap between appearance and essence, negativity is nothing but the essential self-fracture of the appearance itself. In Hegel, essence is therefore to be found in the radical displacement/inconsistency that cuts across the field of phenomena.

11. This logic can have surprising effects on censorship, as Žižek recalls apropos of the release of *Ben Hur* (1959) in Communist Yugoslavia, when the cutting of substantial parts of the film transformed 'a rather insipid Christian propaganda piece' into 'an existential drama about the ultimate nullity of our accomplishments, about how in the hour of our greatest triumph we are utterly alone' (Žižek, 1993, p. 127).

12. See Eco (1968, pp. 150–60), Garroni (1968, pp. 14–7 and 43–4) and Heath (1973). All these scholars chastise Pasolini's essays as semiologically naive, arguing that his persuasion that elemental cinematographic signs coincide with the real objects reproduced on the screen contradicts the basic aim of semiology, which is that of reducing the facts of nature to facts of culture, and not vice versa (see particularly Eco, 1968, p. 151). Pasolini replied specifically to Eco's critique with his essay 'Il codice dei codici' (The code of codes) (in Pasolini, 1995, pp. 277–84), insisting on the fundamental cultural importance of the "non-rational" foundation of the notion of reality.

13. Metz's text was translated in Italian three years later (see Barthes et al, 1969, pp. 205–25).

14. For a Lacanian reading of *Stromboli, terra di Dio* centred on the notion of the feminine act, see Žižek (2001b, pp. 42–6).

15. This, again, reminds us of Rossellini, as in the "Neapolitan episode" of *Paisà* (Paisan, 1946) we have a similar sequence where a black American soldier intervenes in a marionette staging of the Crusades to help the Moors against the Christians.

16. Which, incidentally, belongs fully to the Italian popular tradition, as it can be linked to Carlo Collodi's famous *Pinocchio*.

17. Critics have often praised *Partner*'s pictorial allure, which appears as a striking follow-up to Antonioni's earlier experiments with colour in *Deserto rosso* (Red Desert, 1964) and *Blow-up* (1966). More generally, it seems to me that since his debut with *Prima della rivoluzione* (Before the Revolution, 1965), the key aspect of Bertolucci's cinema lies with its intrinsic formalistic excesses, which imply less an overshadowing of the content than a displacement of unresolved narrative impasses.

18. Does this reading not throw some light on Bertolucci's self-confessed inclination 'to remove *Partner*' from his filmography (in Socci, 2003, p. 20; see also Ungari, 1982, pp. 51–2), as if it was a shameful blemish unsettling his recollection of the first phase in his directorial career? Today, favouring the practice of Buddhism over that of psychoanalysis (let us not forget that the year after *Partner* he started Freudian analysis), Bertolucci's interest in the correlation between psychoanalysis and cinema (let alone in the unconscious) has inescapably waned.

19. The big Other is to be understood as synonymous with the socio-symbolic order, essentially the order of language and communication. In *Seminar III* Lacan states that 'the Other must first of all be considered a locus, the locus in which speech is constituted' (Lacan, 2000, p. 274).

20. It is evident that suture and *objet petit a* operate at the same level, since the latter is nothing but the ever-elusive, fantasmatic, exceptional feature on account of which *there is* external reality (or, in cinematic terms, representation).

21. Let us not forget that Freud regarded the dream as 'the guardian of sleep', an attempt to strike a compromise with the essentially psychotic emergence of unbearable unconscious demands: 'In a certain sense, all dreams are *convenience-dreams*; they serve the purpose of continuing to sleep instead of waking. *The dream is the guardian of sleep, not its disturber*' (Freud, 1997, p. 130).

22. Perhaps the fact that in the film, contrary to what we read in the script, Thomas remains nameless, is to be related to the fragility of his subjective status as emphasised by the last shot.

23. 'Expressionist painting, and this is its distinguishing feature, provides something by way of a certain satisfaction – in the sense in which Freud used the term in relation to the drive – a certain satisfaction of what is demanded by the gaze [...] Indeed, you saw clearly enough last time that after declaring that there is in painting a certain *dompte-regard*, a taming of the gaze, that is to say, that he who looks is always led by the painting to lay down his gaze, I immediately introduced the corrective that it is nevertheless in a quite direct appeal to the gaze that expressionism is situated' (Lacan, 1998a, pp. 101 and 109).

24. Here, see also Žižek's ironic quip directed at cognitivist critics such as Bordwell and Carroll: their complaint about the mythical status of the Lacanian gaze, Žižek argues, completely misses the point, insofar as 'this gaze, effectively, is missing, its status is purely fantasmatic' (Žižek, 2001b, p. 201).

25. After being "visited" by the stranger Emilia returns to her country village and starts performing miracles.

26. In Tolstoy's novel, Gerasim is the butler's assistant, an unassuming country boy who looks after Ivan Ilych during his fatal illness. Symbolically, he represents a refreshing alternative to the hypocrisy of the main character's world. Pasolini saw in Gerasim an earlier version of his own contemporary sub-proletarian models, someone who stands for the purity and freshness of a world uncorrupted by bourgeois values.

27. A similar displacement of visual perspective takes place at the start of David Lynch's *The Lost Highway* (1997), when Fred and Renee receive a videotape with a creepy black and white film of the outside of their house. What is evoked there is precisely the impossible viewpoint of the gaze, whose externality structures the visual field. Incidentally, the same idea in developed in Michael Haneke's *Caché* (Hidden, 2005).

28. However plausible it might be to think of the stranger as a student (he reads books and lecture notes), any direct association with the 1968 students movement would be utterly misplaced; however close to the sub-proletariat, he is also far from just another representative of the director's favourite class.

29. This predicament is given a succinct socio-political emphasis in the cinéma-vérité sequence which works as a prologue to the actual film. Before the unfolding of title and credits against the backdrop of a red desert, we see a television crew interviewing a group of workers after their boss has bequeathed his factory to them. As we discover later, this short prologue belongs chronologically to the end of the film, as the generous boss is none other than Paolo (the father) after his personal epiphany. In addition to consolidating the chosen narrative structure (the flash-forward helps conveying the notion that a theorem has been demonstrated), the passage also works as a reminder that the allegory of the "second coming" has been triggered by a real, urgent socio-political dilemma, for, as the journalist suggests to the workers, the general tendency of the modern world is to erase the last traces of class struggle and impose a global capitalist order. If in narrative terms the sequence comes last, one can argue that its position at the start of the film is legitimate, insofar as the burning question of the universalisation of capital is the initial concern of the film itself.

30. Rinaldi, for example, claims that there is no connection between Pasolini's theory and his film practice, for in his writings on cinema Pasolini 'attempts to construct an imaginary justification for his films' (Rinaldi, 1982, p. 271).

31. It is worth remembering that in 1968 Pasolini was also working on the script for a film on Saint Paul, which was never completed due to the producers' diffidence after the meagre box-office returns of *Medea* (1969).

32. More specifically, in the third (very Hitchcockian) episode of *I vinti* (1952), set in London, we have the same association park-murder that will return in *Blow-up*.

33. Suffice it to recall the final sequence of *La notte* (which I shall discuss extensively in part 3) where Giovanni and Lidia, walking out into a seemingly endless park, finally find the courage to confront the impasse in their relationship.

34. We find a similar passage, although much longer, in *Identificazione di una donna* (Identification of a Woman, 1982), when Mavi (Daniela Silverio) disappears in the thick fog after a heated discussion with her lover Niccolò (Tomas Milian). As in *Deserto rosso*, the fog is used to achieve derealisation and therefore as a medium to invoke the Real.

35. If we take Antonioni's representation of nature (including human nature), we can see how it always retains an uncannily artificial character, which in many ways echoes Pasolini's paradox on the portentous, utterly mysterious and unnatural quality of what appears natural (see Pasolini, 1995, pp. 242–47).

36. All this despite his notoriously sceptical address to the students during the May 1968 uprising in Paris: 'Revolutionary aspirations have only one possibility: always to end up in the discourse of the master. Experience has proven this. What you aspire to as revolutionaries is a master. You will have one!' (in Stavrakakis, 1999, p. 12).

37. The perceptiveness of this observation is later emphatically demonstrated by the famous explosion sequence of *Zabriskie Point* (1970), which involves precisely the use of the same shot from different angle and with different lenses.

38. Antonioni himself always talked about *Deserto rosso* as his first colour film, conceding that it was meant, first of all, as an experimental attempt to put into practice his reflections on the use of colours in cinema. As far as the theme of industrialisation is concerned, he said: 'I am not against progress. But there are people who [...] cannot adapt. It is as if a phenomenon of natural section took place: those who survive are those who manage to keep up with progress, the others disappear swallowed by their own crises. For progress is inexorable, like revolutions' (in Antonioni, 2001, pp. 252–53).

39. This is the way in which Žižek understands, for example, the two Russian revolutions of 1917 (February and October): 'the fundamental lesson of revolutionary *materialism* is that revolution must strike twice, and for essential reasons. The gap is not simply the gap between form and content: what the first revolution misses is not the content, but *the form itself* – it remains stuck in the old form, thinking that freedom and justice can be accomplished if we simply put the existing state apparatuses and its democratic mechanisms to use' (Žižek, 2002b, p. 7).

40. This is why from the very beginning of the film Julian's father questions himself on the ambiguous nature of his son, defining him 'neither obedient nor disobedient'.

41. The palace (il palazzo) is a recurrent symbolic cipher in Pasolini, a metaphor for shady political power (see Pasolini, 1987, pp. 63–7).

42. In *The Ticklish Subject*, for example, we read that 'the death-drive [...] is the very opposite of dying, it is a name for the "undead" eternal life itself, for the horrible fate of being caught in the endless repetitive cycle of wandering around in guilt and pain' (Žižek, 2000a, p. 292).

43. A similar result was achieved by Antonioni's early documentary *Gente del Po* (People of the Po River, 1943–47).

44. I would also argue that the erotic charge of the narrative originates, first and foremost, in the film's visual ambiguity, which is eminently a formal feature, insofar as it could be defined as the constant intrusion of the vacuum of the image. Given the melodramatic and seedy narrative context of the film, this vacuum can only be filled by *jouissance*, by illicit sexual fantasies. There is some truth, therefore, in the unconfirmed anecdote according to which Vittorio Mussolini, son of the dictator and head of Cinecittà, stormed out of the cinema, at its premiere in Rome in spring 1943, shouting 'questa non è l'Italia!' (this is not Italy): what the film, which was generally judged by the pro-Fascist press as repulsively lascivious, actually focuses on is precisely the repressed (dirty) underside of Fascism, the structural gaps in an official discourse that projected the image of a functional, healthy, martial country.

2

ENJOYING THE REAL: UNCONSCIOUS STRATEGIES OF SUBVERSION

2.1 THE VRAIE FEMME'S REDEMPTIVE VIOLENCE

In *Medea* (1970), Pasolini's passionate defence of the Real is summed up by the Centaur (Laurent Terzieff), who at the start of the film claims that 'only those who are mythical are realistic, and only those who are realistic are mythical'. Despite Pasolini's dismissal of Hegel, this sentence functions as an unequivocal endorsement of the Hegelian notion of *reflexivity*, for its apology of myth is thoroughly dialectical: 'the sacred world is in no way superseded by its own desacralisation, as the centaur points out. The sacred and the profane continue to exist side by side' (Pasolini in Willemen, 1997, p. 68). Hegelian reflexivity here implies that the sacred and the profane (or, in Lacan's terms, the Real and the Symbolic) only exist through their own reciprocal over-determination: just as it is impossible to portray the sacred without referring to the profane, by the same token any cultural context hinges upon that which resists cultural integration absolutely. The Lacanian implications at stake here are self-evident, for the Real is the very blotch whose displacement allows for the cultural (symbolic) field to surface, while simultaneously precluding its universalisation by antagonising it from within. In *Medea*, as in *Porcile*, Pasolini's strategy appears driven by a determination to dialecticise the couple Real/Symbolic, starting from the empirically based assumption that the socio-symbolic order (late-capitalistic liberal democracy) is engaged in a global project aimed at eliminating any reference to pure externality. The point made by Pasolini's mythical films, *Teorema* included, is undoubtedly a prophetic and extremely pressing one: the more reason imposes itself as a purely instrumental tool that administers democracy and civilisation, the more aggressively tragedy will strike; the more the very notion of knowledge is a dead letter in the hands of capitalism and its relentless effort to convert social antagonisms into regulated market competition, the more hatred and destruction will spread.

Pasolini, therefore, uses myth to comment on modernity, for myth allows him to address the questions of violence, trauma and evil from a dialectical perspective. Oedipus kills his father, Medea kills her sons, the split protagonist of *Porcile* kills and eats human flesh, the mythical guest in *Teorema* brings separation and the collapse of bourgeois subjectivity. What must not be overlooked is that this sacred violence is invariably linked to, and over-determined by, the explicit reference to the contemporary world: in *Edipo re* (Oedipus Rex, 1967) an autobiographical Oedipus grows up in the North of Italy during the 1920s and, after a detour through ancient Greece, returns, blind, to the Bologna and Milan of the 1960s; in *Porcile* and *Teorema* the contemporary bourgeois setting is constantly pinned back against its meta-historical underside; in *Medea*, the ancient and barbaric universe of the heroine is juxtaposed onto the modern world founded by Jason. Pasolini is not interested in mythical violence *per se*, but only insofar as these ancient traumatic narratives give him a chance to comment on his world. The standard criticism should thus be reverted. It is not that these films depict 'the dilemma of a subject caught between historical consciousness and the temptation to escape into metahistory. [...] of a man who has lost faith in history and finds shelter in the Manichaean myth of a timeless conflict between irreconcilable opposites' (Viano, 1993, p. 237). On the contrary, they attempt to demonstrate that there can be no historical consciousness without the positing of an ahistorical kernel. More precisely, the gap between history and meta-history is reflected back into history itself, which therefore appears "traversed" by its own lack. In this respect, Pasolini's entire work has been the object of a critical misunderstanding of colossal proportions, for his insistence on the sacred and the irrational was never the measure of an egotistical retreat into an imaginary world; instead, it was meant to historicise (i.e. dialecticise) the Real *qua* ahistorical bar of impossibility, whose primordially-repressed status is precisely what sustains the framework of the possible. Thus, when in late 1960s Pasolini confessed his fascination with such notions as 'barbarism' or 'the heroism of evil' (in Duflot, 1993, pp. 83–5), he was addressing, admittedly in a partial and theoretically unsatisfactory way, the fantasmatic core of his own desire, the kernel of *jouissance* confronted in his cinematic production.

Put differently, we could argue that these so-called mythical films do not try to contain the horror of pure violence, for they "know" that what is at stake in this horror is nothing less than the fundamental feature of the revolutionary act. Walter Benjamin's essay 'On the critique of violence' provides a useful framework within which to situate Pasolini's representation of violence. The basic premise of the essay, which emanates from the bedrock of Benjamin's messianic utopianism, is the profoundly pessimistic criticism of lawmaking and law-preserving violence, i.e. of any form of violence related to the exercise of law and power. Instead of dispensing *tout court* with violence, Benjamin elaborates upon the idiosyncratic notion of 'divine violence', which he defines as a form of violence absolutely disengaged from means and ends, and yet inherently political. For example, he is prepared to subscribe to Sorel's defence of the redemptive violence perpetrated in the proletarian general strike (as opposed to the violence of the political general strike), but only because this violence can be conceived as a "purer" form of destructive intervention (its aim being the annihilation of the state) that is absolutely detached from any reference to law and power. Furthermore, it is interesting to notice that before arriving at the definition of divine violence, Benjamin criticises what he calls 'mythic violence' for its explicit link with the lawmaking function: 'Far from inaugurating a purer sphere, the mythic manifestation of immediate violence shows itself fundamentally identical with all legal violence, and turns suspicion concerning the latter into certainty of the perniciousness of its historical function, the destruction of which thus becomes obligatory' (Benjamin, 1997, p. 249).

In this context, the question indirectly raised by Pasolini's films can easily be seen as concerning the reconfiguration of the classic Marxian notion of proletarian violence into the strictly speaking theological notion of divine violence. Apropos of Benjamin's differentiation between divine and mythic violence, then, Pasolini's films of the late 1960s speak for the former despite having myth as their subject matter, since violence is performed by a subject who "disappears behind the act", in the specific sense that the grounds for his or her involvement cannot be known in advance. More than the irreconcilable opposition between Western teleology and myth, and more than a Jungian retreat into archetypes (see Viano, 1993, pp, 238–40), these films express Pasolini's partially unconfessed desire for a violent intervention that "wipes the slate clean", just like in Benjamin's vision: 'Mythic violence is bloody power over mere life for its own sake; divine violence is pure power over all life for the sake of the living. The first demands sacrifice; the second accepts it. [...] if the existence of violence outside the law, as pure immediate violence, is assured, this furnishes proof that revolutionary violence, the highest manifestation of unalloyed violence by man, is possible, and shows by what means' (Benjamin, 1997, pp. 250–52).

The choice of Medea is in this sense an exemplary one: the character of the barbaric high priestess of Colchis brings to fruition the subversive potential already at work in films such as *Edipo re*, *Teorema* and *Porcile*. The very fact that *Medea* was regarded by many commentators as a failed film, and thus a kind of exception in Pasolini's filmography, paradoxically confirms its vital importance (in Lacan it is always in the exception that we find the repressed truth of a given signifying chain). The film's aesthetics and narrative shortcomings (the lack of narrative cohesion, its endless ellipses, the superficial treatment of most of the characters) are functional to the absolute centrality of the character of Medea. No wonder this is the only one of Pasolini's films where we do not feel the director's encumbering presence, where the autobiographical baggage seems to disappear! With *Medea*, Pasolini confronts head-on the inassimilable core of *his own* desire, which coincides with the destructive *jouissance* unleashed by his heroine; as a consequence, the director is "erased from the picture", his *aphanisis* literally deriving from an excess of enjoyment. If *Edipo re* did stage a desire that Pasolini was fully aware of (the Oedipal complex), *Medea* goes a step further into the uncharted (unconscious) territory of the feminine act, which reveals the true scope of Pasolini's subversive stance. What Medea's enigmatic final words ('Nothing is possible anymore!') allude to is precisely the limit of expenditure, the pure void of subjectivity where the sacred overlaps with unthinkable evil.

From a different angle, it would appear that Medea accomplishes the Kierkegaardian "religious suspension of the ethical", which, as Žižek often reminds us, designates the formal dimension of the ethical gesture *par excellence* (see Žižek, 2001d, pp. 148–51): first she kills her brother Absyrtus out of love for Jason; later, out of hatred for him, she kills their two sons. What we need to emphasise here is that the formal structure of Medea's cruel acts makes visible the liberating potential of a sovereign gesture of self-relating violence. Let us consider these two acts more closely. The explicit motivation behind the killing of Absyrtus is one of survival: having stolen the Golden Fleece, Medea and Jason escape from the land of Colchis, but are followed by Medea's father (Aeetes) and his soldiers; by dismembering Absyrtus' body and scattering its pieces along the way, Medea effectively delays the chasing army. However, the real aim of this act is a much more subtle one: what Medea wants to achieve is not just a break with the pursuing army, but, more crucially, a break with her own emotional attachment to her family, which would enable her to dedicate herself unconditionally to Jason. By the same token, the final killing of her sons cannot be simply liquidated as a gesture of supreme vindictive cruelty, for no hatred would justify such a monstrosity. Instead, the real target is, again, Medea's own libidinal attachment: the only way for her to overcome her love for Jason (i.e., to traverse and dispel the libidinally invested fantasy of their relationship, which is the only passionate attachment she has left) is by killing the dearest thing they have in common: after such a shock, 'nothing [between them] will be possible anymore'.

We must therefore value both of Medea's acts as horrifying confrontations with the abyss of the Real, to be intended literally as the formless, pulsating life-substance of the human body, that which Freud refers to in his famous analysis of his dream about Irma's throat (see Freud, 1997, pp. 20–33). Lacan describes the object of Freud's account as 'the flesh one never sees, the foundation of things, the other side of the head, of the face, the secretory gland *par excellence*, the flesh from which everything exudes, at the very heart of the mystery, the flesh in as much as it is suffering, formless, in as much as its form itself is something which provokes anxiety' (Lacan, 1988, pp. 154–55), and later as the 'lamella', that is, 'libido, *qua* pure life instinct, [...] immortal life, or irrepressible life, life that has need of no organ, simplified, indestructible life' (Lacan, 1998a, p. 198).[1]

With this premise, it does not seem exaggerated to claim that Medea is the first fictional subject to come face to face with the abyss of negativity that *is* the subject. Her predicament is one of progressive isolation: having first betrayed her family for Jason, she is later betrayed by her husband, and finds herself utterly alone and dejected. As a result, she is forced to face the paradox of subjectivity: either "live in loss" (in eternal mourning), or outsource loss through loss itself, i.e. through an act of violence that effaces the very memory of loss. The subversive potential of this situation can be grasped by transposing the situation itself onto a political level: Medea can either accept her condition of subordination/marginalisation within Jason's newly-founded modern state (and, for example, piously devote herself to her children), or she can "out-violence" Jason's power by assuming the very negativity that marks her state of exception/exclusion. Only by choosing the second option, a radical limit-position, does she manages to truly antagonise her husband-rival. As often argued by Žižek, this masochistic logic of "striking at oneself" indicates that the first and fundamental step towards the emancipation from a certain symbolic predicament lies in resorting to an act of self-relating violence, whose aim is to break the disavowed libidinal attachment that sustains the subject's double-bind to a given symbolic configuration, while also exposing the very inconsistency of the power edifice itself.

What rightly appears as Medea's cruelty, her barbaric inscrutability, is thus the very structural condition that sustains the groundbreaking dimension of the act proper. Nietzsche had already laid out in no uncertain terms (see Nietzsche, 1995, p. 89) that any act worthy of this name always depends on a degree of forgetting, of detachment from one's own historical awareness or symbolic mandate – a concept that echoes what Lacan calls separation, the over-identification with the negativity of the unconscious desire. Strictly speaking, Medea is able to perform the abominable final murder because she can suppress the knowledge that the two creatures in front of her are her sons. Her power to break the spell of time and memory, which signals the inscription of the infinite in the finite, is correlative to the endorsement of the traumatic dimension of *jouissance*: in order to bring herself to accomplish the killing of her brother and sons, Medea has to assume the explosive surplus of enjoyment that structures her attachment to them. And what do Pasolini's heroes and heroines suggest if not that what takes place in the ahistorical domain of their *jouissance* is the only adequate response to a true passionate attachment? The paradox is that passion for reality can only be adequately expressed as "passion for the Real" – attachment can only fulfil itself as traumatic dis-attachment.[2]

Also, could we not argue that Medea goes a step further than Antigone, the Lacanian "heroine of the act" *par excellence*? If Antigone's self-destructive inflexibility was still aimed at safeguarding a certain symbolic constellation (the family mores as opposed to the law of the paternal state), Medea's act dissolves the last vestiges of symbolic unity, exposing the abyss at the heart of the subject interpellated in the family network. Jacques-Alain Miller, despite some restraint, was the first to recognise that the figure of Medea has all the credentials to satisfy the Lacanian definition of *une vraie femme*: 'For Lacan, the act of a true woman is not necessarily as extreme as Medea's, but it has *the same structure*, in that she sacrifices what is most precious to her in order to pierce man with a hole that can never be filled' (Miller, 2000, p. 19, my emphasis). What Pasolini focuses on in his film is not quite the divine cruelty of a true woman, but a much more troubling question – which, one might add, he was very familiar with: the fact that the condition of exclusion can only be truly redeemed through an act that *must* be perceived not only as scandalous but also, strictly speaking, as impossible. In a way that can only remind one of Pasolini's own personal predicament, Medea does not negotiate her position of victim within the socio-symbolic order; on the contrary, she radicalises the attitude of victimisation by assuming the libidinal attachment embedded in her subordinate position. This is the only way she can free herself from what she seemed irredeemably attached to.

Luchino Visconti's *Senso* (The Wanton Countess, 1954) presents us with another prototypical cinematic incarnation of *une vraie femme*. Desperately in love with young and handsome Austrian

Lieutenant Franz Mahler (Farley Granger), Countess Livia Serpieri of Venice (Alida Valli), a proud patriot actively involved in the Italian Risorgimento, ends up abandoning both her husband and her political cause in persuit of a self-destructive love affair with the debauched and callous Austrian officer. Her complete devotion to Mahler blinds her to his opportunistic behaviour, until one day, after having saved his life and helped him hide as a deserter, she catches him in bed with a

Senso

prostitute. Drunk, Mahler brazenly derides her, launching into an obscene tirade against womankind. Finally awoken to the truth about her lover, Countess Serpieri reports Mahler for desertion, and the Austrian court-martial immediately have him arrested and executed. More overtly than in Medea's case, what matters here is the self-relating violence sustaining the Countess' act. It would be a mistake to see her denunciation of Mahler as a gesture of cruel revenge, for it is a gesture that aims, essentially, at breaking down *her own* attachment to the object of desire.

Dillinger è morto

The unconscious logic of striking at one's own libidinal attachment in order to gain some freedom from a given symbolic context is, I believe, also silently at work in one of the most startling Italian films of the 1960s, Marco Ferreri's *Dillinger è morto* (Dillinger is Dead, 1969). This claustrophobic tale of human alienation revolves around Glauco (Michel Piccoli), an industrial engineer who suddenly decides to break with his modern and empty life. Upon returning home after a day's work, he finds his wife (Anita Pallenberg) in bed with a headache, and a cold meal on the table. Unhappy with the food he looks for a recipe and decides to cook himself a sophisticated dinner. Whilst searching for the necessary ingredients he comes across an old gun, which he cleans carefully and paints red. After eating his meal he sets up his projector and watches some disconnected images on the wall, then flirts with the maid, listens to music and eventually shoots his sleeping wife dead. In the surreal final scene of the film he leaves his flat and drives to the seaside; there he swims out to a boat bound for Tahiti, discovers that the cook has just died, and manages to get his job. What should not be missed about Glauco's psychotic act of liberation (the killing of his wife) is that it is preceded by the staging of his suicide, as repeatedly in the narrative he points the gun against himself, faking his own death. These instances of staged suicide tell us that by murdering his wife he actually aims to kill off what is "in him more than himself", i.e. his attachment to his bourgeois milieu. This is why the psychotic act of liberation is fundamentally self-directed: without it, he could never have found the strength to leave.

2.2 FROM THE VIRTUAL REVOLUTIONARY TO THE REVOLUTIONARY VIRTUAL

It is a striking coincidence that whilst Pasolini was filming *Medea* amongst the breathtaking rock formations and subterranean dwellings of Cappadocia (Turkey), Antonioni was shooting at Zabriskie Point, in the Death Valley National Park of California, a similarly estranged and spectacular location made of gullies, mud hills and canyons. *Zabriskie Point* also compares to *Medea* as an even more conspicuous box-office flop, ignored and ridiculed by critics and rejected by the public (although today it has gained the status of cult movie). My claim is that such concurrences originate in the overwhelming attraction these two films display towards the previously discussed dimension of "the desert of the Real", a dimension one can hardly avoid relating to the late 1960s cultural and socio-political climate of widespread unrest and utopianism. However, ahead of sharing a magnetic and ultimately lethal attraction to the cinematic potential for "representing void", these films also manage to dialecticise such potential into a subtly subversive ploy. If Medea's act of self-contraction culminates in a psychotic stance of separation, *Zabriskie Point* stages a similar instance of self-directed violence.

Antonioni's treatment of revolutionary American youth focuses on Mark (Mark Frechette), a college drop-out who attends student meetings but declares himself 'bored stiff' with their organised revolutionary rhetoric a la Black Panther, as well as with their intellectual counter-cultural strategies. Rather than wasting his time attending long political debates (such as the one that opens the film), he buys himself a gun under a false pretext and goes back to the campus, where the police are trying to force a group of students out of an occupied library. There, we witness the first event of the film, as a policeman mistakenly shoots dead one of the students exiting the library, thinking that he was reaching for a gun when he was simply tucking his shirt in his trousers. At this precise point the camera cuts to Mark, who, having observed the whole scene, instinctively tries to get hold of his own gun. Then a shot is fired and the policeman falls down dead right in front of Mark's eyes. Who is responsible? Although everything happens very quickly, the attentive viewer will have noticed that Mark has nothing to do with the assassination, for by the time the policeman is shot he has not managed to grab hold of his gun, which he keeps hidden in his boot. Later on in the film Mark tells Daria (Daria Halprin), the female co-protagonist, that *he would like to have shot the policeman, but someone else did it first*. His bold statement confirms what by then had become fairly clear, i.e., that he is prepared to fully assume the consequences of an act which he did not but would have performed had he been given the chance. From this moment on, Mark embarks on what can only be defined as a suicidal or psychotic journey, progressively detaching himself from his world: he steals a small private airplane, joyrides it through the desert, fortuitously meets Daria, engages with her in a short-lived and surreal love adventure at Zabriskie Point, and eventually provokes his own death at the hands of the police.

Within such a seemingly disconsolate portrayal of organised student revolts, what risks going unnoticed is the key question concerning Mark's reaction to the killing of the policeman. As often with Antonioni, we are confronted with a non-subjectivisable event, an act that remains enigmatically deprived of its empirical agent, and which therefore acquires a virtual status.[3] In *Zabriskie Point*, Antonioni's reflection on the virtual status of the act is brought to fruition through a simple logic: since the subject of the act does not exist (at least in narrative terms) anyone who shares the desire to accomplish it (Mark) may well appropriate it, willingly assuming its consequences. More precisely, it is the vertiginous openness of the revolutionary act that occupies the pivotal place in this narrative, a feature recalling Walter Benjamin's anti-historicist apology of Messianic time in his *Theses on the Philosophy of History*. In thesis XVII, Benjamin writes:

> Thinking involves not only the flow of thoughts, but their arrest as well. Where thinking suddenly stops in a configuration pregnant with tensions, it gives that configuration a shock, by which it cristallizes into a monad. A historical materialist approaches a historical subject only where he encounters it as a monad. In this structure he recognizes the sign of a

Messianic cessation of happening, or, put differently, a revolutionary chance in the fight for the oppressed past. He takes cognizance of it in order to blast a specific era out of the homogenous course of history – blasting a specific life out of the era or a specific work out of the lifework (Benjamin, 1968, p. 263).

Benjamin's 'revolutionary chance' against 'the homogeneous course of history' is correlative to the radical openness of the concrete historical situation as subtly vindicated by Antonioni. Mark fully endorses the abyss of the act that suddenly opens up before his eyes, and does so by assuming the traumatic content of his desire. Crucial to this is the virtual dimension involved, for had Mark actually killed the policeman, the groundless character of the revolutionary chance would have been partially lost. In other words, the revolutionary chance is qualified by the shock effect it produces on the subject suddenly confronted by it.

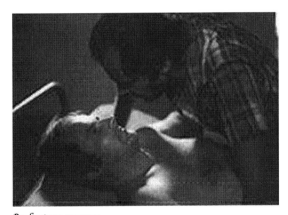

Professione reporter

And is not the same virtual logic at work in Antonioni's following film, *Professione: reporter* (The Passanger, 1975)? Whilst in an unspecified African country to interview a group of guerrilla rebels, television reporter David Locke (Jack Nicholson) accidentally finds himself in an analogous position to that occupied by Mark. Having failed to contact the rebels, he returns to his hotel to discover that David Robertson (Chuck Mulvehill), a fellow guest whom he had previously befriended, has suddenly died, apparently of natural causes. It is at this early stage that the virtual dimension comes into play: taking advantage of his physical resemblance with Robertson, Locke opts to exchange identity with him. He swaps the passport photos, drags Robertson's body into his room, and calmly goes to the reception to report the sudden death of David Locke.[4] As in Mark's case, the protagonist here is presented with the opportunity to enter the virtual space of radical otherness, thus fulfilling his long-repressed desire to do away with an unsatisfactory life (we find out later that Locke is unhappy with his job and private life, as the many references to his failed marriage demonstrate). Despite the fact that he will not succeed in becoming Robertson, what counts is that the revolutionary dimension of virtuality – the zero-level where life and death miraculously coincide – is inscribed in the narrative.

The subversive character of this operation finds corroboration in two crucial elements. Firstly, we have the politically significant reference to the African rebels, which is strengthened by the subsequent knowledge that Robertson was taking part in their struggle by selling them weapons (and Locke, despite a degree of self-restraint, will remain faithful to this "inherited" role, right down to his death at the hands of the counter-revolutionary secret services).[5] Secondly, as always with Antonioni, the most vital part of the content is sublimated into form: through its use of unconventional flashbacks,[6] the narrative ambiguity conveyed by editing, and the radical freedom of camera movements, Antonioni confirms his attraction to the desert of the Real, which does not so much amount to 'a basic sense of the impossibility of sure and fixed knowledge about anything' (Brunette, 1998, p. 133), but rather to an irresistible fascination with void, with the violence of a break that has the potential to thoroughly transform a given symbolic situation. If therefore the film is centred on David Locke's death-drive (see Chatman, 1985, pp. 187–89), we need to add that such a drive conveys an extraordinary liberating potential – which, as Sam Rohdie (1990, pp. 150–51) has rightly emphasised, comes to full fruition in the remarkable penultimate shot at the Hotel de la Gloria.[7] Antonioni himself hinted at the correlation between death-drive and freedom:

> I could say that the desire to die has simply become nestled in his unconscious, unknown to him. Or that Locke begins absorbing death from the moment he leans over Robertson's corpse. But I could also say that he keeps the appointment for the opposite reasons: in fact, it's Daisy he is going to meet, and Daisy is a character from his new life (in Brunette, 1998, p. 144).

Back to *Zabriskie Point*. The hostility with which the film was received can be explained through Antonioni's lack of interest in the revolutionary mystique of active student organisations. In *Zabriskie Point* he follows the less directly political logic of virtuality, which is operative from the beginning of the film and can be summed up as follows: from the virtual core of the commodity to the virtual core of the act. With particular reference to the commodity, one should not underestimate the visual energy generated by *Zabriskie Point*, particularly with regard to its emphasis on advertising. Far from adopting a moralistic attitude towards the commodification of American life, Antonioni aestheticises the object-commodity, thus drawing our attention to its form, which, as Marx pointed out in Volume I of *Capital* (see Marx, 1970, pp. 76–80) is precisely what confers upon it such a spellbinding lure. If the aesthetic elusiveness of the object-commodity is what fascinates Antonioni's camera in the first part of the film, where he focuses on a breathtaking succession of massive publicity posters flanking a Californian road, by the end this fascination has exploded into a delirious apology of the structural enigma of the commodity. I am referring, of course, to the famous sequence of the explosion of Allen's house, shot from thirteen different angles, followed by the minimalistic slow-motion framing of the detonation and disintegration of a series of household products such as a box of Kellogg's Special K, a loaf of Wonder Bread, etc. It is with this deliriously formalistic final sequence that Antonioni's cinema confirms its fundamental attraction to the imaginary status of *objet a*.

One should nevertheless be careful not to disregard this attraction as a purely pathological whim of Antonioni's art. The political significance to be retrieved from the formalistic excesses of *Zabriskie Point*'s final sequence depends on its crucial insight into the very meaning of commodity fetishism: what sustains the commodity, and consequently the logic of late capitalism, is its "virtual soul", the empty core of the (sublime) object that sets desire in motion. As Žižek points out,

> the real problem is not to penetrate to the "hidden kernel" of the commodity – the determination of its value by the quantity of the work consumed in its production – but to explain why work assumed the form of the value of a commodity, why it can affirm its social character only in the commodity-form of its product (Žižek, 1992, p. 11).

And again:

> In other words, classical political economy is interested only in contents concealed behind the commodity-form, which is why it cannot explain the true secret, not the secret *behind* the form but *the secret of this form itself*. In spite of its quite correct explanation of the "secret of the magnitude of value", the commodity remains for classical political economy a mysterious enigmatic thing – it is the same as with dreams: even after we have explained its hidden meaning, its latent thought, the dream remains an enigmatic phenomenon; what is not yet explained is simply its form, the process by means of which the hidden meaning disguised itself in such a form (Žižek, 1992, p. 15).

Žižek's wager here is that the enigma of the commodity-form can only be solved by bringing Lacan's unconscious into the equation, that most fundamental and sublime of abstractions which allows us to perceive ourselves as subjects capable of articulating a certain relationship with knowledge.[8] Expanding on Žižek's parallel between commodity and dream, could we not claim that it is the same with film, and that Antonioni's specific merit is that of pinpointing for us *the form of film-thought*, which is strictly speaking external to the narrative and yet has to be posited in advance if we are to critically engage with the actual content of the film?[9]

It is easy to see how this critical approach can be elaborated further in psychoanalytic terms through the dialectics of the gaze. If, expanding on what established in the last section of part 1, we consider the very location that lends the film its title, we realise that it designates nothing but the gaze: Zabriskie Point is simply a blind spot, another one in the series of places/non-places functioning as figurations of *objet a* in Antonioni's filmography.

Zabriskie Point

As anticipated, the representation of the subversive impact of the virtual in *Zabriskie Point* is clearly at its most convincing in the final sequence. The explosion of Allen's house allows the director to bring together the two main themes: on the one hand, we have the equation between the commodity and its empty kernel; on the other, the virtual dimension of the act. The complicity between Mark and Daria is articulated against the background of virtuality, which explains (and partly redeems) the psychedelic portrayal of their lovemaking in the desert: what if the sudden and imaginary multiplication of couples in this famous "love-in" is simply a way to suggest that love is also a virtual dimension, where the particular miraculously coincides with the universal? Perhaps what this sequence surreptitiously indicates, over and above its falsely idealistic (but also, as the script points out, 'slightly ironic', see Antonioni, 1970, p. 67) connotations, is the classic Antonionian theme of the "impossibility of communication between the sexes", the fact that love between two human beings hinges on its sublimation into a virtual dimension *that can be assumed but not subjectivised*. In short, there seems to be no solution of continuity between the three main moments of the film: Mark's assumption of guilt, Mark and Daria's lovemaking, and Daria's imagined explosion; what unites these moments is *the thread of virtuality*, the fact that they belong together in a de-realised domain – which, conversely, is exactly what endows them with a subversive potential.

As well as providing an insight into the meaning of commodity fetishism, the explosion of Allen's house also tells us something about Daria. Let us first briefly summarise the plot from the point of view of the female protagonist. Daria's story runs parallel to Mark's, to the point that almost half of the film is an extended crosscut sequence between the two subjective points of view. Having been eyed up by Lee Allen (Rod Taylor), the owner of a real estate company called "Sunnydunes", Daria accepts a job as a secretary in Allen's company. One day she drives out into the desert on a business trip; along the way she meets Mark in exceptionally bizarre circumstances, and escapes with him to Zabriskie Point, where they make love. Later, on the way back, Mark decides to return the stolen plane, consequently leaving Daria. As she is driving back to Allen's luxurious home outside Phoenix, she hears on the radio that Mark has been killed. After meeting Allen in his house, she feels enraged and decides to leave. However, she stops her car at a short distance from the house, hesitates for a while, and then gets out to look back at it.

The intensity of Daria's act of looking brings back the question of the gaze. The first observation we should make apropos of this impressive sequence is that the explosion is not a direct consequence (however imaginary) of Daria's incensed gaze, but rather the result of a disarmingly artificial "alliance" between Daria's eye (the way she looks at the house) and Antonioni's camera. The sequence suggests that Daria's rage *is not enough*, it is powerless in itself, as it needs to be articulated from the radically distorted perspective of the Lacanian gaze (hence the repetition of the shot of the explosion from thirteen different angles) which the cinematic eye has a chance to vindicate. Antonioni seems to arrogate to film the privilege of representing the formal structure of the revolutionary act: the cinematic eye activates the virtual logic of the gaze by identifying the blind spot in the visual field, which, similarly to what happens in *Blow-up*, brings about the collapse of the image, i.e. of the world "as we know it".

2.3 MASOCHISM AND THE LAW

If we were to define the radicality of Pasolini's cinema vis-à-vis Antonioni's, we would point out his insistence on the anthropomorphic character of the Real: if Antonioni secretly wishes to erase the subject or dissolve it in the background, Pasolini hangs on to its ponderous presence, albeit in an effort to evoke its excessive and inassimilable nature. More to the point, what qualifies Pasolini's Real is his outrageous insistence on a certain *mode of bodily enjoyment* that could not (and still cannot)[10] be tolerated by society: an unacceptable (homo)sexuality "beyond the norm". It is not Pasolini's homosexuality as such that bothered the public and exasperated the institutions. In fact, could we not argue that as soon as he realised that homosexuality had started being tolerated by the "liberalised" establishment of the late 1960s, he strove to exclude himself by deliberately accentuating the pathologically outrageous character of his Eros? As many of his own highly controversial declarations indicate, Pasolini preferred raw intolerance to the permissive tolerance promoted by late-capitalist ethics. However, this choice was not simply instrumental to the enhancement of his libido (since, as we know from Freud, libido thrives on prohibition); rather, it was both a strategy of resistance and a way to launch a final attack against the establishment. What if the often mentioned "pathological derailment" of Pasolini's libido into shockingly indecent, if not immoral or overtly perverted forms of enjoyment (from his well known predilection for adolescent male prostitutes to the alleged sadomasochistic rituals), was aimed at avoiding the lure of strategic-pragmatic compromises, thus secretly reiterating his conviction that only the repetition of a scandal *qua* enactment of inadmissible forms of enjoyment can antagonise the (capitalist) establishment? What I argue is that through the explicit assumption of *jouissance*, Pasolini was attempting to expose what Lacan calls the non-existence of the big Other, the foundational inconsistency of the law.

This is the context in which Pasolini's previously mentioned defence of martyrdom must be understood. When he writes that 'freedom can only be expressed through martyrdom', adding that 'each martyr martyrs himself through the reactionary executioner' (Pasolini, 1995, p. 269), Pasolini conflates the notion of "martyrdom" with that of "masochism". Nonetheless, contrary to what most commentators have maintained, his masochism cannot be dismissed as a mere pathology: it would be a terrible oversight to explain it away as the logical result of a guilt complex generated by his own bourgeois beginnings. The analysis of his cinema and work in general suggests the overlapping of the notion of masochism with a strategy founded upon what we have already designated as the politicisation of the death-drive, which is attained through the repeated endorsement of that "reference to Nothingness" best epitomised by the word *jouissance*. To speak about Pasolini's masochism means to speak about the cold, detached, meticulously planned repetition of the same excessive gesture that characterises, for example, Julian's mode of enjoyment in *Porcile*. As in Julian's case, we have masochism as a domain "beyond the pleasure principle", where pleasure turns into pleasure in displeasure, reiteration of a gesture that *misses its object* (i.e. assumes its object as a lack). Rather than simply recreating the conservative domain of the pleasure principle, as suggested by Deleuze (1991, p. 120), the repetition that qualifies the masochistic gesture circumscribes the domain of *jouissance* as the destabilising force at work in the death-drive.[11]

We shall return to the question of the correlation between repetition and death-drive when examining *Salò*; for the time being, let us focus on the specific character of Pasolini's masochism, which can be linked to a strategy aimed essentially at two objectives. Firstly, as already suggested apropos of *Medea*, a masochistic act represents to him the first step towards liberation, since the staging of self-inflicted violence is the only way for the subject to cut the Gordian knot of his or her libidinally-invested subjection to the symbolic law; secondly, and simultaneously, the masochistic act brings into contention the insidious figure of the Sadean executioner, the representative of the dark underside of the law – or, more precisely, the necessary supplement who takes upon himself the unbearable weight of the law's inconsistency. We shall now examine this enigmatic figure and its specific role more closely.

In his 1962 essay 'Kant avec Sade' (see Lacan, 1966, pp. 765–90), Lacan objects to the fact that Kant, in his positing the autonomous and self-determining character of the law, conveniently forgets to include in the picture the law's obscene addendum, that is, the underworld of perverted enjoyment (*qua* practices of domination) introduced by Sade. This disturbing appendix to Kant's moral construct had already been identified by Freud, who in his 'The economic problem of masochism' explicitly links Kant's categorical imperative to the cruelty of the superego:

> [...] this super-ego is as much a representative of the id as of the external world. It came into being through the introjection into the ego of the first objects of the id's libidinal impulses – namely, the two parents. In this process the relation to those objects was desexualized; it was diverted from its direct sexual aims. Only in this way was it possible for the Oedipus complex to be surmounted. The super-ego retained essential features of the introjected persons – their strength, their severity, their tendency to supervise and to punish. [...] The super-ego – the conscience at work in the ego – may then become harsh, cruel and inexorable against the ego which is in its charge. Kant's Categorical Imperative is thus the direct heir of the Oedipus complex (Freud, 1961, p. 167).

My contention is that Pasolini's masochism targets the structural imbalance of the law as a set of empirical prescriptive measures supplemented by superegoic (sadistic) stimuli. The point not to be missed is that, as Deleuze has noted in *Coldness and Cruelty*, what supremely frustrates the sadistic executioner is the masochistic fervour of his victim: 'a genuine sadist could never tolerate a masochist victim' (Deleuze, 1991, p. 40). The immediate reason for this frustration is that masochism forces the sadist to acknowledge that the object of his desire – the body of the other – is *already the object of the other's desire*, and as such it can only function as ersatz or at least secondary enjoyment; and what is the awareness of this missed encounter with the Thing if not the very distinctive feature of *jouissance*? The point is that the masochist martyr steals (and stages) the secret *jouissance* of the law, thus making visible the extent to which the law is enslaved to the lack that pertains to the logic of desire.[12] The *jouissance* of the martyr affirms its speculative identity with the *jouissance* of the law-enforcing executioner, hence revealing the strict correlation between the neutral but self-affirming character of the law and the groundlessness of desire. From a different angle we could say that the masochist effectively objectifies the law, turning it into an instrument for his own enjoyment – and, of course, this being reduced to an object is what frustrates the law, compelling it to expose its obscene libidinal underside. As Lacan puts it at the start of Seminar XX, the law basically enjoys (see Lacan, 1998b, pp. 2–3). If the law, in its deepest connotation, is about *jouissance*, this means that it is sustained by a scandalous, irrational and strictly speaking unlawful will to enjoy. What emerges from this picture is the law's fundamental imbalance: its vulnerability and changeability. Pasolini understands that it is not enough to denounce the existence of, as he often put it, *il palazzo* (the "anarchy of Power", the shadowy underside of the law); the only way to challenge the functioning of the law is by assuming, in a supreme act of masochistic expenditure, the Real of its obscene *jouissance*, the vertiginous dimension of enjoyment.

We can now see how Pasolini turns around Kant's claim that the moral law is the measure of the subject's freedom: it is not that the unbearable pressure of the moral law coincides with disinterestedness and freedom, but that freedom can only be posited as an unbearable pressure to face the empty kernel of the law. The equation between freedom and martyrdom thus targets the tautological foundations of the law: the real scandal is that, as Deleuze put it apropos of Kant's *Critique of Practical Reason*, 'the law [...] is self-grounded and valid solely by virtue of its own form. [...] the object of the law is by definition unknowable and elusive.' Such a perspective implies the psychoanalytic awareness that 'the object of the law and the object of desire are one and the same, and remain equally concealed' (Deleuze, 1991, pp. 82–5); or, as Lacan put it at the end of *Seminar XI*, that 'the moral law [...] is simply desire in its pure state, the very desire that culminates in the sacrifice, strictly speaking, of everything that is the object of love in one's human tenderness – I would say, not only in the rejection of the pathological object, but also in its sacrifice and murder. That is why I wrote *Kant avec Sade*' (Lacan, 1998a, pp. 275–76).

By coupling Sade with Kant, Lacan underlines the non-pathological thrust of the categorical imperative: Sade's "unconditional injunction to enjoy" is correlative to Kant's "unconditional injunction to do one's duty", as both are ultimately 'pure desire' – they are delivered from any utilitarian concern with the actual attainment of the object. The truth of Sade's injunction to enjoy the body of the other beyond any possible limit is to be found in Kant's moral law, since the latter presupposes a fracture between the positive content of the law and its (empty, frustratingly unattainable) form: the encounter with the object of desire, whether it is body or law, is necessarily a missed encounter, an encounter in the Real of *jouissance*. And, again, the distinctive feature of Pasolini's position is that the scandal of the law's inconsistency can only be fully articulated from the point of view of the masochist martyr vis-à-vis the Sadean executioner. Ultimately, if the secret of the law is that it is sustained by an obscene superego command to obey regardless of the content, this secret can only be challenged through its redoubling *outside the law*, in a place where the executioner is, as it were, exasperated by the "strange fervour" of the masochist victim.

This position can also be elaborated in terms of guilt (well beyond the cliché concerning Pasolini's bourgeois background). If the gap that separates the law from its positive content makes the subject *a priori guilty* (for, as in Kafka's novels, the subject never knows where he stands with respect to the "irrational" law), it is the subject's full assumption of this indelible guilt that can break the vicious circle of the law and its transgressive superego supplement.[13] What counts here is, again, the Pasolinian *topos* of the Christian martyr, which signals the intervention of a mode of enjoyment that calls into question *the law in its totality*, including the disavowed libidinal core. The emancipatory potential of this intervention resides in the fact that it suspends the law's unbearable pressure, for it reveals how this pressure is always-already connected with an obscene injunction to enjoy (the superego command). Thus, when a subject says "I am a priori guilty, and therefore I *enjoy* being punished!", it is the law in its neutral universalistic framework that, in effect, reveals its impotence and frustration. If a subject enjoys being punished, the law inevitably loses its coercive character and exhibits its fundamental lack of purpose, its being anchored in enjoyment. The masochist therefore teases out and identifies with the libidinal (fundamentally irrational and self-destructive) kernel of the law itself.

In *Revolution at the Gates*, Žižek approaches the above theme through David Fincher's film *Fight Club* (1999). The basic question posed by the film's hero (Norton) is extremely simple and yet absolutely pressing: how is the modern subject to break out of 'the futility of a life filled with failure and empty consumer culture' (Žižek, 2002b, p. 250)? The suggested answer is equally simple, although apparently absurd: through self-beating. This strategy is epitomised in what is perhaps the most significant scene of the film, when the hero, whilst arguing with his boss over his salary, decides to act out the latter's repressed anger and suddenly starts beating himself up in his office. According to Žižek, this apparently masochistic act represents the only way 'to suspend the fundamental abstraction and coldness of capitalist subjectivity', the reason being that:

> we cannot go directly from capitalist to revolutionary subjectivity: the abstraction, the foreclosure of others, the blindness to the other's suffering and pain, has first to be broken in a gesture of taking the risk and reaching directly out to the suffering other – a gesture which, since it shatters the very kernel of our identity, cannot fail to appear extremely violent (Žižek, 2002b, p. 252).

Radical agency is here linked to a self-damaging act 'which is equivalent to adopting the position of the proletarian who has nothing to lose'. In Žižek's words, the emergence of pure subjectivity coincides with an 'experience of radical self-degradation' whereby I, the subject, am emptied 'of all substantial content, of all symbolic support which could confer a modicum of dignity on me' (Žižek, 2002b, p. 252). The reason why such a humiliating and potentially perverse position is to be assumed, Žižek argues, is that within a disciplinary relationship (i.e. between "master and servant") self-beating is nothing but the staging of the other's secret fantasy; as such, this staging allows for the suspension of the disciplinary efficacy of the relationship by bringing to light the obscene supplement which secretly cements it. Žižek's key point, however, is that this obscene supplement ultimately cements the position of the servant: what self-beating uncovers is 'the servant's masochistic libidinal attachment to his master', so that 'the true goal of this beating is to beat out that in me which attaches me to the master' (Žižek, 2002b, p. 252). Thus, it is not enough to be aware of our state of subjection to change things, for that very subjection, insofar as it is part of a power mechanism, is inevitably eroticised, sustained by the disavowed pleasure we find in being caught in it:

> When we are subjected to a power mechanism, this subjection is always and by definition sustained by some libidinal investment: the subjection itself generates a surplus-enjoyment of its own. This subjection is embodied in a network of "material" bodily practices, and for this reason we cannot get rid of our subjection through a merely intellectual reflection – our liberation has to be *staged* in some kind of bodily performance; furthermore, this performance *has* to be of an apparently "masochistic" nature, it *has* to stage the painful process of hitting back at oneself (Žižek, 2002b, p. 253).

Ultimately, the passage from "oppressed victim" to "active agent of the revolution" requires a move whereby the subject endorses that excess/symptom which anchors his identity in the socio-symbolic order *qua* power mechanism: '*the only true awareness of our subjection is the awareness of the obscene excessive pleasure (surplus-enjoyment) we derive from it*; this is why the first gesture of liberation is not to get rid of this excessive pleasure, but actively to assume it' (Žižek, 2002b, p. 254).

It is in this context that Pasolini's frequent reference to Christianity, and particularly his sacrilegious identification with Christ, should be accounted for. In the collection of poems entitled *L'usignolo della chiesa cattolica* (The Nightingale of the Catholic Church), written between 1943 and 1949, Pasolini openly confesses his sexual immorality and abnormity, together with his desire to be punished like Christ, exposed and humiliated on the cross (see Pasolini, 1993, pp. 283–413). In cinema, his fascination with the image of the crucifixion returns powerfully in *La ricotta*, which combines it with the theme of unlimited libidinal expenditure. The point is that Christianity for him is truly the religion of Revelation, in the sense that *everything in it is revealed*, including the excessive, scandalous *jouissance* of the victim!

La ricotta

La ricotta re-writes the story of the crucifixion by shifting the main focus on the character of Stracci (literally, "rags"), a poor sub-proletarian extra who interprets the good thief in a lavish production directed by Orson Welles. Similarly to *Che cosa sono le nuvole?*, it concentrates on what goes on underground, behind the scenes. The significance of this insight could be summed up in the following two points: firstly, on a sociological level, the film suggests that the advent of the consumer society implies the ruthless exploitation and mortification of the sub-proletariat, the excluded subjects; secondly, it presents the passion of Christ as a subversive narrative against capitalist hegemony, provided it is intended as a way of fighting "excess with excess" – that is to say, provided it portrays Christ as a sublime figure of reckless expenditure who suspends the law by fully assuming its repressed *jouissance*. In view of this, it should not surprise us that the film opens with the following quotation from Mark's Gospel: 'For there is nothing hid, which shall not be manifested; neither was any thing kept secret, but that it should come abroad. If any man have ears to hear, let him hear'. Essentially, the film "reveals" both Stracci's social exploitation and his abnormal appetite. Sub-proletarian exclusion comes to coincide with bodily excess, a compulsion to "enjoy beyond the pleasure principle" that symptomatically culminates in the crucifixion. As with Pasolini's first two male sub-proletarian heroes, Vittorio in *Accattone* (1961) and Ettore in *Mamma Roma* (1962), Stracci becomes the embodiment of an immoderate and scandalous passion for life that eventually overlaps with the death-drive. The question of self-degradation is crucial: instead of turning his sub-proletarian characters into pathetic victims of social exploitation, Pasolini suggests that their wretchedness is self-inflicted, masochistically assumed. As his scandalous novels of the late 1950s had already made more than explicit, his abject sub-proletarians essentially revel in their condition of exclusion and depravity, and the decisive point is that only such an apparently perverse mode of enjoyment can challenge the perverse mechanism that sustains the functioning of the law.

The paradox embodied by Pasolini's "defence of martyrdom" was also developed by George Bataille, who stated that Sade's language is that of a strange victim who stages his own domination, for only such a victim can show us the true face of power (see Bataille, 1986, p. 187). Endorsing Bataille's point, Deleuze writes: 'The tyrant speaks the language of the law, and acknowledges no other, for he lives "in the shadows of the laws". The heroes of Sade are inspired with an extraordinary passion against tyranny; they speak as no tyrant ever spoke and could ever speak; theirs is the counter-language of tyranny' (Deleuze, 1991, p. 87). Could we not claim that, in a similar manner to Sade (though not necessarily sharing his anarchism) Pasolini at a certain point started speaking 'the counter-language of tyranny?' The self-damaging gesture staged by his cinema is essentially the gesture of *a victim who refuses to be victimised*, for he knows that the logic of victimisation leads to an even more coercive form of submission.[14] Instead, the victim aims at staging a masochistic over-identification with the disavowed *jouissance* of power, thus bringing the latter into light while simultaneously breaking free from its grip. The scandalous excess of Pasolini's cinema is the excess of the law itself, the absolute transgression that shatters the notion of life as idiotic homeostatic balance. The following passage from Deleuze focuses with unequalled accuracy on the subversive potential of masochism:

> We all know ways of twisting the law by excess of zeal. By scrupulously applying the law we are able to demonstrate its absurdity and provoke the very disorder that it is intended to prevent or to conjure. [...] we then behave as if the supreme sovereignty of the law conferred upon it the enjoyment of all those pleasures that it denies us; hence, by the closest adherence to it, and by zealously embracing it, we may hope to partake of its pleasures. [...] A close examination of masochistic fantasies or rites reveals that while they bring into play the very strictest application of the law, the result in every case is the opposite of what might be expected (thus whipping, far from punishing or preventing an erection, provokes and ensures it). It is a demonstration of the law's absurdity (Deleuze, 1991, p. 88).

We need to add that the absurdity of the law is nothing but the excessive force with which it destabilises the domain of the pleasure principle. Not surprisingly, Pasolini's masochistic strategy became particularly urgent with the advent of consumer society and the concomitant "decline of Oedipus". His masochism increased as he became aware that the rigidity of the old patriarchal order was being superseded by the malleability of the postmodern universe: the more symbolic authority was being fragmented, diluted and neutralised through a multitude of formal practices of liberalisation and democraticisation, whose aim was to de-politicise the social field so as to optimise capitalist profitability, the more Pasolini realised that the only way to antagonise power was by assuming its clandestine surplus enjoyment. If at the start of his cinematic career (*Accattone*, 1961) he had placed all his bets on the sub-proletariat as a sublime and excluded subject, he later concluded that the very notion of excluded class was being rendered ineffective by the co-optative logic of late-capitalism. By the end of his career (*Salò*, 1975), he had completely shifted his focus on the exception *within* power itself, i.e. power's own unacknowledged *jouissance*.

2.4 Drive unbound

2.4.1 Accattone: the excremental remainder

Precisely to identify and debunk the inconsistency of power, in *Salò* Pasolini makes full use of what we might call his ideal thematic couple, drive-*jouissance*. However, this ideal couple is already operative in *Accattone*, Pasolini's first film, although explicitly deployed in defence of the powerless. This brings us straight to the political question of Pasolini's alliance with the excluded subjects of our late-capitalistic universe, which could be summed up by three lines of one of his many poems on the subject: 'There's no lunch or dinner or satisfaction in the world / equal to an endless walk through the streets of the poor, / where you must be wretched and strong, brothers to the dogs' (Pasolini, 1984, p. 213).

Pasolini in Rome's borgate

Anyone even slightly acquainted with the work of Pasolini knows that his lifelong attachment to the underprivileged, from the Roman sub-proletariat to the African peasants, has always been the true catalyst for his political concerns. No other Italian (left-wing) intellectual has so obstinately strived to bring to the heart of public awareness the existence of those unacknowledged netherworlds inhabited by the abject subjects of our Western geopolitical universe, whose inconspicuous lives unfold away from our gaze, outside what we commonly know as civilisation. In this sense, it is certainly accurate to hold that Pasolini's critique, especially from the 1960s onwards, bears extraordinary significance in today's global constellation as, despite being conceived during the cold war years, it is essentially founded on a pressing concern with the universalisation of our liberal-democratic and late-capitalistic experience. Pasolini's social outcast, in other words, are today's social outcast. Yet, one thing is to state that Pasolini was "the poet of the poor", quite another to investigate the political dimension of his attachment. If doubting the authenticity of his commitment would be misleading, critics have often cast more than a skeptical glance to the political significance of his passionate attachment.

The key term to emphasise here is exclusion. According to Pasolini, the anti-social condition of non-participation that typified the Roman sub-proletariat of the 1950s and 1960s, was a proper status to be upheld and promoted as it implied a radical opposition to the codified, institutionalised order of the Italian bourgeois society. More to the point, Pasolini's protest was based on his protracted identification with those social groups that had not yet been co-opted into the specific socio-symbolic order defined politically by the liberal-democratic ideology, and economically by capitalism.

In this respect, *Accattone* is a crucial work, in that it offers a particularly powerful representation of the Italian author's long-lasting alliance with the subproletariat as the endangered foreign body situated right at the heart of Italy's late-capitalist modernisation. In accord with its literary predecessors (the novels *Ragazzi di vita* and *Una vita violenta*) the film functions as a clear example of Pasolini's 'imperterrita dichiarazione d'amore' (unflinching declaration of love) for the sub-groups of the Roman slums (*borgate*), which he describes through an emphatic endorsement of their social, linguistic and psychological experience (Pasolini, 1958, p. 210). This act of mimetic identification with the social outcasts, a unique phenomenon in the traditionally elitist scene of Italian culture, epitomises well what Žižek has identified as the leftist political gesture *par excellence*:

> The leftist political gesture *par excellence* (in contrast to the rightist slogan 'to each his or her own place') is thus to question the concrete existing universal order on behalf of its symptom, of the part which, although inherent to the existing universal order, has no "proper place" within it (say, illegal immigrants or the homeless in our societies). This procedure of identifying with the symptom is the exact and necessary obverse of the standard critico-ideological move of recognizing a particular content behind some abstract universal notion, that is, of denouncing neutral universalities as false ('the "man" of human rights is actually the white male property-owner…'): one pathetically asserts (and identifies with) *the point of inherent exception/exclusion, the 'abject', of the concrete positive order, as the only point of true universality* (Žižek, 2000a, p. 224).

This definition of 'true universality' has been defended by Žižek against fellow political theorist Judith Butler in the volume *Contingency, Hegemony and Universality*:

> I perceive the shadowy existence of those who are condemned to lead a spectral life outside the domain of the global order, blurred in the background, unmentionable, submerged in the formless mass of "population", without even a proper particular place of their own, in a slightly different way from Butler. I am tempted to claim that this shadowy existence is *the very site of political universality*: in politics, universality is asserted when such an agent with no proper place, "out of joint", posits itself as the direct embodiment of universality against all those who do have a place within the global order (in Butler, Laclau and Žižek, 2000: p. 313).[15]

With regards to the precise socio-political location of universality, the most palpable evidence of Pasolini's leftist stance, at the time of his cinema debut, is to be found in his scandalous (one would be tempted to say *fundamentalist*) identification with the constitutional other of the hegemonic bourgeois order. Rather than just fighting for the socio-economic and cultural improvement of unprivileged social subjects (the sub-proletariat) and neglected social space (the Roman slums), Pasolini took a much more radical step by way of, in Žižek's words, '*identifying universality with the point of exclusion*'. The political force of this identification lies in the uncompromising challenge it poses to the liberal-democratic hegemony: it does not say to the sub-proletariat 'I will fight for your rights to be recognised by the existing hierarchy' (liberal leftist); rather it says 'you, the displaced and exploited, are the universal measure of progress insofar as you are excluded'. More precisely, what is universally valid for Pasolini is the concrete existence of the excremental/particular subject, the subject representing the exception, without a place within the socio-symbolic order. This conflation of the Universal and the Particular demarcates, according to Žižek, the domain of politics proper, in as much as the paradox of a particular content incarnating universality inevitably undermines the normal functioning of the social body. What the Italian ruling class perceived as a danger to be removed was precisely Pasolini's "fanatic" over-identification with this shameful remainder of the country's late-capitalist modernisation. As is widely acknowledged, Pasolini's persistence in his limit-position turned him, especially from the 1960s, into the target of a strategy of permanent persecution (see Betti, 1978).[16]

Pasolini's defence of the excluded/excremental part of the social whole (the utopian space of the Roman borgate) finds resonance in Žižek's recent book on Iraq, where he launches into a vindication of the Canudos, a late 19th century 'outlaw community deep in the Brazilian heartland which was home to prostitutes, freaks, beggars, bandits and the most wretched of the poor':

> The echoes of Canudos are clearly discernible in today's favelas in Latin American megalopolises: are they not, in some sense, the first "liberated territories", the cells of future self-organized societies? [...] The liberated territory of Canudos in Bahia will remain for ever the model of a space of emancipation, of an alternative community which completely negates the space of the state. Everything is to be endorsed here, up to and including religious "fanaticism". It is as if, in these communities, *the Benjaminian other side of historical Progress, that of the vanquished, acquires a space of its own* (Žižek, 2004b, p. 82).

As Žižek reminds us time and time again, Lacanian psychoanalysis theorises how the constitution of a given socio-symbolic field is decided by way of a primordial exclusion, whereby the existence of a pathological antagonising excess is fundamentally foreclosed. Only through the repression of this fundamental antagonism does social reality emerge as the battlefield for hegemonic struggle (see Žižek in Butler, Laclau and Žižek, 2000, pp. 110–11). In order to challenge a given socio-symbolic network, it is therefore necessary to fully assume its repressed point of exclusion.

As we have evinced from Pasolini's theorisation of editing, this concept of identifying universality with the symptom is immensely fruitful if we are to grasp the emancipatory character and ideological scope of cinema. In Pasolini's case, what critics have often refused as his deep-seated irrationality,[17] his purely pathological inclinations towards the poor, acquires a totally different meaning if only we filter it through the theories on symbolisation developed by Lacan in the second phase of his career (starting from the late 1950s). Essentially, we are engaging once again with the Real as the impossible limit of the process of symbolisation, the limit which, in Žižek words, '*reveals the ultimate contingency, fragility (and thus changeability) of every symbolic constellation that pretends to serve as the a priori horizon of the process of symbolization*' (in Butler, Laclau and Žižek, 2000, p. 221).[18]

Paradoxically, then, those who lamented the scandalous character of Pasolini's intellectual propositions where absolutely right: he was scandalous, provided we understand his "will to scandalise"[19] as tantamount to the Lacanian act, consisting in the subject's assumption of the unworkable limit of the socio-symbolic field. The scandal originates precisely in Pasolini's universalisation of the sub-proletariat, in view of his conviction that 'the elements at play in the psychology of the abject, the poor, the sub-proletarian, are always in a certain way pure and essential,' in that 'they exist outside the historical conscience, and, more specifically, the bourgeois conscience' (Pasolini, 2001, p. 2846). What bothered most of his contemporaries (including many fellow leftists) was less his defence of the excluded as underprivileged than his determination to equate the excluded with the universal subject. However, far from following the proverbial Romantic who simply cherishes the wholeness of primitive cultures, or the postmodernist who speaks up for the pluralisation of narratives and discourses of otherness, Pasolini's solidarity with the underprivileged was meant to be truly shocking.

To understand the full political implications of Pasolini's solidarity with the poor, we must remember that, in Lacan, the point of exclusion of any symbolic field coincides with universality *only insofar as universality is perceived as an abyssal void*, as the impenetrable kernel of the Real of *jouissance*. The survival or collapse of a given symbolic configuration is decided precisely in the Real of *jouissance*, as it is either the repression or the assertion of its traumatic content that determines or undermines its viability. Now, the radicality of Pasolini's operation lies in *making thematic*, that is, in filling with anthropological or anthropomorphic substance, Lacan's notion of the Real of *jouissance*: in identifying the Roman sub-proletariat first, and later the modern, trans-national *lumpenproletariat*, with universality as the excremental remainder of the hegemonic order. This is why Pasolini's sub-proletariat is not only excluded, but also released from working-class consciousness, which he sees as inevitably overdetermined by the liberal-democratic discourse. Rather than playing the game of the endless contingent re-signification of the liberal-democratic context, by then pervasively controlled by late-capitalist ideology, Pasolini assumed the impossible and yet properly political task of forcing a radical break with that context.

At one point in *Uccellacci e uccellini* (Hawks and Sparrows, 1966) we are offered a concise, understated, and yet somewhat literal definition of the author's strategy, when we realise that the streets walked by the two sub-proletarian protagonists (Totò and Ninetto Davoli) are named after unknown people with revealing epigraphies such as "unemployed", or "run away from home at 12 years of age". These bizarre pointers suggest that the sub-proletariat becomes a true political agent the moment its presence at the heart of the symbolic network (street names) is emptied of all pathological content and frozen into pure nominalism. The term sub-proletariat comes to coincide with a linguistic referent which *speaks nothing but its own void* – its own absence, the impossible limit of signification. Pasolini's sub-proletariat, functioning as the dislodged structuring principle of the liberal-democratic network, is precisely the name for this paradoxical condition.

This brings us to what is perhaps the most palpable Pasolinian contradiction, the conflation of the themes of wretchedness and sacredness, which runs through his entire *oeuvre*. The dynamic aspect of this oxymoron can be discerned by considering Agamben's notion of *homo sacer*. As Agamben (2000, p. 3) reminds us, the ancient Greeks used to oppose *zoē*, the biological fact of life common to all living creatures (naked life), to *bios*, which instead indicates 'the form or manner of living peculiar to a single individual or group'. Agamben observes that the problem with the concept of human being promoted by the 1789 Declaration of Human Rights is that it does not leave any autonomous space for the notion of *zoē*, by way of dissolving it completely into the juridical and political order. As soon as a human being is born, naked life vanishes into the notion of *bios* as the condition of belonging to a given national identity: 'Rights, in other words, are attributed to the human being only to the degree to which he or she is the immediately vanishing presupposition (and, in fact, the presupposition that must never come to light as such) of the citizen' (Agamben, 2000, p. 21). The obvious upshot of this repression of the pure human is that modernity, at least since 1789, has consistently identified the status of man stripped of citizenship with the notion of *homo sacer*, 'in the sense that this term used to have in the Roman law of the archaic period: doomed to death' (2000, p. 22). It is from this vital definition of *homo sacer* as today's disfigured version of the pure human that Agamben develops his critique of late-capitalism – which in turn enables us to articulate our analysis of *Accattone*.

The closest Pasolinian version of *homo sacer* as 'the pure human' who is 'doomed to death' for the simple reason of not belonging to the civilised congregation is Accattone, the quintessential beggar (*accattone* means beggar) of his eponymous film.[20] On first impression, the film does not seem directly political. Vittorio Cataldi nicknamed Accattone (Franco Citti) is a pimp of the Roman outskirts who desperately struggles for survival after his woman, the prostitute Maddalena (Silvana Corsini), is thrown in jail. Initially, he turns to his ex-wife Ascenza (Paola Guidi) for support; after she has rejected him, he falls into despair until he accidentally meets Stella (Franca Pasut), a young girl who instantly wins him over with her naivety and candour. Thought attracted to her, Accattone plans to turn Stella into a prostitute, a replacement for Maddalena. However, he is eventually overwhelmed by a mixture of love and remorse, and resolves to take her off the streets. To provide for Stella, Accattone, for the first time in his life, decides to find employment. Yet, his first day's experience as a *manovale* (labourer) is enough to make him change his mind and quit his job. In the meantime Maddalena, still in jail, is informed about Accattone's new girl, and reports him to the police in revenge for his betrayal. Finally, out of work and with Stella to support, Accattone decides to turn to thieving, like many of his friends from the slums. On his first mission with two friends (nicknamed Balilla and Cartagine) he tries to steal a load of meat from an unguarded truck. The police, however, who had been keeping and eye on his moves, are quick to intervene on the scene of the theft. As he is being arrested, Accattone tries to escape on a random motorcycle, but he is crushed in an accident and dies.

The most obvious reading of the film reflects quite literally the previously illustrated politicisation of the sub-proletariat: Accattone is the miserable leftover of the booming Italian society of the 1960s whom Pasolini transposes into a sacred dimension. Yet, we only need to take a closer look at the cinematic rendering of this scandalous association of the sacred and the profane to realise that, far from constituting a self-evident political position, it involves a specific, if unconscious, theoretical apprehension of subjectivity. My contention is that Pasolini's treatment of Accattone compels the viewer to focus on the character's specific psychological experience, to the extent that it is only by observing the development of Accattone's self that we are given an insight into the authentic meaning of Pasolini's identification with the sub-proletariat. This perspective implies a surprising reversal of the standard materialistic reading of the film: Accattone is not only mediated by the socio-political field, but he also mediates reality *tout court*, since he functions as a sort of Hegelian self-consciousness whose movement discloses for us the meaning of external events. On the one hand, we could say that Accattone's subjectivity is determined precisely by the social circumstances that cause his segregation: he is an outcast, a pimp, a thief and eventually dies because the Italian society ostracises him, denying him a viable alternative.[21] However, such interpretation is compromised by the formal configuration taken by the narrative, more specifically by the predominance of the lyrical-introspective register over the sociological one. It is enough to observe the widely acknowledged mimetic pathos that qualifies Pasolini's focused study of his leading character, reinforced by the sacred musical comment accompanying his *via crucis*, to realise that more than just the Lukacsian characterisation of the "typical" Accattone is seen *sub specie aeternitatis*: a universal, Christ-like subject representative of humanity as a whole.

To clarify this fundamental aspect of the film, it is worth noting that Accattone is estranged even amongst his fellow sub-proletarians, as his gnawing anxiety is unmistakably at odds with the atavistic indifference that presides over the self-enclosed universe of the Roman slums. More precisely, his uniqueness lies in a sort of masochistic attitude, or more precisely on his determination to face what Bataille (1988, pp. 6–9) calls the impossibility/insufficiency at the heart of inner experience. Žižek's theorisation of subjectivity is in this sense very close to Bataille's, in that it postulates, via Lacan, the presence of an impenetrable hard kernel: 'The leftover which resists "subjectivation" embodies the impossibility which "is" the subject: in other words, the subject is strictly correlative to its own impossibility; its limit is its positive condition' (Žižek, 1992, p. 209). Pasolini's deep-seated political claim rests on his shifting of the notion of 'leftover', analogous to that of symptom, from the sub-proletariat as a social body, to Accattone as a subject/body of the sub-proletariat. According to Žižek, it is only through this shift that an accomplished account of materialism can emerge:

> True *materialism* does not consist in the simple operation of reducing inner psychic experience to an effect of the process taking place in "external reality" – what one should do, in addition, is to isolate a "material" traumatic kernel/remainder at the very heart of "psychic life" itself (in Butler, Laclau and Žižek, 2000, p. 118).

The opening scene of the film immediately focuses on this material kernel at the heart of psychic life. After a sarcastic reference to the Metro Goldwin Mayer (a *borgataro*, imitating the MGM lion, yawns epically and then staring into the camera exclaims: 'What are you waiting for, join the Metro Goldwin Mayer!'), we are immediately thrown into a seemingly facetious

Accattone

conversation between Accattone and his unoccupied friends from the *borgate*. Despite the typically light and mordant exchange of remarks in Roman jargon, the central issue is a serious one: death. Fulvio has just returned from his new job and Alfredino, leisurely sat at a bar table, sarcastically addresses him thus: 'Aren't you dead yet? Strange, they told me that work kills people!' Fulvio, out of frame, replies: 'At least it's an honest death', and immediately adds: 'You all look as if you've just come out of the morgue!' At this stage Accattone cuts in to make his own point, claiming that their friend Barberone's drowning in the river was caused by exhaustion and not indigestion. Giorgio, however, relying on medical erudition, calmly explains that swimming with a full stomach causes a failure in the digestive system, which eventually leads to drowning. It is at this point that Accattone makes the decisive wager: if they buy him a meal, he will eat it and then dive into the river to prove them wrong – which is exactly what happens in the next scene.

What is significant in this *incipit*, culminating with the prodigious dive from atop the tall bridge, is the intrinsic nature of Accattone's challenge. While Fulvio redeems death through work (he is an honest flower vendor), and Giorgio neutralises it through scientific knowledge, Accattone is the only one who dares to take on the titanic challenge that death poses to self-preservation.[22] In other words, we are immediately faced by what Alberto Moravia (1961) aptly called 'Accattone's unconscious death-drive', in my opinion the film's central theme. As the narrative progresses, the incidence of Accattone's death-drive becomes increasingly pervasive. Not only is he constantly tempted by suicide (in the police headquarters, he tries to jump off the window; later, drunk, he threatens to throw himself off a bridge; he repeatedly calls on death as the only solution to his suffering), but he also cannot help fantasising about it: first, when spellbound he witnesses the procession of a mysterious funeral in a deserted *borgata*; and later when, after his first day of work, he dreams of attending his own funeral.

Given its permeating presence in the narrative, Pasolini's recourse to the death-drive can be interpreted according to the previously identified materialistic-idealistic double measure: both as a denunciation of social oppression (it is the bourgeois society that causes the death of the sub-proletariat and the disappearance of the *borgate*, see Pasolini, 1998, p. 1460) and, at a deeper level, in correlation with the constitutional lack that defines the subject. This second reading, I would argue, is by far the more productive, and indeed complements the first one. Pasolini seems to suggest that the process of subjectivation can be properly accomplished only if the subject comes to terms with its own kernel of constitutive negativity. Abolishing from subjectivity the fundamental antagonism posited by drive is, in Žižek's words, 'precisely the source of totalitarian temptation: the greatest mass murders and holocausts have always been perpetrated in the name of man as a harmonious being, of a New Man without antagonistic tension' (Žižek, 1992, p. 5). Accattone's intimate refusal of subjective stability is therefore a key narrative factor, which we could also explain through Žižek's critique of Althusser's notion of "subjective interpellation":

[…] far from emerging as the outcome of interpellation, the subject emerges only when and in so far as interpellation liminally *fails*. Not only does the subject never fully recognize itself in the interpellative call: its resistance to interpellation (to the symbolic identity provided by interpellation) *is* the subject (in Butler, Laclau and Žižek, 2000, p. 115).

Accattone embodies this 'resistance to interpellation' both as a member of the sub-proletariat, and as a prospective member of the working class. The significance of Pasolini's position with regard to the sub-proletariat, and also to political participation as such, is decided by the step his character takes in trying to resolve the tension between these two (negative) poles. Rather than postulate the humanistic notion of self-appropriation through social identification, thus possibly affirming a (sub-)proletarian positivity *vis-à-vis* bourgeois order, Pasolini concludes that negativity (lack) is the constitutive element of free subjectivity: Accattone chooses freedom as "freedom to choose death", as is confirmed first by Accattone's dream, and eventually by his real death.

Accattone's dream is undoubtedly the most revealing moment of the film, for it enables us to grasp the relationship between drive and the Real of *jouissance*. After his first day of work he dreams about attending his own funeral. First, however, he witnesses the death of the Neapolitan pimps, which we can read as the collapse of his previous identity (this becomes clear when his friends give him the news of his death calling him by his real name, Vittorio, as if a new individual was born from the ashes of Accattone the pimp). We then see him following a hearse to the gates of the cemetery. Whilst everybody proceeds inside, the guardian orders him to remain outside. Alone, bewildered, he looks around and then resolves to climb over the cemetery wall. Once inside, he sees an old man intent on digging a grave in the shadow. Realising that it is his own grave, Accattone asks the old man, deferentially, whether he could move it a few yards down, into the sunny part of the cemetery. As the old man agrees to restart his work, the camera pans out on the hilly countryside basked in sunshine, and the dream vanishes.

According to Lacan, the subject regulates its relationship with the non-discursive kernel of the Real through fantasy, an imaginary construction that allows the subject to avoid the lethal encounter with *jouissance*. So what is Accattone's dream if not an explicit representation of the Lacanian "going through the fantasy" aimed at disclosing the void around which the process of subjectivation is structured? The very narrative position occupied by the dream (after Accattone's first day of work) seems to confirm this interpretation, as it effectively effaces the symbolic networks that the subject is striving to activate: it not only explodes Accattone's old identity (pimp), but also annihilates his attempt to stabilise his new identity as a labourer, and consequently his position in society. Not surprisingly, Accattone immediately quits his job to fall back on thieving.

The traumatic content of the dream-work can be isolated in what is, symbolically, the most crucial part of this "narrative within the narrative": the moment Accattone, disobeying the guardian's injunction, climbs over the cemetery wall. A fairly straightforward Freudian reading tells us that the guardian is correlative to Accattone's ego, whose injunction is clearly self-protective, a warning against the dangers of facing the unconscious object of the drive. We need Lacan, however, to explain Accattone's transgression. His decision to overcome the wall that separates the ego from the id (or, in Lacanian terms, the Symbolic from the Real), could be legitimately equated to the Lacanian act proper: the act which brings the subject to over-identify with what is "in him more than himself" (see Lacan, 1998a, pp. 263–76), the hard kernel of subjectivity. Confronting his own death, Accattone effectively experiences the impossible object of drive as something that is both utterly external and absolutely intimate, and the whole film is essentially a meditation on this idea of becoming intimate with the Real of *jouissance*. When Pasolini says that death is the subversive notion *par excellence*, and at the same time 'the only thing that confers true dignity on a human being' (in Magrelli, 1977, p. 59), he is simply reiterating *Accattone*'s main claim: that freedom can only be conceived of as the endorsement of the self-relating negativity constitutive of the subject.

Predictably, therefore, after his dream Accattone grows increasingly disaffected with his previous attempt to find a place in society through work. Instead, he chooses thieving, and with a couple of layabouts like him he organises an expedition into Rome's city-centre. Here the spatial dimension becomes significant, as the movement from periphery to centre implies the contamination of the bourgeois universe (also emphasised by the three character's dialogue about Cartagine's smelly feet). Yet, even more significant is the fact that this contamination is constantly monitored, and eventually neutralised, by the "panoptical" gaze of the police (after Maddalena's denunciation, the narrative is regularly punctuated by extreme close-ups of a policeman's eyes). The swift intervention of the police as soon as the trio manage to carry out their first theft is tantamount to a textbook illustration of the Foucauldian notion of the articulation of power through 'permanent visibility' (Foucault, 1977, p. 201). However, Accattone's reaction to the arrest is truly symptomatic. While his friends do not oppose any resistance, since after all it is a common event in their lives, Accattone jumps on a random motorbike and attempts an impossible escape, disappearing out of field. We then hear the noise of an accident, screams and on the background the leitmotif from Bach's *St Matthew's Passion*. Everyone runs to the scene of the accident only to hear Accattone's last words: 'Ahh, now I'm fine…'. In a nutshell, Accattone's self refuses to be defined by the hegemonic Gaze.[23] By choosing death he fully assumes the destructive power of *jouissance*, an act that, however tragic, manages to disturb the socio-symbolic totality. The political significance of this death, the ultimate accomplishment of the character's suicidal tendency, is all in the paradoxical positivity of Accattone's last words. These words not only allude to Accattone's release from a life of utter misery, but tapping into a deeper subjective level they sanction the foundational role of negativity for self-consciousness. Ultimately, Accattone's death retains a positive value because it signals that the struggle for emancipation must pass through the radical displacing of subjectivity.

Despite the initial Dantean allusion to his ascendance into heaven,[24] Accattone dies like Hegel's Christ: behind his death there is no suprasensible bliss, no transcendental salvation, but rather the universalisation of humanity through the sublation of negativity (see Hegel, 1977, pp. 779–85). As Žižek (1993, p. 50) notes, the death of Christ reverses the logic at work in the Kantian Sublime, as what we get is divine essence shining through a 'wretched "little piece of real"', the 'counterpart […] of pure spirituality'. In Hegel the death of Christ effectively designates the death of God as an abstract essence, pure externality. Accattone's "Christ-like" sacrifice is significant precisely because it fully endorses negativity as immanent substance, quite differently from the Christian dogma of transcendence and sublimation (see Pasolini, 1995, p. 252). The very last shot is, in this respect, emblematic: Balilla's awkward failure to reproduce the sign of the cross should be read as a displaced Catholic cipher, indicating that the sacredness of the sub-proletariat must be located in immanence, not in an idealised transcendental domain. Once again we ought to stress the political implications of 'such a reading'. Accattone, a sub-proletarian, is the universal historical subject because he embodies antagonism in the form of the constitutive split that cuts across subjectivity. Only in this sense can Pasolini see him as the saviour: his mere presence as universal antagonistic substance restores true dialectics against the positivity of the hegemonic order.

In conclusion, *Accattone* works as a demonstration that identifying universality with the point of exclusion implies assuming the repressed kernel around which the socio-symbolic space is structured. It is this shocking encounter with the repressed other of a given symbolic universe that, in Žižek's words, exposes the ultimate failure of 'the ideological function of providing a neutral, all-encompassing space in which social antagonism is obliterated' (in Butler, Laclau and Žižek, 2000, p. 113). In the context of 1960s Italy, Pasolini "bets" on the sub-proletariat as he believes that this social group can act as the anthropological breaking point (the symptom) of capitalist ideology. However, this is not Pasolini's conclusive stance. With *Accattone* he adds a fundamental turn to his main argument by shifting its focus from external reality to the question of subjectivity, the sphere of psychic life itself. Against "vulgar" materialism, and against historical relativism, his film shows that the subject is not entirely determined by the objective, external circumstances of his existence. Quite on the contrary, *Accattone* tells us that *the subject is already its own externality*, as the (im)possibility of identity is decided by the encounter with the Real, the activation or repression of the hard nub of impenetrable matter situated at the core of any subjective configuration. Thus, Accattone's "sacredness" does not designate a condition of positive fullness outside the social contract, the idealised status of a modern-day *bon sauvage*; instead, it circumscribes the non-symbolisable fracture where "the barred subject meets the big Other".

2.4.2 *Salò: the executioner's whip*
During World War II, four representatives of power (the Duke, the President, the Monsignor, and the Magistrate) conceive an intricate plan to kidnap eighteen teenagers and abscond with them to a beautiful Renaissance villa in an isolated retreat, taking along their own daughters (whom they swap and take as wives), an entourage of guards, and four mature prostitutes. Once in the villa, they meet regularly to listen to stories from the prostitutes. Each prostitute has a different specialty, from fairly ordinary sexual passions to coprophilia and sadistic torture. Each libertine has a small number of adolescents at his disposal, whom he can use as he pleases while the stories fan the flames of his desires. What follows is a nightmarish vision of subjugation, degradation, and destruction of the human spirit as the four libertines continually assault their prisoners to satisfy their desires.

The first question we are bound to ask ourselves when watching this film is: what about its metaphorical significance? A degree of symbolisation is what we desperately strive for in order to avoid its gnawing nihilism. However, the somewhat comforting reference to Fascism provided by the title does not really pull it off for us, and perhaps it should be regarded as the weakest point of an otherwise extremely lucid dissection of power. Despite the setting, it is not the Nazi-Fascist "Republic of Salò" that the director is really targeting, but rather *our* contemporary universe of late-capitalism and consumer society. *Salò*'s bleak prophetic pledge is that nothing can stand in the way of capital anymore, and that, to put it bluntly, the new generations of Italians are reduced to mere mass material for the ruthless capitalistic machine. Pasolini connotes our late capitalistic constellation as a form of barbarism, to the extent that *Salò*'s negative theodicy can be said to have its condensed equivalent in Adorno's famous statement about Auschwitz: 'Genocide is absolute integration' (Adorno, 2000, p. 362). Precisely in this sense the horrors that take place inside the beautiful Renaissance villa are meant to expose the dark truth about the universalisation of capitalism's inner dynamics.

Substantiating this reading from a psychoanalytic angle, one would take as a focal point the signing of the contract performed by the four libertines at the start of the film. As argued in the previous section of this book, the juxtaposition of the law and sadomasochistic practices highlights the dominant role played by the superego, the "obscene underbelly" that supplements the public law as its nightly shadow. The reason why Pasolini takes Sade as its primary narrative source is that the latter allows him to focus on this normally disavowed excess, showing us how the field of the law is effectively split into its pacifying symbolic function and its sinister superegoic double. The properly psychoanalytic point is that what is potentially a hindrance to the working of the law becomes its most powerful weapon: as was already shown by Mikhail Bakhtin, periodic transgressions of the law are inherent to its proper functioning (see Bakhtin, 1968); or, in Žižek's terms, it is not so much the identification with the public law that holds together a given community, but rather the community's secret reliance on specific forms of transgression, i.e. on certain ritualistic modes of enjoyment outside the law.[25] Both Lacan's 1962 essay 'Kant avec Sade'[26] and, before that, Adorno's attacks on Kant's doctrine of freedom,[27] constitute valuable material for the evaluation of the repressive character of the superego. However, in line with what I have argued in the section on masochism, my claim is that *Salò* goes beyond the denunciation of the complicity between the law and its transgressive superego injunction to enjoy.

Let us acknowledge, first, that some narrative elements in *Salò* actually suggest the possibility of a break in the vicious circle of the symbolic law and its clandestine supplement. Two characters in particular, Ezio and the pianist, incarnate an instance of (tragic) withdrawal from the normative double bind of the law. Having been caught breaking the rules (i.e. having heterosexual sex) Ezio meets his death with the clenched fist of the Communist salute. One cannot fail to recognise here the same kind of heroic passionate attachment displayed by Giorgio Manfredi (Marcello Pagliero), the communist leader of the resistance in Rossellini's *Roma, città aperta* (1945). We realise that Pasolini is explicitly quoting from Rossellini's masterpiece when the libertines, stunned by Ezio's act of defiance, freeze and step back like their Nazi counterparts in *Roma, città aperta* after Manfredi's death – an image that inscribes a moment of vacillation in their otherwise mechanical persistence in evil. The second act of defiance occurs with the pianist's apparently unmotivated suicide. Having so far accompanied the horror-tales on the piano, she suddenly leaves her instrument, walks to a window, looks out, sits on the window sill and suddenly puts a hand to her mouth, as if struck by a disturbing sight; she then recaptures her cool expression and throws herself out of the window. However shocking and capable of conveying the paradoxical Lacanian convergence of ethics and psychosis, these two episodes are too isolated to sustain an alternative reading of the film.[28]

My contention is that to grasp the paradoxical significance of ethics in *Salò* it is necessary to turn to the specific treatment reserved to the film's most outrageous theme, that of raw sexual perversion. What needs to be taken into account is the crucial question of the relation between power and the perverted mode of enjoyment of the libertines, who abuse the beautiful young bodies at their disposal to satisfy their perverted libidinal tendencies. The film does not limit itself to the denouement of the deleterious consequences implicit in the absolutisation of abstract reason over the sensuous dimension of the object, which turns the latter into a commodity, or a fetish. More insightfully, it characterises the libertines' perverted desire to enjoy the other as *jouissance*, that is, as *a form of pleasure beyond the pleasure principle*, a pleasure that cannot satisfy itself as it finds its limit in the empty object of desire. As Lacan put it succinctly apropos of the difference between pleasure and *jouissance*, the latter 'implies precisely the acceptance of death' (Lacan, 1999, p. 189).

It is true that Pasolini's universal libertine society de-individualises and fetishises the body as an instrument for the generation of pleasure. In his interpretation of Sade, Pasolini stages the complicity between modern ratio and perversion denounced by Adorno and Horkheimer: the more civilisation enforces its mastery over nature, the more it administers pleasure as regimented enjoyment; in its rationalised and ritualistic modes of distribution, the truly mythical and alienating quality of pleasure is thoroughly extinguished, together with its profoundly antagonistic core. The nature of sadism, in *Salò*, is unveiled with particular stringency in the recurrent theme of violence against women: the four "civilised" men's co-ordinated effort to separate mind and body, reason and feeling, results in the explosion of the latent patriarchal hatred for women, who are sadistically despised and abused precisely as reminders of the threat posed by nature. As Adorno points out in a passage about Sadean misogyny, 'what lies below draws the attack upon itself: it is most pleasurable to inflict humiliation where misfortune has already hit hard. The less danger there is for those above, the more refined the pleasure they will derive from the anguish they are about to inflict. Domination comes really into its own principle of discipline when the quarry is cornered and desperate' (Adorno, 1997, p. 112).

That said, we need to bear in mind that what is most important in *Salò* is not pleasure in itself, but rather its endless pursuit. It is not surprising that despite their vaunted expertise in any field of sexuality, these libertines practically dismiss their own orgasm (and the homeostatic comfort that derives from it). The truth about their perversion is to be found in the limitless repetition of the act they constantly try to stage, which is based on the rejection of pleasure in favour of *jouissance*. For them, only the endless suspension and delay of pleasure provides the illusion of an absolute control over the object. This also allows us to account for their ban on heterosexuality. The universalisation of the homosexual act in the film is to be approached through what Deleuze (1991, p. 120) calls 'the coldness of desexualization', the fact that homosexuality lends itself to be conceived as disengaged from the utilitarian logic of immediate satisfaction, a concept punctually underlined by the Duke (Paolo Bonacelli): 'The sodomitic act has the advantage of endless repetition'. However, Pasolini eventually departs from Deleuze, holding on instead to the Freudian domain "beyond the pleasure principle": it is not that the repetition of the sadomasochistic act simply reasserts the modicum of balance implied in the pleasure principle from the opposite end; rather, repetition in *Salò* brings about the divisive force of *jouissance*. How? Precisely by accomplishing the passage from desire to drive: from the awareness that the encounter with the object of desire can only be given 'in the intractable Real of *jouissance*', to the awareness that the Real of *jouissance* will stick to us whatever we do, like a curse (drive)! While in the logic of desire *jouissance* defines the impossibility of the Thing that we crave, in the logic of drive it becomes the stain of surplus-enjoyment attached to our every act. *Salò* makes visible that when the wall of prohibition sustaining the economy of desire falls, we enter the shadowy domain of drive, whose circulation implies the nightmare of an endless encounter with *jouissance*, 'since jouissance is, at its most elementary, "pleasure in pain", that is, a perverted pleasure provided by the very painful experience of repeatedly missing one's goal' (Žižek, 2000a, p. 297).

And then? Let us return to the previous question. Does Pasolini suggest, in a Deleuzian way, that the self-enclosed flow of *jouissance* recreates the conditions for the activation of the pleasure principle? Are his libertines satisfied with being caught in the loop of drive, with the fact that their only chance of reaching satisfaction passes through the infinite repetition of the failed encounter with the impossible Thing? Quite on the contrary, *Salò* suggests that drive does not send us back to the gratifying balance of the pleasure principle, but instead it presents us with an exorbitant bill, that is, a traumatic awareness that the impossible Thing sustaining desire is now recast as the very core of the subject caught in the loop of drive. What the libertines discover at the end of their journey into the dark realm of drive is that the Thing *qua* "surplus of sense" that they cannot shake off *is what they are*, the empty hub of their being. The external and ever-elusive Thing comes to coincide with "our Thing", the most intimate place inside us, the object that is "in us more than ourselves". Such a realisation cannot but have a devastating effect on the subject: as the final part of the film suggests, it implies the sudden collapse of the subject's psychic balance.

Salò

An interesting point to note is that throughout the film Pasolini endeavours to align the spectator's point of view with that of his four debauched dignitaries, thus suggesting, or inviting, a certain alliance in evil. Let us take one of the most impressive sequences, the one in which the Monsignor (Giorgio Cataldi) tortures his young victims in the courtyard. Significantly, we see him through the binoculars of the Duke, who is comfortably seated inside the villa, masturbating a boy. Imitating Rossellini's crafty manipulation of the spectator's point of view in *Roma, città aperta*'s famous torture sequence, Pasolini puts us in a voyeuristic position, forcing our visual perspective to overlap with that of the libertines. By looking through the binoculars we not only realise that we are looking voyeuristically, but also that the encounter with the object of our visual desire (the gaze) coincides with its loss: we see partial scenes of torture, something remains excluded, we are forced to resort to our imagination; in short, the object of our voyeurism is enmeshed in the uncanny domain of the Real of drive. Naomi Green has underlined precisely the derealising effect created in this and the following passages:

> One after another, each libertine stands by a window and uses binoculars – which become a stand-in for the camera – to view the scenes of carnage that are taking place below in an inner courtyard. The binoculars are reversed so that each shot witnessed is, quite literally, distanced, but also framed and miniaturized like the iris shots of early films. Reinforcing this visual echo of early cinema, the sequence is silent except for light piano music in the room: the sight (but not the sound) of the victims' cries and screams hightens both the vividness and unreality that characterises not only *Salò* but, also, the very institution of cinema (Greene, 1994, p. 240).

We can add that such a juxtaposition of points of view causes a further complication, for the scopic drive that we are progressively caught into, and which culminates precisely in the "binoculars sequences", eventually calls *us* into question, telling us that the object we strive to see is inside us, in the form of the unbearable inconsistency of our desire. Just as the libertines sense that they are the very missing object responsible for the circulation of drive, so are we, the spectators, forced into the disturbing purview that our scopic drive threatens to explode our subjective balance.

Apart from the partially glimpsed scenes of torture, the truly troubling things we see through the binoculars are the images of the delirious Monsignor as he cracks his whip in the courtyard, screaming furious words that we cannot hear since they are covered by a sombrely sacred musical comment. These images provide clear evidence that the Sadean executioner is left with nothing but a purposeless rage, which of course betrays the groundlessness of his desire. More precisely, the terrifyingly frustrated facial expression of the Monsignor suggests that torture has turned into a strange kind of self-torture, for the more he inflicts pain to his victims, the more he effectively "becomes" the very Thing (the whip) that secretly feeds his perversion.[29] The epilogue in fact indicates that the libertines have endorsed transgression to the extent of reaching *jouissance*, and consequently subjective destitution, the loss of the self. One of the "binocular shots" frames three of the four libertines engaging in an inane and utterly psychotic dance amongst their dead victims. The point is that only then, after this psychotic passage through self-instrumentalisation, we are allowed a glimpse of hope, as eventually the camera cuts to two innocent young soldiers dancing to a foxtrot melody (the last sequence of the film). We go from a mad dance that ratifies subjective annihilation to an innocent image of dance symbolic of rebirth – a gentle image confirmed by the name of one of the soldiers' girlfriend, Margherita, the Italian for "daisy".

But let us return to the parallel between Pasolini's libertines and Sade's executioner. In a twist that I believe to be the trademark of Pasolini's socio-political commitment, *Salò* shows how the over-identification with the excess of the law brings about the law's own undoing. This is because it reveals how the the executioner (the external, unacknowledged and yet fundamental support of the law) is the subject of drive, whose ultimate compulsion is not just to repeat endlessly the failed encounter with the impossible Thing, but, in a reflexive turn, to assume the impossible *jouissance* of the Thing as the explosive libidinal core of what he is. The point that Pasolini seems to be making is that the more pervasive the grip of power on individuals becomes, the more the question of *jouissance* will come back to haunt power itself.

This uncovering of the inner inconsistency of power acquires an even more stringent significance if observed from the perspective of Pasolini's notorious anti-capitalistic stance. When resisting or escaping the rule of capital becomes an impossible proposition, he seems to suggest, the most effective attitude lies in assuming capitalism's own explosive imbalance. If *Salò* is, as Pasolini intended it to be, a political act, this is because it accomplishes the full endorsement of the destructive potential of *jouissance* inherent in capital. And precisely because it over-identifies with the obscene superego supplement of power, Pasolini's strategy is at the opposite end of today's predominant postmodern attitude of taking an ironic distance towards anything concerning power and ideology. This strategy is echoed in Pasolini's shocking declaration that, despite the horrors therein portrayed, he enjoyed making *Salò*. When, during the shooting, he was asked why he chose Sade, his reply was: 'Well, I am surely not planning to create an ascetically political, puritanical film. Obviously I am fascinated by these sadistic orgies in themselves too' (in Bachmann, 1975, p. 40). The Italian public and media had been long obsessed with the true nature of Pasolini's desire, more or less secretly toying with the following question: 'what if he really is a (Sadean kind of) pervert?' Again, we should insist that it is precisely the ambiguity of Pasolini's position vis-à-vis the seedy underbelly of power that poses a threat to the ideological machine. Along these lines, *Salò*'s most crucial indictment is perhaps that, far from amounting to a subversive stance, post-ideological cynicism is in fact the highest form of conformism, since a degree of cynical distance is exactly what capitalism requires to function smoothly.

In a nutshell, this is how Pasolini holds on to the antagonistic potential of *jouissance*: not by associating it with an external act of resistance, but by "smuggling" it inside the enemy's camp and identifying with it. To do so, he bestows on Sade's depiction of mechanical evil the kind of tragic self-awareness triggered by the absolutisation of disenchantment. As he himself noted (see Pasolini, 2001, pp. 3019–22), his libertines depart from Sade's insofar as they are intellectually aware individuals capable of introspection, to the extent that their philosophical digressions are nothing short of interpretative accounts of Sade's work enriched by quotations from Klossowski, Barthes and Blanchot (see Pasolini 2001, pp. 3155–59).[30] Their distress generates the awareness that their infinite power is sustained by a fundamental powerlessness. For instance, whilst observing the masturbation of two adolescents, the Duke, quoting Klossowski (see Klossowski, 1995, pp. 27–9), laments that, however unlimited is their power over the two adolescents, they feel powerless when confronted by the inexpressible language of obscene gestures. This also explains why their execution of Franchino (one of the victims) is only feigned. After the shot goes blank, the Monsignor shouts at the terrified boy: 'Imbecile, how could you think that we would kill you? Don't you know that we would like to kill you a thousand times, until the end of eternity, if eternity had an end?' (Pasolini, 2001, p. 2055). This acting out clearly betrays the libertines' failure at neutralising, through ritualistic control, the transcendental, inherently subversive excess of death. Death, like pain and pleasure, cannot be seized, for these terms belong in the domain of *jouissance*. But what counts here is Pasolini's ability to bring to light *the scandal of the law*, the fact that the neutral configuration of the law is moored in the pure, self-destructive desire of its nightly supplement. This is why the director can claim that 'the pages of Sade are extremely revolutionary. I have created this lucid, extraordinary scandal of reason, *a limitless and boundless scandal that I admire*' (in Greene, 1994, p. 208 my emphasis).

The 'scandal of reason', incidentally, was also the subject matter of a film that Pasolini had genuinely appreciated (see Pasolini, 1996, pp. 129–33), and which could certainly be paired with *Salò* in terms of its bleak nihilism (although much more ironic): Marco Ferreri's *La grande bouffe* (Blow-out, 1973). The story of another set of four male characters (a magistrate, a choreographer, a pilot, and a chef) who this time decide to "eat themselves to death", *La grande bouffe* shares with *Salò* precisely the focus on the enigmatic excesses of reason, on its fundamental *cupio dissolvi*. Pasolini commented that the shock-value of Ferreri's film rests on the ontological arbitrariness of the characters' "will to die": not once in the film are we given an insight into the reasons behind these characters' 'obscure fanaticism' (Pasolini, 1996, p. 130). Even more explicitly than in *Salò*, death-drive aims here at the impossible *jouissance* of one's own body, in as much as the four libertine-like protagonists are driven by the immoderate enjoyment of food and sex, as well as of an endless chattering.[31] A metaphor for our consumer-society, Ferreri's film anticipates and perhaps influences *Salò* in exposing the dark side of capitalism's normative regulation of pleasures. The truth about the regulated, imposed-from-above freedom to consume is, as already envisaged by *La ricotta*, a lethal drive to confront the Real of *jouissance*, the encounter with the radically non-utilitarian, pure injunction of the Kantian moral law. The force of films like *La grande bouffe* and *Salò* is that of not shirking from the traumatic-liberating power of this abyssal injunction, which exemplifies the challenge that Lacanian ethics poses to the notion of "service of goods", the utilitarian, market-driven ethics of liberal tolerance. Lacanian ethics are by definition beyond the service of goods, for they are beyond the good *tout court*, that is to say, beyond any purpose that may be articulated in positive terms.

2.5 KAFKAESQUE ENCOUNTERS IN THE LAW

'Whatever impression he may leave on us, he serves the law, and therefore he belongs to the law and eludes human judgement'. We find this quotation from Kafka at the end of one of Elio Petri's most impressive works, *Indagine su un cittadino al di sopra di ogni sospetto* (Investigation of a Citizen Above Suspicion, 1970). Many Italian films, especially those made in the aftermath of 1968, have measured their subversive ambitions against that implacable conundrum represented by the notion of the law as popularised by Kafka. In most of Elio Petri's films, for example, the confrontation with the enigma of the law occupies a privileged position, to such an extent that his best works, from *L'assassino* (The Assassin, 1961) to *I giorni contati* (The Days are Numbered, 1962) to the abovementioned *Indagine*, are articulated around a (partially disavowed) desire to enjoy the scandalous and transgressive *jouissance* of the law. However, if *Salò* fully assumes this *jouissance*, Petri's films tend to maintain a much more uncertain relationship to it, based on an ostensibly contradictory interplay of avowal and disavowal. *Indagine* offers itself as the clearest illustration of Petri's ambiguous attitude towards the law.

This remarkable work tells the story of a nameless police inspector (Gian Maria Volontè) who kills his debauched lover Augusta Terzi (Florinda Bolkan) and then proceeds to leave clues as if purposefully placing himself in the line of investigation. On the same day of the killing, he is promoted from head of the homicide department to head of the political police, where he is admired for his repressive methods. The first part of the film can be viewed as a demonstration of the limitless and utterly discriminatory power of the law, at least in the socio-historical context in which it is represented (post-1968 youth rebellion): the inspector kills Augusta Terzi, it seems, precisely to prove to himself that as an representative of the law he is untouchable. In the second part, however, his theorem on the granitic might of power slowly falls apart, as the very factor that makes power absolute and irresistible is exposed as the cipher of its boundless fragility. The libidinal foundations of the law, in other words, are shown to be the very cause of the law's own undoing. Not unlike Pasolini, Petri exposes the link between criminal authority and the erotic fascination it exerts, suggesting that the "letter of the law" owes its power to an unconscious libidinal investment based simply on its senseless enunciation.[32]

What brings about a change in our perception of the law's representation in *Indagine* is the neurosis that suddenly creeps into the inspector's disciplined *forma mentis*.[33] The person responsible for this neurosis is none other than his deceased lover. Though not explicitly emerging as the key character of the film, Augusta Terzi stands for that vital reference to masochism which forces power to confront its inconsistencies. In this respect, the main weakness of the film may be said to lie in its failure to fully capitalise on its intuition concerning the correlation between masochism and the undoing of the law. The narrative proposes that the progressive erosion of the inspector's certainties is instigated by his repressed jealousy for Augusta, who has sexual relationships with other men, including young anarchist Antonio Paci (Sergio Tramonti). Exploiting the theme of jealousy to unmask the fragility of the authoritarian personality, however, appears as a rather banal solution both in narrative and in psychoanalytic terms. What remains unconvincing is the central dissimulation of the film, whereby the inspector's crime is motivated, first, as a "perverted" plan to prove his untouchable position of law-enforcer, and later as the psychotic culmination of his grotesque jealousy.

Instead, the film's unconscious kernel should be uncovered by pursuing its central symptomal feature, i.e. the "masochistic fervour" of the victim. Formally, this symptom fragments the narrative through a number of flashbacks telling us precisely how much Augusta enjoyed masochistic rituals, with a particular preference for necrophilic fantasies.[34] It is through these flashbacks that the partly disavowed desire of Petri's film emerges, for what really breaks down the subjective defences of the inspector is the fact that *he is unable to forget the enigma of his victim's masochistic enjoyment*. As we have argued apropos of Pasolini, the only thing that proves unbearably frustrating for the sadistic executioner is the possibility that his victim might actually enjoy being punished! This awareness of the other's *jouissance* is what drives the Volontè character insane, thus uncovering the thoroughly specious if not overtly perverted nature of his inflexible practice of the law.[35]

In this respect, the film's final scene shows us the extent to which the institutions are engaged in dissimulating their own transgressive core. In this nightmarish, quintessentially Kafkaesque passage the inspector fantasises about being paternalistically forgiven by higher-level authorities. In his fantasies, the Volontè character penetrates the essence of the law, the fact that it constantly supplements transgression with its dissimulation. On the whole, Petri's film suggests that the law is essentially a formal fact invested by *jouissance*, and not merely a question of content; from this angle, *Indagine* goes well beyond its explicit (conscious) intention, i.e. the denunciation of the repressive, proto-Fascist type of power operative in Italy after 1968. Let us take the delirious speech given by the inspector on his first day of work as head of the political police. As one can gather, the efficacy of the speech is successfully linked to an instance of excessive enjoyment:

> What difference is there between a bank robbery and organised, legalised insubordination? None, for both tend to subvert the status quo. We, on the other hand, are the guardians of the Law, and we want it immutable, engraved in time. The people are immature, the city is ill. Others have the task of educating the people, we must REPRESS! REPRESSION IS OUR VACCINE. REPRESSION AND CIVILISATION!!!.

After the final words are pronounced, the crowd of subordinates erupt in an enthusiastic applause accompanied by shouts of "Bravo, bravo!", which seem to confirm Lacan's insight that '[c]e qui pense, calcule et juge, c'est la jouissance' (Lacan, 2001b, p. 551; that which thinks, calculates and judges is the *jouissance*).

This also accounts for the fact that the equation between "repressive Law" and "Fascism" advocated many post-1968 political films in their anxiety to denounce the corruption of the Italian system, is essentially misplaced. The common mistake of films like *Salò*, *Indagine*, *Il conformista*, as well as Marco Bellocchio's *Sbatti il mostro in prima pagina* (Slap the Monster on Page One, 1972) and Francesco Rosi's *Cadaveri eccellenti* (Illustrious Corpses, 1976) – to mention but a few – is that they tend to disregard the fundamental fact that *law is law* regardless of its fascistic excesses. This is why *Salò* functions much better as a metaphor of our tolerant consumer society than a direct indictment of Fascism. The point is that the core of the law is Real irrespective of its different historical or geo-political frameworks: whether liberal-democratic or explicitly totalitarian, the law remains rooted in its tautology, in the enigma of its form so eloquently narrativised by Kafka. In denouncing the intrinsically fascistic trait of the law, what we risk overlooking is precisely its universal formal dimension.

Let us consider Francesco Rosi's *Cadaveri eccellenti*. As in most of Rosi's films, we are presented with a clear-cut ethical divide between the morally upright subject and the abysmally corrupted system: Amerigo Rogas (Lino Ventura) is a hardened but honest police inspector who, while investigating the mysterious assassinations of a series of prominent judges, uncovers a conspiracy of epic proportions aimed at creating the appropriate conditions for a right-wing coup. As soon as he discovers that the police are also involved and colluding with the government, he is taken off the case, but only to doggedly continue the investigations on his own. Eventually, he is gunned down by a mysterious sniper whilst passing on some crucial information about the coup to the leader of the Communist Party (who is also killed). Rosi, as always, tells us that power goes hand in hand with corruption, and that hope can only come from the moral dignity and civil dedication of a few, isolated men like Rogas. However, the ethical implications of his film are undermined by two latent themes: firstly, the inspector's zeal goes well beyond his sense of moral duty, and so can only be fully comprehended as an unconditional (over-zealous) fascination with a seemingly insoluble enigma; secondly, power itself, despite its immorality, is unconsciously narrativised as an object of desire – exactly like the Kafkaesque law, with its labyrinthine, indestructible, and as such irresistibly attractive structure. In short, Rosi's cinematic ethics, the so-called "civil commitment" of his cinema, are founded on the displacement of strictly speaking amoral *jouissance*.

Such a pervasive displacement of *jouissance* also features in Petri's first film, *L'assassino* (1961). Here we start another Kafkaesque situation, with the seemingly inexplicable arrest of Nello Poletti (Marcello Mastroianni), a wealthy antique dealer later accused of murdering his rich and older mistress Adalgisa De Matteis (Micheline Presle), who had set him up in business only to be cast aside in favour of a younger woman, Antonella Nogara (Cristina Gaioni). Poletti is eventually sent to jail where he has a chance to reflect on his shameful life of deceit and selfishness. Overcome by guilt he decides to confess, but at that very moment the real killer is found. Once he is set free he returns (after a brief introspective phase) to his old lifestyle, jokingly referring to himself as "the assassin".

The first thing to note is the previously mentioned Kafkaesque notion that, when confronted by the law, the subject is always-already guilty regardless of whether he has committed a crime or not. Poletti has not killed anyone and yet he feels guilty, to such an extent that he is willing to confess a crime he has not committed. As with *Indagine*, however, Petri tends to betray Kafka's lesson by over-historicising Poletti's guilt, deriving it from his socially driven opportunism. The Lacanian insight about guilt is that it functions in exactly the opposite way: we feel remorse not because we break the law, but because we give up our desire (to break it). So if there is anything Poletti is guilty of, it is his having "escaped into guilt" – he has chosen to be culpable so as to circumvent the traumatic content of his desire.[36] Are there any symptoms in the narrative that might alert us to this interpretation? Perhaps the key figure is the very ordinary looking detective Palumbo (Salvo Randone). From the start he is depicted as the capricious, if not openly vicious executioner of the law, as one can clearly detect an unjustified sadistic edge in his aggressive behaviour against Poletti. The point is that his sadism belies *jouissance*, the fact that power for him 'is the ultimate "transgression" of an idiotic life of modest pleasures' (Žižek, 2004b, p. 174).[37] Even more symptomatic is the final shot of the film, with Poletti attempting to strike a car deal on the phone and referring to himself as "the assassin". This finale suggests that the "escape into guilt" has not worked, and the traumatic content of desire *has remained in excess of its representation*: the signifier *assassino* has turned into a hystericised linguistic nucleus of irreducible enjoyment.

With Bertolucci's *Il conformista* (The Conformist, 1970) a psychoanalytic approach to the question of power is almost inevitable. Initially, the analysis seems straightforward, conforming to one of psychoanalysis' uncontested theorems: the more we seek the balance of the pleasure principle, the more we compromise our desire, whose libidinal potential is bound, sooner or later, to re-emerge in explosive fashion. Marcello Clerici (Trintignant), another executioner of the law, fits perfectly the Freudian logic of the "return of the repressed". The main flashback of the film tells us that as an adolescent he had undergone a traumatic homosexual experience that had *stained* his life, forcing him to perceive himself as "different", and therefore prompting him to seek the norm at all costs. However, we may still legitimately question the exact motives behind Marcello's desperate choice of the norm, since the latter implies embracing the excesses of the Fascist rule (most of the narrative is set in 1930s Italy). The key passage is of course Bertolucci's enigmatic representation of Marcello's "close encounter" with Pasqualino (Lino) Semirama (Pierre Clementi), his personal chauffeur. One day Pasqualino abducts Marcello to an isolated retreat and, as far as we can gather from the nebulous flashback, lures him into a sexual act that, once performed, induces the young boy to shoot his depraved seducer. Whether Marcello seeks normality (an average family, social respectability, etc.) because of this early crime, or to avoid the disturbing thought of his latent homosexuality, the main psychoanalytic line of reasoning holds: it is the repression of a non-symbolisable psychological remainder that eventually causes the law to "lose its head". The flashback seems to confirm this reading, as Marcello's memory is fragmented and elliptical, unable to focus with clarity on the Real of *jouissance* (the homosexual act) that structures the entire narrative. By joining the fascist majority, Marcello wants to erase this shameful and obscene stain of *jouissance*.

Marcello's obstinate pursuit of ordinariness thereby results in his stumbling upon an utterly abnormal reality, rendered perfectly through Bertolucci's stylistic excesses. This abnormality is also connoted through narrative ambiguity (especially as far as the constant condensation and displacement of the characters' sexual identity is concerned) and, more specifically, through the emphasis placed on the invasive perversion of the very social environment that Marcello believes to be sane and well ordered. Marcello's distorted vision is ultimately reflected in his decision to enter the secret police and volunteer for a mission that involves eliminating his former university lecturer, professor Quadri (Enzo Tarascio), an anti-fascist militant who has escaped to Paris. As Bertolucci himself stated, professor Quadri carries 'the weight of the paternal figure' (in Kline, 1987, p. 82) for Marcello, an observation which brings us to the typical psychoanalytic situation of Bertolucci's cinema: the Oedipal theme of the son's rebellion against the authority of the father.[38] In Paris, however, things get even more complicated for our hero, as he falls in love with the androgynous Anna Quadri (Dominique Sanda), the professor's wife.[39] Eventually he manages to repress his emotional involvement and dutifully carries out his murderous task. In fact, in a clear reprise of the initial incident with Lino, Anna Quadri, the new impossible/traumatic object of desire, is also eliminated. Back in Rome, on the day of Mussolini's deposition (25 July 1943), Marcello accidentally bumps into none other than Pasqualino Semirama, whom he believed to have killed. Only then does he realise how futile his endeavours to rid himself of the trauma related to their encounter had been, and in a fit of panic starts blaming Lino for the killing of Quadri, confirming that this killing was nothing but a desperate attempt to uproot and erase an indelible traumatic excess.

The main problem with Bertolucci's *tour de force* is precisely the positioning of the Real of *jouissance*. Over and above the barrage of often complacent references to the ambiguity of the signifier – which turn every character into a potential double and the whole action into a blurred, insubstantial, artificial

Il conformista

reflection of some true but foreclosed kernel of reality —[40] Bertolucci seems to put forward the thesis that the Real encounter that threatens the subject coincides with the Freudian primal scene, which Freud regarded as a universal traumatic experience linked to early childhood's scopophilia.[41] However, in the second part of his career Lacan progressively distanced himself from the Freudian belief in the primal scene as the *original* trauma related to events that are repressed and yet pervasively operative in the subject's psychic apparatus (whether they had really happened or were merely fantasised about). Instead he proposed that the Real, the trauma itself, is in a way consubstantial with the Symbolic, i.e., that it emerges as a result of the subject's attempt to achieve a degree of balance in the big Other. From this angle, the portrayal of Marcello Clerici's endeavours to erase the *jouissance* at work in his primal scene by immersing himself whole-heartedly in the law should be reversed: it is by submitting himself to the (paternal) law that *jouissance* emerges as the traumatic Real. In Lacan, the starting point is the acceptance of the paternal metaphor (of the symbolic order), a necessary choice that inevitably splits the subject, condemning it to perpetual encounters with *jouissance*.

This reading also allows us to comment on Bertolucci's depiction of Fascism. Can we really reduce Fascism (or the fascistic/authoritarian personality) to Marcello's desire to conform? Here, again, the film appears rather ambiguous, since Marcello is not portrayed in entirely negative terms, but also endowed with a degree of intelligence and sensitivity that his fellow comrades unquestionably lack. What I suggest is that the unconscious dimension of Bertolucci's film has to do with the displaced significance accorded to Marcello in his function of "executioner of the law". Had Bertolucci excluded the Freudian reference to early childhood trauma, the fundamental structure of *Il conformista* would come to resemble very closely that of *Salò*, in as much as both films develop the notion that the essential feature of the (not necessarily Fascist) law can be uncovered by focusing on its inherent excess, i.e. the figure of the executioner. Not dissimilarly to *Salò*'s libertines, Marcello Clerici is an intellectually aware individual *whose desire to conform to the law eventually turns into (subversive) desire pure and simple*. Marcello's uncompromising submission to the law, his fetishistic self-instrumentalisation, is ultimately correlative to a shattering injunction (to do his duty) that destabilises any preconceived idea of symbolic balance. We are therefore back to 'Kant avec Sade'. According to Lacan, Kant's "categorical imperative" (if developed to its extreme consequences) is the highest form of transgression, desire in its purest form; this means that duty, in its most categorical and disinterested manifestation, coincides with crime, the ultimate form of disobedience.

Hence, the unconscious dimension of *Il conformista* resides in the disavowed knowledge that Marcello Clerici does not simply stand for a pitiful compliance with an evil social order, but that he represents the very shattering force of subversion that sustains the law. The film is highly significant for our approach, especially if read against the socio-historical awareness that, in our postmodern, "liberated" universe, *just about everyone wants to appear as a non-conformist*. What Bertolucci unwittingly tells us is that the truly anti-conventional stance comes from conforming, from adhering unconditionally to the letter of the law.

A similar notion of fetishistic self-instrumentalisation is in place in Petri's *La classe operaia va in paradiso* (The Working Class Goes to Heaven / Lulù the Tool, 1971). Ludovico Massa, nicknamed Lulù (Gian Maria Volontè), plays a metal piece worker whose total dedication to his mind-numbing job makes him the pride of the management as well as an embarrassment for his fellow workers, who regard him as an enemy setting a frantic pace of work for them all, and also a threat to their struggle against factory exploitation. Similarly to the tramp in Chaplin's *Modern Times* (1936), Lulù appears as an utterly dehumanised and subjugated individual whose only aim in life is to work faster and faster so as to produce more pieces and add a meagre pay supplement to his pitiful salary. However, one day he loses a finger in an accident caused by overworking, and from then on he becomes a radical protester, to such an extent that he joins a cluster of extremist students in an organised insurrection against the factory. Consequently, after losing his finger he also loses his job, only to be eventually re-hired thanks to the trade unions' intervention.

The central feature of Petri's impressive working-class epic is to be found in the subtle initial reference to the correlation between his bedraggled hero's categorical commitment to do his duty, and his sudden transformation into a diehard anti-capitalist militant. Petri suggests that these two apparently opposite positions are much closer than they might seem, for the degree of *jouissance* spent by the subject who fanatically obeys the law can easily be converted into a subversive libidinal force.[42] Along the same lines, Lulù incarnates the Chaplinesque attitude of coarse and even obtuse vitality which, however, is almost magically turned into a sublime fascination with the ideal of justice. As with Chaplin, an imperceptible subjective property demarcates the sublime from the vulgar, a property that here finds its objective correlative in Lulù's finger. As soon as he loses it, his vulgar existence suddenly acquires noble connotations. In terms of this radical subjective ambiguity, the sequence that epitomises Lulù's repressed potential for a libidinally-invested revolutionary act is the one in which he demonstrates his working technique: in order to produce more pieces, he has to focus his imagination on fellow-worker Adalgisa's (Mietta Albertini) backside, whilst simultaneously repeating to himself: 'Un pezzo, un culo, un pezzo, un culo, un pezzo, un culo...' (one piece, one arse...). Far from hindering the break to a subversive position, the shameless endorsement of this vulgar libidinal attachment is precisely what makes it possible.

Pasqualino settebellezze

In Italian cinema, the director who best epitomises this reference to a universe of unrestrained masculine vulgarity/vitality is Lina Wertmuller, a woman who has often been accused (by feminist critics) of promoting a cynical, male-chauvinistic vision of the world. However, what if her "vital worms",[43] so many preposterous, pathetic and utterly tasteless male heroes, often played by the histrionic Giancarlo Giannini, represent such an excessively sexualised attachment to life that, in its very offensive, often traumatic character, successfully embodies the potential for a revolutionary act?

2.6 PASSIONATE ATTACHMENTS IN THE TORTURE ROOM

What 'Kant avec Sade' reveals is that, if developed through to its "bitter end", Kant's revolutionary insight into morality conflates with Sade's notion of absolute excess. Lacan claims that the moral law cannot serve as a stabilising device which prevents us from encroaching upon the abyss of the noumena; quite on the contrary, it represents the Real "in disguise", an irresistibly transgressive injunction sustained by a certain traumatic excess. My contention here is that Lacan's reading of the moral law is the essential starting point if we are to grasp Rossellini's lesson on the ethical act. We shall now focus on some elements concerning the moral dimension of Rossellini's *Roma, città aperta* (Rome, Open City, 1945), and then attempt a comparative analysis of the film that signalled the director's return to the early period, *Il generale della Rovere* (General della Rovere, 1959).

My initial assumption is that Rossellini's neorealist "trilogy of war" is constructed around a symptomatic attraction to a kernel of traumatic negativity. If *Roma, città aperta* ends with the portrayal of the Italian Resistance as an event sustained by a violent act of self-sacrifice, the following *Paisà* (Paisan, 1946) and *Germania anno zero* (Germany Year Zero, 1947) repeat this negative move by focusing on the spectacle of ruins produced by the war. More precisely, in these war films negativity paradoxically overlaps with freedom, since Rossellini's insistence on destruction and sacrifice is exactly what sustains the awareness that things can start anew.

In 1955, Rossellini stated that as a rule his films are centred on 'a humble human being overwhelmed by something that, all of a sudden, hits him inexorably, in the precise moment when he finds himself free in the world' (in Bruno, 1979, p. 26). I propose that this coincidence of trauma and freedom be reformulated as follows: the liberating force of these narratives is closely related to the emergence of that unconscious formation which Lacanian psychoanalysis knows as *jouissance*. If my analysis proves correct, the usual stereotype "Rossellini the *viveur*" – the quintessential Roman bourgeois cynically and hedonistically indulging in a life of pleasures – needs to be replaced by "Rossellini the *jouisseur*", for the simple reason that his war films hinge on a repressed nucleus of *jouissance*. Rossellini's secret aim in the trilogy of war is that of "hitting at the Real of enjoyment" by way of anchoring a fictional subject's (and/or the viewer's) point of view to a disturbing element whose sudden emergence provokes a short circuit that subverts the standard legibility of the narrative.[44] Perhaps the most effective intervention of *jouissance* takes place in the second part of *Roma, città aperta* (a title which, if read with Lacan, should immediately reveal the film's link with the clandestine potentialities of the unconscious).[45]

The central question of the attachment to the cause – to symbolic fictions or ideological beliefs – rests precisely on the characters' diverging relations to *jouissance*. The Nazis, first of all, are presented as completely subjected to the pleasure principle, or to what Kierkegaard in *Either/Or* calls the 'aesthetic dimension' (see Kierkegaard, 1972). Rossellini conveys this when he brilliantly juxtaposes Nazism and narcissistic hedonism (with strong homosexual undertones), giving us a perfect illustration of the perverted force behind the Nazis' passionate attachment.

At a crucial stage of the deservedly famous torture sequence, Major Bergmann, the Head of the Gestapo in Rome, steps out of his office and walks straight into the adjacent room, crowded with Nazi officers intent on drinking, smoking, playing cards and listening to music. Through this understated but poignant association of torture and pleasure seeking, Rossellini uncovers the horror of what does not look horrible at all, a surprisingly modern representation of evil camouflaged as seemingly normal self-gratification. The following outburst of drunken angst on the part of Major Hartmann, who decries the self-destructive nature of Nazism and yet will callously execute Don Pietro at the end of the film, not only confirms Kierkegaard's prediction that hedonism eventually leads to dread and despair, but also pinpoints the self-contradictory core of ideology. More specifically, however, what is valuable here is the correlation between enjoyment and ideology, in the sense that Nazi ideology in *Roma, città aperta* functions precisely through its vital link to a displaced nucleus of enjoyment, which ranges from smoking, drinking and playing cards to sadistic torturing.

If we stay for a moment with Kierkegaard's *Either/Or*, Rossellini's representation of the Resistance implies that the aesthetic deadlock in which the Nazis are caught can be overcome through the choice of the ethical, which is based on the strict adherence to a moral code. Nonetheless, this reading only comes to fruition if we accomplish Kierkegaard's next and conclusive step, which involves the passage from the ethical to the religious 'suspension of the ethical', fully developed in his *Fear and Trembling* (Kierkegaard, 2003, pp. 83–95).

If there is a place for the suspension of the ethical in *Roma, città aperta* – beyond the standard reading of its reliance on tragic, ethical heroism – this is to be found, firstly, in the uncanny manifestation of the Real during the torture sequence. The detail not to be missed is that when Don Pietro (Aldo Fabrizi), the parish priest who collaborates with the Italian Resistance, is brutally pushed into the prison cell, he falls to the ground and breaks his glasses. From now on, and especially when forced to behold the painful spectacle of Manfredi's torture, his visual impairment becomes the narrative channel enabling Rossellini to stage the intrusion of *jouissance* in the scopic field. How does the Real manifest itself here? On first impression, one would certainly opt for the most obvious answer: in Manfredi's agony. However, Rossellini forces a slight narrative detour, placing the main emphasis on Don Pietro's fantasy. What we realise is that the trauma of torture relates to Don Pietro's blurred vision of Manfredi's tormented body – a vision that triggers, in the priest as well as in the audience, the distressing compulsion *to imagine the act of torture*. Rossellini, in other words, provides a tremendous insight into what Žižek calls 'the plague of fantasies' (see Žižek, 1997), for he knows that the compulsion to imagine torture is far more distressing than the sustained visual disclosure of brutal violence.[46] As shown by Pasolin's *Salò*, the Real of *jouissance* is to be strictly related to fantasy.[47]

With the torture sequence, therefore, Rossellini radicalises the function of fantasy by disturbing what Lacan calls the *fundamental fantasy*, the displaced libidinal affection that sustains the subject's very existence. Žižek's defines the fundamental fantasy as

> the primordial "masochist" scene in which the subject "makes/sees himself suffering", that is, assumes *la douleur d'exister*, and thus provides the minimum support to his being [...]. This

fundamental fantasy is thoroughly *inter-passive*: in it, a scene of passive suffering (subjection) is staged which simultaneously sustains and threatens the subject's being – which sustains this being only in so far as it remains foreclosed (primordially repressed). From this perspective, a new approach opens up to the recent artistic practices of sadomasochistic performance: is it not a fact that, in them, this very foreclosure is ultimately undone? In other words, what if the open assuming/staging of the phantasmatic scene of primordial "passionate attachments" is far more subversive than the dialectic rearticulation and/or displacement of this scene? (Žižek, 2000a, p. 265).

My claim is that the ultimate purpose of Rossellini's torture sequence is to unravel the sado-masochistic kernel of subjectivity. Don Pietro, this kind of prototypical spectator, is inescapably drawn towards that limit-dimension where fantasy (triggered by his inability to see clearly) dissolves into voyeuristic *jouissance*, and it is precisely the excess of this radically ambiguous point of view that ultimately sustains his passionate attachment to the ideals of the Resistance! Put it another way, his readiness to die for the cause (his heroism) is necessarily supplemented by the (excessive) voyeuristic experience of *his own demise as mirrored in Manfredi's agony*, insofar as visual *jouissance* is a libidinal tension driven against the subject's symbolic identity: a kernel of libido that needs to be disavowed if we are to attain subjective fullness, and assumed (as in Don Pietro's case) if we are to break out of a given symbolic predicament.

This secret reliance on visual *jouissance* also helps us understand the implications of the death of another central character, Pina (Anna Magnani), a working class woman who actively supports the Resistance. In what is arguably the most famous sequence of the film, Pina's desperate run towards Francesco (her bridegroom, the Resistance fighter who is abducted on a Gestapo jeep in front of her eyes) is also characterised by what we might well call an explosion of *jouissance*. Firstly, as in Manfredi's and Don Pietro's cases, death implies the subject's assumption of the unconscious goal of desire, as Pina's run is clearly staged as a suicidal confrontation with the very excess that sustains her desire. The bottom line, however, is that the director subtly connotes this tragic event (just like Manfredi and Don Pietro's deaths) as a painfully voyeuristic situation, and he does so by exposing the inconsistency of the fantasy support that sustains, visually, the identification with the victim. If what generates visual *jouissance* in the torture sequence is the fact that Don Pietro's perspective is impaired, Pina's killing creates a similar effect, as it is half-watched by Don Pietro, Francesco and Marcello, Pina's young son. The emotional impact of her death originates in the way Rossellini exploits the points of view of these characters: the killing is shot from different perspectives, aiming to suture the partial gazes of the priest, the fiancée and the son. Contact with the Real of *jouissance* is made, again, through a certain voyeuristic compulsion to fantasise about the horror: Francesco's point of view is blocked (as he is held inside the jeep), Marcello's is impaired (Don Pietro instinctively hides the boy's face in his cassock) and finally Don Pietro is framed as he turns his head away from the killing. What matters is that the viewer is forced in the position of "seeing and yet not seeing", and is therefore compelled to rely on a certain libidinal investment in fantasy.

This reading, which supplements the standard view of the scene as one that simply creates affective stimuli in the spectator, is confirmed by a couple of crucial details: first, the often noted raw sensuality of Pina's run towards Francesco, preceded by an allusion to her being sexually molested by a Nazi soldier; then, the posture of her dead body, which reveals the scandalous nakedness of her thigh (a detail which, at the time of the film's release infuriated Marxist critics!). In this respect, the equivalent of Pina's naked thigh is the Christ-like posture of Manfredi's naked body in the torture chamber, in as much as both function as *objet a* for the voyeuristic economy of the gaze. The overlapping of the two contrasting dimensions of death and voyeurism is essential for the emergence of visual *jouissance*. I would therefore argue that, rather than just 'providing Symbolic identification' with the victims (Rocchio, 1999, p. 47), the deepest underlying aim here is to make this identification problematic through the conflation of "obscene" visual enjoyment and affective attachment to the victims. Rossellini cunningly relies on the camouflaged insistence of an obscene subtext, situated precisely where one would least expect it. To put it somewhat light-heartedly, his resistance epic is founded on a central instance of self-sabotaging.

To contextualise the disturbing "excess of enjoyment" that characterises Rosellini's representation of the heroic stance, we can focus on the fact that the victims' attachment to their political goal is eventually nourished by the death-drive. As previously suggested, one should of course avoid understanding the term death-drive as a pathological impulse toward self-annihilation. The opposite is true: despite their tragic demise, Pina, Manfredi and Don Pietro uncannily live on in a radically different future (this is exactly what the end of the film hints at, with the kids witnessing Don Pietro's execution). In Lacanese, death-drive is an indomitable thrust that persists beyond biological life, none other than the unshakeable stain of *jouissance* itself, which opens the way for the reconfiguration of the socio-symbolic order. Borrowing from Lacan, Žižek defines the death-drive as 'not merely a direct nihilistic opposition to any life-asserting attachment; rather, it is the very formal structure of the reference to Nothingness that enables us to overcome the stupid self-contented life-rhythm, in order to become "passionately attached" to some Cause – be it love, art, knowledge or politics – for which we are ready to risk everything' (Žižek, 2000a, p. 108).

Paradoxically, the victims' passionate attachment to the Resistance, in *Roma, città aperta*, is ideologically significant *insofar as it turns radically against the subjects*: it turns into dis-attachment, into a confrontation with the abyss that sustains their belief.[48] Despite what may appear at first sight, the ethical act here does not simply coincide with the classic and intrinsically pathetic "dying for the cause", but with the overcoming of the cause itself through the identification with the impossible dimension of pure lack that secretly supports it. Manfredi's refusal to collaborate with the Gestapo despite the horrors of torture (and despite the absence of any guarantee that his sacrifice will actually achieve anything concrete), dovetails with a passionate attachment that, in order to assert itself fully, must overcome itself fully in the Real of desire. And is not this excessive surplus of desire already discernible in Manfredi's relationship with Marina (Maria Michi), the much younger actress-prostitute who eventually betrays him to the Gestapo? Is not Manfredi's love for Marina, despite her obvious unreliability, already a symptom of his excessive / self-destructive desire? More generally, does not such excess qualify *every* ethical subjective position in the film, from that of the priest who strikes a scandalous alliance with a communist, to Pina's sacrifice, or even the kids' own attempt at organising an improbable revolutionary committee? Ultimately, this 1945 film is still extremely significant today because it stages a notion of subjectivity which, being founded on the politicisation of the death-drive, provides a radically alternative perspective to the postmodern subject, who by definition shrinks away from any instance of ideological involvement. As Žižek puts it: 'What if we are "really alive" only if we commit ourselves with an excessive intensity which puts us beyond "mere life"? What if, when we focus on mere survival, even if it is qualified as "having a good time", what we ultimately lose is life itself?' (Žižek, 2002, p. 88).

Roma, città aperta

This question can also be approached through what Nowell-Smith calls the constant dialectics of "communication" and "failed communication" in Rossellini's cinema (see Nowell-Smith, 2000, pp. 11–12). It can be argued that in *Roma, città aperta* we do have true communication between Manfredi and Don Pietro, as their collaboration against Nazi-Fascism represents the pivotal theme and the emotional core of the narrative. However, the standard reading of the heroic spiritual alliance between the Catholic priest and the communist fighter needs to be developed through to its traumatic end. Such a miraculous encounter between two conflicting ideologies is not simply legitimised by the common background of anti-Fascist commitment (a view at the heart of the typically idealistic and ultimately misleading interpretation of the film), but rather by its taking place in the excessive domain of torture and death. What cements Manfredi and Don Pietro's alliance is the fact that *they meet in the Real of their desires*, the strictly speaking inaccessible dimension whose fundamental repression sustains their respective ideological stances. Thus it is not surprising that, just prior to the torture sequence, their attempt to confess to each other their beliefs, and therefore construct some kind of "communicative alliance", is abruptly cut short by the intervention of a Nazi soldier who takes Manfredi away for interrogation: their encounter, Rossellini suggests, can only be understood in relation to the disturbing surplus of their subjective (physical, psychic and linguistic) economy, which emerges in the torture room.[49]

If the finale manages to project a harmonious idea of the Italian Resistance as the successful alliance of two seemingly incompatible ideological domains, such a result is ultimately represented as a miraculous event that belongs in the Real of the subjects' desire. In contrast to Vincent Rocchio's criticism of the director's attempt 'to contain the subversive utopian impulse of the Resistance' through various strategies of symbolisation (Rocchio, 1999, p. 50), it seems to me that the emphasis needs to be placed on the disruptive and subversive quality of Rossellini's realism, which calls for a radical reassessment of the first phase of his work by suggesting that its moral significance hinges on the question of subjectivity as a fundamentally split context.

The basic message of *Roma, città aperta* was replicated fifteen years later with *Il Generale della Rovere*. Notwithstanding the plausibility of all that has been written on Rossellini's opportunistic reasons for making *Il Generale della Rovere*,[50] one should at least consider the director's statement that the film was inspired to him by the need 'to re-introduce the great feelings that moved men when they were confronted face to face with final decisions' (in Brunette, 1996, p. 211). In this respect, making too sharp a distinction between Rossellini's neorealist period, the Bergman era, and the following production before the turn to didactic films would be misleading, for the simple reason that even the arguably most conventional amongst his works invite reflections that take us beyond the conventional and the opportunistic. It seems to me that the main question could be posed in the following terms: with Rossellini, as with Antonioni and Pasolini, what appears on the surface of film is much more profound than what we might wish to find in its depth.

There is a crucial phrase in *Il generale della Rovere*, one of those phrases that have the dramatic potential to sustain an entire narrative: 'in moments of grave moral indecision between two ways, we should take the harder one'. The first point to make is that this sentence appears uncannily de-subjectivised, for its original bearer – the military and Resistance leader General della Rovere – only features in the film for a few seconds, in an extreme long shot depicting him as an indistinguishable figure gunned down by the Nazis whilst running away from a road bloc. The fact that the central character is practically missing is by no means insignificant, and should immediately prompt us to ask questions concerning subjectivity. What is Rossellini's subject if *the* subject of his film is missing?[51] The General's phrase is quoted in a letter written by his wife, who is lead to believe that her husband is still alive, but in prison. When Bertone – who in the meantime has been forced by the Nazis to take up the General's identity – receives the letter, he has to have it read to him by a nameless Italian prison guard owing to the physical impairment he carries from heavy torture. The effect of this reiterated displacement of the bearer of the message reinforces the underlying idea that the bearer is actually missing – or, in psychoanalytic terms, that the message comes from the unconscious. But what is, exactly, the "harder of two ways" alluded to in the letter? Well beyond the immediate historical reference to Marshal Badoglio's controversial choice of 8 September 1943,[52] I would suggest that, given the clear suspension of the narrative between reality and fiction, essence and appearance (the General's real identity and Bertone's mask; the real footage sequences scattered here and there, and the fairly obvious studio artificiality of most of the film), the harder and properly ethical way is the choice of the "truth of fiction", the one eventually endorsed by Bertone.[53]

Rossellini's brilliant intuition in this vastly underrated film lies in the way in which the fictional dimension ultimately overlaps with the real: the mask (Bertone) not only becomes what he is not (the General), he also tells us that this presumed "real identity", behind a name or a title, is nothing but a stop-gap in the ever sliding signifying chain, a missing link that sustains an entire series of identificatory processes through the paradox of its empty presence. This is why Bertone's final decision to die with the partisans cannot be explained in rational terms: it is the choice of the "hardest way", a choice of self-contraction whereby the subject discovers that what lies behind the endless play of fictional selves (let us not forget the ambiguity implicit in the use of De Sica himself, famous both as actor and as director) is nothing but an empty, non-symbolisable fracture, a kernel of vertiginous negativity. And the point is that this abyssal core of negativity stands for the power of freedom, for it miraculously turns an ignoble con man (Bertone) into a self-sacrificing hero. The standard Marxist complaint that Bertone's choice lacks socio-historical credibility (see Aristarco, 1961, pp. 15–17) should therefore be counteracted by the Kierkegaardian argument that every true choice takes place in an ahistorical domain, where the ethical dimension is suspended in order to make room for the religious "madness" of the act.

2.7 ON NEOREALISM: EXCURSUS 2

In Italy, questions concerning Rossellini's realism have always been raised, never more so than in the highly politicised 1950s. One of the first debates on the issue saw the Italian critic Guido Aristarco and the French critic André Bazin exchanging their views between 1952 and 1955. Aristarco, a Marxist, upheld an essentially Lukacsian notion of realism which led him to criticise the involution of Rossellini's cinema in the 1950s,[54] whereas Bazin, a moderate leftist, strenuously defended the consistency of Rossellini's method (see Forgacs, Lutton and Nowell-Smith, 2000, pp. 9–13).[55] In the most convincing part of his articulated defence, Bazin addresses the wider issue of neorealism, maintaining that the defining feature of the genre is its ability to connote 'a certain globality of the real':

> Neo-realism is the global description of reality by a global consciousness. I mean by this that neo-realism is opposed to the realist aesthetics that preceded it, and specifically naturalism and verism, in that its realism is directed not at the choice of subject-matter but at the process of awareness. If you like, what is realist in *Paisà* is the Italian Resistance; but what is neo-realist is Rossellini's *mise-en-scène* and *his elliptical and at the same time synthesising presentation of events*. To put it in yet another way , *neo-realism [...] considers reality as a bloc, not incomprehensible but indivisible* (in Forgacs, Lutton and Nowell-Smith, 2000, p. 159, my emphasis).

For Bazin, neorealism does not just rely on moral, historical or politico-ideological presuppositions, but also on the director's (in this case, Rossellini's) unmediated love 'for the real itself', for reality in its *indivisible guise*. Bazin suggests that 'the neo-realist film has a meaning, but a posteriori, to the extent that it allows our consciousness to pass from one act to another, from one fragment of reality to the next, whereas meaning is given a priori in classical artistic composition: the house is already there in the brick' (in Forgacs, Lutton and Nowell-Smith, 2000, p. 160).

This is not a naive phenomenological approach. What we must appreciate is the implicitly Hegelian flavour of Bazin's argument, as it entails a notion of realism that affirms itself as a retroactive, *a posteriori* phenomenon sustained by an elliptical (i.e. *not* grounded in the shared knowledge of a certain historical context) presentation of events. To put it differently, we could say that Rossellini's highly intuitive, unplanned directing style (testified by his well-known on set improvisations) is correlative to what Sandro Bernardi calls the Hegelian 'positivity of the negative' that characterises his cinema,[56] which comes forward as a radically idiosyncratic feature that cannot be integrated into any previously existing vision of reality and therefore "clears the slate" for the new to emerge.

If we radicalise this view we get an even more cunning and properly Hegelian paradox, which lies in the acknowledgement that Rossellini's unique and irreducible approach ultimately coincides with the very truth-content of his cinema. This paradox can be mapped against Bazin's claim that the term neorealism represents nothing but an empty signifier, a linguistic place-holder for individual directors who incarnate, and thus redeem, its significance, by giving its universally abstract status a concrete value: 'If my analysis is correct, it follows that neo-realism should never be used as a noun, except to designate the ensemble of neo-realist directors. *Neo-realism does not exist in itself*: there are only neo-realist directors, whether they are materialist, Christian, Communist, or what have you' (in Forgacs, Lutton and Nowell-Smith, 2000, p. 160, my emphasis). Similarly to what has been argued by Žižek apropos of film noir (see Butler, Laclau and Žižek 2000, p. 243 and Žižek, 2001a, pp. 149–56), this position reproduces the Hegelian notion of "concrete universality", whereby every contingent, particular reality (a neorealist film) represents a certain content that is necessarily distorted by its own attempt to fulfill the demand of its abstract universal (neorealism).

Far from being either a conceptually practicable or a transcendentally intangible framework, however, this abstract universal is thoroughly immanent to its concrete counterpart, and as such it exists *in the form of its own impossibility*, the hindrance/gap exerting a gravitational pull on any concretely existing phenomenon.[57] Thus Rossellini's idiosyncratic approach *is* the truth-content of his filmmaking, for, to go back to Bazin's argument, it functions as the elliptical feature that intrinsically "curves" the space of his cinema (a consideration which confirms Gilles Deleuze's claim that Italian neorealism exposes the virtual dimension at the heart of the cinematic image).[58] With this in mind, it comes as no surprise that Bazin's argument develops into the defence of the Rossellinian act as an apparently meaningless gesture that suddenly reveals its symbolic significance: 'The Rossellinian universe is a universe of pure acts, insignificant in themselves, but preparing almost behind God's back, as it were, the sudden dazzling revelation of their meaning. [...]' (in Forgacs, Lutton and Nowell-Smith, 2000, p. 160).

These observations are meant to bolster my claim that the emergence of a symbolically-constituted subject in Rossellini's neorealist films (a subject which elicits or discourages identificatory processes in the viewer) is to be linked dialectically to an utterly heterogeneous feature that critics have variously named epiphanic, miraculous, elliptical, sacred,[59] which ultimately stands for the Rossellinian subject's unconscious assumption of his or her fundamentally repressed desire. I would suggest that this feature corresponds to what Bazin calls 'pure act', and as such it can also be defined in terms of realism and authenticity. Apropos of Rossellini's "Bergman films", for example, Žižek (2001b, p. 54) contends that they are all, in different degrees, structured around a deceptive reference to authenticity, whether the latter is the isolated rural community (*Stromboli*, 1950), the poor and their faith (*Europa '51*, No Greater Love, 1952) or the sensuality and magic of southern Italy (*Viaggio in Italia*, Voyage to Italy, 1953), all themes that can be deemed interchangeable. He develops his analysis by suggesting that authenticity here does not relate to a substantial and well-defined understanding of reality, or even civilisation, but to the excess of the Real, to "what is in reality more than reality itself", an inassimilable and non-symbolisable surplus.

The best way to track this passage from reality to the Real is by looking at what many consider the most accomplished of the Bergman films, *Viaggio in Italia*, which chronicles the breakdown of an

English couple's marriage during their trip to the South of Italy. The unconventional narration reminds one of Antonioni (and particularly of *L'avventura*) for the plot is reduced to the bone and filled with *temps morts*, while the camera focuses on the smallest and apparently insignificant details concerning the journey south of the increasingly detached Alex (George Sanders) and Katherine Joyce (Ingrid Bergman). As with Antonioni's films, we are denied access to primary narrative information (the reasons behind the couple's falling-out). The emphasis shifts instead on the Italian landscape, which gradually fills up and widens the gap between the man and the woman. Of the two, Katherine is the one who indicates a potential way out of the stifling sentimental impasse, as she gains a distance from it by directing her attentions to the external world. Alone, she goes for a drive through Naples, she visits museums and catacombs, and eventually – this time with her husband – the ruins of Pompeii, growing more and more engrossed in the natural spectacles she beholds, i.e. 'the physicality and rawness of the ancient world, the ubiquity of death in life' (Brunette, 1996, p. 166). The visit to Pompeii leads to the controversial final sequence, where the Joyces, whilst driving out, drift into a religious procession in honour of San Gennaro, the town's saint. The car is forced to stop, eaten up by the crowd. Then somebody shouts 'Miracolo! Miracolo!" (Miracle! Miracle!), which propels the crowd forward, snatching Katherine away from Alex. After a few minutes of panic Alex manages to rescue his wife and, reunited in a comforting embrace, the couple finally declare their love to each other.

Critics have been fairly unanimous in spotting the intrinsically false character of this reconciliation, on the grounds that it does not appear to be a spontaneous one, but engendered by fear and estrangement. Rossellini himself went in this direction when he commented that 'the only way a *rapprochement* could come about was through the couple finding themselves complete strangers to everyone else. [...] The couple take refuge in each other in the same way as people cover themselves when they are seen naked, grabbing a towel, drawing closer to the

person with them, and covering themselves any old how' (in Brunette, 1996, p. 169). However, in line with our previous argument, what if it is precisely in the somewhat forced and unnatural context of the final embrace that the dimension of true love is to be found? What if the notion that love is the result of a harmonious and transparent consolidation of mutual feelings between two individuals is ultimately false? Rossellini's film provides us with the ideal link to the next section

Viaggio in Italia

on Antonioni precisely because it makes the implicit statement that sexual relationships are ontologically impossible, insofar as they are fraught with an objectal excess that cannot be integrated into a whole, a Real remainder whose indelible persistence in the intersubjective field throws any pre-conceived idea of harmony off-balance.

Going back to Žižek's insight, this excess is exactly what is at stake in Rossellini's representation of "authentic" Italy. Authenticity is here a misnomer, and as such it ought to be supplement with the indestructible, "undead" quality of the external world as it appears to Katherine's eyes. As in James Joyce's eponymous short-story, the dead here (particularly in the Pompeii sequence where an archaeologist digs out a man and a woman caught by the volcanic eruption whilst in bed together) *are more alive than the living*, but precisely in the sense that they embody the Lacanian lamella, the libido-object that cannot die, persisting after biological death and undermining any attempt at symbolic signification. This lamella is the lifeblood of Rossellini's Italy, constantly intruding, slipping through the fractures of the narrative – as epitomised in the wonderful passage where Katherine, whilst visiting mount Vesuvio, takes cognisance of the boiling lava and the process by which it produces the uncanny phenomenon of ionisation: when lighting a torch or a cigarette in proximity of the lava, thick smoke immediately arises from every nearby crater, as if by magic. What better figuration of the Lacanian Real! A formless, slimy, dangerous substance endowed with the power to change instantly the configuration of external reality.[60] *Viaggio in Italia* is, essentially, a voyage to *this* Real.

NOTES

1. In Italian cinema, one of the most hilarious and accurate rendering of this "anxiety of the flesh" is the sequence in Lina Wertmuller's survivalist Holocaust drama *Pasqualino settebellezze* (Seven Beauties, 1975), in which the protagonist Pasqualino (Giancarlo Giannini) kills Mafia boss Totonno and cuts his body up so as to fit it into a suitcase and make it disappear. Despite its comical/grotesque register, the passage epitomises well Lacan's insight that the human body in its formless, mucous, anonymous throbbing coincides with the Real *qua* immortal substance: as he tries to position Totonno's cadaver on a table in order to start the cutting, the fat dead body emits a series of prolonged farts, whose effect on the already heavily distressed Pasqualino proves devastating. Paradoxically, it is in the Real of these inconsistent and yet traumatising bodily excesses that the unfortunate character meets the abyss of the self, as these "undead farts" are symptoms of that very life-substance (lamella) which, later, allows him to survive an interminable string of life-threatening circumstances.

2. Perhaps this is what Pasolini meant when he claimed that 'those who, like me, love reality too much, inevitably end up hating it, subverting it, and sending it to hell' (Pasolini, 1995, p. 255).

3. Antonioni's first feature, *Cronaca di un amore* (Chronicle of a Love, 1950), presents us with two paradigmatic cases of "virtual murder": the death of Guido's previous girlfriend and of Paola's rich husband. In both cases Paola and Guido, the two lovers, feel responsible despite technically not having committed the crimes.

4. The closest literary reference here is Luigi Pirandello's famous novel *Il fu Mattia Pascal* (The Late Mattia Pascal, 1904), where the eponymous protagonist takes advantage of a similar chance and attempts to refashion himself as an entirely new man.

5. Antonioni noted that 'when [Locke] discovers that the man whose identity he has assumed is a man of action, who acts rather than simply witness events, he tries to assume not only his identity, but also his role, his political role. But this other man's story, so concrete and built on actions, becomes too much of a burden for him' (Antonioni, 2001, p. 308). Perhaps the key to understand Locke's indecisiveness is to be found in his name, which is also that of the English philosopher John Locke (1632–1704). Locke's radical empiricism led him to theorise the mind as a *tabula rasa*, an empty recipient filled with sensuous impressions and their subsequent rationalisation. As for Antonioni's Locke, what seems to be decisive for him is precisely this "revolutionary" insight into the essential blankness of the mind, which inevitably implies changeability and regeneration. To forget his past (his wife, his job and the people he knew) and to refashion a new self, Locke comes to terms with the emptiness of his mental framework. The early shot that depicts him stranded in the desert, screaming in sheer frustration (not dissimilarly from Paolo at the end of *Teorema*), signals the first encounter with the "ground zero" of the mind.

6. I am referring particularly to the sequence following Locke's discovery of Robertson's dead body, where Antonioni recounts the first encounter between the two men. What we have here is the type of "disguised flashback" (a flashback within the same shot, i.e. without apparent cuts) also used, for example, by Visconti in *Le notti bianche* (White Nights, 1957) or Petri in *L'assassino* (The Assassin, 1961). Whilst Locke is exchanging the passport photos, we hear a voiceover conversation between him and Robertson; then the camera pans from Locke to the tape recorder, thus revealing the true source of the conversation; finally, it moves back to Locke and then slowly across the room to frame the open window and, beyond, the balcony, where we see the back of a man (Robertson) who is soon joined by Locke himself. The effect of this gliding flashback, as well as of other stylistic and narrative features of the film (unconventional flashbacks, disjointed editing, the constant change of

setting, etc.), is that of producing a strong sense of detachment, which is functional to the film's central idea that time and space, as it were, "can be reset to zero".

7. I refer to the tracking shot through the iron bars of the window at the Hotel de la Gloria (from inside to outside), whilst Locke, lying on his bed, out of frame, is killed by the secret services.

8. 'Here we have one of the possible definitions of the unconscious: *the form of thought whose ontological status is not that of thought*, that is to say, the form of thought external to thought itself – in short, some Other Scene external to the thought whereby the form of the thought is already articulated in advance' (Žižek, 1992, p. 19).

9. Lacan's claim that Marx invented the symptom (see Lacan, 1975, p. 106) retains therefore a surprising significance if we are to grasp the political function of Antonioni's formalism. Perhaps we could even risk suggesting that Antonioni was aware of the clandestine Marxist relevance of his formalism in *Zabriskie Point*, for at one point in the narrative the signifier "Marx" indeed does make a furtive appearance: when a police officer asks Mark for his details, since he suspects him of participating in the campus upheavals, he replies scathingly that his name is Karl Marx (written with a capital C by the police officer, who simply does not recognise the magnitude of the signifier).

10. It is quite significant that, in a time when memory is glorified as the most effective instrument to garner historical knowledge, Pasolini has been almost totally removed/erased from the official palimpsests of Italian culture, (apart from occasional and generally distorted "exhumations"), as if to corroborate the final two lines of one of his late 1960s poems: 'Dopo la mia morte, perciò, non si sentirà la mia mancanza: / l'ambiguità importa fin che è vivo l'Ambiguo' (After my death, therefore, I won't be missed: ambiguity counts only insofar as the Ambiguous is alive, Pasolini, 1993, p. 899).

11. The mixture of attraction and revulsion that typifies *jouissance* is summed up in Freud's famous description of the Rat-Man: 'horror at pleasure of his own of which he himself was unaware' (Freud, 1973, p. 160).

12. The relationship between the executioner and the masochist offers itself as an interesting variation on the classic Hegelian couple lord-bondsman (master-slave). In the *Phenomenology of Spirit*, Hegel claims that it is through his complete submission to the lord that the bondsman actually gains self-consciousness, insofar as he externalises himself in the objects of his labour: 'the bondsman realizes that it is precisely in his work wherein he seemed to have only an alienated existence that he acquires a mind of his own' (Hegel, 1977, p. 119). As the standard Marxist interpretation has it, it is therefore the bondsman, and not the lord, who can claim to occupy an autonomous subject-position. However, does not the figure of the masochist challenge the lord/executioner precisely by undermining the belief in such autonomy? What the masochist makes manifest is the fact that his "being-for-itself" is grounded in the unfathomable abyss of his own enjoyment, which is homologous to the Hegelian notion of absolute negativity. Hegel emphasises this crucial point by insisting on the tie between the bondsman's self-consciousness-through-labour and 'absolute fear': 'If consciousness fashions the thing without the initial absolute fear, it is only an empty self-centred attitude; for its form or negativity is not negativity per se, and therefore its formative activity cannot give it a consciousness of itself as essential being' (Hegel, 1977, p. 119).

13. The question of how to suspend the vicious circle of law and its transgression was of course confronted by Saint Paul, whose writings Pasolini had become acquainted with during his Friulan years (1940s). Saint Paul's answer is that the only way to break out of the superego's irresistible injunction to sin is via Love; however, what should be emphasised is that Pauline Love coincides with the Christian dimension of the Fall (i.e. Christ on the cross), the traumatic moment when we "lose everything", when we renounce our pathological attachment to the world. From this angle, masochism is therefore a strategy to attain precisely this paradoxical coincidence of freedom and loss which suspends our capitulation to the rule of the law.

14. Žižek often refers to 'the paradox of victimization', whereby 'the Other to be protected is good *in so far as it remains a victim* [...]; the moment it no longer behaves like a victim, but wants to strike back on its own, it magically turns all of a sudden into a terrorist/fundamentalist/drug-trafficking Other... The crucial point is thus to recognize clearly in this ideology of global victimization, in this identification of the (human) subject itself as "something that can be hurt", the mode of ideology that fits today's capitalism. This ideology of victimization is the very mode in which – most of the time invisible to the public eye – the Real of Capital exerts its rule' (Žižek, 2000b, p. 60).

15. In *Did Somebody Say Totalitarianism?*, Žižek explicitly relates this notion of exclusion to political agency, by claiming that 'we are to look for today's proletarians [...] where there are subjects reduced to a rootless existence, deprived of all substantial links' (Žižek, 2001c, p. 140).

16. 'The fear of "excessive" identification is therefore the fundamental feature of the late-capitalist ideology: the Enemy is the "fanatic" who "over-identifies" instead of maintaining a proper distance towards the dispersed pluralities of subject-positions' (Žižek, 1993, p. 216).

17. See Pasolini's defence of his use of the term "irrationality" in Pasolini (1960) and Magrelli (1977, p. 80).

18. Furthermore, one finds in Pasolini certain recurrent, seemingly tautological definitions such as '*reality only speaks to itself*', or 'one cannot escape reality, because reality speaks to itself, and we are enclosed in its circle' (Pasolini, 1995, pp. 238 and 246), which seem to match the Lacanian notion of the kernel of the Real as the non-discursive, unfathomable foundation of every process of symbolisation.

19. In an interview with French television before *Salò*'s premiere, Pasolini summed up his position thus: "I believe to give scandal is a duty, to be scandalized a pleasure, and to refuse to be scandalized is moralism."

20. This is of course by no means the only Pasolinian *homo sacer*, as his entire filmic and literary production is marked by the unignorable presence of an utterly displaced and abject humanity.

21. Accattone's only way out of his destitute existence in the Roman slums is to sell his labour as a *manovale*, the lowest rank in the productive machine. When, indeed, he gets a taste of class-exploitation, he determines immediately to go back to his desperately anarchic existence by hinting, hyperbolically, at the complicity of capitalism and nazi-fascism: 'Ma che siamo a Buchenwald qua?' ('Is this Buchenwald?').

22. It should be noted that the metaphor of "life as ingestion-assimilation" is a recurrent one in Pasolini, reinforcing his understanding of reality as an endless process of change rather than as a static structure. A similar situation occurs in *La ricotta*, where Stracci dies of indigestion on the cross. Metaphorical treatments of the act of eating are also central in films like *Il vangelo secondo Matteo* (1964), *Uccellacci e uccellini* (1966), *Porcile* (1969) and *Salò* (1975). The Pasolinian metaphor of life as a process of endless ingestion-assimilation-renewal is suggestively summarised in a 1960 autobiographical observation: 'I love life with such violence and such intensity that no good can come of it. I am speaking of the physical side of life: the sun, the grass, youth. It is an addiction more terrible than cocaine. It does not cost anything and it is available in boundless quantity. I devour it ravenously... How it will end, I don't know' (in Ragusa, 1976, pp. 136–37).

23. The dynamics of absolute and decentred vision in *Accattone* are acutely investigated by Maurizio Viano (1993, pp. 76–8).

24. I refer here to the Dantean quotation that preface the film: 'The angel of the Lord took me and Satan / cried out: why do you rob me? You take / for yourself the eternal part of him for / one little tear which takes him from me'.

25. In recent cinema, one of the most effective representations of such disavowed modes of obscene enjoyment outside the official law can be found in Kubrick's *Eyes Wide Shut* (1999), specifically in its crucial "orgy scene", when Bill (Tom Cruise) manages to sneak into a lavish, and yet profoundly aseptic, Masonic sex party attended by powerful people covered in masks and cloaks.

26. Lacan first developed the link between Kant and Sade in his 1958–59 *Seminar, The Ethics of Psychoanalysis* (see Lacan 1999, pp. 71–84).

27. See, for example, the excursus 'Juliette or Enlightenment and Morality', in *Dialectic of Enlightenment* (Adorno, 1997, pp. 81–119); or the section 'Freedom' in *Negative Dialectics* (Adorno, 2000, pp. 211–99).

28. Also, we should remember that, in Pasolini's own words, the film is not meant to evoke any sense of pity for the tortured (see Pasolini, 2001, p. 3021), for, morally, he considered the libertines to be on the same level as their victims (pp. 2063–67).

29. Gary Indiana (2000, p. 59) rightly notes that 'the libertines experience arousal almost exclusively as a species of rage [...]. There is, of course, nothing tender or romantic in Sade; but there is, in everything, selfish pleasure. Pasolini's heroes appear to experience their own depravity as an unassuageable irritant, no less than their victims' experience of submission'.

30. In the opening credits Pasolini acknowledges Roland Barthes, Maurice Blanchot, Simone de Beauvoir, Pierre Klossowski, Philippe Sollers as his main sources.

31. The cinemas of Ferreri and Pasolini would seem to ratify the Lacanian maxim that 'Ce n'est pas à sa conscience que le sujet est condamné, c'est à son corps' (Lacan, 2001, p. 206. The subject is not condemned to its consciousness, but to its body). Given the current cultural studies fascination with "the body", this notion of bodily *jouissance* cannot but appear as a refreshing radicalisation of an academic cliché.

32. Let us recall Žižek's reading of Pascal's argument in favour of symbolic authority: 'According to Pascal, the interiority of our reasoning is determined by the external, nonsensical "machine" – automatism of the signifier, of the symbolic network in which the subjects are caught [...]. It follows, from this constitutively senseless

character of the Law, that we must obey not because it is just, good, or even beneficial, but simply *because it is the law* – this tautology articulates the vicious circle of its authority, the fact that the last foundation of the Law's authority lies in its process of enunciation' (Žižek, 1992, pp. 36–7).

33. There is a clear resemblance between the Volontè character and Marcello Clerici (Jean-Louis Trintignant) in Bernardo Bertolucci's *Il conformista* (The Conformist), also made in 1970, in as much as they both combine supreme authority with absolute vulnerability.

34. The extensive use of the flashback is another common trait between *Indagine* and *Il conformista*, insofar as it serves the aim of destabilising the psychic balance of their protagonists.

35. We have a wonderful example of this "other's *jouissance*" in Pasolini's *Che cosa sono le nuvole?*, when Desdemona, having been slapped by Othello, unexpectedly replies with a libidinally invested 'Mmh, not bad at all this slap of yours!', which of course increases Othello's frustration.

36. I am borrowing this expression from Žižek, who uses it to describe Irene's subjective position in Rossellini's *Europa '51* (see Žižek, 2001b, pp. 37–42).

37. The contradiction inherent to the law emerges again when Poletti is released from prison, for Palumbo's words to the probing host of journalists are 'I've always known he is a very nice guy'.

38. The second twist to this father-son relationship can be found in Bertolucci's identification of Quadri, Marcello's "master signifier", with Jean-Luc Godard, Bertolucci's own muse, which is revealed by Bertolucci's famous admission that Quadri's address and telephone number in Paris were actually Godard's (in Goldin, 1971, p. 66).

39. In Alberto Moravia's novel of the same title, from which the film is adapted, the connection between Anna and Lino, the chauffeur, was openly revealed by the fact that Quadri's wife is actually called Lina.

40. The central metaphor of Plato's myth of the cave is used precisely to achieve this meta-cinematic purpose: to develop the idea that all representations, cinema *in primis*, are but reflections of something that remains radically concealed. The very assassination of the Quadris is shot in such an unrealistic way so that, in Bertolucci's own words, the audience would be tempted to think that it was all 'a fantasy' (in Kline, 1987, p. 97).

41. The classic example here is Freud's Wolf Man, who was one and a half when he witnessed his parents' coitus *a tergo*.

42. It only takes an accidental encounter with the Real (the loss of a finger) for Lulù to invest his *jouissance* in the opposite goal.

43. I am paraphrasing the corpulent Nazi commander from *Pasqualino settebellezze*, whom Pasqualino tries to seduce so as to escape death in a concentration camp. This passage provides a near-perfect exemplification of the function of fantasy in Lacan, particularly in its correlation to sexuality. If he wants to survive, Pasqualino is required to make love to the repulsive and sadistic Nazi commander. After a first failed attempt, he realises that he can only succeed in this ordeal by closing his eyes and reminisce scenes of seduction and arousal from his past. Overall, his strategic recourse to fantasy proves successful, except for those comical and yet traumatic instances when the huge woman pulls up Pasqualino's eyelids by force, informing him that she wants to look him straight in the eyes. Whilst demonstrating the function of fantasy, the passage also confirms the Lacanian thesis, which we shall develop in the following section, that "there is no such thing as a sexual relationship", insofar as in place of the sexual rapport there is rapport with the phallus. In other words, in the sexual act the subject is a variable of phallic *jouissance*, which functions as an unsurmountable wall between the partners. The rapport that gets established is thus the one between the subject and phallic *jouissance*, whilst the real partner, the other, is fundamentally instrumental to this rapport.

44. As claimed by Bernardi, 'Rossellini's realism always follows this procedure: it builds up a stereotype then suddenly demolishes it. The result will be, as we shall see, an epiphanic instant when the film stops because it is impossible for it to go any further' (Bernardi, 2000, p. 53).

45. I am tempted to claim that Rossellini's Rome, *the* open city, should be seen as nothing less than the quintessential openness/otherness of the unconscious: a place not only literally ravaged by utterly foreign forces (the Nazis), but also metaphorically representative of clandestine potentialities.

46. Incidentally, this is also why the censorship issue is not an issue here. In 1945, Rossellini would certainly not have been able to show a sustained act of torture. However, my point is that he would not have done it anyway, since it is through fantasy that he achieves his aim.

47. Lacan (1984, p. 16) states that 'there is no other entry for the subject into the real except the fantasy.'

48. The crucial moment of Manfredi's demise, after lengthy physical torture, can thus be read as a radical assertion of negativity, the affirmation of the kernel of the Real against the simulacra of the Imaginary. The interesting point is that the Nazis themselves, however momentarily, cannot elude the displacing power exerted by the sudden

materialisation of the Real. For a few seconds, Rossellini shows with emphatic intensity how the traumatic sight of Manfredi's dead, ravaged body suspends the perfunctory efficiency of the Nazis' imaginary configuration. The result is that officers and torturers alike appear utterly shocked, as they realise the enormity of what has just happened.

49. Is not the same communicative principle in place in Mario Monicelli's *La Grande Guerra* (The Great War, 1959), where the true encounter between Giovanni Busacca (Vitorio Gassman) and Oreste Jacovacci (Alberto Sordi), two cowardly and opportunistic Italian soldiers, concurs with their unexpected heroic decision not to commit treason and therefore perish at the hands of the Austrians? Beyond the over-sentimental tone of their sacrifice, it is the displaced emphasis on the paradox of communication that matters here.

50. One consideration should be enough: is not Bertone (Vittorio De Sica), the desperate gambler of *Il generale della Rovere*, the alter-ego of Rossellini, who made the film because of severe financial difficulties? Here of course mirror images abund, for De Sica was not only a director himself, but also a notoriously addicted gambler.

51. Are we not, from this angle, on a surprisingly parallel plane with Antonioni's *L'avventura* which, incidentally, was made in that same summer of 1959?

52. As is well known Marshal Pietro Badoglio became Italy's Prime Minister after Mussolini's deposition in July 1943. On September 3 he had secretly agreed on an unconditional armistice with the Allied forces, and five days later he made an official radio announcement which, due to its remarkably contorted nature ('The Italian forces will cease all acts of hostilities against the Anglo-American forces, wherever they may be. They will, however, oppose attacks of any other forces') caused great uncertainty amongst the Italian troops.

53. Žižek (2001b, p. 33) makes this point by quoting Leo Braudy's claim that 'the importance of the film lies in its acceptance of artifice – role-playing, the assumption of disguise – as a way toward moral truth' (see Braudy, 1978). Žižek (2001b, p. 34) then adds that '[s]uch a dialectic – developed by Rossellini even more pointedly in his *Rise to Power of Louis XIV* – implies that there is more truth in a mask than in what is hidden beneath it: a mask is never simply "just a mask" since it determines the actual place we occupy in the intersubjective symbolic network; what is effectively false and null is our "inner distance" from the mask we wear (the "social role" we play), our "true self" hidden beneath it.'

54. As is well known, Georg Lukács sustained that the role of art is to reflect and represent the historical forces at work in a given historical moment.

55. In the first issue of his new journal *Cinema Nuovo*, on 15 December 1952, Aristarco harshly criticised Rossellini's *Europa '51* (No Greater Love, 1952), pointing out the progressive involution of his cinema since the highs of *Paisà* (1946). Prompted both by Aristarco's negative review and by his journal's subsequent silence on Rossellini's later films, Bazin wrote an open letter to the Italian critic which was published in *Cinema Nuovo* on 25 August 1955 (see Forgacs, Lutton and Nowell-Smith, 2000, pp. 156–61).

56. 'Rossellini's work is primarily negative and it possesses all the "positivity of the negative" described by Hegel: the opening up of meaning produced by criticism, the destruction of old, dead models which are no longer adequate to make sense of what is happening' (Bernardi, 2000, p. 51).

57. Along the same dialectical lines, we could read Pier Paolo Pasolini's provocative claim that 'cinema does not exist' (see Pasolini, 1995, p. 253). Far from being a pseudo-semiological *boutade*, this claim alludes to the same state of affairs: cinema's non-existence is the necessary presupposition to its concrete existence in the form of particular films.

58. See particularly the final part of Deleuze's *Cinema 1* (1986, pp. 205–15) and the opening of *Cinema 2* (1989, pp. 1–13), where the reference to Bazin is explicit.

59. Particularly insightful is Bernardi's reading of the sacred in Rossellini: 'If Rossellini's cinema is realistic, then it is in the sense that it reflects on the state of western culture and evokes, in order to comprehend it, the experience of the sacred not in the religious menaing but in the way that Pasolini (who was deeply indebted to Rossellini) or Bataille spoke of the sacred. There is nothing transcendental, supernatural or divine about the sacred in this sense. It is completely immanent' (Bernardi, 2000, p. 50).

60. The magical charm of this extraordinary sequence reminds us of the passage in Fellini's *Roma* (1972) where, during the excavations for the underground system some workers discover ancient Roman dwellings. When a team of archaeologists is called upon, they are faced by the breathtaking spectacle of a number of extremely well preserved frescoes of beautiful and melancholic figures; however, as soon as these paintings come in contact with gusts of wind from outside, they immediately vanish. As in Rossellini's film, albeit in a stylistically more enchanted manner, the Real is visualised as a sublime object that cannot be approached directly.

3

ADVENTURES IN THE REAL OF SEXUAL DIFFERENCE

3.1 NEGOTIATING THE IMPOSSIBLE

According to Lorenzo Cuccu, Antonioni's characters tend to move within two main poles of attraction: money and eroticism (see Cuccu, 1988, p. 30). To develop this insight we note that Antonioni's female characters are generally defined by their hysterical obsession with anything concerning the universe of feelings, whereas the male ones are split between their professional (or societal) role and their predatory instinct towards women. Antonioni's account of gender difference dramatises the fundamental operative framework of Lacan's theory of sexuality, which could be summed up with his bombshell motto of the late 1960s: *il n'y a pas de rapport sexuel*, there is no such thing as a sexual relationship.[1] My starting hypothesis is that the driving inspiration of Antonioni's production of the early 1950s – which will take different directions in his mature cinema – revolves around the unbreakable deadlock known by Lacanian theory as the Real of sexual difference, as each one of these films owes its relative narrative practicability to the partial obfuscation of the trauma engendered by the realisation that relationships between the sexes are constitutionally dysfunctional. To use a well-known Lacanian paradox, one could surmise that in Antonioni the sexual relationship "does not stop not being written",[2] i.e. *it can only be written as the impossibility of being written*. It is on this impossibility that I shall focus.

In *Cronaca di un amore* (Chronicle of a Love, 1950), Paola and Guido vainly try to build on a past infatuation to start a new life together. The three episodes of *I vinti* (The Vanquished, 1952) surreptitiously centre on the deadlock of the sexual rapport, thus bypassing the pedagogical tone imposed by the Catholic production company. *La signora senza camelie* (Camille without Camelias, 1953) weaves its melodramatic plot around an unhappy marriage between a rich entrepreneur and a young actress. In *Tentato suicidio* (Attempted Suicide, 1953), an episode of the compilation film *Amore in città* (Love in the City), the central theme is that of women attempting suicide as a consequence of failed love affairs. With *Le amiche* (The Girlfriends, 1955), sentimental frustration is so pervasive that it culminates in a suicide. *Il grido* (The Cry, 1957), finally, while signalling a turning point in Antonioni's cinema, is more openly infused than any of the previous films with the tragic awareness of the impracticability of the sexual relationship.

Il grido

In fact, it could be argued that *Il grido* attempts to resolve the narrative compromises negotiated by the films that preceded it by fully committing to a head-on confrontation with the shattering Real of sexual difference. This Real materialises in Aldo's (Steve Cochran) final death, but only if we concede that this death cannot be reduced to a conscious decision to commit suicide. Having been humiliated and abandoned by his wife Irma (Alida Valli) after eight years of marriage, Aldo, a sugar refinery worker, decides to leave town with his daughter Rosina. Wandering aimlessly through the Po valley, he spends some time with an old girlfriend and drifts through a couple of equally unsatisfactory affairs, until one day, back in his village, he catches sight of Irma with her new baby. Exhausted and in a state of utter dejection, he turns away and heads for the blast furnace where he used to work, while Irma follows him from a distance. He then proceeds to climb the tower of the furnace, and as he moves up Irma calls his name aloud – a call that, to quote the screenplay, 'is the only thing in the world that could pull him out of his depression'. The screenplay continues: 'He leans over the railing and reels for a moment as if to resist a sudden vertigo. Irma looks up from below. [...] She emits a bloodcurdling scream. In the silence, her loud, long outcry accompanies Aldo's fall, covering the sound that his body makes as it strikes the ground' (in Chatman, 1985, p. 40).

The strong visual and narrative ambiguity about this death arises from the fact that Aldo's fall is not a conscious leap into the void, but the result of the vertigo he suddenly experiences, and which in my opinion is meant to capture the impossibility of his relationship to Irma. Chatman (1985, p. 42) has emphasised that Aldo's fall is the consequence of 'a movement of yearning toward Irma, the only woman who could ever satisfy him'; the crucial point, however, is that this yearning can only fulfil itself, metaphorically speaking, *in the vertiginous abyss of the Real*, the non-symbolisable, lethal sexual divide that Antonioni's (very Hitchcockian) finale ultimately aims to depict.[3] At a deeper level, this works as an example of Antonioni's penchant for turning the gaze into a fetish: since what is at stake is, strictly speaking, an impossible object (the harmonious representation of the sexual rapport), this impossibility is displaced onto the gaze, the blind spot in the image. This idea is successfully captured by the last shot of the film, with the camera tilted above Aldo, framing the back of his head in a medium shot that also includes Irma as she looks up at him, but reduced to little more than a black point on a white surface. This shot, which comes after an unusual parallel montage (Aldo's exiting the frame as he walks up the tower is repeatedly matched by Irma's entering it as she walks towards him) achieves an effect that is both objective, since both characters are in it, and unreal, since it frames the missing object of Aldo's visual desire from an unnaturally suspended/distorted position.

If we consider the films that precede *Il grido*, it is interesting to see how they adopt a different approach to the Real of sexual difference, in that they all exhibit a basic tendency to narrativise it, that is to say, to neutralise (or in any case gentrify) its traumatic impact. Antonioni's escamotage takes a variety of forms: on the one hand he relies on the proven durability of both film noir (*Cronaca di un amore*) and melodramatic formats (*La signora senza camelie*); on the other hand he smugly pretends to embrace the pedagogical (*I vinti*) and literary frameworks (*Le amiche*).[4] With *Il grido* this narrative straitjacket loosens up, and a more formalistic strategy affirms itself. In terms of content, all these early films demonstrate a socio-psychological aptitude to uncover a bourgeois universe of ennui, arrogance and existential malaise. Considering the highly politicised climate of 1950s Italy, two opposing ideological interpretations have emerged from this basic assumption: the Marxist one, with its insistence on the historically determined character of bourgeois alienation, and the existential one, which tends to read the Antonionian cipher of despair and solitude as a metaphysical truth about the human condition. However, what about approaching the question through the opposite hermeneutical strategy? What if the ideological content of these films were nothing but a masquerade, a secondary fantasy formation correlative to the director's unconscious attempt to avoid *another* dimension, that is, the trauma of sexual difference?

Here we should recall Žižek's lesson on what we might label "the ruse of ideology": questions regarding a given ideological content should be reformulated as questions regarding *the modes of appearance of a certain ideological space*. This means that before we engage with concrete ideology critique (say, Antonioni's account of bourgeois alienation), we should concern ourselves with the mechanisms through which the possibility of engaging with one or conflicting ideological positions has materialised. In the case of cinema, this amounts to saying that the narrative framework of a given film, inclusive of the ideological poise or restlessness that it harbours, is the expression of a pre-existing (unconscious) operation of foreclosure. Or, to put it even more comprehensively: film as a combination of ideological, stylistic, economic, etc. factors, which can all be accounted for from a given historical perspective, is already the product of a Kantian transcendental turn of sorts, which corresponds to the basic condition for the appearance of film. Not surprisingly, Žižek contends that one of Kant's most crucial contributions to philosophy corresponds to his insight that knowledge needs to presuppose something if it is to exist as a commonly shared human experience. The immortality of the soul, for example, is the disavowed but fully operative form of knowledge that allows us to behave, at least in principle, as ethically responsible agents. In film we are faced with a similar situation, not only in the sense that something hidden foregrounds what we see, but because a narrative framework can only emerge as the effect of a preceding act of displacement.

With the above in mind, I would suggest that the great appeal of Antonioni's 1950's films is that despite their awareness of the impossibility to conceal the sexual deadlock, *they strive to do exactly that*. Such an attitude also implies that these films give us a chance to investigate some meaningful questions concerning Antonioni's "negotiations" with the cinematic unconscious. In other words, we have a chance to observe the shaping up of a fascinating confrontation between the domain of filmic representation and its unacknowledged underside – a confrontation whose understanding requires locating apparently insignificant details loaded with symptomatic value.

The first remarkable thing to note is that Antonioni's symptoms express themselves in purely formal terms from the very start of his directing career.

Let us pick a symptomatic shot of *Le amiche* whose mere function appears to be that of unobtrusively linking one sequence to the next. It occurs in the second part of the film, when Cesare (Franco Fabrizi) pays a visit to his fickle lover Momina (Yvonne Furneaux), who had lured him over with a veiled promise of sexual gratification. On his arrival, however, he finds his lover busy entertaining some friends. When the two are finally alone, Antonioni cuts to an external shot of the flat, revealing his intention not to intrude on the intimacy of this encounter (a few years later, he would have no doubt remained with his characters). The point is that this external, deceptively unassuming shot is much more than just a connective between two sequences, for it takes on a noir significance of its own. The camera is placed outside in the evening dusk, slightly tilted upwards, framing the lit window of Momina's flat, through which we catch sight of the silhouettes of the two lovers. Suddenly an unknown man enters the frame, looks up at the window, and slowly makes for the entrance of the building. Perhaps as a result of this unwanted gaze, Cesare moves towards the window and pulls the Venetian blinds, a peremptory gesture which creates an uncanny visual effect, as the shadow of his silhouette is suddenly skewed into a distorted dark blotch and then instantly disappears.

Such a seemingly inconspicuous shot tells us more about Antonioni's film than endless discussions about its sociological content. The simple fact of Cesare's disappearance behind the blinds demands that we rectify substantially our previous line of argumentation. The impossibility of the sexual relationship is here expressed by way of another deadlock, which we have already (apropos of *Blow-up*) identified as a key catalyst of Antonioni's cinema, namely the radical inconsistency of the subject *qua* object of the scopic drive. This is therefore one of the first opportunities we have to realise how Antonioni's cinema concerns itself with *the erasure of the subject*, whether we choose to look at this issue from a formal or content-related perspective. From a formal angle, the apparently meaningless vanishing of Cesare's silhouette foreshadows Antonioni's "fatal attraction" to the blind spot in the picture (the gaze). Here, in fact, the voyeurism of the camera is fully operative, for what the camera gets back from the object of its visual desire (with the presence of the unknown man simply reinforcing the desire to see) is the negativity of the gaze: the camera looks, keeps looking, and its scopic drive is reciprocated by a pure semblance embodying the negative capacity of the gaze.

This early Antonioni already underscores the importance of the "surface of things": reality *is* an image, on condition that this image expresses a potential to uncover the enigmatic presence of the gaze, the repressed kernel of reality itself. In *Le amiche* the "realness" of Rosetta's (Madeleine Fischer) love for Lorenzo (Gabriele Ferzetti) – so overwhelming that it leads up to her suicide – originates in the immaterial image of her portrait: 'I've started to love you as you were painting my portrait [...] I've never felt like that before, you were painting my face [...] and it was as if you were caressing me, without realising it'. Fiction here is already designated as the privileged medium to access the concealed core of the extant, while women become fictional subjects *par excellence*, constantly flirting with the negativity of the Real. In *Cronaca di un amore*, Paola's (Lucia Bosè) "being-there" coincides with the inert presence of her luxurious dresses, so many emphatic masks working as captivatingly insubstantial envelopes for the traumatic emptiness of the self. Antonioni's outlook on the world of Milanese fashion, then, is less a sociological cipher than a fascinated attempt to reveal the strange coincidence of fiction and truth. This is even more evident in *La signora senza camelie*, where the central narrative theme of the contamination between fiction and reality, incarnated in the character of Clara (Lucia Bosè), is functional to the unravelling of the painfully empty truthfulness of fiction. As Clara states apropos of her fictional roles: 'I'm scared when I see myself on screen, I have to repeat to myself ten times every minute "it's me, it's me!"'.

Going back to the question of sexual difference, another observation imposes itself at this stage. At different points in his writing, Lacan claims that the deadlock pertaining to the sexual is not as apocalyptic as it might seem, and can indeed be overcome in the Symbolic. In his *Seminar* on the psychoses he states: 'It is insofar as the function of man and woman is symbolized, it is insofar as it's literally uprooted from the domain of the imaginary and situated in the domain of the symbolic, that any normal, completed sexual position is realized' (Lacan, 2000, p. 177). He refines this stance at the end of *Seminar XI*, where he claims that 'any shelter in which may be established a viable, temperate relation of one sex to the other necessitates the intervention – this is what psycho-analysis teaches us – of that medium known as the paternal metaphor' (Lacan, 1998a, p. 276). Lacan's point is that the drama of sexual dissymmetry can only be staged in the field of the big Other: it is "out there" that the couple can attempt to dodge the Real by externalising it into 'a viable, temperate relation'.

Now, can we relate this avowal of symbolisation to Antonioni's early films? What comes to the fore is that his "paternal metaphors" fail miserably: older husbands such as Enrico (*Cronaca di un amore*) and Gianni (*La signora senza camelie*) cannot provide any viability or relief to the relationship. Not only do Antonioni's couples fail to find a conciliatory solution in the big Other; normally, these relationships are also tragically truncated when one of the two either commits or threatens to commit suicide. Nonetheless, we should not overlook the fact that what is missing at the interpersonal level is recuperated at the structural level: the trauma of intersubjective lack is "absorbed" by narrativisation. Confronted with the dilemma of how to deal with the Real of his filmmaking, Antonioni resorts to inserting his characters into a well-defined narrative context, which allows him "to keep the enemy at a safe distance". While the sexual fracture is clearly not recomposed, its traumatic impact is deflected onto the structure and the reassuringly ambivalent ideological preoccupations it purports.[5] Finally, however, even this attempt at narrative/socio-ideological symbolisation fails, to the extent that Antonioni's early cinema could be said to provide a perfect illustration of the Freudian-Lacanian thesis of the return of the repressed: what is foreclosed by the process of symbolisation inevitably returns to haunt the very consistency of the structure. And my thesis here is that this "ghost of the Real" manifests itself through what I would be tempted to call "formal fetishism".

The primary stylistic features of Antonioni's cinema have been meticulously and eloquently described. His much praised modernism can be summed up with what French critics called *de-dramatisation*, a general avoidance of grandly spectacular and over-dramatic gestures, coinciding with a penchant for extraneation, detachment, understatement, intellectual coldness and rigor.

Even when engaging with a melodramatic plot like *La signora senza camelie*, Antonioni's camera carefully prevents us from identifying with the dramatis personae, or from indulging in sentimentalism. It would be improper and intellectually sluggish, however, to liquidate the question of Antonioni's style with the tautological remark that "this is his method". I would rather suggest that his stylistic detachment functions as a symptom of a deeper anxiety related to the prospect of a shattering encounter with the proverbial object of desire. More exactly, it functions both as a defence against the deadlock of the Real, and as a way to negotiate some kind of compromise with it, which essentially results in its sublimation into autonomous formal configurations completely delivered from the diegetic function of the film.[6]

Furthermore, if we apply Hegel's concept of reflexivity we could maintain that, since it is through form that Antonioni manages to "strike a deal" with the foreclosed dimension of his filmmaking, the filmic content inevitably sets itself up as a grandiose metonymy of form: what is the treatment of such themes as existential aimlessness, lack of purpose, social inertia and stagnation – all characteristic of Antonioni's portrayal of the postwar bourgeois universe – if not a metonymical prefiguration of the director's obsession with form as *objet petit a*, which will explode with *L'avventura*? Content itself ultimately conveys Antonioni's founding obsession with the unconscious side of filmmaking: just as these narratives cannot be fully reconstructed without taking into account their formal excesses, so are these excesses always-already registered in the narrative content.

Let us examine what is arguably the most memorable sequence of *Cronaca di una amore*, Antonioni's first feature film. The two reunited lovers Paola (Lucia Bosè) and Guido (Massimo Girotti) drive out to the countryside in order to plot the murder of Paola's rich and jealous husband Enrico (Ferdinando Sarmi). Suddenly they seem to falter, to lose their resolve. This existential hesitation coincides with the beginning of the famous four-minute long-take of the two characters as they move slowly on a small bridge overlooking a dry canal (the Naviglio), surrounded by a vast, misty and deserted plane. The passage, which echoes a similar long-take in Visconti's *Ossessione* (see Bernardi, 2002, p. 141), has been rightly hailed as paradigmatic of Antonioni's original use of the landscape in terms of its relation to the characters foregrounding it. In this specific case, the barren background both heightens the sense of realism and, more importantly, emphasises metaphorically the mixture of apathy and fear that suddenly seizes the couple. More accurately, the passage reflects the constitutional tension between content and form that typifies Antonioni's filmmaking: the feeling of void generated by the slow 360–degree long-take unobtrusively manipulates our perception of the characters' subjective universe, revealing the emptiness of their bourgeois existence (Paola) and aspirations (Guido); simultaneously, their class-related weariness projects itself on to the landscape, conferring upon it an utterly desolated feel. Antonioni's choices are crucial: rotating on its axis, this single shot determines a remarkably inconspicuous "internal editing" by following the characters' slow movement and dialogue, while avoiding the dramatic effect of shot-reverse-shots and close-ups.[7]

This pivotal sequence confirms that the key to access the content of Antonioni's early cinematography is form, for it is form that reveals the director's attraction to the cinematic Real. The most flagrant example of the function of formalism in *Cronaca di un amore* can be found in the sequence that leads to the one just described: whilst Enrico is testing a fast car on a country road, Guido and Paola, waiting inside another car on the side of the road, realise that they are still in love, and for the first time after their reunion kiss passionately. The rebirth of their love-story is accompanied by an uncanny element in the mise-en-scène: two publicity posters placed on each side of the road and shaped as two enormous bottles of a famous 1950s Italian liqueur ("amaro Cora"). As Cuccu notes, while these posters are historically realistic, at the same time, given the specific emotional tension created by the passage, they cannot fail to appear odd, mysterious and even disquieting (see Cuccu, 1988, p. 36). The reason for this effect, I would add, is that they speak for Antonioni's fundamentally fetishistic fascination with non-symbolic figurations, particularly with the spectrality of modern urban shapes and architectural patterns that, in their purely affirmative efficacy, function as a metonymical sublimation of the non-figurative Real. What we have in this sequence is the emergence of the cinematic unconscious of the sexual relationship, which materialises as a sublimated configuration that provides its positive support to what is beyond representation. This is why these enormous bottles play the role of *objet a*: their presence is correlative to the trans-semantic excess that underscores the entire narrative.

To recapitulate our argument so far: it is not that Antonioni's stylistic mastery is purposely designed to achieve a specific content-related result, but that his obsessive insistence on form is unconsciously and surreptitiously aimed at pinpointing the very libidinal kernel of his cinematic desire, whose fundamental repression allows him to make films. Ultimately, the dialectical tension between form and content is secondary with respect to the self-relating persistence of form, which is why any explanation attempting to locate the disproportioned "Cora" bottles back into symbolic reality misses the significance of their fantasmatic role.

One more twist needs to be added here. Is there not a surprising homology between these bottles as *objet a* of the visual drive, and the same bottles as commodities pure and simple? Significantly, the first time we see Paola and Guido together – when Guido arrives in Milan to inform Paola that she is being followed by a private eye – the encounter is accompanied by a somewhat disproportioned reference to the commodity-form, as Guido is depicted against another enormous publicity poster ("Tessuti Filati"). If we recall Marx's theorisation of commodity fetishism – already employed in our discussion of *Zabriskie Point* – the most fundamental connotation of a commodity is its uncanny aura, not its material status as embodiment of the social relations of production. Marx's key intuition is that the essence of the commodity belongs in its exchange-value rather than in its use-value. This allows us to consolidate our argument on the existence of a "Marxist nerve" in Antonioni's cinema. In terms of commodity criticism, Antonioni is closer to Marx than he would have envisaged himself, for he makes visible how the true secret of the commodity, its irresistible co-optive power, dwells in its form (its *Schein*) rather than in its content. It was Adorno who took the question of the formalistic essence of the commodity to its extreme consequences, when he claimed that the degree of abstraction at work in great art is coterminous with the abstraction of the commodity form; which, in turn, is what prompts Jameson to claim that 'the absolute work of art [...] coincides with absolute commodification', insofar as 'the overwhelming objectivity of the commodity form [...] is syncopated with that objectivity of the work of art which is prior to living subjectivity' (in Jameson, 1990, p. 167). In this respect, the insistence on commodity *qua* pure form, one of the distinguishing features of Antonioni's cinema, can be said to target nothing less than the secret mechanism that propels today's late capitalistic ideology.

In equating the fundamental dimension of modern art and the commodity form, Adorno is keen to emphasise the so-called "predominance of the objective" – which is in effect the theoretical backbone of his entire philosophical production, amounting to an attempt to reconcile materialism with the idealist theme of the subjective mediation of objective reality. My aim, however, is to give Adorno a Lacanian twist, that is to say, to interpret his "object" as *objet a*, the elusive feature that is not only "other" in the sense that it belongs to the impenetrable opacity of matter, but in the more specific sense that its alterity represents the disavowed abstraction stealthily operative in any field of knowledge. Hence, the "Cora" bottles in *Cronaca di un amore* represent both the abstraction underscoring the paradoxical consubstantiality of art and commodity, and the very sublime object that deceptively "bolsters" the space of narrativisation. This formalised feature unravels the mystery of Antonioni's fascination with "the surface of things": what we encounter on this surface is the imperceptible blot that allows for the symbolisation of the fictional space. The supposedly hidden content, the enigma of the narrative, is always-already condensed in a tiny, elusive detail right in front of our eyes.

Along these lines, the most effective way to tackle the central critical concern of Antonioni's formalism is to translate it into proper philosophical terms: is Antonioni's reliance on form not akin to a sort of Kantian transcendentalist strategy, positing the object of his visual desire as an unreachable Other (Kant's *das Ding*), whose elusiveness can only be accounted for in terms of an a priori loss? And if so, does this logic not imply a fundamental melancholy, since it breeds the notion that every empirical object will never coincide with the Thing? Far from being of secondary importance, this question can be regarded as the common theoretical denominator between German idealism, Lacanian psychoanalysis and Marxism. In Lacanian terms, Kant's transcendentalism cannot be disjointed from the problematic of the Real. In fact, Žižek holds that, from an ethico-political prospect, transcedentalising Lacan is equivalent to 'a celebration of failure' (Žižek, 2002c, p. xii). His thesis is that the Lacanian Real does not simply amount to an out of reach Other regulating the symbolic field through its unapproachable presence. Rather, it ought to be conceptualised as a traumatic event, in the precise meaning that encounters with the Real do happen, but they are impossible to make sense of, any attempt to integrate them into a symbolic economy is destined to fail. Thus, asserting that *the Real is impossible* is not enough, for it leads us to a neo-Kantian, deconstructionist, Levinasian/Derridean logic of Otherness, elevating the Other into an unattainable target (with a regulative function). One should instead accomplish the opposite analytical operation and state that *the impossible is Real*.

Within these parameters, my aim is to establish whether Antonioni's formalism actually contrives to impinge upon the Real. On first impression the director would seem to be trapped in the transcendentalist logic of desire and the elusiveness of the object of representation, which implies that the encounter with the Real is endlessly postponed as fundamentally impossible. In Antonioni, one of the clearest metaphorical figuration of this attitude is the image of the staircase, a recurrent visual reference suggesting a kind of "winding up" of the subject around its

Amarcord

own unreachable and empty kernel.[8] This logic is also regularly articulated in most of Fellini's films, which can be seen as fully blown fantasies precisely because the distance between the camera and the impossible Thing is consciously filled by a thick smokescreen of fantasmatic apparitions. In actual fact, one could legitimately claim that the true face of Fellini's earlier pseudo-realistic/sociological films such as *I vitelloni* (Spivs, 1953) and *La dolce vita* (The Sweet Life, 1959) lies in the most hallucinated and deliriously visionary parts of later films like *Giulietta degli spiriti* (Juliet of the Spirits, 1965), *Satyricon* (Fellini Satyricon, 1969), *Casanova* (Fellini's Casanova, 1976) or *E la nave va* (And the Ship Sails On, 1983), where the imaginary thrust is at times so overwhelming that it encroaches upon the fundamental fantasy, activating its traumatic legacy. Generally speaking, however, Fellini's fantasy remains a protective screen.[9]

To focus back on Antonioni's object of desire, I would argue that it re-emerges as the sublimated image of his visual drive right from his early production, finding an outlet in a series of highly formalised objects situated on the surface of our world – such as, for example, the commodity. In any event, another "formalised object" starts stealing the scene in these early films: woman.

3.2 The Lady who wasn't there

With *La signora senza camelie* (1953), Antonioni starts deploying the conspicuous meta-cinematic resources of his filmmaking for the exploration of femininity, opening up a series of interrogations that will remain the focal point of his cinema. The plot is deceptively sentimental, verging on the melodramatic. Clara Manni (Lucia Bosè), a Milanese shop assistant, is turned into a successful actress of commercial films by rich producer Gianni Franchi (Andrea Cecchi), who also takes her as his bride. Increasingly distressed by the fact that his wife features in second-rate productions as a scantily dressed *femme fatale*, Gianni concocts to change Clara's image: he suspends her participation in a melodrama fittingly called *The Woman without Destiny* to recast her as a virginal Joan of Arc. This new lavish production, however, soon turns out to be a colossal box-office flop. Her career seriously damaged, Clara is now forced to play the role of a rich and increasingly unhappy housewife, which leads her into an affair with Nardo (Ivan Desny), a playboy diplomat. Gianni's jealousy, in the meantime, results in his attempted suicide, at which point Clara resolves to leave him in order to start a new life with Nardo. The handsome diplomat, however, soon reveals his true colours: rather than letting a scandal ruin his career, he opts to "return" Clara to her husband. Unhappy with her marriage and rejected by her lover, Clara decides to fend for herself. She is helped by friend and colleague Lodi (Alain Cuny) and begins to study acting, turning down a number of work offers for commercial films. Eventually, after a few months away from the screen, she resolves to approach Gianni, who in the meantime has managed to get over her and is now financing a big production. Despite not holding a grudge against her, Gianni is unable to secure Clara a role in his new film. Instead, he advises her to hang on to her career in undistinguished productions, for, as he puts it, 'actresses age quickly'. Dejected and disenchanted, Clara accepts a part in a second-rate costume drama called *The Slave of the Pyramids* and, succumbing to fate, telephones Nardo offering him to resume their dismal affair.

The most obvious interpretation of the film demands that we read it alongside works of the same period such as Fellini's *Lo sceicco bianco* (The White Sheik, 1951, the script was co-written by Tullio Pinelli and Antonioni himself) and Visconti's *Bellissima* (also made in 1951), which expose the cynicism of the film industry by linking it to the naive idealism of women seduced by the irresistible power of the star system. Clara is surrounded by a number of predatory men, most associated with the film industry, who endeavour to take advantage of her good looks in one way or another, either for sexual/sentimental reasons (Gianni and Nardo) or for purely financial ones (directors and producers). As a victimised female forced to accept her fate in a world dominated by male power and opportunism, Clara seems to fit perfectly into a narrative that indicts what, years later, Guy Debord would dub 'the society of spectacle' (see Debord, 1992). Most critics, particularly Marxist ones, have been quick to underline this dimension of social criticism. Alternatively, *La signora senza camelie* can be viewed as a reflection on the discrepancy between fiction and reality: on the one hand the frivolity and inauthenticity of the fictional world from within the film studio, on the other the passions and tribulations of real life. However, our task here is to resist the temptation of searching for explicit messages (all the more crucially a "social message", which was always, at best, a secondary preoccupation for Antonioni); instead, we shall attempt to locate the unconscious core of this underestimated narrative.

From a psychoanalytic viewpoint, the fact that Clara appears as a victim should instantly set our alarm bells ringing, for victimisation here clearly relies on a displaced knowledge which, if endorsed, would lead us to a radically different perception of the heroine's subject-position. To contextualise and circumscribe this displaced knowledge I propose that we take into account one of Antonioni's main stylistic features, namely his use of *temp morts*, 'chronological gaps of considerable duration' (Chatman, 1985, p. 31) that disrupt the linear development of the narrative. The point is that once we start focusing on these cinematic "knots", Clara's identity can no longer be taken for granted.

Let us take the considerable temporal gap between Gianni's marriage proposal to Clara and the sudden reappearance of the newly-wed couple on the set of the film, whilst the director had been desperately looking for the missing starlet: what is suppressed by this ellipsis is an account of Clara's decision to accept Gianni's proposal, especially if we bear in mind that earlier on she had seemed reluctant to do so. From this angle, Clara suddenly "sheds her sacrificial skin" and, to an extent, becomes responsible for her downfall. The possibility of this reading is somewhat silenced by the logical development of the narrative, precisely because Antonioni knows that the plot has to be secured through the concealment of a certain knowledge: if we were explicitly told that Clara marries a rich producer for opportunism, the main narrative motif would suddenly collapse. To his merit, then, Antonioni's provides us with a key insight into the dialectics of representation: for something to be seen and understood, a part of its content has to be foreclosed.

Nevertheless, to claim that the excluded part is Clara's opportunism would amount to a glaring oversight. What remains foreclosed about Clara's identity is, rather, something that *is and remains unaccountable* (*foreclosed* in the proper Lacanian sense of the term). Not only is the audience denied access to it; it is *Clara herself* who does not seem to be fully aware of the reasons behind her crucial decisions (for example, her choice to marry Gianni)! The general point to make here is that Antonioni sees women as being much more readily in touch with the unconscious than men – in touch, that is, with a form of knowledge that makes itself available only as a traumatic encounter with freedom. In *La signora senza camelie* he often intimates that Clara (who in this respect reminds us of later Antonionian heroines such as Anna in *L'avventura*; Lidia in *La notte*; Vittoria in *L'eclisse*; etc.) is simply detached from the meaning of her actions.

In the last scene of the film, for instance, Clara goes to meet Gianni at the Cinecittà studios to ask him for a part in his new production. How are we to account for this decision? Is she being merely opportunistic? Has she got something to prove to her husband? Is she trying to get back with him after realising that he was the only one who loved her? Those who criticised the film for its confused melodramatic plot and overall lack of clarity are missing the crucial point. The fact that we cannot answer the above questions proves that we have located, lead by Clara (a name by no means meant ironically!), the unconscious side of the narrative. Paradoxically, her determination to re-invent herself as a good actress can only be explained as a desperate attempt *to secure her own identity in fiction*, within the supremely fragile jurisdiction of the image. Consequently, her final decision to accept a role in a second-rate film should appear in a much more ambiguous and deceptive light than we might have thought: Clara has not just reluctantly accepted "the way of the world", the fact that she lacks proper acting talent; on the contrary, her choice suggests that *depth and superficiality coincide* – that the most profound point in the subject is its automaton-like dimension (the script itself stresses this: 'she behaves like an automaton'). No wonder Chatman (1985, p. 29) laments that Clara's behaviour is irritatingly incomprehensible ('even the Laurence Oliviers and Bette Davises of the world have played their share of awful roles')! What he overlooks is the fundamental detail that her decision-making is incomprehensible *pour cause*, for it touches on a disavowed form of knowledge that, if on the one hand permits Antonioni to set up his melodramatic narrative, on the other it boycotts it from within, betraying the real stakes of the director's desire.

Clara's acceptance of a second-rate role ought to be seen as *the very form of her choice*, a gesture aimed at sanctioning her radically fictional status. To fully comprehend this gesture we need to grasp its meta-cinematic significance, in as much as it allows Antonioni to assert the paradoxical superiority of appearances over reality. Clara steps from one symbolic mandate to another: she is a shop-assistant, then an actress, a wife, an unfaithful wife, a drama student, and eventually she is forced to acknowledge the futility of her search for the proverbial "true identity". In this respect, the final shot where she is flattened against the cheap and artificial set of her new film sums up Antonioni's deep-seated conviction that the truth about the subject is, as it were, "hidden on the surface". What fascinates Antonioni is precisely the enigma of superficiality, an enigma that threatens to subvert cinema's representational status.

3.3 OF LOVE LETTERS AND UNDELIVERED MESSAGES

On eloping with her lover Nardo, Clara leaves behind an explanatory letter for her husband. Significantly, what matters here is not the explicit content of the letter (as it is the narrative that suggests it: Clara has fallen in love with another man, she is unhappy in her marriage, etc.); the emphasis, rather, falls on the actual presence of the letter on the table, on the envelope/form containing the message for the heartbroken husband. Immediately before stepping into Nardo's car, Clara tells him about the letter. Cowardly, Nardo reproaches her for being too uncompromising, suggesting that she go back in and tear the letter apart. Despite the fact that Clara *does* rush back inside with the intention of getting rid of the letter, another narrative gap prevents us from knowing whether she actually accomplishes the act or not (only later do we learn that she had opted not to do it). This ellipsis is crucial: its point is not that our non-knowledge (what is repressed in this sequence, i.e. Clara's decision to leave the letter on the table) is to be linked to a certain (more or less hidden) content (the content of the letter), but that this non-knowledge corresponds to the actual letter *qua* pure form, to the presence of a signifier which, in itself, means absolutely nothing, it simply serves as a place-holder for the message. The passage thus illustrates the dialectical function of the unconscious: it is the unconscious (the envelope/form) that determines the conscious content (the message of the letter), and not vice versa. This is one of the meanings of Lacan's famous motto, in his *Seminar* on Poe's 'The Purloined Letter', that 'a letter always arrives at its destination' (see Muller and Richardson, 1988, p. 53): the letter is not the explicit message, but the unconscious desire repressed in the message. In Clara's case, the letter arrives at its destination when Clara hears the news of her husband's attempted suicide.

Italian cinema presents us of course with many other cases of letters that always arrive at their destination. A paradigmatic example, to stay with Antonioni, is the type-written letter read by Lidia (Jeanne Moreau) to Giovanni (Marcello Mastroianni) at the end of *La notte* (The Night, 1961): the very fact that Giovanni, a writer, does not recognise his own message ('who wrote this?'), implies that the message was simply "imprinted" in the form of the letter, i.e. that Giovanni's sophisticated declaration of love to Lidia (the content of the letter) was a mere sham, a pretext to practice writing a romantic piece. No wonder that when the letter truly arrives at its destination, Giovanni, the bearer of the message, suffers a proper shock, which compels him to assume the consequences of his conduct! The letter arrives at its destination when the bearer receives its own message back in inverted form.

Mastroianni also features in a similar case of "unconscious delivery" in Visconti's *Le notti bianche* (White Nights, 1957), an adaptation of Dostoevsky's 1848 short story *White Nights (of a dreamer)*, which narrates an impromptu romance on the streets of Petersburg between an unnamed businessman (the dreamer)

Le notti bianche

and Nastenka, an attractive young woman desperately seeking comfort and advice for her troubled relationship with a man who has not returned from an extended trip after promising to marry her. Visconti's adaptation remains quite faithful to Dostoevsky's narrative, except for the fact that the unnamed Dostoevskian dreamer is now called Mario (Mastroianni), Nastenka is Natalia (Maria Schell), and 19th century Petersburg becomes a spectral studio reconstruction of present-day Livorno (Leghorn).[10] In a decisive passage of the film, Mario offers to deliver Natalia's letter to her fiancée (who, despite having returned to town, had not contacted her), but instead rips it off. After such an impulsive gesture, Mario inevitably develops a feeling of guilt, which becomes unbearable the moment he realises that Natalia has started reciprocating his attentions. When he confesses to her that her letter never reached its destination, she has already decided to forget her old lover and devote herself to Mario. Overwhelmed by joy, Mario takes Natalia on a night trip through the town canals, on a small rowboat; meanwhile, heavy snow starts falling, adding a fairy-tale feel to the new romance. At the end of the enchanted journey through the "white night", however, the mysterious fiancée (Jean Marais) suddenly reappears. As Natalia runs away with him, Mario, his face inundated with tears, pronounces the famous final words of Dostoevsky's novel: 'God bless you for the moment of happiness you gave me, for it was worth an entire life!"

How does Visconti manage to render the subtly masochistic intention of Dostoevsky's hero (a prefiguration of the later "Underground Man"), a lonely man divorced from reality who favours his romantic reveries over their realisation? The key change to the written source has to do with the fate of Natalia's letter: while Dostoevsky's hero dutifully delivers the letter, Mario destroys it, and the allure of Visconti's reading lies in his (unconscious?) intuition that "the letter always arrives at its destination", insofar as the secret message carried by the letter is precisely Mario's unacknowledged (masochistic) desire *for things to go wrong*.[11] As Žižek puts it, 'the real letter is not the message we are supposed to carry but [...] the object in us that resists symbolisation [...] a surplus, a material leftover circulating among the subjects and staining its momentary possessor' (Žižek, 2001b, pp. 7–8). In the space of the long nightly (de)tour, Mario consumes his unconscious desire to deliver Natalia back to her fiancée. The reappearance of Natalia's lover tells us that the letter has finally arrived at its destination: the real purpose of Mario's gesture of tearing the letter apart was Mario's desire to free himself of his attachment to Natalia. First he tries to "escape into guilt", then he simply waits for the reappearance of Natalia's lover. Contrary to the standard interpretations, the film (and the short-story) is not so much about a romantic dreamer bent on endlessly postponing the encounter with reality so that he can keep fantasising about it. It is rather about a man who unconsciuosly escapes from the Real dilemma that pertains to the sexual relationship. Fantasy seems to function, for him, not as a way to keep his desire alive, but as a protective shield against the explosive encounter with the gap of sexual difference.

However, throughout the film Mario's behaviour remains thoroughly ambiguous. In fact, in the most captivating sequence of the entire film, which is set in a (disturbingly promiscuous) dance hall where couples perform their numbers as if spellbound, transfixed by the spectral and sexually-charged atmosphere, the Mastroianni character comes very close to the traumatic *tuché* with the Real. In this sequence Mario desperately tries to imitate the hauntingly beautiful style of a handsome male dancer who has caught Natalia's eye. He bravely steps into the centre of the dance floor, performs a series of clumsy moves, falls flat on his face making a fool of himself, and yet he persists in what becomes an embarrassingly hopeless show and impossible enterprise. Far from qualifying the behaviour of an idealistic dreamer, Mario's dancing performance (which we do not find in Dostoevsky's story) stands as a moving and convincing illustration of the Lacanian ethics of the Real: the subject must try to make the impossible happen, must attempt to tamper with what threatens to deprive him of that minimum of inner balance which allows him to have a certain idea of who he is.

3.4 *La Femme n'existe pas!*

With *L'avventura* (1959) Antonioni for the first time abandons any attempt to displace the central impasse of his filmmaking onto elements of narrativisation, which is here a secondary preoccupation. After *Il grido*, he openly accepts the challenge posed by his own desire to push cinema beyond the strictures of symbolisation, beyond conventional forms of cinematic rationalisation such as dialogue and genre. If Aldo's fall from the tower starts undermining the linearity of the narrative, Anna's soundless, implosive disappearance radicalises that gesture by placing itself truly beyond narrative comprehension, outside a meaningful symbolic context, to the extent that it might be said to encroach upon the unconscious abyss of the text. From a Lacanian angle, the only possible answer to the standard question "where has Anna gone?" is that "she has plummeted into the film's unconscious". All other attempts at explaining this event, including those given by the characters, are to be regarded as mere fantasies, whose primary aim is to conceal the founding narrative deadlock (fantasy always comes into play where interpretations fails – which is why, incidentally, it is an eminently political dimension). Perhaps for the first time in the history of cinema a character fully "comes to be where the cinematic unconscious is", over-identifying with the lack that sustains the filmic system of symbolic representations.[12] Roland Barthes was right when he mentioned 'fragility' as one of the three modernist characteristics of Antonioni's work (see Chatman and Fink, 1989, p. 212; Barthes, 1988), but only as long as we regard this fragility as the effect of a *stricto sensu* psychotic intervention into the vertiginous void of the image.

Bearing in mind our previous account of editing, we could say that the structural focus of *L'avventura* is the invisible line that separates the "before" from the "after" of Anna's disappearance. What happens in between Anna's last words to Sandro, her fiancée, and the beginning of the next sequence, when the remaining characters slowly come to realise that she has gone missing? The trap to avoid, of course, is to think that she has gone missing *somewhere in the actual text*. Instead, it is much more fruitful to bring the analysis to the meta-cinematic level, suggesting that *she has slipped in between the junctures of the text*, in those underlying "cracks of editing" whose invisibility opens up the space for representation. The episode of the shark also points in this direction. Why does Anna, whilst swimming with her friends, suddenly shout that she is being threatened by a shark if, as she tells Claudia a few minutes later, that danger never existed in the first place? Despite all the metaphorical interpretations that the figure of the shark may evoke (as we know from many a reading of Steven Spielberg's *Jaws*, 1975), and despite the fact that Anna is effectively a bored and spoilt bourgeois woman who might well be "looking for kicks", I would suggest that the fantasmatic shark is quite simply a symptom of Anna's unconscious desire to disappear from the text.

This brings us to the fundamental challenge of Antonioni's cinematic desire: how to represent absence. In the brilliant sequence that follows Anna's disappearance, the director recurs to what Kant, in the *Critique of Judgement*, calls the dynamically sublime in nature, that is to say, the immeasurable might of nature whose manifestation causes in man a feeling of helplessness so great and boundless that it defies imagination. Antonioni's sublime is exactly of the kind discussed by Kant, as Anna's vanishing coincides with a sudden worsening of the conditions of the sea, followed by a violent thunderstorm and even a hurricane.[13] Kant, of course, resolves the failure of aesthetic imagination vis-à-vis the natural sublime by bringing into contention the moral law, with its ability to absorb the shock of this failure and recoup it in the unbearable pressure of the moral injunction to do one's duty: precisely because the feeling of the sublime conjures up the impossibility of reaching the Thing, we must submit to the moral law. However, contravening the solution indicated by Kant, Antonioni sticks to the very negativity introduced by the Kantian "inadequacy of the imagination". Let us consider that, precisely in its sensuous connotations, Kant's sublime acquires the shape of a miraculous object through which the impossible dimension of the Thing shines – as Žižek explains in the following passage:

> The Sublime is therefore the paradox of an object which, in the very field of representation, provides a view, in a negative way, of the dimension of what is unrepresentable. It is a unique point in Kant's system, a point at which the fissure, the gap between phenomenon and Thing-in-itself, is abolished in a negative way, because in it the phenomenon's very inability to represent the Thing adequately *is inscribed in the phenomenon itself* (Žižek, 1992, p. 203).

Given that the sublime coincides, effectively, with *objet a* (insofar as, to say it with Lacan, it represents *the paradox of an object elevated to the dignity of a Thing*),[14] should we not argue that, in *L'avventura*, the truly sublime object, the mediator between the phenomenal world and the impossible Thing, is Anna herself? In other words, the miraculous connection with the Thing is engendered by Anna, who disappears and thus brings about… what, exactly?

The shocking effect of Anna's effacement, to go back to Pascal Bonizer's excellent definition, is 'the disappearance of the disappearance of Anna', i.e. a kind of "loss of loss": if a "simple" disappearance means that someone has gone missing and can, at least in principle, be found, "disappearance of disappearance" implies that what has gone missing is Nothing – that the object of the search was always-already missing, since it is primordially lost. Does this mean that Anna never existed? From the start of the film we are presented with a quintessential case of feminine hysteria: what does Anna want? Like most of Antonioni's heroines, Anna is troubled by the elusiveness of her desire. Notably, she constantly complains (to her father and to her friend Claudia) that there is something wrong with her relationship to Sandro, and yet she is unable to locate the problem and act upon it, to the extent that she prefers to elude it through sex.[15] In other words, it is not enough to say that Anna is an enigma to the people around her, for we could surmise that Anna's desire remains an enigma to Anna herself, since Antonioni never allows for a hint of self-consciousness to emerge. Instead, he suggests that the mystery of his character's desire cannot be explained. Anna's desire projects us into a bottomless abyss which is *nothing* in the precise sense that it determines the disappearance of the mystery itself (as we always start from the presupposition that every mystery has or requires a solution). Oddly enough, the only plausible solution is that there was no enigma in the first place, in the sense that Anna, *qua* Lacanian *Femme*, simply does not exist: her elusive essence, the core of her desire, coincides with *the very void that "erases her disappearance" from the narrative*. We should therefore endorse the properly Hegelian paradox here: the failure of the subject to live up to its notion bears witness to the inherent weakness of the notion itself – that is to say, Antonioni's feminine subject *is* fundamentally empty.

It seems pointless to try and develop a critical reading of the film (or indeed of Antonioni's cinema) by questioning ethical attitudes attached to gender representation. To discuss whether Antonioni's camera is more or less phallic ('the supreme technological embodiment and extension of the already powerful male gaze', Brunette, 1998, p. 38) than Rossellini's or Fellini's, is already a way to avoid the central deadlock of sexual difference. Antonioni's aim is definitely *not* that of emphasising the priority of the masculine over the feminine. He focuses instead on the impossibility of the sexual relationship, a conviction that arises from his perception that masculinity is defined by phallic enjoyment, whereas femininity implies the possibility of a subversive encounter with the Real of desire beyond the Phallus.[16] We are dealing here with Lacan's (in)famous "formulas of sexuation", which in my opinion find a clear cinematic exemplification in Antonioni's portrayal of sexual difference.

L'avventura

To begin with, Antonioni's males are all invariably alienated, i.e., split between their phallic function (their predatory instinct towards women) and symbolic role (their career, economic and social status, moral and intellectual convictions, etc.).[17] His female characters, on the other hand, are generally depicted as hysterical individuals (radically unsure about their, as well as the other's, desire), with a strong tendency towards psychosis – a condition that Antonioni endows with a rebellious potential. With *L'avventura*, the schism of sexual difference becomes particularly prominent, and every couple can be seen as providing evidence for it: Sandro and Anna, Sandro and Claudia, Giulia and Corrado, Raimondo and Patrizia, the Sicilian pharmacist and his wife from Viterbo. With the following *La notte* and *L'eclisse*, as we will see, this schism acquires a properly compulsive magnitude.

For the time being, we should insist that, in Antonioni, sexual difference is Real in the precise sense that it is a universal, indivisible and ineliminable surplus parasitising every relationship between the sexes. Only if we start from the Lacanian assumption that the bar of sexual difference is an

L'avventura

ontological fact can we appreciate the immanent stoicism implicit in Antonioni's understanding of love. Let us take the closing shot of *L'avventura*, where the emotional deadlock between Claudia and Sandro is actually visualised as the sharp contrast between the cement wall filling up Sandro's side of the picture, and the view of Mount Etna behind Claudia. The director himself stated apropos of this finale: 'I really don't know if the relationship between these two halves will endure or not, though it is quite evident the two protagonists will remain together and not separate. The girl will definitely not leave the man; she will stay with him and forgive him. For she realises that she too, in a certain sense, is somewhat like him' (in di Carlo and Tinazzi, 1996, p. 34). Elsewhere he added that the only way for his two characters to stay together is by 'establishing a relationship based on reciprocal compassion, or comprehension, which implies a form of resignation that is not weakness, but rather the only force allowing them to remain together, to stay alive, to be opposed to catastrophe' (in Tinazzi, 1976, p. 83). It seems to me that at the heart of this understanding of love there is none other than the director's full awareness of the impossibility of the sexual relationship, which Žižek sums up as follows:

> In so far as sexual difference is a Real that resists symbolisation, the sexual relationship is condemned to remain an asymmetrical non-relationship in which the Other, our partner, prior to being a subject, is a Thing, an "inhuman partner"; as such, the sexual relationship cannot be transposed into a symmetrical relationship between pure subjects. The bourgeois principle of contract between equal subjects can be applied to sexuality only in the form of the *perverse* – masochistic – contract in which, paradoxically, the very form of balanced contract serves to establish a relationship of domination' (Žižek, 1994, p. 109).

If therefore, due to the different modalities in which man and woman are internally split (alienated), sexual antagonism cannot be eliminated, the only way to achieve love between two individuals is to establish 'a relationship of "partnership" that is animated by a different, non-sexual goal' (Žižek, 1994, p. 153). Sandro and Claudia seem to arrive at this conclusion, for they realise what other couples in Antonioni's earlier films had not realised: that the 'catastrophe' (in Antonioni's words) of sexual difference can only be overcome through 'reciprocal compassion, or comprehension'. This implicitly validates Žižek's claim that 'I am truly in love not when I am simply fascinated by the agalma ["treasure", *objet a*] in the other, but when I experience the other, the object of love, as frail and lost, as lacking "it", and my love none the less survives this loss' (Žižek, 1994, p. 104). Or even, in a more militant fashion:

> Today, more than ever, the lesson of Marguerite Duras's novels is pertinent: the way – the *only* way – to have an intense and fulfilling personal (sexual) relationship is not for the couple to look into each other's eyes, forgetting about the world around them, but, while holding hands, to look together outside, at a third point (the Cause for which both are fighting, to which both are committed) (Žižek, 2003, p. 38).[18]

Prior to this conclusion, however, the catastrophic Real of sexual difference is often wilfully confronted in Antonioni's mature films, as Anna's choice emphatically proves. In fact, can we not claim that the common denominator between *L'avventura*, *La notte*, and *L'eclisse* is their fascination with the abyss opened up by Anna's disappearance? The representation of the Real of sexual difference returns in the extraordinary final sequence of *La notte*, and particularly in the conclusive tracking shot that slowly takes us from the desperate embrace between Giovanni and Lidia (which repeats the open-ended finale of *L'avventura*) to the emptiness of the park – an emptiness that resonates with a piece of jazz ambiguously situated between the diegetic and the non-diegetic. In *L'eclisse*, the passage from the dramatic evocation of the impossibility of the relationship to impossibility pure and simple is even more manifest, since at the end the couple is simply erased from their environment.

The fundamental role played by the Real of sexual difference, which supports Antonioni's search for the filmic unconscious, entails the endorsement of the "mad choice" implicit in psychosis. The point that critics have generally missed is that Anna's quintessentially psychotic contraction is structurally tantamount to the basic revolutionary gesture, for it breaks the narrative stalemate and opens the space for a distinctly different symbolic configuration: it is her vanishing "into the Real of film" that sets up the relationship between Sandro and Claudia, despite all the difficulties that such a new beginning involves.

However, perhaps things are not this simple in *L'avventura*. If Antonioni's originality lies in his shifting the emphasis from the question of Anna's disappearance to the development of the relationship between Claudia and Sandro (which, one might add, was latently active from the beginning), it is also true that this shift of perspectives does not happen seamlessly. More precisely, the second part of the film appears to revert to a typically Kantian transcendentalist mode, in as much the director re-inscribes the lost object (Anna) into the story-line *precisely as a loss*, a ghostly presence whose insistence in the field of representation hystericises the field over again. Anna becomes nothing less than a Kantian ghost, lingering in between the phenomenal and the noumenal world.[19] Her eerie presence is demonstrated with particular efficacy when Sandro and Claudia arrive at the newly built and yet abandoned location near the baroque Sicilian village of Noto. As they leave the empty, sun-beaten piazza, Antonioni cuts to a long shot of Sandro's car taken from a narrow alley in the shade, with the camera slowly advancing and nevertheless remaining concealed, so as to produce the effect of an unseen gaze. Is it Anna looking? Although we never find out, she is clearly alluded to as a spectral presence/absence hanging over the new couple's attempt to develop a meaningful relationship. The very choice of a ghostly setting adjacent to Noto, in as much as this name literally means "known", uncannily suggests that Anna is interfering from an "unknown", unconscious/Real domain situated somewhere at the very boundary of the text.

The return of the lost object, the Lacanian *fantasme* that conditions Sandro and Claudia's arduous struggle to detach themselves from the past (exactly the same type of malaise that affects Paola and Guido in *Cronaca di un amore*), prompts Antonioni to introduce a second traumatic event, whose significance has been regularly missed by critics. The point is that the first encounter with the Real of sexual difference (Anna's disappearance) *must be repeated* in a second shattering encounter, which takes place in the last scene of the film, when Claudia discovers Sandro in a post-coital embrace with Gloria Perkins, a high-society prostitute-writer. *This* is the key event of the film, the displaced and yet fundamental traumatic kernel that allows the couple, at least potentially, to "lose the loss of Anna", to rid themselves of her spectral gaze, and thus truly invest in a new relationship. I am referring here to Hegel's theory of repetition (in history), often popularised by Žižek (see for example Žižek, 1992, pp. 131–49). In the excerpt below Žižek's analysis of repetition could well be read as an acute elucidation of Antonioni's film:

> The crucial point is here the changed symbolic status of an event. When it erupts for the first time, an event is experienced as a contingent traumatism, as an intrusion of a certain non-symbolized real. It is only through its repetition that this event is recognized in its symbolic necessity […]. It is not, then, only that people need time to understand, to grasp, it is not only that in its first form of appearance, the event […] was too traumatic for people to grasp its real signification. The misrecognition of its first advent is immediately "internal" to its symbolic necessity, it is an immediate constituent of its final recognition. To put it in a traditional way: the first murder […] opened up the guilt, and it was this guilt, this debt, which was the real driving force of the repetition – the event did not repeat itself because of some objective necessity, independent of our subjective inclination and thus irresistible, but because its repetition was a repayment of our symbolic debt (in Ragland-Sullivan and Bracher, 1991, p. 194).

With reference to the final scene of *L'avventura*, then, the main enigma we are dealing with concerns Sandro's betrayal: why does he spend the night with Gloria Perkins? Reducing everything to either pure contingency or Sandro's rapaciousness would be far too simplistic. Much more productive, however paradoxical this may sound, is to read his betrayal as an ethical act whose shock potential aims at the cancellation of the couple's debt towards Anna – at the liquidation of Anna's ghost. What ought to be acknowledged is that Sandro "wants" this second trauma, for he unconsciously knows that it is only through such a risky repetition of the encounter with the Real that he can try and convert the perception of the radical contingency of the first trauma into a necessary event, thereby legitimising himself as Claudia's fiancée. Put differently, only by endorsing the radical freedom implicit in the Real of sexual difference is he able to detach himself, and Claudia, from their "perverse" attachment to the enigma of Anna's disappearance, thus creating the viable conditions for a fresh start.

In conclusion, it is the Real of *jouissance* that leads Sandro and Claudia out of their impasse, as *jouissance* here implies a repetition of the first failure to make sense of Anna's disappearance. The miracle accomplished by such "repetitions in the Real" is that the abyssal openness of contingency is retroactively posited as necessary. From this perspective, *L'avventura*'s finale invites us to draw a surprising parallel with Pasolini's typical endorsement of wretchedness. Sandro's self-destructive act of betrayal obeys the classic Kierkegaardian *topos* of the identification with the scandalous and humiliated Christ on the cross, for only through such a radicalisation of failure as the endorsement of radical subjective destitution, can the symbolic network be radically reactivated.[20]

At this stage it becomes evident that Antonioni's intention in *L'avventura* is definitely *not* that of deploring the alienating power of contemporary society, nor of lamenting the audacity of modern individuals who have grown insensitive towards the tragic. His intention is rather to criticise the modern subjects' *inability to forget* (in the truly Nietzschean sense of the term).[21] In his criticism of the romantic attitude of guilt, melancholy and nostalgia, Antonioni demonstrates how his cinema hinges on an anti-humanistic rejection of the traditional vision of man as a fixed entity anchored in reason and morality. If there is essentialism in Antonioni, it is the essentialism of the unconscious, of the absolute impenetrability that qualifies the most intimate core of the subject. The most convincing piece of evidence for this reading of subjectivity is contained in the statement circulated by Antonioni himself at Cannes film festival in 1961, when his film debuted. Here, Antonioni states that his characters reflect the utterly inadequate moral standards of modern man:

> For even though we know that the ancient codes of morality are decrepit and no longer tenable, we persist, with a sense of perversity that I would only ironically define as pathetic, in remaining loyal to them. The moral man who has no fear of the scientific unknown is today afraid of the moral unknown. Starting out from this point of fear and frustration, his adventure can only end in a stalemate (in Chatman and Fink, 1989, pp. 177–79).

Do we need a more explicit defence of the subversive potential stored in the unconscious? The 'moral unknown' of which Antonioni speaks is nothing but the empty centre around which his films (starting from *L'avventura*) *explicitly* rotate, prompting us to endorse a traumatic encounter with the Real that, alone, can unlock the stalemate. The standard view of Antonioni as the quintessentially modernist director whose artistic sensibility is correlative to the classic hermeneutic deadlock – the existential impasse between the aspiration to truth and the impossibility of reaching it – needs therefore to be reviewed. Far from being a melancholic pessimist or a cold aesthete cynically embracing a deterministic vision of the world, he is driven by a passionate search for the truth, provided we are willing to conceptualise truth as the unacknowledged element that *ex-sists* in (any) symbolic representation.

As anticipated, this search for truth depends on the director's ability to focus on non-symbolic figurations within a given narrative. It also implies the progressive denouement of the Cartesian subject as empty, and the consequent privilege accorded to landscape, with which the empty subject of the unconscious entertains an utterly enigmatic relationship. Let us take the case of Antonioni's use of actors, which is in many ways similar to Pasolini's. When he claims that 'the cinema actor must not understand, he must be' (for 'the more his effort is intuitive, the more he will appear spontaneous', in Tinazzi, 1976, p. 49), is he not reiterating, almost *verbatim*, the Lacanian theme of the separation between "thinking" and "being"? The reason why his characters are not instructed about the plot, and are rather treated as "objects" by the director,[22] can be found in Lacan, who tells us that "thinking" pertains to consciousness, whilst "being" is a prerogative of the unconscious. We are therefore back to the original question: Antonioni's subject is, essentially, the Lacanian *Femme*, since 'women constitute a thinner filter to reality than men' (Antonioni in Miccichè, 1980). This claim should be taken very seriously indeed, for the way in which Antonioni's female characters reflect reality is, ultimately, *by matching void with void*, by "coming to be" where the Real is. What better reading of Anna's gesture of self-contraction than Lacan's controversial statement that 'if the sexual relationship doesn't exist, there aren't any ladies' (Lacan, 1998b, p. 57)

3.5 MIMESIS AND SUBLIMATION

By and large critics agree in reading Antonioni's early 1960s trilogy as a comprehensive attempt at screening the reification of human relationships in late-capitalist Italy. It is widely acknowledged that themes, characters, settings and environments in these films all partake in the representation, however ambiguous and problematic, of the loss of identity of the contemporary subject – and particularly of the spiritual erosion of the bourgeoisie, the class directly linked to production. Antonioni himself has always confirmed that these films deal with a historically determined sense of crisis (see Antonioni, 2001, pp. 20–46, 56–65, 69–95, 245–50). Moving beyond sociological observations, however, I have so far been arguing that ideology, in Antonioni, should not be looked for in the explicit narrative content, but mainly in the aesthetic dimension, *provided we regard the latter as the recipient of displaced unconscious drives*. This is nowhere more evident than in *La notte* and, particularly, in *L'eclisse*, the most formalistic of Antonioni's films.

One way to approach formalism in these two films is by revisiting Theodor Adorno's notion of mimesis. As is well known, in Adorno mimesis does not indicate the rationally conceived imitation of the external world, the naive referentialism adopted by naturalist or realist aesthetics that brought a sickening feeling to Roland Barthes' stomach (see Barthes, 1970, p. 145), and has since then been dismissed by post-structuralism as an absurd faith in the fixed meaning of reality. Possibly inspired by Benjamin's brief 1933 essay 'On the mimetic faculty' (see Benjamin, 1989, pp. 332–36), Adorno keeps faith with mimetic behaviour as 'the nonconceptual affinity of a subjective creation with its objective and unposited other' (Adorno, 1984, p. 80). In contrast to the false mimesis imposed by the culture industry, whereby everything human is struck with the bane of identity, art's mimetic impulse provides, in one of Adorno's favourite quotations, a 'promesse du bonheur', a promise of happiness.[23] Aesthetic mimesis, therefore, becomes the locus for the articulation of a crucial utopian urge. Fully aware of Schelling's lesson, Adorno believes that art can accommodate reconciliation as a fleeting, immensely fragile formal configuration evoking the material unity of subject and nature. By the same token, he draws on Freud's unconscious to define his notion of aesthetic mimesis as 'all that has been violently lopped off by centuries of civilisation' (Adorno, 1984, p. 465), which implies that 'to this day rationality has never been fully realised' (Adorno, 1984, p. 453).

But how relevant is this philosophical argumentation for the comprehension of Antonioni's cinema? Significantly, in his essay 'Transparencies on film' Adorno briefly referred to Antonioni's style. Despite his well-known denigration of the film-industry, in the above essay he sought to uncover an emancipatory potential in the medium itself by defending a cinematic style that he considered analogous to the interior monologue technique in writing. Choosing Antonioni to articulate his point, he wrote:

> The most plausible theory of film technique, that which focuses on the movement of objects, is both provocatively denied and yet preserved, in negative form, in the static character of films like Antonioni's *La notte*.[24] Whatever is "uncinematic" in this film gives it the power to express, as if with hollow eyes, the emptiness of time. Irrespective of the technological origins of the cinema, the aesthetics of film will do better to base itself on a subjective mode of experience which film resembles and which constitutes its artistic character. [...] As the

objectifying recreation of this type of experience, film may become art. The technological medium par excellence is thus intimately related to the beauty of nature (Adorno, 2001, p 180).

As Gertrud Koch (1993) has shown, and as it is clear from the quoted passage, Adorno truly believed that film had the potential to wriggle out of its commodity status. Praising Antonioni's inclination to freeze narrative movement in order to force it to implode in a constellation of mimetic fragments, Adorno was consciously criticising the representational character of Hollywood cinema as well as of realist aesthetics.[25] What is particularly significant for our argument is that the viewer's emancipation from the reductionist realism of the film industry is linked to cinema's potential to evoke a mimetic dimension that is 'intimately related to the beauty of nature'. In *Aesthetic Theory*, Adorno writes that natural beauty is 'undefinable' as it 'flashes out, only to disappear when one tries to pin it down'; he then adds that art should not 'imitate nature [...] but rather natural beauty as such' (Adorno, 1984, p. 107). In view of this, I argue that Adorno's appreciation of Antonioni's work must have stemmed from the latter's ability to conjure up this notion of natural beauty through a fleetingly enigmatic and nonconceptual *mode of appearance*, that is, through what Lacan calls *objet a*. Ultimately, in fact, Adorno's mimesis and Lacan's *objet a* both designate the breaking point of a given signifying field, whether it is the symbolic order (Lacan) or the domain of instrumental rationality (Adorno).

Let us take the long, experimental opening sequence of *L'eclisse*, which focuses on the break-up between Vittoria (Monica Vitti), a woman in her twenties, and Riccardo (Francisco Rabal), a writer in his thirties. The sequence is characterised by Vittoria's anguished failure at coming to terms with her emotional drainage, as well as Riccardo's morose ineptitude in responding to it. Antonioni's minimalist long-takes convey a heavy feeling of impasse, imprisonment and estrangement. As the camera slowly pans over various apparently insignificant objects scattered in the room, the viewer realises that he/she is denied any assistance in accessing the narrative. It is a reflexive cinematography, made of limited and obscure dialogues, ambient noises and long, static takes that seem unrelated to any plausible attempt at signification. Indeed, the sequence can be regarded as a classic example of Antonioni's ability to sabotage narrative continuum and cinematic logic from within the shot, by progressively eroding the conventional perception of space and time. The mimetic tension is created precisely by Antonioni's penchant for congealing the narrative into apparently meaningless, lifeless formal configurations, which lend his films their oft-noted coolness and abstraction. However, my argument is that the extremely formalistic character of this opening, with its mimetic focus on insignificant objects, is nothing but a way to cope with the impossibility of (representing) the sexual relationship, Antonioni's crucial thematic concern – to the extent that the two lovers are actually objectified as zombie-like creatures unable to communicate.

The Lacanian reference that springs to mind apropos of these "stylised zombies" is the section of *Seminar VII* referring to Antigone's relegation into the domain 'between the two deaths' (see Lacan, 1999, pp. 270–83) – that is, between symbolic death (exclusion from the community) and real death. My claim is that Vittoria belongs precisely in this suspended zone, which in Lacan designates the intervention of the death-drive, 'the dimension of what horror fiction calls the "undead", a strange, immortal, indestructible life that persists beyond death' (Žižek, 2000a, p. 294). From the initial break-up sequence to the final effacement of the characters, *L'eclisse*, more than any other film by Antonioni, concerns itself with this estranged place in between Symbolic and Real.

This is confirmed by the wonderful opening sequence of *La notte*, where the main characters (Lidia and Giovanni) are depicted as they descend the Pirelli Building in Milan in an external lift, entering what Lidia calls 'the domain of the living dead'. It is a descent into hell that will fully accomplish itself with the couple's participation in the opulent summer party thrown by the Milanese industrialist Gherardetti. If in the opening sequence of *L'eclisse* the impossibility of the relationship between the sexes appeared utterly formalised, here it is still partially sustained by external narrative elements: after the opening shot of the lift, perfectly balanced between its mesmerising formalism (the reflection of the cityscape on the glass of the modern lift) and its metaphorical significance (the couple's descent into hell), Giovanni and Lidia pay a visit to their moribund friend Tommaso (Bernard Wicky), an embittered intellectual who languishes in a hospital bed with an incurable disease. The point to note is the way in which the narrative "excess" of this sequence, namely the crisis in the relationship between Giovanni and Lidia, is displaced onto specific formal coordinates, as the next sequence of Lidia's solitary walk through Milan will confirm.

However, we may also gather from two main episodes that the traumatism inherent in the failed relationship is still disguised through narrativisation here: firstly, Giovanni's double encounter with the neurotic nymphomaniac, whose disproportioned desire he willingly complies with until the arrival of two nurses; secondly, the less obvious but equally effective hint at Tommaso's love for Lidia, who indeed leaves the hospital before her husband presumably to avoid inflicting further distress on his suffering friend. Nevertheless, despite the presence of these "markers" which (timidly) try to provide a minimum of narrative depth, the non-representational status of the sexual impasse between Giovanni and Lidia tends to acquire a certain formalistic autonomy, as the shot of Lidia gazing out of the open window at an helicopter streaking across the cityscape demonstrates. What we have in this shot is an anticipation of the main formal concern of both *La notte* and *L'eclisse*: the visualisation of a mysterious mimetic relationship between femininity and the modern city.

In *L'eclisse*, mimesis is synonymous with the eclipse of the characters – or their figurative merging into the urban environment. Antonioni's typical shot from behind the female characters (*di spalle*) not only creates a gulf, a baffling distance between them and the viewer, but more crucially suggests their strange complicity with the object of their hidden gaze. This underlying intention already emerges in full in the highly stylised opening of the film. If the slowness and unnatural movement of both cameras and characters create a feeling of stasis, this is ultimately aimed at de-realising the two lovers, for their figures, as anticipated, are progressively turned into lifeless shapes. This becomes particularly poignant when the back of Vittoria's head, forming a semicircle at the bottom of the shot, is juxtaposed to Riccardo's figure as he is sat facing her, with his face pale and expressionless. Apart from the metaphorical reference to

Riccardo's inability to understand Vittoria, this shot also prompts us to question the actual existence of the characters, especially as a section of Vittoria's head is eventually superimposed to Riccardo's unnaturally motionless body. Not only are we forced to perceive the fragility of the modern subject (particularly Riccardo), but most of all we witness its evanescence, which is to be read as correlative to the Real of sexual difference.

Later on in the same scene we see Vittoria drawing the living-room curtain to look outside. This is a crucial shot that perfects the one of Lidia looking at the helicopter, summing up Antonioni's representation of femininity: Vittoria's figure is framed against a wide rectangular window, rigorously from the back, while outside looms an oddly shaped water tower resembling a still of the mushroom effect created by the explosion of the atomic bomb. The symbolic meaning of this shot is fairly obvious: Vittoria's outward gaze suggests her attempt to escape the claustrophobic atmosphere in Riccardo's flat, but all she finds is a reminder of atomic danger, a particularly pressing threat at the start of the 1960s.[26] Yet, apart from reinforcing the no-escape symbolism, this shot also testifies to Antonioni's obsessive preoccupation with the form, especially in relation to femininity. For a few seconds Vittoria's silhouette is flattened out and situated right next to the water tower, looking at it, thus suggesting a mysterious correspondence between the shape of her body, her gaze, and the abstract architecture outside.

There are two implications to note regarding this correspondence: firstly, it confirms that Antonioni's *objet a* has to do with a formalistic obsession involving women and landscapes, or cityscapes; secondly, it alludes to what Lacan calls feminine *jouissance* 'beyond the phallus': 'There is a jouissance that is hers, that belongs to that "she" that doesn't exist and doesn't signify anything. There is a jouissance that is hers about which she herself perhaps knows nothing if not that she experiences it – that much she knows' (Lacan 1998b, p. 74). If Antonioni's *objet a* is a formalistic concretion of femininity, this concretion is homologous to an act of sublimation, a formal configuration founded on the assumption that feminine *jouissance* is indefinable, for it is 'a good that is not caused by a little *a*' (Lacan, 1998b, p. 77). While masculine sexuality hinges on *objet a*, feminine sexuality in Lacan has a chance to enter the realm beyond the phallus (i.e. beyond the rigid exclusionary logic that sustains masculine sexuality), and it is this feminine realm that Antonioni's films of the early 1960s focus on, allowing the male director to encroach upon the unfathomable Real of feminine *jouissance*.

This crucial shift from male to female desire is what both *La notte* and *L'eclisse* are about. The long scene of the summer party, in *La notte*, is aptly conceived against the background the radical dissymmetry between masculine and feminine desire. Whilst Giovanni is courting Valentina (Monica Vitti), the daughter of the rich Milanese industrialist, Lidia prefers to remain aloof. Later she is told about Tommaso's death, she mourns him quietly and then, all of a sudden, inexplicably, her mood changes: she starts enjoying the party to the extent that she happily consents to sneak away with Roberto, a perfect stranger who had eyed her up since her arrival. Despite the fact that after sustained flirting she turns down Roberto with the classic 'I'm sorry, I can't', we are left in the dark as to what actually happens between them, since Antonioni cuts back to Giovanni's story, suturing Lidia and Roberto back in the narrative only at a much later stage. If Giovanni's desire is clearly spelt out as pertaining to the phallic kind, Lidia's remains radically enigmatic right through to the very end.

La notte

When, on leaving the party at dawn the disconsolate couple meander through the park, Lidia's intentions finally seem to become clear, as she tells Giovanni that she does not love him anymore, that she only feels pity for him. Upon realising that he is about to lose her, Giovanni desperately tries to embrace her.[27] At first Lidia resists him, but eventually she appears to give in (seemingly starting to return Giovanni's embrace and kisses). As the open ending suggests, however, the truth about Lidia's desire remains utterly concealed, and ultimately it is this fascinating kernel of non-knowledge that Antonioni sublimates into form. In this brilliantly constructed finale, the Real of the sexual relationship is deflected onto two main formal features: two trees in the park, and the jazz music played by the band outside the Gherardettis' mansion. In one of the last shots of the film Giovanni and Lidia are framed in an artificially rigid position next to two tree trunks, whose presence creates the effect of an abstract composition while simultaneously suggesting a metaphorical parallel with the couple, since one is perfectly straight and the other curved, replicating Giovanni's slightly unnatural posture. Then, as the final tracking shot moves from the embraced couple lying on the ground to the haunting emptiness of the park, the jazz piece returns and the film ends. The status of this music could be said to constitute the most ambiguous element of the finale, since it remains suspended between the diegetic and the non-diegetic. The detail not to be missed here is Lidia's comment on the persistence of the band, who have kept playing through the whole night: 'do they think it's going to be a different day if they continue playing?' The somewhat absurd insistence of this music functions precisely as the medium through which the Real of the sexual relationship uncannily materialises: the impossibility of the relationship is sublimated into jazz.

We can now see how, in a 1963 piece entitled 'La realtà e il cinema diretto' (Reality and cinema-vérité), Antonioni defends his formalistic practice against the naturalistic canon of the then in vogue "cinema-vérité":

I stop for a drink in a village near Valdagno. The building is situated on a very windy square. How photogenic the wind is! [...] From inside, the scene is all the more suggestive. Through an enormous glass-window the square is visible almost in its entirety, closed at the end by a wall that hides the landscape. The dust carried by the wind dims the blue of the sky, above the wall. [...] I move through the parlour looking for the right angle, but I can't find it. I wouldn't quite know how to shoot what I see. Perhaps it's because I have no story to tell and my imagination finds no outlet. I go back to the bar where a girl has delivered my order. She is a brunette, with clear, melancholic eyes. […] She sits on a stool and rests her arm on the coffee machine, her head leaning against the arm. She seems tired, sleepy, or indifferent, or maybe pondering. In any event, she is still, and being still she gradually turns into a character. I think this is also "cinema-vérité". To find a story for an individual, that is the story which coincides with the appearance of such individual, with his or her position, weight, the relationship of his or her volume to the surrounding space. I move slowly so as to reach the end of the bar, behind the girl who is now framed in a close-up. At the end of the parlour the slightly tilted window, the dust driven against the glass and then slipping down as if liquid matter. From this position, the rapport between inside and outside is right, the image is loaded. Everything makes sense: the white outside (a non-existent reality) and the dark shapes inside, girl included. By now, the girl has become an object herself. A character without a face, without a story. The shot is so beautiful that we don't need anything else to know it (Antonioni, 2001, pp. 54–5).

The essential quality of Antonioni's style is here successfully summed up, the director's realism is brought down to its very mimetic truth: the scene slowly taking shape culminates in a mimetic shot from behind the female character, who is therefore intentionally projected against the background, deprived of subjective autonomy, and *reduced to the unconscious truth of her enigmatic gaze*.[28]

Turning to the actual content of *La notte* and *L'eclisse*, we could argue that Antonioni's use of mimesis uncovers two intentions, a symbolic and a non-symbolic one, both perfectly plausible and interrelated. Symbolically, mimesis targets the reification of social and emotional relationships in the modern world. Non-symbolically, it designates a purified formal dimension with no obvious connections to the narrative. From a psychoanalytic point of view, Antonioni sutures the non-symbolic element into the symbolic order of the narrative. Mimesis is thereby inscribed into the film content, and yet it remains what it is: a nonconceptual, impenetrable feature. This strategy of constant suturing the mimetic *objet a* in the narrative shows the extent to which Antonioni's cinema (not necessarily Antonioni himself) is aware of the dialectical mechanism sustaining the functioning of the symbolic field, for *objet a* could be equated to the "door of the law" in Kafka's famous parable: the stability of the socio-symbolic order depends on the distance we keep from the object-cause of desire. Conversely, the closer we get to *objet a*, to the void that it embodies, the more the symbolic field releases its magnetic hold on us, revealing the abyssal hole at its centre: things fall apart, reality decomposes.

In *L'eclisse*, the stock exchange sequence provides us with the film's most powerful example of the interaction between mimesis as social reification (content) and mimesis as non-symbolic sublimation (form). What we have here is a realistic reproduction of a stock exchange, with professional brokers playing themselves in real life.[29] Yet, a few crucial elements challenge the realistic effect of the sequence. Firstly, this episode is redundant, as the sequence is repeated twice in the film, with the second one protracted much longer than any realist aesthetics would require. But the importance of Antonioni's recourse to mimesis is confirmed by another detail: the insertion of a reference to death, as a voice from the speakers suddenly invites the brokers to stop their activity and pay homage with a minute of silence to a suddenly deceased colleague.

After the minute has elapsed, business automatically resumes in its loud, merciless impetuosity. The *suprema ratio* of modern capitalism is successfully related to the irrationality of a system ruled by the abstract value of money. The message is perfectly captured in the sudden petrifaction of the crowd, which metaphorically tells us the truth about their activity: the frantic movement of the stockbrokers around a centre occupied by a machine suggests insanity rather than progress. Likewise, it indicates that the absolute subjugation of time to practical ends corresponds to timelessness – that is, death. Unassumingly and unrhetorically, aesthetic mimesis reflects the director's intuition that in modernity history turns into myth, life into death, reality into virtuality; it exposes the cadaverous absurdity of the stock exchange as the essence of life in a capitalist world.

Apart from its socially critical value, this minute of chilling silence that suddenly falls on the motionless crowd is also emblematic of Antonioni's fascination with form alone. Along with social reification, mimesis here points to the "secret happiness" of *temps morts*: frozen fragments of reality that stand as purely formal constellations, thus exposing and at the same time resolving the unworkable antagonism that subtends the narrative. Antonioni's films are crowded with such rigidified, sublimated and transient moments of crystalline brightness that seem to require contemplation rather than symbolic classification.[30] However, it is precisely in resisting conceptualisation that Antonioni's mimesis becomes meaningful. Let us take the shot of Vittoria and Piero standing motionless during the minute of silence, separated by a massive cement pillar that occupies most of the shot. The Real impossibility of their relationship is successfully reflected by the hard opacity of this pillar, which is reminiscent of the obtrusive wall in the final shot of *L'avventura*, or the massive pylon absorbing the shock of Agostino's suicide in Bernardo Bertolucci's *Prima della rivoluzione* (Before the Revolution, 1965). In Antonioni the complete shattering of individuation does not liquidate knowledge and hope. On the contrary, the contraction of subjectivity is correlated to a fragile formal figuration representing the director's intuition that thought must venture into the taboo zone of the Real if it is to become truly rational and challenge the bad infinity of what Adorno dubbed the administered world (*verwaltete Welt*).

This is why the image of the strange bond between the female character and the environment is the opposite of a sociological critique of modern alienation. When Vittoria, and before her Lidia, fall into a kind of psychotic trance, establishing a mysteriously solipsistic connection with the their surroundings, Antonioni is not attacking the alienating power of modern society, he is rather hinting at the subversive potential implicit in this condition of self-contraction. The progressive quality of Antonioni's cinema is to be found precisely in its consummated ability to conjure up the contour of a radically estranged subjectivity. This is the way we should understand the director's eerie sounding admission of his preference for things, objects, over human beings (see Biarese and Tassone, 1985, p. 121). Far from being the preference of a cold formalist disinterested in the human destiny, this acknowledgment conceals a highly significant (albeit unconscious) attempt to rekindle the political impact of cinematic aesthetics. Stripped of their identity, inexorably flattened against their surrounding ambient, his female subjects not only reproduce and consequently unveil the infernal reification of social life, but more importantly seek to break the spell *by becoming the spell itself*. In those uncanny moments when mimetic transfiguration coincides with formal plenitude, Antonioni's female characters contrive an image of salvation by over-identifying with their unconscious desire. It is in the shuddering, evanescent and cool appearance of void that the ethical value of Antonioni's artistic operation lies.

The highly formalised last shots of *L'eclisse* are emblematic of the director's method. Antonioni's fascination with the natural phenomenon of the eclipse, which gave him the idea for the film, had originated in his imagining that during such a phenomenon everything must come to a halt, including people's feelings (see Antonioni, 2001, p. 58 and p. 174). A metaphor for social alienation though it may be, the final eclipse also aims at reproducing the ephemeral and indefinable kernel of what Adorno calls 'natural beauty'. In the end, the disappearance of the characters does not speak for the sad fate of the contemporary subject in a totally integrated society, but it crystallises hope in the mimetic image that swallows up subjectivity itself. By disclosing hope in hopelessness Antonioni offers here an acutely condensed theoretical model of cinema's dialectics.

3.6 WAR OF THE SEXES

To return to the question of sexuality, let us now explore its impact on Rossellini's neorealist cinema. What is particularly striking in Rossellini's "trilogy of war" is that the divisive potential of the Real does not only relate to the devastation of war, but also to sexuality pure and simple – a theme hardly investigated by critics. It seems to me that in his famous trilogy Rossellini develops a connection between feminine subjectivity and kernel of a troubling enjoyment (*jouissance*), which would indicate strong continuity with the following "Bergman films".[31] The characters I am referring to are Pina, Marina and Ingrid in *Roma, città aperta*; Carmela and Francesca in *Paisà*; Edmund in *Germania anno zero*.[32] The following analysis concentrates specifically on Carmela and Francesca, respectively from the first and the third episode of *Paisà*.

The first episode is set in 1943, during the landing of the Allies in Sicily. A small contingent of American soldiers arrives in a Sicilian village and starts inquiring about the Nazis. Language difference, however, severely hinders their communication with the local people. As a consequence, the Americans decide to take an Italian girl as a guide through the German mine fields, though they continue to distrust her throughout the episode. One soldier ("Joe from Jersey") is left to guard the girl (Carmela) in a dark and decrepit tower, whilst the others move on in search of the enemy. A bond is quickly made between the two, until the Nazis are alerted to their presence in the tower and kill them both in rapid succession.

Carmela, the heroine of the episode, represents an almost paradigmatic case, although rather unobtrusively, of what is normally regarded as Rossellini's typically male-coded depiction of femininity. The customary feminist reproach to Rossellini is that his camera, as well as that of most Italian male directors, tends to frame female characters as either sexual objects (of desire), or neurotic/hysterical subjects at the mercy of their emotions. To expand on the basic argument of this chapter, however, I would argue that the fundamental subjective inconsistency that qualifies Rossellini's feminine subject needs to be related to the specific relationship the character entertains with the physical and symbolic space in which she operates. In Carmela's case what counts is her radical defiance with respect to symbolic over-determination. To start with, she is clearly instrumentalised, portrayed as a tool in the hands of the foreign forces fighting for territorial control over Sicily. The Americans use her as 'little more than a device, employed for the purpose of avoiding German land mines' (Brunette, 1996, p. 66), and by the end of the episode they scornfully brand her as a 'dirty Eye-Tie', holding her responsible for Joe's death. Similarly, the Germans, connoted as lecherous harassers just like in *Roma, città aperta*, treat her as nothing more than a sexual distraction to their mission. The nodal point, however, is that, as Brunette timidly notes, Carmela generates sexual tension in a manner that is altogether new, at least to American audiences. Despite being too allusive, Brunette hits the target when he claims that 'the very presence of the girl [Carmela] – slovenly and directly sensual in a way no real actress would ever chance – gives an edge to her encounter with Joe that *makes the film seem bracingly out of control*' (Brunette, 1996, p. 72 – my emphasis). More explicitly, then, we could say that Carmela's sensuality, powerful and yet so rough and primitive to appear slightly repulsive, produces the basic effect of *jouissance* by provoking the viewer (as well as the fictional characters in the film) into literally "losing control of the plot", i.e. fantasising about a thoroughly different (disturbingly promiscuous) scenario.

This representation of femininity can be approached from the thematic point of view of "failed communication", insofar as the character engenders such a strong narrative tension that the emphasis quickly shifts from "the war of the Allies against the Nazis" to "the war of the sexes". Rossellini, in other words, succeeds in staging a battlefield where Americans and Germans are paradoxically *on the same side*, since the very symbolic space which functions as a framework for their fight is threatened by the intrusion of a thoroughly alien body: the kernel of *jouissance* incarnated by the heroine. Contrary to what critics have often noted, Rossellini does not seem overly interested in questioning the ideological barrier separating the Americans from the Germans, nor, for that matter, in passing a judgement on the native Sicilians with their Fascist legacy. The truly divisive question concerns the proximity of a sexual signifier that undermines communication radically by generating what Žižek (2004a, p. 140) calls 'little jolts of enjoyment'. The end of the episode is emblematic, with the image of Carmela's dead body thrown against the rocks by the rough sea, at night, suggesting that she should be seen as a "sublime" character that exceeds signification.

Paisà

Such a connotation is confirmed by the extraordinary central scene of the episode, where Carmela and "Joe from Jersey" find themselves alone in the abandoned tower by the sea. Both ignorant of the other's language, they slowly manage to communicate on a gestural level, quickly developing a mutual attraction. Then, when Joe shows Carmela a photo of his sister, she misunderstands her for his lover and turns jealous. To reassure her, Joe points out his own resemblance to his sister: he holds the photo next to his face and, as it is dark, fatally ignites a lighter. A quick cut to a German outpost frames a soldier who sees the light inside the tower and prepares to shoot. What should be noted here is that the question of failed communication is successfully sexualised, as during the brief interlude between Joe and Carmela, Rossellini subtly shifts the emotional focus of the narrative from the question of linguistic difference (the fact that they can hardly communicate) to the question of sexual difference (the fact that "there is no such thing as a sexual relationship").

Perhaps it should not surprise us that when the two are on the verge of overcoming their communicative deadlock, we get what Brunette fittingly calls 'a startling intrusion of otherness' (Brunette, 1996, p. 63), i.e. the German bullet that kills Joe. If we were to qualify the nature of this otherness, however, the central element would not be the bullet itself but rather the fire that attracts it. Firstly, the intrusion of otherness remains thoroughly elliptical, as we do not see what actually happens, we can only imagine it – which again, echoing the torture sequence in *Roma, città aperta*, provides evidence that Rossellini's realism hinges on the Real of fantasy. Secondly, what causes Joe's death is, literally, the flame next to his face. Beyond the fairly obvious metaphorical reading of fire as passion, we should not be afraid to apply the Lynchean lesson and see in this signifier precisely a symbol of the inaccessible (Real) domain of true communication between the sexes. As in most of Rossellini's films, harmony between men and women either proves impossible or is located in a realm beyond reality and representation. Couples such as Karin and Antonio (*Stromboli*), Katherine and Alex (*Viaggio in Italia*), Irene and George (*Europa '51*), all represent explicit examples of Rossellinian failed relationships. The centrality of this theme should prevent us from considering it simply an effect of historical circumstances (the war), for in the "Bergman films" of the 1950s gender relations are still seen as constitutionally thwarted by a radical incompatibility caused by the different way in which men and women relate to desire. Far from being the point of view of an embittered pessimist, such an insight paradoxically allows Rossellini to suggest how inter-subjective alienation can be overcome. If on the one hand it seems plausible to argue that Rossellini's subject is, similarly to Antonioni's, by definition alienated and therefore unable to truly communicate with the other, on the other hand his cinema constantly undermines such a view by radicalising its impact: alienation can be overcome through *separation*, through the subject's traumatic encounter with the Real of his or her desire.

Carmela's example gives us a chance to clarify this further. The depiction of her death as a heroic act inscribed in a sublime context seems to suggest that the way out of the universe of failed communication can be found in the Real of some shattering (self-)destructive choice. As with Pina's suicidal run towards Francesco in *Roma, città aperta*, we have here a paradigmatic instance of Lacanian separation: the (feminine) subject over-identifies with the unconscious, thus inscribing a break in the domain of symbolic alienation (typically masculine). The "madness" of Carmela's act, her getting in touch with the unconscious, is exactly what is at stake in her decision to confront the Nazi soldiers who had killed Joe (a confrontation which, significantly, Rossellini avoids to represent, in what is one of the clearest examples of his elliptical editing).[33] Although she knows that she is going to die, at the same time *she does not know it*, for she is literally not herself anymore, in the sense that *it*, the subject of the unconscious, has taken over. Ultimately, Carmela's dead body, in a similar manner to the dead bodies in *Roma, città aperta* (Pina, Manfredi and Don Pietro), and Edmund's dead body at the end of *Germania anno zero*,[34] reminds us not only that the socio-symbolic order is a contested space occupied by clashing forces, but also, more insightfully, that a truly subversive act aims at antagonising the very framework which makes such clash possible.

It is revealing that the question of failed communication between the sexes is at the heart of two other episodes of *Paisà*, the third and the fourth. The third episode is set in Rome immediately after liberation, and begins with a drunk American soldier, Fred, meeting an Italian prostitute named Francesca. Once in Francesca's room, Fred starts telling her in a clumsy mixture of Italian and English about his arrival in Rome on liberation day. As the flashback starts he describes his meeting a young and innocent local woman he had immediately fallen in love with, but whom he had not been able to see again ever since. Despite realising that she is the woman Fred is referring to, Francesca decides not to reveal her identity out of shame for her new occupation. Instead she watches Fred falling asleep, and then leaves the room, asking the landlady to give him her old address when he awakes. In the final sequence Francesca waits in vain for her man outside the house where they first met, while Fred is shown ripping and throwing away the piece of paper with the address – 'the address of a whore', as he comments to a friend.

In a nutshell, true love remains a chimera for the two characters, as they literally fail to recognise each other. One can legitimately argue that what hampers their love is the brutality of war, which turns Fred into a cynical drunk and Francesca into a prostitute. However, what if the episode were to be read in the opposite way? What if, in conformity with my discussion of the first episode, misrecognition originates in the very gap of sexual difference, the Lacanian "il n'y a pas de rapport sexuel" which causes "wars" between the sexes? What I would like to insist on is the ontological character of such *méconnaisance*. Fred idealises Francesca into an innocent girl and ends up believing, predictably, that all women are whores; Francesca on her part is subtly portrayed as a fundamentally hysterical woman, as her desire remains inaccessible. In fact, Francesca is much more ambiguous than what she might appear at first impression.[35] Rossellini juxtaposes to her romantic side an ambiguous and sharply contrasting surplus of promiscuity: far from appearing as a victim of war forced into prostitution, from the outset Francesca quite simply *seems to enjoy it*, and it is only when she recognises herself in Fred's story that she radically modifies her behaviour. The political potential of Rossellini's neorealist subject, then, rests on the emergence of *jouissance*, on the endorsement of the Real of failed communication, the universal gap of sexual difference. This justifies the seemingly paradoxical argument that the defining feature of Rossellini's neorealist cinema resides in the representation of subjectivity as a field marked by the traumatic encounter with the inaccessible Real.[36]

3.7 THE ABYSS OF FEMININE SEXUALITY: UNCONSCIOUS FIGURATIONS UNLIMITED

In the mid-1980s many believed that Marco Bellocchio had completely fallen under the sway of his psychoanalyst Massimo Fagioli. From the start of the 1970s, Fagioli had been organising seminars of "collective analysis" (Analisi Collettiva), through which he openly attacked psychoanalytic theory and practice in Italy. These attacks eventually led to his expulsion from the Italian Society of Psychoanalysis (SPI). Bellocchio started attending Fagioli's seminars in the late 1970s, and soon developed with him a number of collaborative projects in film. Critics were often very harsh on this partnership, denouncing Bellocchio's films of the 1980s as mere applications of Fagioli's anti-Freudian theories, which are based on what he calls 'immagini interiori' (inner images) – images corresponding to figurations of a "healthy and accessible" unconscious (see Fagioli, 1972). If we recall that Freud's rejection of the cinema was instigated by his scepticism towards the idea that the unconscious could be expressed figuratively, then it is clear that Fagioli's belief in the beneficial potential stored in the unconscious and its non-traumatic representability could not be more remote from the Freudian tradition. Fagioli believes that the unconscious *can* be represented, which implies that visual arts, cinema *in primis*, are able to perform an explicitly subversive function. With reference to Fagioli's thought and his influence on Bellocchio's work, my argument develops as follows.

As repeatedly admitted by both parties, the collaboration cannot be taken to imply that Bellocchio's cinema became a mere reflection of Fagioli's theories. The relationship remained open and antagonistic, as the two constantly provoked and challenged each other. Moreover, even if we admit that Bellocchio's films are articulated around the need to accommodate Fagioli's *immagini interiori*, this does not prevent these films from developing an unconscious side *beyond* their conscious strategy. Especially with regard to the notion of the feminine unconscious – Fagioli's key reference – Bellocchio seems to me more Lacanian (and thus implicitly Freudian) than his mentor, for Bellocchio's narratives constantly funnel their meanings into a hidden kernel which ultimately appears to relate to a traumatic, non-figurative domain. Rather than exhausting its function at the figurative level, Bellocchio's cinematic unconscious presents itself as correlative to the bar of the Real. The limits of the notion of *immagine interiore* can be accounted for by exploring the issue of femininity in two films where the collaboration between Bellocchio and Fagioli proved particularly intense: *Il diavolo in corpo* (Devil in the Flesh, 1986) and *La condanna* (The Conviction, 1991).

Let us begin with the scene in *Il diavolo in corpo* where Giulia Dozza (Marushka Detmers) unexpectedly materialises in her psychoanalyst's study. The camera is placed behind the couch, framing a male patient as he lies down; a few seconds into the same shot Giulia emerges in his place stark naked, to the understandable bewilderment of the analyst. What we have here is an illustration of Fagioli's inner image, an unconscious fantasy expressing the psychoanalyst's repressed desire to sleep with Giulia. The first thing to note is that despite being elaborated on an anti-Freudian basis, this image functions nevertheless according to the Freudian theme of the return of the repressed: the father – who has warned his son against seeing Giulia, his hysterical patient – has to face the hallucinated return of his own repressed desire. My point, however, is that this image is not correlative to the unconscious as such, but at best to the Lacanian *objet a*, or the fundamental fantasy, the subject's ultimate mode of defence against psychosis. Fagioli's *immagini* seem to function precisely as screens between symbolic meaning and the disavowed desire to stare the Real in the face. Along these lines, we could also argue that Fagioli gets the point right for the wrong reasons, in the sense that his images are Real only as long as we conceive them as distorting screens. According to Žižek,

> we should not forget the radical ambiguity of the Lacanian real: it is not the ultimate referent to be covered/gentrified/domesticated by the screen of fantasy; the real is also and primarily the screen itself as the obstacle that always already distorts our perception of the referent, of the reality "out there" (Žižek, 2001b, pp. 220–21).

It is worth noting that this logic is the same one at work in Freud's already mentioned theory of dreams: the real kernel of the unconscious is not the latent message of the dream, but the unconscious desire that inscribes itself through the very distortion made manifest by the latent content of the dream / narrative. That is to say: the unconscious is, in its deepest connotation, the *form* of the desire that attaches itself to a certain narrative (the dream in itself is the guardian of sleep, a narrative that absorbs the shock potential of the unconscious). The image of Giulia's naked body works therefore as a gentrified unconscious formation (*objet a*), since the unconscious cannot be reduced to "the analyst's desire to sleep with her", but it is rather the very *form* of this desire, which in its deepest connotation can only be defined as a deflagration of *jouissance*, a leap into a radically different temporality. The Real / unconscious desire at stake here is the desire for the abyss of an Event that intervenes *ex nihilo*, out of a different time frame. Ultimately, Giulia's body needs to be related to a violent, non-representable wish for a break with the symbolic structure: negativity at its purest.

We can put this concept in a slightly different way: this negativity coincides with the invisible transfiguration that takes place between the male patient and Giulia. The unconscious desire manifests itself in that "unimaginable image" underpinning Fagioli's inner image. In philosophical terms, the unconscious does not operate at the level of Kant's transcendentally synthetic imagination, the spontaneous and purely intuitive faculty of apprehension which "prepares the ground" for the intervention of understanding. What is at stake in the fundamental fantasy is, in fact, the opposite of a (no matter how intuitive) synthetic function: the negative, destructive force of imagination, 'the capacity of our mind to dismember what immediate perception puts together' (Žižek, 2000a, p. 30). In short, Giulia's miraculous "rising from the couch" is an image that works as a visual prop to the unconscious wish *qua* dismemberment and transfiguration, a potentiality for a break that can only be conceived of against the background of an absolutely changed temporal framework.

The impressive initial sequence of *Il diavolo in corpo* helps us contextualise further the central question of unconscious agency. Here Bellocchio contrasts the signifier "reason" (law, order, culture, consciousness, masculinity, etc.) with the signifier "irrationality" (the unconscious, desire, transgression, the sacred, femininity, etc.), a typical binary opposition in his cinema. Whilst a schoolteacher is explaining Giovanni Pascoli's poem 'La tovaglia',[37] a scantily dressed black woman appears on the roof adjacent to the school, uttering incomprehensible words that attract the attention of the whole class and specifically of the film's young protagonist, Andrea (Federico Pitzalis). Long-held close ups show tears on her terrified face, suggesting she may be about to commit suicide. In the meantime, the clamour resulting from the incident awakens Giulia in the flat opposite the school. As she steps out onto the balcony overlooking the roof, pale and bedraggled in her nightgown, Andrea catches a glimpse of her face behind the suicidal woman. The moment she enters Andrea's visual field, Giulia turns into an exemplary case of *objet a*, for she is unobtrusively connected with the traumatic appearance of the mysterious woman on the roof, and consequently sets Andrea's desire in motion. More to the point, Giulia confirms that the notion of *objet petit a*

comprises itself and its own *opposite / dissimulation. Objet a* is simultaneously the pure lack, the void around which the desire turns and which, as such, causes the desire, *and* the element which conceals this void, renders it invisible by filling it out. The point, of course, is that there is no lack without the element filling it out: *the filler sustains what it dissimulates* (Žižek, 1994, p. 178).

From the moment he sets his eyes on Giulia, Andrea he is fatally hooked, and the film develops as a wholehearted glorification of the transgressive power of love between two improbable partners, against the repressive normality imposed by modern reason through state institutions and the family.

Il diavolo in corpo

More to the point, the film suggests that "feminine irrationality" can be practised as a thoroughly reasonable vehicle for liberation in the cold, aseptic, lifeless and ultimately irrational universe of "male rationality". *Il diavolo in corpo* is thus meant to turn around the proverbial Freudian fear of hysteria, expressing an optimistic and fairly unproblematic endorsement of the "abyss of femininity", an allegedly more authentic dimension where unconscious desires and unconstrained libido have a chance to free man from the repressive yoke of instrumental reason.[38] Here, however, we encounter the first problems, as this reading is partly contradicted by certain symptomatic deadlocks secreted by the narrative itself. To a closer inspection, the unfurling of the relationship between Giulia and Andrea (and particularly the sequence where Giulia, armed with a long pair of scissors, stages Andrea's castration while he sleeps) seems to point to the Lacanian impasse concerning sexuality: how can we articulate our sexual relation without stumbling into the wall/interdiction of phallic *jouissance*? Lacan holds that our true partner in the sexual act is less the flesh and blood other than the phallus, the ghost of *jouissance* that can only be consciously experienced as lack, thus working as an insuperable obstacle against our plea for "oneness", or true harmony:

> Love is impotent, though mutual, because it is not aware that it is but the desire to be One, which leads us to the impossibility of establishing the relationship between "them-two" – the relationship between them-two what? – them-two sexes. [...] Phallic jouissance is the obstacle owing to which man does not come, I would say, to enjoy woman's body, precisely because what he enjoys is the jouissance of the organ (Lacan, 1998b, pp. 6–7).[39]

Despite its deliberate attempt to endorse a positive and practicable "unconscious fantasy", the film betrays its "Real desire" by constantly alluding to the divisive nature of *jouissance*. The previously described opening scene provides us with more clues as to what mars the film's intention to link the subversive power of the unconscious to ordinary situations, as Andrea is an intelligent, mature, controlled boy, whilst it is his father, the psychoanalyst, who grows progressively paranoid and "irrational". A standard interpretation of the opening scene would focus on the potentially redeeming intervention of the mad woman as the incarnation of man's ancient bond with the sacred, which however is undermined by the fact that the modern world (symbolised by the school as the institution producing shared symbolic values) has grown insensitive to such calls. In many ways this can be read as another instance of the return of the repressed: Bellocchio and Fagioli suggest that the sacred survives/returns in the modern world through the feminine. As the opening juxtaposition of the two "out of sync" women suggests, Giulia is nothing but a modern version of the ancient, diabolical witch, deprived of her immense powers and yet able to awaken, if only in one individual, a wealth of subversive unconscious wishes.

If this is the case, we should also note that this initial sequence stages the paradigmatic psychoanalytic scene of original seduction popularised by Laplanche (see Laplanche, 1998). The child (Andrea) is confronted by an Other that he is unable to fully make sense of, for it retains some incomprehensible libidinal connotations. The heart of the matter, however, is that these connotations *are impenetrable to the Other itself*: 'the primordial encounter of the Unconscious is the encounter with the Other's inconsistency, with the fact that the [...] Other is not actually the master of his acts and words, that he emits signals whose true libidinal tenor is inaccessible to him' (Žižek, 2000a, p. 284). In this sense, the fantasmatic intrusion of the woman on the roof and the strange signals she emits suggest the (re-)birth of the unconscious *qua* traumatic encounter with the Other's radical libidinal inconsistency: looking from the window, Andrea is challenged precisely by "what is in the other more than the other herself". Following this line of reasoning, Giulia appears to be the gentrified reflection of an unconscious desire, i.e. an *immagine interiore*.

To radicalise the argument, we could say that the problem lies precisely with "the beginning of the whole thing", for one should not be afraid to ask the naive question: how did the image of the unconscious come about in the first place? What is it that, from a purely diegetic point of view, causes the strange materialisation of the hysterical woman (the Other) who then hands over her mandate to Giulia? My contention is that not only Giulia but even the cinematic image of the hysterical woman is strictly speaking *secondary*, in as much as its emergence depends on a mechanism of fundamental displacement. Our question should therefore be reformulated thus: what needs to be repressed so that the film can begin with such an astonishing image? As in the previous example where Giulia rises from the couch, the answer can only be one: the film's unconscious in the form of an impossible desire to transfigure time, to register a different temporality into our linear perception of time, which would cause/allow us to disconnect violently with "what we know".

More generally, does not every creative effort require a similar "Big Bang" event, whereby the artist violently detaches himself or herself from the self-contented immersion in everyday life through some kind of perturbing experience that opens up a different symbolic configuration? The great merit of Bellocchio's openings is that they invariably produce the uncanny feeling that some pre-existing peace has been disturbed — *and that it is such a disturbance that kick-starts the film*. Along these lines, could we not argue that his scandalous first film *I pugni in tasca* (Fists in the Pocket, 1965) — where the lone Alessandro (Lou Castel) kills his blind mother to liberate his older brother from his burden of responsibility towards his emotionally crippled family – functions precisely as a psychotic act creating the space for Bellocchio's filmmaking career?

Theoretically, the point is that every conscious figurative effort necessarily relies on its obverse: on the reference to a spark of pre-synthetic, non-symbolisable imagination, whose negative power is, to quote Hegel, 'the energy of thought, of the pure "I"' (Hegel, 1977, p. 19). And the Lacanian unconscious belongs precisely to this Hegelian framework, insofar as it stands for a kernel of self-relating negativity which coincides with life-giving substance. Hegel described this coincidence in a famous passage from the Preface to his *Phenomenology*:

> But the life of Spirit is not the life that shrinks from death and keeps itself untouched by devastation, but rather the life that endures it and maintains itself in it. It wins its truth only when, in utter dismemberment, it finds itself. It is this power, not as something positive, which closes its eyes to the negative, as when we say of something that it is nothing or is false, and then, having done it, turn away and pass on to something else; on the contrary, Spirit is this power only by looking the negative in the face, and tarrying with it. This tarrying with the negative is the magical power that converts it into being (Hegel, 1977, p. 19).

Paraphrasing Hegel from a Lacanian angle, we could say that Bellocchio's images find a way to the unconscious when they manage to convey a sense of their tarrying with the negative which magically converts them into images. Here we encounter one of the paradoxes of the Lacanian Real: on the one hand, it functions as a pre-synthetic and primordially disruptive force always-already at work, attached to everything we do or think; on the other hand, it is also the product of our synthetic intellectual activity, the "indivisible remainder" or "excremental leftover" (to use two of Žižek's favourite expressions) of reason's endeavours to bring together the multitude of raw sensuous intuitions. The paradox is that these two definitions mutually exclude and feed off each other in a vicious circle, as they make it impossible for us to establish whether the Real comes before the intervention of synthetic imagination or vice versa. Žižek resolves this paradox by bringing together Hegel and Lacan – by claiming that the primordial/mythical aspect of the Real is less a detached and pre-existing force than the very activity of understanding at its purest, the Hegelian pure I, the subject's abyssal freedom "to look the negative in the face", which heralds the creation of a new symbolic framework.

Let us take a key formal cipher of *Il diavolo in corpo*, its insistence on long-held, almost interminable close-ups on Giulia's face. What are we supposed to read into these distressing and frustrating shots? Presumably, following Fagioli, nothing but reflections of purely subjective figurations regarding something which does not have a place in our universe of sense and yet has the potential to come into being.[40] Nonetheless, I would refine such explanation by adding that these close-ups achieve a degree of anamorphotic concreteness. The grimaces on Giulia's face – emotionally charged and yet strangely impassive facial expressions – are Real in that they reflect the distortion they suffer from a constitutionally displaced and invisible desire.[41] Fagioli and Bellocchio's images are imaginary formations perturbed or even besieged by an unconscious wish.

We are faced with a similar logic in *La condanna*, a film that compulsively stammers against the wall of phallic *jouissance*. Like in *Il diavolo in corpo*, Fagioli's intervention can be detected in those passages where the fairly linear narrative appears disrupted by disconnected or inchoate inner images. Perhaps the most obvious of these takes the form of a strangely incorporeal shot towards the end of the film, when the "man of reason" (the judge Malatesta: *in nomen omen*, literally "bad head") is confronted by the hallucinated return of his repressed desire, a fantasy of a sexually provocative woman from the country – the equivalent of Giulia. But is this surreal image to be regarded as a figuration of the unconscious? Or are we not faced, again, with a secondary formation (*objet a*, fundamental fantasy) mediating between the subject and a more radical impasse? The effectiveness of this image is correlative to its ability to relate to the gaps that unwarrantedly invade and distort the narrative, showing it for what it always is: a curvature of space, what Žižek calls 'the swerve of the Real' (see Žižek, 2003, pp. 58–91). It is in these gaps that the unconscious desire generated by the film is lodged.

The returns of the repressed are also symptomatic of the role of fantasy in man's relation to woman. In one of these hallucinations, judge Malatesta meets an unnamed woman in a field, surrounded by a group of sexually aroused men. The judge's instinctive reaction is to try and rescue the woman from the danger she is in. As soon as the danger is dispelled, however, the woman has nothing to say to her saviour other than laughing provokingly in his face. This sequence captures the problematic rapport between feminine enjoyment and masculine gaze, insofar as the masculine gaze is split between fascination and repulsion with respect to a modality of enjoyment that remains beyond symbolisation.[42] By fantasising about the woman's need to be rescued, the male simply constructs a fantasy-scenario to avoid the traumatic confrontation with the inaccessible domain of feminine *jouissance*. In other cases, the reaction may of course be of a psychotic kind.[43]

In this respect, the baffling opening of *La condanna* is as impressive a piece of filmmaking as the opening of *Il diavolo in corpo*. As Sandra (Claire Nebout) finds herself locked inside a castle after visiting its museum, Bellocchio suggests that *there is no cause* for this turn of events, in the sense that it is impossible to establish whether Sandra has deliberately provoked her fate or whether it all happened accidentally. Once again, Bellocchio (clearly inspired by Fagioli) opens up his female character to the paradox of her sexuality, to the fact that *woman does not know what she wants*, for she entertains a privileged relationship with the empty core of her desire. To contrast and thus emphasise the specific quality of the feminine position, we are immediately introduced to woman's asymmetrical partner. While Sandra, locked inside the castle, is looking at Leonardo's famous painting *Madonna Litta*, Giovanni (Vittorio Mezzogiorno) suddenly appears behind her, proceeding to explain the meaning of the painting (an explanation which, inevitably, Sandra does not share). Interestingly, Sandra does not seem at all surprised by the presence of this complete stranger, the point being that not only are we left with an utterly inexplicable situation, but the paradox of not knowing the cause of a certain narrative outcome *also qualifies Sandra's position*, i.e. the position of the bearer of the main action. In sharp contrast to Sandra's enigmatic desire, Giovanni knows full well what he wants: as we discover later, he had planned things in detail so as to remain alone with his chosen prey.

The ambiguity relating to feminine sexuality and its proclivity to get in touch with the unconscious is explored further in the following sequence, which focuses on the sexual act between the two characters. The first thing to note is that the sexual encounter is presented in ambiguous visual terms, as it is impossible for us to make out whether the couple is actually having sex or it is all just an act. Their movements and noises suggest a real copulation, but the whole scene also amounts to something akin to a theatrical masquerade, the kind of ceremonial mating foreplay performed by animals. Crucially, it is impossible for us to establish the amount of violence involved. True, at one point Sandra runs away, Giovanni chases her and takes her rather aggressively; yet, it is evident that we are not watching a rape scene, as Sandra is portrayed in such a way as to suggest that she is willing to be taken by force.

The obvious feminist counter-argument would be that we are watching a rape scene from a male (chauvinist) point of view. However, what about Liliana Cavani's "post-Holocaust" drama *Il portiere di notte* (The Night Porter, 1974), where Lucia (Charlotte Rampling), a concentration camp survivor, openly endorses her scandalous "desire to be raped" by her former SS captor/torturer Max (Dirk Bogarde)? Twelve years after the end of World War II Lucia chances upon Max while in Vienna with her husband, an accomplished orchestra director. Despite her initial horror, she is unable to resist the fascination that the memory of Max (now the night porter in the hotel where she is staying) exerts on her. One brief rendezvous is enough for Lucia to bring back irresistible recollections of the violent abuse Max used to inflict upon her, to the extent that she immediately leaves her husband and ties herself completely to her vicious lover. Liliana Cavani, a woman, does not shirk away from what she clearly regards as the feminine fundamental fantasy, a masochistic primal scene in which the Freudian "a child is being beaten" is turned into "a woman is being beaten".[44]

Going back to the Lacanian 'il n'ya pas de rapport sexuel', we can now see how this motto works in the above two films. Firstly, *La condanna* and *Il portiere di notte* disclose the problematic character of the very notion of rape, suggesting that the sexual act is in itself essentially traumatic (since, deprived of its traumatic dimension, sex would be utterly desexualised and dehumanised).[45] Secondly, by emphatically presenting the sexual interplay as a *staging* of repressed traumatic fantasies, they correlate it to the question of the gaze. *La condanna*, for example, not only makes clear that Giovanni and Sandra are "doing it" for an imaginary witness (ultimately, the spectator), but that *this third party is what enables them to engage in the sexual act:* without a fantasised imaginary gaze, this act (his staging) would be utterly inconceivable. In both cases (rape and gaze) the Lacanian thesis on the non-existence of the sexual relationship is confirmed – sex between two (or more) human beings is never simply sex, it always implies, as its key factor, a certain displacing excess that problematises while simultaneously enabling the rapport.

The entire film narrative is built on the irreducible sexual antagonism evoked so poignantly in the opening scene. In spite of this, Bellocchio does not endorse the popular maxim that "men are from Mars and women from Venus", i.e., that the masculine and the feminine fields are made up by two sets of radically different and conflicting contents. The problem, rather, is that they are both traversed by a structuring impossibility that pertains to their respective subjective economies, and it is the non-coincidental character of this impossibility that makes their relationship impossible. That is to say: what hinders the relationship are not two contrasting sets of positive features, but two contrasting sets of differently antagonised features. When, during Giovanni's trial, Sandra states that 'he [Giovanni] stirs deep-seated realities that everyone has the right to keep hidden', the referent is the very abyss of femininity, the gap behind the network of appearances securing the symbolic consistency of woman. Sandra's tears, at this point, cannot but remind us of Giulia's tears, since they are provoked by the collision with the Real (void) kernel of what she is. Ultimately, Sandra's desire to be locked in the castle with a male stranger functions at a pre-conscious level, and as such it is "only" a latent thought, which is in turn parasitised by the reference to void that typifies the truly unconscious wish.

Sandra's double in the film is Monica (Grazyna Szapolowska), judge Malatesta's sexually frustrated girlfriend, who openly contests the judge's accusations against Giovanni at the trial. Her role is that of clarifying (often to an excessively didascalic extent) the central question of feminine enjoyment. Half way through the film, for example, Monica and her partner are embraced in bed, apparently asleep after making love. He then wakes up and moves to the living room. There he starts leafing through a book on painting, where we catch a glimpse of the Leonardo's *Madonna Litta*. As she joins him, we understand that their love-making must not have been particularly successful, for in the ensuing heated conversation on the Colajanni trial she reproaches him thus: 'you are the rapist, you rape me every time you disappoint me', adding that she resents his lack of desire, his inability to let himself go, to 'bring her to orgasm'. Malatesta, who eventually manages to have Giovanni condemned (only to go and visit him in prison for advice on women!), offers us therefore a clear illustration of how, in Lacan, the law and *jouissance* are inextricably connected: 'I will remind the jurist that law basically talks about what I am going to talk to you about – jouissance. Law does not ignore the bed. Nothing forces anyone to enjoy except the superego. The superego is the imperative of jouissance – Enjoy!' (Lacan, 1998b, pp. 2–3).

NOTES

1. "There's no such thing as a sexual relationship" indicates precisely the radical dissymmetry between genders, or, to put it in Fink's words, the fact that 'no conceivable relationship between the sexes can thus be postulated, articulated or written in any form whatsoever' (Fink, 1997, p. 121).
2. 'The "doesn't stop being written" [...] is the impossible, as I define it on the basis of the fact that it cannot in any case be written, and it is with this that I characterise the sexual relationship – the sexual relationship doesn't stop not being written' (Lacan, 1998b, p. 94).
3. The Hitchcock film I am referring to is, of course, *Vertigo* (1958), which was made the year after *Il grido*. What links the two films is their common reliance on the vortex of vertigo, a metonymy for the impossible Real that cuts across the sexual relationship.
4. *Le amiche* was adapted from a famous novel of the same title written by Cesare Pavese.
5. Once again, we should stress how misleading it is to seek a pervasive ideological message in these films: ideology, here, clearly functions as a kind of "safety net" for an otherwise potentially explosive, and thus paralysing, encounter with the Real.
6. The ultimate consequence of Antonioni's formalism is that it gets caught in the loop of drive, which leads either to the "catatonic" freezing up of the image typical of films like *L'eclisse*, or, in terms of contents, to potential, imaginary psychotic outbursts such as the explosion in the final sequence of *Zabriskie Point*.
7. On a different level, the idea of rotation around a fixed axis, which this type of shot represents, reminds one of Lacan's understanding of revolution in its "celestial" meaning, as a 'retour au départ' (Lacan, 1991, p. 62, a return to the start).
8. In *Cronaca di un amore*, the impossibility of the relationship between Paola and Guido is perfectly captured in the shot of their secret encounter on the stairs of a building: here, the presence of the lift reminds them of their responsibility for the death of Guido's ex-girlfriend, Giovanna, who stepped into a defective lift before their very

eyes. Similar uses of winding staircases can be found in *Il grido* (in the previously discussed final sequence), *L'eclisse* and *Identificazione di una donna* (Identification of a Woman, 1982).

9. One of the most emblematic cases of fantasy as a protective screen is *Amarcord* (1973), where even Fascism is ultimately represented through the dreamy eyes of the characters. However, in *Amarcord* we also have at least one exception to this general attitude. I am referring to young Titta (Bruno Zanin) – supposedly Fellini's alter ego – whose first sexual experiences bring him face to face with the traumatic Real of desire. First he follows Gradisca (Magali Noël, the collective object of desire) into an empty cinema, moves closer and closer to her, even finding the courage to put his hand on her knee, but eventually, when Gradisca turns around and somewhat invitingly acknowledges his presence, simply freezes up 'come un pataca' (like an idiot). Later on, his much-desired sexual encounter with the big-bosomed tobacconist proves to be just too much for him, and as a result he falls ill.

10. I am tempted to suggest that the coupling of Leghorn, the place where the Italian Communist Party was founded back in 1921, and the utopian content of Dostoevsky's story would seem to conceal Visconti's wish for a rebirth of Communism after the blow it suffered from the 1956 Kruschev report at the XX Congress of the Soviet Communist Party, where he delivered his famous speech on Stalin's crimes.

11. An analogous mechanism is in place in Bertolucci's enigmatic *La tragedia di un uomo ridicolo* (Tragedy of a Ridiculous Man, 1981), where Primo Spaggiari (Ugo Tognazzi), owner of a cheese factory, forges a letter from his son Giovanni (Ricky Tognazzi), who has been kidnapped, with precise details concerning the payment of the enormous ransom. His aim is simple: to pay the ransom to himself. The point, however, is that the true message of the letter is Primo's hope that *the son is really dead*, or at least vanished, for he suspects that the abduction has been staged by Giovanni himself together with his left-wing extremist friends in order to raise money for political ends (the setting is Italy during the "leaden years" of political terrorism). However, after the ransom has been deposited and Primo is waiting to get it back from the two people he had planned with (who are also Giovanni's friends), the son does reappear, and the father, to his great embarrassment, can only feign to be pleased. It is with this final embarrassment that the forged letter arrives at its destination, carrying its inverted message: the father knew that the son was conspiring against him, and would have preferred to lose him rather than his money and factory.

12. The bitter irony is that, while shooting, Lea Massari, the actress who plays Anna, actually *did* "fall into the Real", for she suffered a heart attack that left her in a coma for two days (see Brunette, 1998, p. 28).

13. See Kant's famous definition: 'Bold, overhanging, and, as it were, threatening rocks, thunderclouds piled up the vault of heaven, borne along with flashes and peals, volcanos in all their violence of destruction, hurricanes leaving desolation in their track, the boundless ocean rising with rebellious force' (Kant, 1914, p. 125). Incidentally, the hurricane we see in the film was a real one.

14. What we need to add is that 'there is nothing intrinsically sublime in a sublime object – according to Lacan, a sublime object is an ordinary, everyday object which, quite by chance, finds itself occupying the place of what he calls *das Ding*, the impossible-real object of desire. It is its structural place – the fact that it occupies the sacred/forbidden place of *jouissance* – and not its intrinsic qualities that confers on it its sublimity' (Žižek, 1992, p. 194).

15. It is not that by taking her clothes off in front of Sandro, at the start of the film, 'Anna directly expresses female desire' as part of her search of 'authentic existence' (Brunette, 1998, p. 34). The opposite is true: sex functions here as a stopgap preventing the encounter with the Real of desire, exactly like in the final sequence of Kubrick's *Eyes Wide Shut* (1999), when Alice (Nicole Kidman) tells Bill (Tom Cruise) that what they urgently need to do (so as to stop thinking about the traumatic fact of sexual difference) is 'fuck'. In *L'avventura* sex acquires a distorting and at the same time defensive function.

16. 'A woman is not split in the same way as a man: though alienated, she is not altogether subject to the symbolic order. The phallic function, while operative in her case, does not reign absolutely. With respect to the symbolic order, a woman is not whole, bounded, or limited' (Fink, 1997, p. 107).

17. Whether his male characters are intellectuals like Sandro (*L'avventura*), Giovanni (*La notte*), Riccardo (*L'eclisse*), or modern professionals like Piero (*L'eclisse*), their universe remains rigidly divided into the sexual and the symbolic. The split is even more evident with ordinary males: in the second half of *L'avventura*, the Sicilian males are repeatedly represented as a horde of predators. The paradox of the male division is that 'man subordinates his relationship to a woman to the domain of ethical goals (forced to choose between woman and ethical duty – in the guise of professional obligations, etc. – he immediately opts for duty), yet he is simultaneously aware that only a relationship with a woman can bring him genuine "happiness" or personal fulfilment' (Žižek, 1994, p. 152).

18. Is this not the ultimate point made by Bertolucci's *The Dreamers* (2003), where the deadlock afflicting the intimate relationship between Matthew (Michael Pitt), an American student in Paris, and French twins Isabelle (Eva Green) and Theo (Louis Garrel), appears surmountable only if displaced onto the conflict taking place outside, in the streets of Paris during May 1968?

19. I am referring here to Kant's ambiguous (fascinated) evaluation of Emmanuel Swedenborg's spiritualism in his 1766 *Dreams of a Spirit-Seer* (see Kant, 2003).

20. Incidentally, this emphasis on the necessity of subjective destitution is also at the heart of Federico Fellini's Catholic inspiration, and perhaps nowhere more visibly than in his *La strada* (The Road, 1954), where the brutish strongman Zampanò (Anthony Quinn) gains a minimum of self-consciousness only after undergoing two traumatic experiences in rapid succession: first he unintentionally kills the character called "il matto" (the fool, Richard Basehart) and then loses his servant Gelsomina (Giulietta Masina). It is only after the second trauma (Gelsomina's death) that he develops a proper conscience, tragically realising how much he was attached to his servant. *La strada*, therefore, is a clear testament to Fellini's belief in the Christian *topos* of decadence and rebirth. In response to the objection that films like *La strada* and, on a different level, *La dolce vita* deal essentially with moral decadence and *not* rebirth – since their heroes are plunged into a seemingly irreversible condition of despair and alienation – we should recall Pasolini's insight that Fellini's cinema is intrinsically pervaded (especially thanks to its style) by a strong sense of Catholic forgiveness, whereby even its most decadent characters appear to us in a sympathetic light, as if blessed by grace (see Pasolini, 1966, pp. 50–9). Perhaps this is the reason why the traumatic dimension in Fellini, if at all present, invariably appears assuaged and gentrified.

21. Claudia, for instance, is horrified by the prospect of forgetting: 'My God, can it really take so little to change, to forget? Only a few days ago, the mere thought that Anna might be dead almost killed me. Now I can't even cry. I'm afraid she might be alive. Everything is becoming so terribly simple, even getting rid of tragedies'.

22. In 1961 Antonioni explicitly stated: 'as far as I am concerned, the actor is an element in a frame, just like a wall, a tree, or a cloud' (in di Carlo and Tinazzi, 2001, p. 36). In the same interview he revealed that, to try and capture the spontaneity of the actors outside their awareness of their fictional role, he often shouted that the take was over whilst instead protracting the shooting (see di Carlo and Tinazzi, p. 24).

23. 'Stendhal's dictum about art's *promesse du bonheur* implies that art owes something to empirical life, namely the Utopian content which is foreshadowed by art' (Adorno, 1984, p. 430).

24. Strangely enough, Adorno is actually mentioned in the opening scene of *La notte*, when Giovanni Pontano (Marcello Mastroianni) comments enthusiastically on an article written by his friend Tommaso (Bernhard Wicki) on the German philosopher. Antonioni also mentions Adorno in *Prefazione a "sei film"*, with reference to the concept of alienation (see Antonioni, 2001, p. 59).

25. 'The reactionary nature of any realist aesthetic today is inseparable from this commodity character. Tending to reinforce, affirmatively, the phenomenal surface of reality, realism dismisses any attempt to penetrate that surface as a romantic endeavour' (Adorno, 2001, p. 182).

26. The theme of the atomic explosion will be reaffirmed in the last sequence of the film, with a shot on newspaper headlines reading 'The Atomic Arms Race' and 'The Peace is Weak'.

27. Giovanni's reaction helps us contextualise the meaning of Lacan's controversial thesis that "woman is a symptom of man". It is not that once man is cured of his symptom he can live happily without woman; on the contrary, it is that man only exists through his relation to woman, insofar as woman, for him, is the elusive externalised formation upon which all his symbolic consistency depends. The Lacanian symptom is the disavowed reflection of the non-symbolisable essence of subjectivity: once the symptom is dissolved, the subject collapses.

28. In her aimless walk through Milan, for example, Lidia dispenses a number of looks that simply defy meaning. What we have in this sequence is a kind of "walking unconscious", which expresses itself through the organ of sight. Again, what matters to Antonioni is the elusive rapport between Lidia's gaze and what she sees.

29. Alain Delon himself, who plays the stockbroker Piero, was sent by Antonioni to learn his role in real stock exchange (see Antonioni, 2001, p. 248).

30. Geoffrey Nowell-Smith (1960–1 and 1963–4) and Pascal Bonitzer (in Chatman and Fink, 1989, pp. 215–18) are amongst the critics who have insisted more convincingly on the importance of the non-symbolic in Antonioni's cinema.

31. Most critics, especially in Italy, failed to understand the link between Rossellini's neorealist production and the Bergman films of the 1950s. In this respect, French critics such as Bazin and Rivette were far more perspicacious

(see Michelone, 1996, pp. 179–82). My specific point here is that if we start by considering Rossellini's cinema (before his didactic period) as primarily concerned with introspection and subjectivity in general, we should also note that there exists a fundamental continuity between the neorealist films and those of the Bergman era.

32. The notion of feminine sexuality is by no means grounded in biology or anatomy, it is rather a psychoanalytic notion which may well apply to males too.

33. In relation to editing, therefore, Pasolini's lesson holds true here, for the Rossellinian ellipsis can clearly be seen as a function of the Real, as it brings into contention what remains beyond symbolisation.

34. Edmund's "act" in *Germania anno zero* (his parricide followed by the suicide that ends the film) is read by Žižek (2001b, p. 35) as a supremely ethical event: 'an act of "absolute freedom" which momentarily suspends the field of ideological meaning'. We shall return to this film in part 4.

35. Incidentally, Francesca is played by Maria Michi, the same actress who played the mischievous Marina in *Roma, città aperta*. Whether or not this is a coincidence, Francesca retains some of the untrustworthyness that belongs to Marina.

36. This is quite different from other films such as the already discussed *Il generale della Rovere* (1959) and *La Prise de Pouvoir par Louis XIV* (The Rise of Louis XIV, 1966), both of which, as noted by Žižek (2001b, pp. 33–4), represent the other, radically heterogeneous logic at work in Rossellini's cinema, since the emphasis there is on the subjective identification with a symbolic role rather than on the epiphanic encounter with the Real.

37. Literally, the "table-cloth", a poem that deals with Pascoli's favourite themes of family and tradition, and which eventually focuses on the image of the dead: 'Lascia che vengano i morti, / i buoni, i poveri morti' (let the unfortunate, good-hearted dead come to us).

38. Which is why, at least to an extent, *Il diavolo in corpo* can be read through Marcuse's *Eros and Civilisation*, with its emphasis on the liberating power of unconscious libido.

39. As discussed apropos of Antonioni's cinema, Lacan endeavours to resolve the "autoerotic" deadlock of sexuality by bringing into contention the social link: the only way to obtain a satisfactory degree of harmony in a relationship is by externalising it into a social bind, for it is only through their awareness of their position within society that the subject and the other have a chance of interpreting each other, thus putting a limit to their fundamental solitude. Unconsciously, this is precisely what the final scene of *Il diavolo in corpo* points towards: Andrea waits in vain for Giulia's arrival on the day of his high school oral exams, which is also the day of Giulia's marriage with Giacomo Pulcini, her repented terrorist / fiancé; it is only during the examination that Giulia appears and, unseen by Andrea, sits among the small audience of family and friends, shedding a tear of (seemingly) real love and affection. What needs to be underlined here is the paradox of love as commented upon by Žižek: 'The message of true love is thus: even if you are everything to me, I can survive without you, I am ready to forsake you for my mission or profession. The proper way for the woman to test the man's love is thus to "betray" him at a crucial moment in his career [...] only if he can survive the ordeal, and accomplish his task successfully, although he is deeply traumatized by her desertion, will he deserve her, and she will return to him. The underlying paradox is that love, precisely as the Absolute, should not be posited as a direct goal – it should retain the status of a byproduct, of something we get as an undeserved grace' (Žižek, 2003, p. 19).

40. Incidentally, after his collaboration with Bellocchio Massimo Fagioli has directed *Il cielo della luna* (The Sky of the Moon, 1998), an anti-narrative film reflecting Fagioli's belief in the figurative potential of the feminine unconscious.

41. It is indicative that in the previously mentioned last sequence of the film Giulia is indirectly compared to Antigone. Whilst Andrea answers the final question of his oral exam, which concerns the passage from Sophocles' *Antigone* on the conflict between human and divine law, we have the conclusive cut to Giulia's face as she sheds a tear. Despite its aleatory nature, this reference to Antigone – the Lacanian heroine of the uncompromising and self-destructive act – seems to confirm that Giulia's role (like Antigone, she chooses to disobey the official law, symbolised here by marriage) is that of mediating between the cinematic image and a more fundamental, libidinally-invested and unrepresentable wish.

42. This theme of "the woman who refuses to be rescued" is at the heart of many famous films such as, for example, *Taxi Driver* (1976) and *Holy Smoke* (1999). It also recurs briefly in a passage of *Il diavolo in corpo*, when Giulia, in a nightclub, engages in a provocative dance with a number of men before Andrea's very eyes.

43. Let us recall the famous passage in Visconti's *Rocco e i suoi fratelli* (Rocco and His Brother, 1960) where Simone (Renato Salvatori) kills Nadia (Annie Girardot) in an attempt to get rid of the unbearable libidinal excess that she represents for him.

44. Also, the fact that Max's friends and ex-Nazi comrades decide to eliminate Lucia, since she knows who they are and could jeopardise their attempt to erase their old identities, works as a misplaced narrative filler: in actual fact, Lucia needs to be eliminated because her masochistic zeal undermines the evil sadistic position they still unashamedly endorse. In this sense we can see how different Max turns out to be with respect to the gang of Nazi henchmen he initially cooperates with: the second encounter with Lucia produces a "miraculous" transformation, changing him from an unrepentant sadist to a faithful lover willing to sacrifice his own life for the sake of the loved one (he hides Lucia away in his flat until the day when – isolated and starved to death by his ex-companions, who monitor the flat day and night – he attempts to escape with Lucia, but both are killed).

45. Sergio Castellitto's recent debut feature, *Non ti muovere* (Don't Move, 2004), also invites reflections on the implicitly traumatic character of the sexual act. When at the beginning of the film Timoteo (Castellitto), a well-off surgeon, rapes Italia (Penelope Cruz), a destitute woman from Rome's outskirts, we should find the courage to grasp the significance of this act beyond its obvious immoral character. At least one crucial observation needs to be added: that by forcing himself on Italia Timoteo is indirectly trying to traumatise himself, so as to gain a distance from his bourgeois milieu (including his deeply unsatisfactory marriage) and start a new life. From this angle, the film tells us precisely that our attempts to free ourselves from a certain socio-symbolic order are never painless and unproblematic, but require us to undergo a traumatic, essentially masochistic experience – which, as Castellitto's film suggests, may not even be enough.

4

THE POSTMODERN REAL:
NOTES ON THE RETURN OF OEDIPUS

One of the recurrent narrative themes in new Italian cinema is the representation of the family as a fundamentally antagonised unit. Against the classic *topos* of the infinite malleability of the Italian family, functioning as an idealised haven of social harmony – from *Ladri di biciclette* (Bicycle Thieves, 1948) to *La vita è bella* (Life is Beautiful, 1997) – a number of recent popular Italian films focus on the family as a divided network struggling to recompose itself. A clear example of this emphasis on fragmentation can be found in Silvio Soldini's *Pane e tulipani* (Bread and Tulips, 1999), where Rosalba (Licia Maglietta), a housewife from Pescara, is accidentally separated from her husband and two children when the coach on which they are travelling makes a routine stop at a motorway garage. Instead of trying to catch up with them, she decides to "take a break" from her family chores. Her hitch-hiking takes her to Venice, where an array of eccentric people fill her life with a renewed *joi de vivre*. Ironically, she even has an affair with the implausible detective sent by her husband. Despite the originality of the plot, Soldini's optimistic take on the changeability of family roles is suspect to say the least, as it plays on the worn out, disingenuous postmodern appraisal of the fluidity and plasticity of the symbolic order – which often turns into the shameless commodification of violent ruptures with shared codes of behaviour (a phenomenon one can detect in almost all aspects of popular culture, from pop music to reality shows).

The main problem with this postmodern insistence on deterritorialisation (in our case, on the crisis of fixed social roles) is that, as Marx had already foreseen, it simply plays the game of capitalism: far from undermining the circulation of capital, deterritorialisation facilitates its universalisation – or, as stressed by Deleuze and Guattari, it is always accompanied by movements of reterritorialisation.[1] This implies that true change is never a question of throwing away the old symbolic identity in order to consciously and freely assume a new one, as if identity were a pair of trousers or a car; one of the lessons of psychoanalysis is that "liberation hurts", in as much as it requires that we gain a painful distance from the unconscious excess of enjoyment that keeps us attached to a certain subject position. Ultimately, a film like *Pane e tulipani* remains caught in harmless postmodern wisdom because its message that the family is an oppressive structure, and that unhappy married women should seek independence from it, reveals a far too optimistic faith in frictionless "socio-symbolic mobility" (ominously similar to today's neo-liberal principle of "economic mobility").

Measured against this anodyne open-mindedness, a substantially conservative depiction of family ties such as the one we find in Roberto Benigni's *La vita è bella* may well elicit a surprisingly penetrating analysis of social relations. In *La vita è bella* we have a protective father who weaves a web of humorous fictions to spare his young son the horrible trauma of the Holocaust, which is precisely why the film has been accused of concealing a historical truth behind a fairy-tale façade (see Gordon, 2005). However, are things really this simple? If we look a little closer at Guido Orefice (Benigni), the father, what we find is less a credible bearer of symbolic authority than a cartoon-like, comical and ultimately derealised character. Put differently, Guido is much more than just the standard father figure (the Lacanian "nom du père") who helps the child mature as an autonomous individual through symbolic castration (prohibition of incest with the mother). In excess of this paternal function, he also performs an over-protective "motherly" role, "benign" and smothering so as to achieve a crucial symptomal value. The problem is that we are not simply dealing with a "normal" father who offers his son Giosuè (Giorgio Cantarini) a symbolic fiction with which to avoid the Real, but rather with a father whose suffocating over-proximity to the son would in real life induce in the latter a series of psychological imbalances likely to culminate in psychotic behaviour. In a sense, therefore, the most profound distortion of truth in *La vita è bella* is that Giosuè does not become a psycho! As Hollywood "disaster-movies" amply testify, excessive protection inevitably leads to psychotic fantasies of catastrophic scenarios.

In this respect, the key moment in Benigni's film is perhaps the shot that magically introduces Giosuè in the narrative: having just rescued Dora from her unwanted wedding with a Fascist official, Guido takes her to his home on a horse. As he is looking for the keys, she disappears into the adjoining greenhouse from which, seconds later and within the same shot, young Giosuè comes running out playing with a toy car, whilst Guido and Dora, by this time married, enter the shot from the opposite direction as they exit their home. I would argue that the real purpose of this suturing shot, apart from compressing a vast time-span, is that it allows Benigni to avoid confronting the central question of the deeply antagonistic nature of family relations – the point being that the depiction of the unproblematic father-son relationship in the film hinges precisely on the exclusion of this underlying antagonism.[2] In conclusion, going back to our initial argument, it is clear how a symptomal reading of the film's reliance on fixed symbolic roles can lead us beyond the enthused apology of their function, permitting us to gain an insight into the inner structural logic that sustains family relations.

The specific merit of the three films I am going to discuss is that they reject the facile postmodern emphasis on the fluidity of symbolic roles and structures, whilst all the same suggesting a politically significant conceptualisation of subjective agency vis-à-vis repressive socio-symbolic conditions. These films are Nanni Moretti's *La stanza del figlio* (The Son's Room, 2001), Marco Bellocchio's *L'ora di religione (Il sorriso di mia madre)* (My Mother's Smile, 2002),[3] and Marco Tullio Giordana's *I cento passi* (The Hundred Steps, 2000). My analysis starts from the consideration that these three films present a similar Oedipal structure, insofar as the son introduces in the narrative an element of disturbance that threatens to explode the consistency of the family unit. More precisely, the common thread in my critical investigation is provided by a question concerning the type of knowledge possessed by these sons: to what extent are they aware of their subversive roles?

4.1 *LA STANZA DEL FIGLIO*: RADICALISING NEUROSIS WITH NANNI MORETTI

4.1.1 *The narcissism of the Beautiful Soul*

If there is a feature of Nanni Moretti's cinema that has always divided critics is its pronounced self-referentiality, the fact that it is founded on an essentially narcissistic impetus.[4] The prominence of Moretti's cinematic ego mainly manifests itself in the authorial control he exercises over the filmic material, as the director is also the leading actor, the screenwriter, and the producer of his films.[5] Perhaps the first question that we should ask when faced by Moretti's overwhelming authorial presence is whether the issue of self-referentiality really matters at all – or, rather, whether it should be taken as a reliable criterion to measure the quality of his work. Despite representing a case of strong authorial control over the filmic and profilmic, and despite the narcissistic drive that compels him to be on both sides of the camera, it seems to me that Moretti's obsession with his cinematic self can be evaluated as a potentially decisive feature only *after* we have tried to discern what the content of the variously reflected forms of his self might be. One thing is to say that Moretti loves to represent himself, quite another to try and understand what the scope of his reflexive gesture is.

The typically postmodern way of tackling Moretti's narcissism would be to suggest that it constitutes a masquerade of constantly shifting "forms of the self", a kaleidoscopic interplay of disguises which ultimately points to nothing but the painful fragility of the authorial 'I', and its inability to achieve a degree of consistency and self-transparency (see De Gaetano, 2002). From this perspective it could be argued that the author's self-obsession paradoxically precipitates the fragmentation of his identity, an endless multiplication of subject positions that is primarily reflected in the adoption of different stylistic registers. If in early films such as *Io sono un autarchico* (I Am Self-Sufficient, 1976), *Ecce bombo* (1978) and *Sogni d'oro* (Sweet Dreams, 1981) we have an aggressively grotesque and satirical type of self-referentiality, with *Bianca* (1984), *La messa è finita* (The Mass is Over, 1985) and *Palombella rossa* (Red Lob, 1989) we shift into a more intensely dramatic and meditative dimension, somewhat purified of the generational angst of his previous production. Later vicissitudes of Moretti's cinematic self can be followed through films such as *Caro diario* (Dear Diary, 1993) and *Aprile* (April, 1998) where the comic verve, coupled with a light-hearted, (self-)ironic inspiration, signals a clear departure from the ponderous inwardness of the previous phase. With *La stanza del figlio* (The Son's Room, 2001), finally, Moretti's self-referentiality displays itself through a completely new approach to the tragic, which again seems to confirm the heterogeneous, shifting and essentially unlocalisable nature of the director's self.

This emphasis on the fragmentation of identity can of course be given a social and (pseudo-)ideological spin: it can be observed that the vicissitudes of Moretti's cinematic self are regularly accompanied by its frustrating inability to relate to any stable "meaning". This can be expressed in abstract and idealistic terms (*La messa è finita*, *Bianca*), wrapped up in a metaphoricoideological frame (*Palombella rossa*), or narrated as variously shared experiences of social and political life (the early films, but also *Caro diario* and *Aprile*). What seems to emerge in all of Moretti's films is an existential-ideological discourse which, if on the one hand often seems characterized by authentic ethical commitment, on the other hand appears vitiated by the subject's deep-seated inhibition towards its full participation in the socio-symbolic order, which is normally ridiculed as a set of stereotypes and clichés. Typically, in *Caro Diario* the Moretti character approaches a complete stranger to tell him that, even if he lived in a better society, he would never believe in the moral majority. In *Aprile*, he famously criticises Massimo D'Alema, then leader of the centre-left coalition, for not being able to say anything truly "di sinistra" (leftist). In the earlier films, from *Io sono un autarchico* to *Palombella rossa*, Michele Apicella (the Moretti character) is essentially portrayed as a social misfit, unable to entertain any kind of meaningful relationship with other people. In a nutshell, the redundant and multifarious presence of Moretti's self reflects a fundamental neurosis: the alienation of the modern subject who finds it impossible to situate himself in a social context which is perceived as essentially hostile.

Another way of grasping this phenomenon of split identity is by considering Moretti's typical way of contrasting fiction and reality. Is not Moretti's fragmented cinematic persona typically caught between reality and a fictional dimension variously connoted as oneiric, surreal or grotesque? In most of his films, the Moretti character eventually enters a domain that is "fictional" for the simple reason that it is detached from what we assume to be "real", and the charm exuded by this character originates in the discordance between the extravagant positions he occupies, and what we inevitably regard as the sense of everydayness around him. One of the best-known examples of such discordance is the scene in *Caro Diario* where Moretti meets Jennifer Beals, the protagonist of the 1980s Hollywood box-office hit *Flashdance* (1983). Here we witness a clever manipulation of the notions of fiction and reality as Jennifer Beals appears as "real" and Moretti as a (lunatic) "fictional" character who suddenly arrives on the scene to disturb the normal course of events. Moretti's subject is therefore constantly displaced and decentred with respect to his environment, and it is precisely this insistence on the fictional *qua* excessive, dissonant, inadequate selfhood that typifies Moretti's narcissism, while simultaneously setting his narrative style between the comic and the grotesque. The director's obsession with portraying his own self implies an equally obsessive determination to represent the fracture that forever prevents the subject from achieving a degree of balance with respect to the social context in which he is immersed.

What if, however, these representations of self-alienation were nothing but a relatively harmless variation on the postmodern platitude of the infinite malleability of identity? What if this insistence on the inescapable neurosis of the self-reflexive modern subject amounted to nothing but a way of avoiding the most fundamental (and traumatic) feature of subjectivity? The aim of the following investigation is to show how the politico-ideological potential of the director's continual representation of an alienated self can only be "redeemed" and truly appreciated if reassessed from the radical perspective on subjectivity indicated in *La stanza del figlio*.

My argument starts from the critical analysis of the pseudo-idealistic concern characterising Moretti's discourse up to *La stanza del figlio*. What typifies subjectivity in his earlier work is a combination of moralistic intransigence towards the stupidity and conformity of contemporary Italian society, and a frustrating inability to articulate a radically alternative vision beyond a feeling of impotent awareness. Thus, Moretti's cinematic subject cannot fail to appear trapped in the Gordian knot of "awareness, impotence, and guilt", which ultimately is what causes him to be deeply dissatisfied not only with the social network in which he operates, but also with his own inability to intervene in it.

Bianca

We find one of the most intriguing representations of guilt-ridden impotence in *Bianca*, the only film in which the director experiments openly with the noir genre. I would go as far as to suggest that *Bianca* stands out as Moretti's major accomplishment prior to *La stanza del figlio*, for it courageously endorses the radicalisation of neurosis, to the extent that by the end of the film neurosis effectively comes to overlap with psychosis. *Bianca*'s protagonist (Michele Apicella, played by Moretti) inhabits the extremely uncertain space between neurosis and psychosis: he can either be seen as a psychotic killer or as an obsessional neurotic who eventually takes upon himself the guilt for a number of mysterious killings (the identity of the real killer is never explicitly revealed). Whether he has committed the crimes or not, his final confession proves that the way out of a neurotic loop – here exemplified by Apicella's proverbial obsession with cakes – lies in the assumption of the traumatic negativity that grounds it. The surreal "nutella sequence" (Apicella wakes up in the middle of the night, goes to the kitchen and starts eating from a massive glass of nutella to compensate for his anxiety) tells us precisely that the neurotic loop hinges on compulsive rituals: anxiety is counteracted by a certain fixation that closes the loop. In this respect, the truth about these fixations is revealed in the comical "Mont Blanc" sequence. Having invited himself to lunch at one of his students' house, Apicella fanatically lectures the whole family on how to eat the Mont Blanc (a cake); his central concern is that one should respect the 'delicate balance' of the Mont Blanc, avoiding the temptation to 'excavate a tunnel' through it. And the point is precisely that Apicella/Moretti's neurosis is correlative to the concealment of the empty core of the Thing – of the awareness that the object of our fixation is fundamentally empty!

In general, however, this reference to void remains foreclosed in Moretti's films. His fictional subject – in a similar manner to Woody Allen's, to whom he is often compared – is neurotic insofar as his awareness of the ills of society is compensated by the excesses and eccentricities of his own behaviour, which ultimately does nothing but increase his sense of impotence and, on a more profound level, guilt.

Perhaps Moretti's filmic representation of subjectivity prior to *La stanza del figlio* can be diagnosed more comprehensively by looking at Hegel's famous definition of the Beautiful Soul in the *Phenomenology of Spirit* (see Hegel, 1977, pp. 383–409). As is well known, Hegel defines the Beautiful Soul as an individual who sees himself or herself as an innocent victim amidst the evils of the world, while at the same time refusing to act, and criticising radical intervention in the name of the impossibility of universalising any such agency. Hegel's point is that this position is inherently false, as the passivity and self-proclaimed purity of the Beautiful Soul is the clearest proof of its participation in the evil universe it purports to reject. The notion that any radical intervention implies loss of innocence, therefore, has to be supplemented with the crucial observation that such innocence was never there in the first place. However, the decisive point is a different one. As Žižek has repeatedly underlined, the main problem with the Beautiful Soul lies in the fact that *self-victimisation breeds narcissistic enjoyment*, as what the Beautiful Soul fears the most is having to sacrifice the role of innocent victim *by actually taking part in the wicked ways of the world*. Similarly, could we not argued that Moretti's films prior to *La stanza del figlio* exemplify a certain attitude of the post-1968 Left in their secretly narcissistic attachment to a sense of loss and impotence, coupled with a condemnation of any attempt to rearticulate a radical ideological project with a universal application? My central argument in what follows is that the neurotic vicious circle in which Moretti gets caught is radically and comprehensively challenged by the new insight into subjectivity suggested by *La stanza del figlio*.

4.1.2 'Father, can't you see I'm burning?'
A way to appreciate the originality of the director's view of subjectivity in *La stanza del figlio* is to acknowledge how he sacrifices what up to that point in his career had been his constitutive epistemological tool: irony (including self-irony). In this overtly tragic narrative, irony is reduced to a bare minimum. Far from being accidental, this sacrifice signals a clear-cut break with Moretti's previous cinematic work, a shift that can be visualized by subtracting irony from self-referentiality. What we get is the representation of a subject who, whilst still narcissistically intent on contemplating his own self, has nevertheless lost the attitude of ironic detachment from the outer world, which allowed him, at least unconsciously, to safeguard his moral integrity.[6] We are instead presented with an utterly de-politicised subject, in the sense that the director does not turn the subject's alienation in the world into an *a priori* condition for a cinematic narrative centred on a mixture of impotent moralism, existential angst and neurotic comicality. On the contrary, the subject is now compelled to face what remains of the self *without* the external support of the corrupted social framework. Unable to lament the oppressive character of the modern world (and, conversely, also unable to say 'I exist because I am different from you')[7] this new Moretti forces himself and the film's spectators to question the very foundations of subjectivity. The crux of my argument is that, in so doing, he paradoxically discovers the most fundamentally political dimension of subjectivity itself.

La stanza del figlio tells the story of a tight-knit Italian family forced to come to terms with the devastating loss of Andrea (Giuseppe Sanfelice), the son, who suffers a fatal accident whilst scuba-diving. Moretti plays Giovanni, a psychoanalyst happily married to Paola (Laura Morante) with two teenage children, Irene (Jasmine Trinca) and Andrea. Tragedy strikes on a Sunday morning, when Giovanni opts to make a rare house call instead of going for a run with his son. As a consequence of this choice, he cannot help blaming himself for his Andrea's death. He starts having difficulty listening to and caring about his patients, and also progressively distances himself from his wife.

In this film, Moretti's representation of subjectivity clearly depends on the emergence of the Real, which coincides with the unexpected death of the son. The effect of this death can be measured in terms of the traumatic void it opens up at the heart of the social institution that in Italy best embodies symbolic identification: the family. As the second part of the film shows, Andrea's disappearance threatens to disintegrate the seemingly impeccable harmony of family life. In a similar manner to Pasolini's *Teorema*, the incendiary intrusion of the Real ushers in fragmentation, disorder and suffering, forcing each family member out of their symbolic roles, and obliging them to question the very foundations of their identities and relationships, which up until that moment had seemed natural and unbreakable.[8] As the marriage between Giovanni and Paola faces potential dissolution, Irene becomes unduly aggressive and finds it increasingly difficult to relate to her parents. If we compare this narrative scenario to those of Moretti's previous films, we immediately notice a simple but decisive difference: the representation of the subject here does not start with a painful awareness of his alienated condition, but with a serene immersion in his environment, which is only later disturbed by trauma.

If the question of the effect produced by the Real on the Symbolic is a central one in *La stanza del figlio*, this is because Moretti is not afraid to confront the Real's traumatic impact. Rather than merely "banking" on the emotional aftermath of Andrea's death, the director asks us to examine the position that trauma occupies with respect to the Symbolic *before* exploding in all its nauseating horror. In fact, it is precisely the problem of the location of the traumatic event that differentiates this potentially banal narrative from a trite TV drama. It is crucial to acknowledge that in Moretti's film the Real (the void of death, the non-symbolisable event *par excellence*) sits latently within the symbolic structure of the family itself, rather than attacking it from outside. Moretti deliberately reproduces what the Roman poet Horace called *aurea mediocritas*, as a sense of idyllic normality seems to envelop everyday situations. Giovanni and Paola are what we may call the perfect (post)modern couple: both well educated and with rewarding careers, their marriage flourishes in seemingly unbreakable spiritual and sexual harmony. Predictably, they spend a lot of time with their children, either following and supporting their sporting activities, or helping with school homework. Everyone at home enjoys a healthy diet, and of course nobody smokes, although the father, demonstrating typically post-Oedipal (marking the decline of paternal authority) tolerance, does not get overly upset when he discovers that his daughter's boyfriend uses cannabis.

To emphasise this sense of placid middle-class normality, Moretti's camera focuses with minimalist, even neorealistic precision on the most ordinary incidents. As with the most accomplished neorealist films, however, what matters is to go beyond the apparent coincidence of reality with its representation, and question instead the smoothness and seamlessness of the narrative. Thus, the subtle feeling of foreboding that seeps through the opening sequence – where a Hari Krishna parade catches Giovanni's attention after his jogging session – works as a kind of deforming mirror for the protagonist, secretly warning him that the smooth running of his life might be the result of a distorted perception. Similarly, the portrayal of the family's harmonious coexistence is from the outset charged with a surplus of enigmatic tension – effectively conveyed, for example, by the noir-coded shots of Giovanni as he walks through his flat, the camera tracking him from behind, creating a sense of suspense in relation to what might emerge in front of him.[9]

The first part of the narrative seems therefore to confirm the Lacanian insight that the Real is not a pre-given dimension which is simply repressed by the Symbolic, but that it is produced by symbolisation itself, nothing but a constitutional excess inherent to the very process of subjectivation: the more we identify with a symbolic role (the more we compromise our desire to attain consistency as subjects), the more we also secrete a non-symbolisable residue that sooner or later emerges from within our pacified symbolic universe, forcing us to confront it in all its radically unfamiliar otherness. Alenka Zupančič sums up the concept in the following way:

> It is in this sense that we should understand the thesis according to which the operation of the symbolic (of symbolisation) never comes out right, that it always produces a remainder. It is not that after this operation something pre-symbolic is left over, as "unsymbolisable" or something that "escapes" symbolisation, it is that symbolisation, in its very perfection and completeness, produces a surplus which "undermines" it from within by engendering impasses. To paraphrase Hegel: the remainder is the bone of the spirit itself, not something external that spirit has not been able completely to devour (Zupančič, 2000, p. 191).

The distinctive attribute of the Real also lends itself to be defined by the Lacanian term *extimité* (see Žižek, 1992, p. 132), which describes an intimate psychological formation that nevertheless remains irreducibly decentred, external to the subject's sense of identity.[10]

A whole array of examples spring to mind here, both from fictional and historical patterns. Is it not true that in the film noir tradition, as well as in its equivalent literary genre of crime fiction, the figure of the killer, i.e. the bearer of the traumatic dimension, inevitably and shockingly comes into view as *extimate*, as the most ordinary character epitomising universally shared notions of normality, lawfulness and respectability? Today's media also provide us with paradigmatic notions of "pure folly" and "radical evil" precisely when they comment on the eruption of incomprehensible violence from within the most harmonious and respectable family environment. The long series of much publicised domestic killings emerging from within our postmodern universe suggests precisely that the Symbolic opens up the wound it professes to heal.

The specific conceptualisation of otherness as *extimate* helps us to grasp the full significance of Moretti's film. What we should not overlook is how the traumatic event that strikes at the heart of the symbolic field *was always-already present (at the heart of this field)*, coinciding with the very void around which any symbolic order, from family to social contract, is structured.[11] My point is that nowhere before *La stanza del figlio* had Moretti so lucidly uncovered the mechanism upon which the functioning of both the subjective and the socio-symbolic field hinge. In his previous films, contemporary society was by and large represented as an obscurely alienating force for a subject whose only answer was a feeling of neurotic powerlessness. Now, instead, the otherness that stained the world outside is repositioned at the heart of subjectivity. As a result society disappears, reduced as it is to "family" first, and then to "subject". And it is in the intimacy of the smallest socio-symbolic unit that the self-referential, narcissistic subject (Moretti) finds himself, as he summons up the courage to confront the fact that the otherness of the external world actually belongs within the self. The introspective dimension of *La stanza del figlio* is ultimately functional to the film's central claim that the original condition of subjectivity is one of radical imbalance and displacement. One can therefore finally appreciate the significance of Moretti's narcissism: rather than representing the (alienated) self as the *effect* of the (alienating) social substance, here he chooses to stage a self who, to paraphrase Hegel, *is* Substance, in as much as his potential intervention in the network of socio-symbolic references is only truly warranted by his coming to terms with his own constitutional imbalance.

In *La stanza del figlio*, the manifestation of the Real can be measured in terms of the change of fortunes affecting the father's work after the death of his son. Moretti's emphasis on therapeutic treatment depends on the question of *transference*, the dialectical relationship between analyst and analysand. According to the Lacanian understanding of transference, the analyst's role is to sit in as a silent cause for a desire that only the patient is aware of, and which he or she will discover in the time it takes to unravel repressed traumas and impasses (to probe, that is, the underworld of the unconscious). During treatment, the analysand transfers expectations for help on to the analyst, believing that the latter knows how to access his or her psychological domain. The ultimate goal of transference, however, is to undermine the illusion that the analyst possesses a stable base for knowledge, showing how the displacing dimension of lack is ontological, as it already pertains to the domain of the other *qua* analyst.

Within this context, it seems legitimate to assume that through an experience of counter-transference Giovanni realises what he should have already known:[12] that the subject is thoroughly alienated in the symbolic order, and that such alienation depends on the emergence of an utterly foreign body (in Giovanni's case, of course, this foreign body is none other than his son Andrea) that is responsible for the activation of desire. Strictly speaking, then, the film demonstrates how Andrea finds himself occupying the position of the analyst, whereas the father becomes the analysand. Visually, this rapport is rendered in the repeated jogging sequence where Giovanni struggles to keep up with Andrea's pace. This scenario serves to illustrate what happens in the final stage of the analysis, when the analyst, who up to that point had simply feigned to occupy a position of absolute knowledge (the position of the Master, the 'sujet supposé savoir'),[13] all of a sudden renders visible his imposture, and only then encourages his patient to confront his or her repressed symptoms. The paradox is that the discourse of the Master is unexpectedly brought to an end by an event that is external to the relationship of transference. Giovanni, in other words, is given a "Real taste" of his own medicine, as he is reminded of the painful truth lurking behind the mask of the *sujet supposé savoir*.

In his portrayal of therapeutic interaction, Moretti suggests that the unconscious, the target of the analysis, is always characterised by its radical negativity. We could say that *La stanza del figlio* carries out the full hystericisation of the postmodern subject by forcing him to confront his own foundational lack; with this film Moretti accomplishes the passage from a superficial representation of modern neurosis to a specific radicalisation of hysteria as the encounter with the non-symbolisable, decentring Real. It was Freud first, then followed by Lacan, who insisted on the subversive quality of hysteria (see Feher Gurevich, 1997), on the ground that the subjective attitude of the hysteric is one where the self is perennially questioned on behalf of its constitutive "wound". More precisely, 'we are dealing with hysteria only in so far as the victimized subject entertains an ambiguous attitude of fascination towards the wound, […], in so far as the very source of pain exerts a magnetism – hysteria is precisely the name for this stance of ambivalent fascination in the face of the object that terrifies and repels us' (Žižek, 2000a, pp. 248–49). If from the opening scene Giovanni's behaviour is latently caught up in the loop of a certain drive towards an enigmatic question (later exacerbated by his nagging doubts regarding Andrea's innocence in relation to the theft of the fossil), the hysterical drive fully comes into play only after Andrea's death, when Giovanni appears inexplicably attracted to 'the very source of pain', the void that has swallowed up his son. When his wife tries to convince him that he cannot go back in time, he replies that this is exactly what he wants to do: 'tornare indietro' (go back), and confront the enigma of the lack which irrationally materialised through Andrea's disappearance. Perhaps the most suggestive metaphorical rendition of Giovanni's hysterical tension is encapsulated in the scene when, alone in his son's room, he keeps rewinding and replaying the same few bars of a Michael Nyman song with the remote control.

The key point is that the uncanny dimension of the nauseating event ultimately reveals to the subject the truth about his own radical dislocation in the symbolic network. What is actually left for Giovanni of what seemed a perfectly balanced, homeostatic Aristotelian universe? Quite simply, Giovanni discovers that the void opened up by Andrea's death *is* the distinctive feature of his own symbolic field. It is only after his son's death that he realises how things – from the teapot to a piece of furniture, from his marriage to his job – are never smooth nor whole: how reality, beyond its fictional functioning, is fundamentally cracked and stained, displaced by its inherent lack. In a nutshell, we are presented with a paroxysm of neurosis: the death of the son drives the father to the verge of an abyss that threatens to swallow him, to reduce him to a lifeless puppet.

If by the end of the film the father finds himself assuming the position of the hysteric, discovering the fundamental arbitrariness of symbolic roles, we could legitimately argue that the original hysteric who poses the first challenge to the symbolic network is the son, Andrea, whose position throughout the film can be summed up with Lacan's definition of the prototypical hysterical question: 'What am I, if I'm what you've just been saying I am?' (Lacan, 2000, p. 279). As Giovanni admits soon after his son's death, there was something in Andrea that resisted interpretation, something that remained untold, impenetrable for the rest of the family, despite their genuine intimacy and closeness. This impenetrability is precisely what "the son's room" eventually comes to represent for the father, who time after time enters the room as if to look for a certain missing truth about Andrea. To be more accurate, the son's demise forces Giovanni to discover the persistence of the *object in the subject*, the disturbing presence of what was "in Andrea more than himself". On closer inspection, in fact, Andrea had been challenging his symbolic mandate within the family well before his death by formulating his own specific version of the hysterical question: 'Are you sure you know who I am?'; or, more precisely, 'Are you sure my role as "son" within the economy of this (post)modern family actually *exhausts* my whole being?' The basic, purest position of the hysteric originates in this split between demand (being the son) and desire (being more/less/something other than the son) through which the subject resists any attempt to fulfil a given symbolic mandate.

Does the initial episode of the stolen fossil not function as a reminder that the symbolic texture was from the outset stained by the Real of desire? Andrea steals the fossil from the science laboratory at school, but when accused by a classmate he adamantly denies the theft. The headmaster summons the parents of both children and a meeting between the conflicting parties ensues. Andrea continues to plead innocent, accusing his classmate of gratuitous malevolence, and Andrea's parents end up believing their son's version of the events, although Giovanni cannot shake off some lingering doubts. Later on, however, it is Andrea himself who confesses to his mother that he had stolen the fossil. Far from working as a narrative filler, the episode of the theft takes us into the duplicitous realm of symbolic identification. First of all, the disturbing realisation that Andrea was actually responsible for the theft starts undermining the illusion of the smooth, organic equilibrium of family life, to the extent that his admission of guilt can be seen as anticipating the trauma to come. However, we should not overlook Andrea's failure to confess to his father, which is caused by his reluctance to disturb Giovanni's tranquillity (as he tells his mother). This detail is important as it clarifies the fact that deep down *the guilty party is the father*, who represses subjective tensions by feigning an illusory stability which, in turn, works against the son as a sort of emotional blackmail. No wonder, then, that Giovanni feels guilty after Andrea's death. As in the Freudian dream re-read by Lacan,[14] the father *knew* that the son was burning (with desire), but simply decided to ignore the question in order to satisfy the requirements of the pleasure principle – the mental device responsible for lowering inner anxieties, therefore moving us towards pleasure and stability.

Here Moretti shows us how well he has learnt the lesson of Kieslowski's cinema, as he himself openly acknowledges (see Bonsaver, 2002). Reproducing one of the most distinctive traits of Kieslowski's filmmaking, the theft works as the uncanny prefiguration of the event that will ruthlessly and unfathomably shatter the symbolic order in which the subject was peacefully immersed. Similar "metaphysical" Kieslowskian forewarnings occur just moments before the tragedy, when Giovanni barely manages to avoid a car crash, Paola is suddenly brushed aside by a man who runs past her (a thief?), and Irene plays dangerously with some school-mates whilst driving her moped.[15] Significantly, as if to underline the intervention of a non-symbolisable dimension (the Lacanian Real), these events seem to take place simultaneously, as Moretti cuts consecutively from one to the next in a stylistically overdetermined fashion.

On a deeper level, the fossil should also be seen as a metonymical materialisation of *objet a*. The detail not to be missed here is that Moretti depicts Andrea, particularly from the moment he perpetrates the theft, as a sort of angelic individual deprived of vitality, objectified, unable to desire. This characterisation of a radically emasculated subject, which Lacanian psychoanalysis calls *aphanisis*, becomes evident when, after watching his son lose a tennis match, Giovanni complains to him that he has lost because he never wanted to win the game in the first place, because he lacked the desire to compete. Giovanni's intuition hits the target. However, what the father does not know is that Andrea's dysfunctional behaviour originates in his sense of guilt towards paternal authority, a guilt caused of course by the theft of the fossil.

The key observation, however, entails a surprising reversal of this reading, whereby guilt is replaced by its necessary correlative, desire. Let us not forget that in its most radical configuration Lacan's notion of symbolic castration coincides with the very theft of the object-cause of desire, which in turn produces *aphanisis*. As a result, Andrea's indifference is not just a consequence of his guilt but more importantly of his intrusion into the impossible domain of the Real.[16] Strictly speaking, the desiring subject wants Nothingness, for his excessive attachment to *objet a* leads to the truncation of all his links with the external world. This is why, as Žižek points out, 'in an authentic act, the highest freedom coincides with the utmost passivity, with a reduction to a lifeless automaton who blindly performs his gestures' (Žižek, 2000a, p. 375): the truly desiring subject frees himself of the constraints of the socio-symbolic network and shifts into a psychotic mode where he literally stops being the master of his own actions. Andrea's position, therefore, finds its theoretical equivalent in what Lacan calls 'destitution subjective' (see Lacan, 1996, pp. 851–54), substanceless subjectivity, a frame emptied, evacuated of all pathological contents. With hindsight we can assume that the son has dared to go beyond the Symbolic (his pre-established role in the family), has stolen the secret treasure (the impossible *objet a*) and as a consequence *has had to disappear* from the symbolic order. It is precisely this (self-)destructive act culminating in separation which, according to Lacan, connects us with the hard core of subjectivity: 'There is no subject without, somewhere, aphanisis of the subject, and it is in this alienation, in this fundamental division, that the dialectic of the subject is established' (Lacan, 1998a, p. 221).

Germania anno zero

Andrea's *aphanisis* reminds us of one of the most shocking sons of Italian cinema, the German child Edmund in Rossellini's *Germania anno zero* (Germany Year Zero, 1947) who poisons his sickly father with cold indifference. As Žižek remarks in his reading of the film, the parricide Edmund stands for 'the subject of the signifier, i.e., for the subject, insofar as it is reduced to an empty place without support in imaginary or symbolic identification' (Žižek, 2001b, p. 36). The point is that far from simply embodying the lethal influence of his homosexual Nazi teacher Henning who has drilled into him the "survival of the fittest" ideology, Edmund's act also stands for a "liberating" event which realises the father's desire to die, since his suffering had become unbearable. After killing his father Edmund enters the Lacanian domain of radical alienation "between the two deaths", a place of utter segregation from the social community that foreshadows his own real death: he meanders pointlessly through the debris of a devastated Berlin and eventually retreats in a half-ruined building; there he refuses to answer his sister's call and, in the last shot of the film, jumps from the second floor of the building with his eyes closed. As in Andrea's case, insisting on the son's guilt (caused by Nazi ideology) is misleading here. On the contrary, Edmund's act demarcates the impossible collapse of meaning, the "anno zero" of ideology:

> What propels him into act is an awareness of the ultimate insufficiency and nullity of every ideological foundation: he succeeds in occupying that impossible/real empty place where words no longer oblige, where their performative power is suspended. This is "Germany, Year Zero": Germany in the year of absolute freedom when the intersubjective bond, the engagement of the Word is broken. True, we can call this – the distance taken from the Other – also "psychosis", but what is "psychosis" here if not another name for freedom? (Žižek, 2001b, p. 36).

Going back to Moretti, the above evaluation of the psychotic act can be developed further through an attentive analysis of Andrea's death. As Paola reminds Giovanni, their son died because he followed a fish into an underwater cave, and once inside he did not manage to find his way out. The fish in question works as a clear equivalent of the fossil, and both objects (*a*) provide evidence for Andrea's destabilising desire. His theft of the fossil represents the first step towards the discovery of the vertiginous abyss of the self, which he then fully assumes through his pursuit of the fish into the cave.[17] This, again, is crucial if we are to grasp the radicality achieved by Moretti's discourse with *La stanza del figlio*, for Andrea signals the passage from *alienation* to *separation*, a passage that the director had always missed in his previous works.

Perhaps the best way to understand this passage is by returning to the notion of *repetition*, another key Lacanian term brought to fruition by Žižek:

> The original position of man *qua* being of language is decidedly that of alienation in the signifier (in the symbolic order): the first choice is necessarily that of the Father, which marks the subject with the indelible guilt pertaining to his very (symbolic) existence. This alienation is best exemplified by the Kantian moral subject: the split subject subordinated to the moral imperative, caught in the vicious circle of the superego where he is all the more guilty the more he obeys its command. Yet Lacan's wager is that it is possible for the subject to get rid of the superego pressure by *repeating* the choice and thus exculpating himself of his constitutive guilt. The price for it is exorbitant: if the first choice is "bad", its repetition is in its very formal structure "worse" since it is an act of *separation* from the symbolic community (Žižek, 2001b, p. 77).

This appraisal of repetition corroborates the claim that Andrea's theft and his chasing the fish are two structurally identical acts which show us how the burden of guilt can be overcome (just as in *Germania anno zero* Edmund's parricide is correlative to his suicide). First, Andrea emerges as a subject through the theft of the fossil, which produces guilt; then he repeats that very (negative) gesture by negating the symbolic frame responsible for his guilt through a second theft, the lethal theft of the object-cause of desire.

This line of reasoning enables us to infer that Andrea is not a typically devitalised postmodern youth in the hands of the late-capitalist social machine; his destitution, rather, overlaps with the emergence of pure subjectivity, the zero-point from which the symbolic field can be radically resignified. So, if we approach the film through the classic Freudian opposition of life and death-drive (see Freud, 1974, pp. 30–7), death-drive would seem to designate Andrea's disattachment from the Symbolic, whereas life would indicate the opposite effort of family bonding, aimed at recomposing the symbolic texture after the tragedy. However, my Lacanian reading suggests that "life" actually coincides with "death-drive", for it is Andrea's act that allows for a reframing of the symbolic field. Hence, the emphasis should be placed on the negative moment of disinvestment, the moment of Andrea's collapse into *objet petit a*. This is why one of the most poignant sequences in the film is the closure of Andrea's coffin in the morgue, shot with a series of disturbing close-ups of the entire sealing operation, focusing in particular the welding and drilling of the coffin lid. The tremendous power of this passage resides in its focus on the inaccessible core of the subject, in the sense that what is here sealed away forever *was always-already sealed away*: Andrea *was* the impenetrable, indivisible leftover correlative to the abyss of the subject.

Uncomfortable as it may sound, we should therefore summon up the courage to discern in Andrea's death a liberating potential, which in the final analysis accounts for Moretti's deep-seated, possibly unconscious (political) desire. The void into which Andrea disappears is none other than the void of freedom, since freedom is successfully actualised as the excessive dimension that opens up a radical fracture in the symbolic order. The question of freedom and its location seems to impose itself here as the nodal point of Moretti's materialistic discourse. Moretti's lack of faith in a transcendental and teleological principle mapping the notions of truth, universality and freedom (a relativism which is the defining feature of his neurotic characters), now for the first time explodes in a powerful narrative that, far from expressing a nihilistic drive, tells us that it is precisely from absolute, "hopeless" atheistic immanence that a new understanding of the word freedom can arise. In *La stanza del figlio*, freedom is nothing but the abyss of absolute negativity through which the subject dissolves every link with its life habitat.

Žižek's combined understanding of Hegel's notions of abstract negativity and concrete universality, as they are articulated in *The Phenomenology of Spirit*, provides another fertile insight into *La stanza del figlio*'s underlying aim. Žižek's fundamental contention is that 'the only way towards a truly "concrete" universality leads through the full assertion of the radical negativity by means of which the universal negates its entire particular content'. As such, the endorsement of abstract negativity acquires a decisive political weight, in that it allows one to undermine radically the *status quo* and consequently 'create the terrain for the new post-revolutionary reconciliation between the demands of social Order and the abstract freedom of the individual' (Žižek, 2000a, pp. 92–4).[18]

My claim, which turns the prevailing reading of *La stanza del figlio* as a sorrowful meditation on human finitude and powerlessness on its head, is precisely that Hegelian negativity represents the implicit truth-content of Moretti's film. In what should be regarded as a typically Hegelian gesture, Moretti tells us that we can only truly define ourselves as subjects the moment we endorse our fundamental alienation in the socio-symbolic order as the universal split which, alone, enables us to thoroughly resignify our life. As strange as it may sound, it is Andrea's death

La stanza del figlio

that, hauntingly symbolized in the empty frame of his room, reveals to the father where freedom is to be found. Of course, Giovanni tries to rationalise the trauma: first he blames himself; then he blames the patient who had called him out on the day of the accident, preventing him from going jogging with his son and thus indirectly provoking the tragic event; then he convinces himself that his son's diving equipment had suffered a mechanical failure. His desperate attempts at making sense of the trauma can be understood through Kant's notion of *Einbildungskraft* (literally, the craft of image-building) which defines the transcendental power of imagination as the power to synthesise incoherent sensory perceptions into images that are suitable to be understood rationally (see Kant, 1996, pp. 164–73). When confronting the nauseating absence of his son, Giovanni tries to do exactly that – he tries to conceptualise what is by definition beyond reason. Eventually, however, his failure to regain a minimum of "cognitive mapping" causes him to leave his job and threatens to destroy his family ties.

Incidentally, this logic of integrating the Real into a symbolic universe is what is at stake in Rossellini's *Europa '51* (No Greater Love, 1952), perhaps the sharpest exploration of the function of guilt in Italian cinema. Irene (Ingrid Bergman) reacts to the sudden death of her son (a suicide?) by "escaping into guilt" (see Žižek, 2001b, pp. 37–42), i.e., by convincing herself that her son committed suicide because of her lack of affection. Consequently, she seeks to atone through self-sacrifice: first she familiarises herself with the Communist ideology, and then Christianity, in an attempt to forsake her selfish bourgeois lifestyle and help the poor. At this stage, however, Rossellini's film strides towards a different outcome with respect to Moretti's, insofar as the subject's escape into guilt becomes unconditional to the point of generating the very non-symbolisable remainder it had set out to conceal: Irene's zeal in detaching herself from her symbolic network is so uncompromising that she is declared insane and locked away in a mental institution, while a cluster of poor people soon assemble in front of the hospital to honour her as a saint. As *Francesco, giullare di Dio* (The Flowers of St. Francis, 1950) emphatically attested, Rossellini's early cinema fulfils its ideological potential through this endorsement of the excessive kernel of the subject, which materialises in the figure of the saint who embodies 'the state of blessed innocence where we "have all" precisely insofar as we have "lost all"' (Žižek, 2001b, p. 36).[19]

To return to the father-son relationship in *La stanza del figlio*, let us now try to assess the meaning of the previously mentioned Freudian dream: it may be argued that 'Father, can't you see I'm burning?' is, contrary to the standard Freudian interpretation, to be taken quite literally: as the equivalent of Andrea's request for a different father figure, one that is aware of the son's inner desires and, more significantly, of the revolutionary potential that they carry into the socio-symbolic order.[20] Does not this uncanny question correspond to Andrea's intimate desire to be seen by his father as culpable of stealing the fossil, i.e. of challenging the homeostatic tranquillity of the family? Again, this confirms that Andrea's death should be inscribed in a narrative logic which (perhaps without the conscious authorization of the director) aims at delineating the contour of a radically antagonistic stance. If we agree with this reading we can perhaps make sense of Moretti's "scandalous" public outburst of 2 February 2002, when he openly attacked leading politicians of the Italian centre-left coalition for their lack of authentic political engagement. Far from being a narcissistic *coup de théâtre*, Moretti's intervention amounted to a sort of painful but necessary "striking at oneself" aimed at exposing the very inconsistency of the current liberal leftist perspective, and thus at opening up the space for a different vision.[21] The point to be emphasised is that Moretti's speech took place during a left-wing rally, producing the uncanny effect of *extimacy*: a disturbing foreign body emerging in the midst of a homely environment where a certain political agenda was universally shared and supported. To have an idea of the symbolic significance of this gesture, one only has to look at the TV footage of Moretti's intervention, where Francesco Rutelli, then leader of the centre-left coalition, can be seen in the background gradually turning pale in shock and disbelief as Moretti proceeds in his angry reprimand.

In the final part of *La stanza del figlio* Moretti shows us how the family attempts to overcome the trauma and refashion its own identity. The decisive factor is the intervention of Arianna, a girl Andrea had met a few months prior to his death during a camping holiday. Despite spending only a single day in her company, Andrea had fallen in love with Arianna, and since the summer the two teenagers had started exchanging secret love letters. The significance of this letter is that it reveals to Andrea's parents their son's desiring nature, in stark contrast with his apparent aloofness and apathy.[22] In what sense, then, does Arianna's unexpected appearance give the family a chance to regroup? The point to note is that this second event prompts them towards symbolising loss. The void left by Andrea's death can now be filled by a minimum of symbolic meaning – just as the emptiness of the son's room is partly refilled with his presence as Arianna shows the family some photographs of Andrea in his room that he himself had taken and sent her.[23] As in the mythical tale, Arianna literally *provides the thread that leads the lost out of the maze*. The final journey through the night, which sees Giovanni with wife and daughter driving Arianna and her friend Stefano to the French border so that they can start their holiday, works as a metaphorical indication that the process of symbolic reconstruction, the suturing of the wound, has finally started. The subjects regain a degree of psychic balance through the fantasy that they invest in their relationship with the stand-in for the lost object. Arianna partly compensates for the void left by Andrea's death and gives them the opportunity, literally, to fantasise again.

The parents now seem to realise that their knowledge of Andrea had always been partial, always structured around a blurred spot. When Giovanni urges Paola not to speculate on the nature of Arianna's relationship with Stefano, her travelling friend, we understand that to them Arianna is to remain Andrea's loved one, thus allowing for trauma to be partly symbolised. The ambiguous ending of the film, however, suggests that the family cannot regain the previous degree of stability. As they gaze at Arianna departing on the coach, these forlorn and isolated figures wandering on the beach, facing the open sea, convey a sense of absolute, incommensurable fragility, suggesting that they now perceive their symbolic space as traversed by a profound and definitive rupture. All they can do, it seems, is endeavour to cope with this imbalance by trying to reconfigure a different fictional structure.

If taken to its extreme conclusion, my analysis brings us back to the question of the director's break with his preceding approach to filmmaking. This is indeed a new Moretti who for the first time steps into that truly uncharted territory defined by Lacanian psychoanalysis as "the discourse of the Other". With *La stanza del figlio* Moretti radicalises the *implicit* achievement of his previous films, namely the idea that subjectivity is constitutionally antagonised by the excess produced by its own self-positing movement. By shunning ironic detachment and instead reaching out to the abyssal lack that grounds the subject, the film accomplishes a gesture of uncompromising self-obliteration which simultaneously opens up a whole new set of potential resignifications. Arguably, the most remarkable aspect of *La stanza del figlio* lies with its determination to evacuate all subject positions and related pathological/idiosyncratic contents, suggesting that the ethical act proper originates in fully assuming the traumatic otherness that dwells in the core of the subject. From this tragedy, Giovanni learns that freedom is nothing but freedom to resignify radically the symbolic field. This happens when the subject finds himself in a position whereby he can release himself from the symbolic burden he had previously undertaken, however traumatic this may be. The road of ethics essentially passes through the groundless abyss around which subjectivity is always structured.[24] In a nutshell, the film tells us that far from being a blissful condition of harmony and balance, freedom is the very act that breaks this presumed balance. Going back one last time to the question of Moretti's self-referentiality, it is tempting to conclude that prior to *La stanza del figlio* Moretti had simply *not been self-referential enough*, in the precise sense that he had always missed the only genuinely reflexive gesture of confronting the abyssal freedom of the subject.

4.2 *L'ORA DI RELIGIONE*: GAZING BACKWARDS WITH MARCO BELLOCCHIO

4.2.1 *The Oedipal legacy*
What is striking about Bellocchio's *L'ora di religione* is that it treats subjectivity as the crucial political context where the fight for change and regeneration takes place, while simultaneously disregarding any direct reference to politics. As with *La stanza del figlio*, the silent postmodern ban on politics turns into the radical politicisation of postmodernism's privileged topic, the subject. In line with Bellocchio's entire production, the exploration of the subversive potential of the subject is here conflated with the exploration of family life. It is highly significant that in almost every one of Bellocchio's previous films the family is portrayed as the network through which the individual experiences the authoritarian nature of social relations (see Bernardi 1998, p. 18). The usual absence of the father allows for a direct critical engagement with institutional forms of power that symbolically perform the paternal function. In *I pugni in tasca* (Fists in the Pocket, 1965), for example, the void opened up by the absent father forces the son into a direct confrontation with the hypocrisy and mediocrity of his middle-class *milieu*, which culminates in a psychotic *passage a l'acte* (the killing of the mother). In later films such as *La Cina è vicina* (China is

Near, 1967) and *Nel nome del padre* (In the Name of the Father, 1972), the disclosure of the basic meanness of family life leads up to a bitterly sarcastic assessment of repressive ideological mechanisms and related institutional practices in postwar Italy. In *Marcia trionfale* (Victory March, 1976), a clear link is established between family and military life in terms of their common repressive nature. In the 1980s, Bellocchio's irreverent deconstruction of the family unit continues to produce remarkable results. Films like *Un salto nel vuoto* (Leap into the Void, 1980), *Gli occhi, la bocca* (The Eyes, the Mouth, 1982) and *Diavolo in corpo* (Devil in the Flesh, 1986) can all be regarded as implacable investigations into the inconsistency of family relations. The central theme here is the irreconcilable animosity between members of the same family, whether brother and sister (*Un salto nel vuoto*), mother and son (*Gli occhi, la bocca*), or father and son (*Diavolo in corpo*). At the same time, exposing such inconsistencies always implies, for Bellocchio, calling into question wider social structures that sustain what the director sees as a squalidly conformistic idea of the family. Hence, it seems legitimate to argue that the ultimate target of Bellocchio's dissection of the Italian family is the bourgeois humus of postwar Italian society as shaped by late-capitalist ideology. Explicit class-related analysis, however, tends to wither in his most recent films, practically disappearing in *L'ora di religione*. Here is a summary of the plot.

The film tells the two intertwining family tales of Ernesto Picciafuoco (Sergio Castellitto), a successful painter and illustrator of children's books. The first tale concerns his extended family and centres on his dead mother, whilst the second revolves around his own nuclear family, focusing on the problematic relationships he has with his wife Irene and his young son Leonardo. The opening is truly Kafkaesque, with Ernesto receiving an unexpected visit from the secretary of an enigmatic cardinal, who tells him that his dead mother, an extremely pious woman, may soon be canonised. As we find out soon after, the candidate for sainthood was killed some years earlier by Egidio, Ernesto's mentally ill brother, who one day, having had enough of his mother's continual reproaching him for blaspheming, stabs and kills her in her sleep. Driven by his atheism, Ernesto slowly unmasks the hypocrisy behind the beatification plan, discovering that his aunt had been lobbying the Vatican for several years, and that each member of his extended family now has a personal stake in the social prestige and material gain that the mother's sainthood would produce. Parallel to the events surrounding his mother's beatification, Ernesto has to deal with the separation from his wife, as well as with some moral questions concerning the upbringing of his little boy. More precisely, Ernesto grows more and more determined that Leonardo, his son, should stop attending the optional session of Catholic doctrine offered in Italian schools. Realising that Leonardo is falling under the influence of the Catholic doctrine, Ernesto resolves to confront his son's religion teacher, whom he expects to be an ugly, wizened old woman. To his surprise, however, the person in question turns out to be young and beautiful. Prompted less by theology than by her dazzling looks, Ernesto cannot help himself falling under her influence too. The result of this mysterious encounter brings new vitality into Ernesto's secluded life, strengthening his opposition to his mother's beatification.

4.2.2 *Virtuality and the demise of the symbolic*

A central feature of *L'ora di religione* is its insistence on the fictional status and potential overthrow of the big Other, the network of symbolic references demarcating the subject's status within the social context. The big Other is represented here by the Picciafuoco family with its vital and ambiguous links with the Catholic Church, and it is antagonised by the film's protagonist, Ernesto Picciafuoco. As his name suggests (Picciafuoco is similar to "arsonist" in Italian, whilst Ernesto is inevitably associated to Che Guevara's first name), this character is a slightly domesticated version of the rebel figures in Bellocchio's early cinema. Ernesto's defiant attitude is confirmed by his painting style, and more significantly by his interest in producing computerised images such as – in one of the key scenes of the film – the virtual simulation of the collapse of Rome's sites of institutional power. This reference to virtuality deserves attention. The first thing to note is that the disclosure of Ernesto's visionary penchant for VR urban devastation coincides with his sexual rapport with Diana, towards the end of the film: he is sitting in front of his computer, absorbed in his virtual endeavour, when Diana magically appears in his studio. She moves lightly, quietly, from room to room, until he suddenly becomes aware of her presence, chases her and eventually makes love to her in a crescendo of emotions. The point here is not that Diana and VR fulfil Ernesto's frustrated desire for subversion – in the sense that he only manages to find an outlet for his subversive desire in love and VR. Rather, we should note, firstly, that *Diana represents virtuality itself* – as Bellocchio suggests by depicting her as a kind of spectre, a strangely insubstantial creature – and secondly that *virtuality is connoted as directly functional to a proper subversive attitude.*

L'ora di religione

As regards the first point, Diana's virtual status is confirmed by a significant detail: her presence in Ernesto's studio is matched by the presence of her uncanny double on computer, for what causes the simulated destruction of Rome is a heavenly-looking virtual woman who glides lightly through crumbling buildings and monuments, just as Diana, unseen, drifts in and out of Ernesto's studio. Again, the obvious passage from virtual (on computer) to real (in the studio) should be reverted: it is the real Diana who is, as it were, already virtual, as the fascination she exerts on Ernesto derives from her fantasmatic and evanescent presence. As regards the second point, what should be acknowledged is that Ernesto's flirtations with Diana and virtuality are tantamount to an encounter with the Real. As Žižek suggests apropos of Deleuze (see Žižek, 2004, pp. 3–9), the simplistic understanding of virtual reality as the imitation/reproduction of material reality through an artificial medium should be replaced by the much more productive notion that every reality originates in some virtual/Real kernel which needs to be disavowed if reality is to emerge as a symbolically consistent field. In our case, Bellocchio's insight consists in his emphasising the non-existence of Diana, or rather the fact that she exists only as pure (spectral) appearance, a virtual signifier whose sudden intervention shatters Ernesto's private universe and compels him to make a radical choice.

To my mind, therefore, Ernesto's confrontation with the divisive power of the virtual suggests that he should be included in the gallery of Bellocchio's formidable rebels. Ernesto is nothing but another variation, and possibly the most poignantly ambiguous and captivating one, on the theme of subjective/unconscious subversion that Bellocchio has been investigating since his directorial debut. To be more precise, *L'ora di religione* narrates the process that brings the subject to face up to his own virtual core, the Real kernel of his own being. Let us take the passage where Ernesto's tigerish aunt Maria (Piera degli Esposti) tries to talk him into backing his mother's beatification. Unexpectedly, Ernesto reacts to his aunt's tirade on the importance of social status by shouting abuse against the very notion of paternal (and maternal) authority, an enraged, acerbic reply that seems to surprise the hero himself, who in fact is unable to substantiate it coherently. Again, this sequence would seem to introduce, at the level of Ernesto's psychic conformation, the interference of an excessive signifier that cannot be brought under control. The vitriolic wager against the paternal role suggests that the subject is flirting with a psychotic stance of radical separation from what he himself is: a father. As acknowledged by the majority of the critics, Bellocchio's rebellious subject is driven by a blind, iconoclastic determination to overthrow the paternal metaphor, which in Lacan is the place of the (supposed) symbolic knowledge – ultimately, nothing other than the law itself. However, the interesting feature of *L'ora di religione*, which encourages the parallel with *I pugni in tasca*, is that the protagonist's iconoclastic fury is directed, first, against the mother, and only then is it reflected back against the paternal metaphor.

4.2.3 Noir is noir

Bellocchio's definition of *L'ora di religione* as a 'very bizarre film noir' calls for a substantial development of my psychoanalytic approach.[25] First of all, can we not argue that the adjective bizarre could be used to designate the central feature of every single film that belongs to the noir genre, in the sense that every film noir is by definition decentred, "out of sync", with respect to the abstract notion of noir which, as is well known, was coined *retrospectively* in France to define certain features of late 1940s American cinema? Today the noir universe is one of the privileged genres for postmodern discourse theory. As pointed out by Žižek (2001b, p. 149), one of the main dangers of the postmodern obsession with noir, namely the theoretical conformity of the critical analysis,[26] originates in the misplaced perception that the noir universe can be positivised, turned into a fully digestible set of features – which, I would add, ultimately aims at guaranteeing its status as cultural commodity. Instead, Žižek's apprehension of noir points to the opposite direction, highlighting the irreconcilable tension between subject and society, which determines 'a radical split, a kind of structural imbalance, as to the possibility of narrativization' (Žižek, 2001, p. 151).

As we have seen in part 3, generally in Bellocchio this narrative split transpires the very moment the film begins. The opening scene of *L'ora di religione* is no exception, presenting itself as a bewildering prelude to the main narrative theme. Whilst Ernesto's wife Irene (Jacqueline Lustig) is leafing through a brochure of her husband's paintings, Leonardo (the son) is out in the garden, apparently talking to himself. Obviously disconcerted, the mother walks out and follows Leonardo, who eventually tells her that he is just trying to escape from God's reach: if He is everywhere, the young boy asks, how can one be free? Irene simply smiles and embraces him in a reassuring way. This scene is highly revealing in summarising the main question posed by the film: what relationship is there between the personal freedom and the overwhelming hegemonic presence of Catholicism? Moreover, the structural role played by the mother's smile is already extremely significant, for it functions as the Lacanian *point de capiton*, the unquestionably authoritative nodal point that "quilts" a series of floating signifiers, structuring them into a coherent symbolic field.[27] This also means that the mother is immediately characterised as the original source of anxiety for the son: in psychoanalysis, the first and fundamental problem faced by the child is how to make sense of this strange situation whereby he/she perceives himself/herself as the object of the mother's enjoyment. The anxiety-generating question is therefore the Lacanian *che vuoi?*: 'What does the (m)other want?', 'why am I an object of the (m)other's desire'? In trying to gain a distance from the baffling opacity and suffocating over-proximity of the maternal signifier with its incomprehensible desire, the child effectively seeks to open up a space where he/she can articulate his/her own desire – i.e. where the child can become a subject.

The following scene introduces Ernesto Picciafuoco. To underline his detachment from the family, he is shown whilst deeply immersed in his work, alone in the emptiness of his spacious studio. As he is reading some comments on his illustrations that have been faxed to him by his commissioner (later identified as a drunken middle-aged man named Baldracchi),[28] Ernesto is paid an unexpected visit by Cardinal Piumini's secretary, who first tells him about the plan to canonise his mother, and then invites him to a meeting with the Cardinal himself. This passage works as a second allusion to the mother-son relationship and its wider implications. The subject (the son: Leonardo in the opening scene, Ernesto in the second) is defined through his potentially conflictual relationship with the all-pervasive proximity of Catholicism – a proximity which is significantly mediated through to the intersubjective level by the figure of the mother, who is nothing but, in Lacan's words, 'the first Other that he [the subject] has to deal with' (Lacan, 1998a, p. 218). What ensues after the two introductory scenes is, essentially, an investigation into the meaning of subjectivation, as Ernesto is followed closely in his efforts to gain a distance from the hegemonic discourse and achieve a degree of self-determination.[29]

Bellocchio's representation of the conflict between subject and society avoids two main commonplaces: moralism and fatalism. The film's central intuition is that the functioning of the hegemonic machine is ultimately secured by the figure of the rebel (Ernesto) himself, *precisely because he proudly believes that he can situate himself outside the reach of the hegemonic discourse*. The paradox is that Ernesto, despite and at the same time because of his disdainful indifference to what is being woven outside (the plan to canonise his mother), was always-already part of the game: the fact that the plan is orchestrated behind his back is functional to the plan's success. In short, Ernesto learns that his choice to play the part of the anti-social artist, somewhat typical of his status of post-1968 non-conformist, does not spare him at all from being included in the symbolic constellation he so intensely despises. In fact, like the Hegelian Beautiful Soul previously referred to, the more he calls himself out, the more he is included. The lesson we get here – one of the key lessons of Italian cinema, as shown in this book – is that the subject is constitutionally prevented from looking at the world *objectively*, from a neutral position, for his point of view is always-already incorporated in the particular historical horizon to which he belongs.[30] Ernesto's initial knowledge about his mother, therefore, leaves him with an apparently insoluble question: how is he to break with the stifling power of a symbolic constellation in which he is fully immersed regardless of how he positions himself towards it? Essentially, this catch-22 situation is what the film is about. The radicality of Bellocchio's cinema hinges on the fact that the rebellious subject sooner or later realises that his true act of defiance coincides with the suspension of his own (subjective) symbolic efficiency. In psychoanalytic terms, this means that the attempt to evade or contrast a certain imbroglio can only succeed if sustained by the subject's overidentification with the central void that structures the symbolic order itself. [31]

Significantly, Bellocchio gives us a number of clues to help us locate the inconsistency of the symbolic sphere. Perhaps the crucial one concerns the issue of sainthood, since the mother's potential beatification, which would greatly benefit the Picciafuoco family, rests on a small piece of information that remains inaccessible throughout the narrative: was she killed in her sleep, or was she awake when she died? Only the second condition would justify the plea for martyrdom, which would in turn lead to her canonisation. The problem is that this knowledge remains out of reach, for it can be disclosed by Egidio alone, Ernesto's mentally ill brother who, since murdering his mother, has been unable to communicate rationally (blasphemy being his only way of expressing himself). It is this coincidence of the structuring truth and the madness of the act (the matricide) that belies the consistency of the symbolic field. And the noir dimension of *L'ora di religione* resides precisely in the film's attempt to expose the fundamental non-existence of the big Other. First, the subject (Ernesto) discovers that he is the central piece in an intricate plan (his mother's beatification) orchestrated behind his back by his extended family; then, this realisation goads him to embark on an arduous journey into the very heart of the symbolic network to find out that, ultimately, this network simply hinges on an empty kernel. What is noir about this is the fact that the big Other loses its presumed innocence and neutrality to emerge as a thoroughly contested space. This also explains Ernesto's growing sense of discomfort and paranoia, highlighted by Bellocchio's use of sudden slow-motion shots, jump-cuts and, generally, an obsessive insistence on dark tonalities. But what is it, exactly, that sets Ernesto against the symbolic order? The answer, as the title suggests, has to be looked for in his relationship with the (dead) mother.

4.2.4 Smile as *objet a*
One of the theoretical points emerged so far is that the antagonistic relationship between the subject and its social environment is characterised by the subject's inclusion into the antagonised field, rather than by its exclusion. This view can be developed critically by revisiting the theory of the gaze in Lacan, particularly as commented upon by Žižek:

> Therein lies the reason of the uncanny power of psychoanalytical interpretation: the subject pursues his everyday life within its closed horizon of meaning, safe in his distance with respect to the world of objects, assured of their meaning (or their insignificance), when, all of a sudden, the psychoanalyst pinpoints some tiny details of no significance whatsoever to the subject, a stain in which the subject "sees nothing" – a small, compulsive gesture or tic, a slip of the tongue or something of that order – and says: "You see, this detail is a knot that condenses all you had to forget so that you can swim in your everyday certainty, it enframes the very frame which confers meaning on your life, it structures the horizon within which things make sense to you; if we unknot it, you will lose the ground from under your feet!" (Žižek, 2001b, p. 15).

This reference demands that we clarify further Ernesto's position vis-à-vis the symbolic order. The news of the beatification plan prompts him to revisit long-forgotten questions concerning his mother's death and, more importantly, the nature of her role and influence over himself. In short, the reappeared mother functions as the knot that threatens to destabilise Ernesto's psychic universe. Even more significant is that this fantasmatic return of the maternal signifier is eventually condensed into what seems to be an inconsequential detail: her smile. Let us take a closer look at this feature which, somewhat eerily, punctuates the unfolding of the storyline. Initially, it takes on the connotation of a frozen, lifeless expression meant to capture the essence of the mother's apathetic docility. Ernesto, for instance, refers to it as something that conjures up a mixture of stupidity, condescension and indifference; the director himself conceded that this smile sums up the worst possible attribute of motherhood: complete disaffection, 'anaffezione'.[32] The viewer is struck by Ernesto's increasing fixation on it, as if he had suddenly been shaken by the encounter with a long disavowed truth. The main point is that Ernesto's obsession with his mother's empty smile eventually becomes an obsession with his own smile, insofar as he realises that it connotes *his own* attitude of indifference and detachment from the world. All this implies that the intervention of the dead mother produces a reflexive effect which forces the subject to acknowledge that the fictional status of the other coincides with the fictional status of the self: both are structured around a disavowed truth that has now materialised in an apparently insignificant detail – precisely the detail that *the subject had to forget so that he could swim in his everyday certainty*.

To expand on the status of this smile, Bellocchio makes it clear that it has to be perceived as an utterly elusive signifier. Ernesto first sees it on the lips of an old woman in a wheelchair. Here, slow motion and a highly-pitched musical comment (the film's main motif) emphasise the importance of the narrative moment. The same technical devices are used again when Ernesto is confronted by what is one of the most poignant shots of the film: the appearance of his mother's face, smiling, printed on an enormous panel visible through the window of Ernesto's aunt's house, where the plans for her beatification (including its publicity) are being woven. It is this extraordinary shot that brings us back to Lacan's dialectics of the gaze: 'in what I see, in what is open to my view, there is always a point where "I see nothing", a point which "makes no sense", i.e., which functions as the picture's stain – this is the point from which the very picture returns the gaze, looks back at me. [...] here I encounter myself, my own objective correlative – here I am, so to speak, inscribed in the picture; this ontic "umbilical cord" of the ontological horizon is what is unthinkable for the entire philosophical tradition, Heidegger included' (Žižek, 2001b, p. 15).

The scene of the publicity poster, a quotation from Kieslowski's *Three Colours: Red* (1994), illustrates the functioning of the gaze, for the gaze is nothing but the fleeting awareness of an eye that seems to look back from outside the picture, outside our field of vision. Here, it is of course the depsychologised smile of the mother that gazes back at Ernesto (as well as at the spectators, since we share Ernesto's point of view) from a displaced

L'ora di religione

position, establishing with him a traumatic link (the image of the umbilical cord is, of course, particularly appropriate here). As a result, Ernesto is effectively 'inscribed in the picture'. If we recall that the Lacanian *objet petit a* is 'a symbol of lack' (Lacan 1998a, p. 103), the paradoxical "something" which gives body to a lack in the other, it should not be difficult to see that this smile functions precisely as the object that embodies the hard, inaccessible kernel of the self. In short, what we (and Ernesto) perceive in this smile is a trace of the Real, an uncanny absence inscribed in the visual field of representation.

As Žižek points out paraphrasing Lacan, the role of *objet a* is taken over by the gaze itself, 'the gaze in the precise sense of the point of view from which the stain [the smile] can be perceived in its "true meaning", the point of view from which, instead of the anamorphic distortion, it would be possible to discern the true contours of what the subject perceives as a formless stain' (Žižek, 1993, p. 66). In our case, the impossibility of *objet a* coincides with the impossibility of Ernesto's gaze *qua* point of view that "discerns the true contours of the mother's smile". Despite his efforts, Ernesto is ultimately unable to symbolise the Real of his mother's disturbingly ambiguous expression. Paradoxically, the only way for him to discern the whole truth about his mother is by endorsing the void that qualifies the displaced kernel of her (and his) self. We can now see how the smile *qua* gaze functions as the Lacanian "vanishing mediator", the last "compromise formation" between the subject and its fundamental emptiness – an agency through which the abyssal void of the subject, the Real, already shines in all its terrifying might.[33] This is crucial if we are to appreciate the subversive edge in Lacan's critique of self-consciousness: 'the function of the stain and of the gaze is both that which governs the gaze most secretly and that which always escapes from the grasp of that form of vision that is satisfied with itself in imagining itself as consciousness' (Lacan, 1998a, p. 74). The subject, in other words, emerges as a conscious self only at the price of the radical exclusion of the (traumatic) truth about its own nature. In turn, this truth can only make itself visible as *objet a* (the mother's smile), demanding from the subject a choice of disavowal or endorsement. For Žižek, who opens up Lacan to the most radical consequences, the solution to the paradox of *objet a* is to be found in the act that fully assumes its underlying negativity. The turning point in Ernesto's life is thus the encounter with his mother's smile, a feature through which he gains an insight into the abyssal emptiness of his own self. Significantly, he refuses to contain the impact of this encounter. Instead of falling back on his family and its attempt to neutralise the meaning of his mother's death through investment in Catholicism, he holds on to its lacerating negativity, a gesture of defiance that eventually results in him breaking with his wife and wider family.[34]

The inherently rebellious dimension of Ernesto's choice manifests itself powerfully in the most evisceratingly intense passage of the film, when the three Picciafuoco brothers pay a visit to Egidio in the lunatic asylum, hoping to extort from him a confession that they can use as evidence for their mother's martyrdom. However, what they get is the angered and blasphemous outburst typical of his condition. It is precisely when Egidio explodes in one of his fits, however, that Ernesto, defying his brothers' plan, impulsively runs to embrace him, while a shrill musical motif reminds us of the pivotal significance of this moment. Ernesto's gesture is homologous to the Hegelian "passage through madness" (see Žižek, 2000a, pp. 34–41), to the endorsement of the disavowed excess (Egidio, who effectively embodies the non-symbolisable Real) that surreptitiously sustains the field of meaning.[35]

At this stage, it is worth revisiting Žižek's argument for an ethical evaluation of the Real: 'Lacan is as far as it is possible from any "tabooing" of the real, from elevating it into an untouchable entity exempted from historical analysis – his point, rather, is that the only true ethical stance is to assume fully the impossible task of symbolising the real, inclusive of its necessary failure' (Žižek, 1994, pp. 199–200). Bellocchio's cinema tends to focus unswervingly on a certain subjective compulsion to overidentify with the Real. As we have seen, the Lacanian name for such a compulsion is death-drive: an irresistible urge to circulate incessantly around a painfully elusive signifier (*objet a*) that has intruded into the subject's symbolic economy, disturbing the smooth balance of the pleasure principle. The passage from desire to drive involves precisely the radicalisation of the subject's relation to *objet a*, or the same relation in a different modality. While desire is the agency that desperately strives to obtain the ever-elusive *jouissance* of the other, drive implies a kind of "pleasure in displeasure", finding a certain satisfaction in repeatedly missing the target, in frustratingly hitting on an empty signifier. In Bellocchio's film, the passage from desire to drive can be traced by following the shifts in Ernesto's attitude towards the elusive presence-absence of Diana, and towards the enigma of the mother's smile.[36]

4.2.5 More paradoxes of feminine inconsistency

In *L'ora di religione* we encounter different modalities of feminine inconsistency: from woman as the proverbial object-cause of desire (a subject characterised by inherent elusiveness), to an illustration of "feminine *jouissance*", or "jouissance of the Other" – phrases with which Lacan aimed to capture the specifically non-phallic potentiality he ascribed to woman's sexuality. Diana Sereni provides a paradigmatic example of feminine inconsistency, to the extent that she can be seen as a modern version of the classic *femme fatale*, since, as in the best noir tradition, her enigmatic presence has a disturbing effect on Ernesto's psychic balance. Bellocchio's characterisation of Diana suggests nothing but ambiguity: upon meeting Ernesto, she recites him a Russian poem on the incompleteness of being; soon after, she confesses to him that she is an unaccomplished individual, unable to fulfil her many ambitions (to be a painter, a writer, a musician). More generally, the question of Diana's elusiveness is mainly centred around her presumed role as Leonardo's religion teacher. When Leonardo tells his father that he does not know anyone by the name of Diana Sereni, adding that the real teacher is in fact an old and far from good-looking woman, we feel that Ernesto may be right in suspecting to have fallen victim to a well-orchestrated conspiracy. In his fantasy scenario Diana is a prostitute sent by his aunt to seduce him and cause him to feel guilty so as to rekindle his Catholic faith – which, eventually, would win him over to the beatification plan. In retrospect, however, there is nothing in the narrative that proves Diana's instrumental role. As a matter of fact, Ernesto's conclusion seems perfectly in line with the paranoid male chauvinist thesis according to which "woman is a whore": a desperate attempt to conceal the inability to come to terms with feminine sexuality. In fact, Bellocchio's film provides us with a near perfect illustration of the interplay between male fantasy and feminine inconsistency: Ernesto's determination to define Diana in relation to the big Other confirms Lacan's theory that male fantasy is nothing but a measure to keep the feminine at a safe distance – just like the hard-boiled detective struggles to come to terms with the threatening presence of the "dark lady".

Again, the point is that whilst both the masculine and the feminine are essentially inconsistent fields (that is, they are split by *jouissance*, which undermines their respective bids for identity), they are so in two radically different ways, i.e. their split is gender-specific. It is crucial to insist that, far from working as an antifeminist slogan, Lacan's theory prioritises the subversive edge of feminine sexuality over the masculine, in as much as the former alone is capable of articulating a truly antagonistic relationship with the symbolic field. How? Whilst man achieves symbolic identity through an exclusionary logic, that is, by way of excluding/repressing the non-symbolisable feature of his self (*jouissance qua* relationship to woman), woman does not depend on a displaced exception, but rather brings the Real of her desire right within the symbolic, thus challenging its totalising function. Whilst in man's universe the positing of the exception creates the illusion that everything is caught within a network of causes and effects, in the feminine context *there is no exception*, and that is precisely why, to Lacan, woman is 'not-all' (or 'not-whole', see Lacan, 1998b, pp. 73–4) – why woman has a chance of not "squaring the circle", of giving the lie to the masculine illusion of positive and consistent totality. Put differently, her being not-all implies that in the domain of the symbolic woman cannot become an object of knowledge. And Lacan's aim is to show that the ethical act is on the side of the feminine, because woman as not-all means that something in her escapes the masculine compulsion to "exclude and identify", thus threatening the spurious universalism of such a position. However, this elusive "something" is not a hidden positive feature ("the way women really are" when freed from patriarchal discourse, for example, or the equally delusive masculine fantasy of the Eternal Feminine); instead, it is the very reference to the void of the subject ('the subject qua $, qua pure "I think" of substanceless self-relating', Žižek, 1993, p. 58) which Lacan defines as a 'supplementary jouissance', a 'jouissance […] "beyond the phallus"', a 'jouissance one experiences and yet knows nothing about' (Lacan 1998b, pp. 73–7). In short, it is the answer of the (feminine) Real to the (male) compulsion to symbolise.

Going back to Diana, we can now see how her being not-all is eventually instrumental to Ernesto's rebellion, for it is Diana's virtual status that enables Ernesto to find the way out of his Kafkaesque maze of paranoid fantasies. From the point of view of intersubjectivity, the film suggests that by "risking everything" and endorsing the abyss of the other (Diana), the subject (Ernesto) has a chance to catch a glimpse of the non-existence of the big Other (the unfathomable emptiness of his extended family's relations with the Catholic church).

It is revealing that the difference between Diana and Ernesto's mother is minimal, for both come to represent the same ambiguous lure which eventually brings Ernesto to the brink of a vertiginous act. Just like with Diana, it is the virtuality of the smile, its derealised insubstantiality, that attracts (and at the same time repels) Ernesto, returning to him the message of the fundamental inaccessibility of his own being. The recurrent image of Ernesto vis-á-vis the smiling mother tells us that drive is the repetition of a failure revealing how otherness (the smile) coincides with utter proximity (the core of the self). However, instead of simply embodying a generic lack this smile stands for a kind of original lack, as it belongs to the mother *qua* first other encountered by the subject. This means that what is at stake here is none other than the maternal Thing, the traumatic core of the mother's desire, for, in Lacan, any lack experienced by the subject eventually comes down to the original impasse generated by the mother's desire. Desire itself is, strictly speaking, correlative to this radical doubt about the desire of the (M)other, i.e., the confrontation with a deadlock 'which announces the abyss of some terrifying, filthy enjoyment. If the Name-of-the-Father functions as the agency of interpellation, of symbolic identification, the mother's desire, with its fathomless "*Che vuoi?*", marks a certain limit at which every interpellation necessarily fails' (Žižek, 2000a, p. 367).

The disturbingly excessive character of the mother's desire is alluded to in the sequence where her murder is staged as part of the beatification stunt. We encounter here the strange image of a mother-martyr who succumbs to the son's stabbing whilst praying and smiling, as if in a state of ecstasy. The passage is truly uncanny. Beyond the obvious ideological function of this staging, what we have here is the Lacanian enjoyment 'beyond the phallus' (see Lacan, 1998b, pp. 74–6), the feminine potential for a *jouissance* that is delivered from the illusion of phallic fulfillment, and that therefore establishes a direct contact with the Real, bypassing castration and the Oedipal configuration.[37] In Lacan, however, feminine *jouissance* has nothing to do with mysticism, that is, with a privileged communicative channel beyond language. On the contrary, woman is fully immersed (without exception) in the symbolic, and that is precisely why she has the chance to expose its structural antagonism. How does this apply to Ernesto's mother? The key point is that she reaches *jouissance* by way of alienating herself in the other, in the sense that her enjoyment is completely externalised, totally reflected in the other's enjoyment (Egidio's, the murderous son). By literally "enjoying through the other", or "disappearing in the other's enjoyment", the mother overidentifies with the gap in the symbolic order, providing a harrowing image of the latter's inconsistency (for the benefit, of course, of Ernesto's fascinated gaze).

Thus, the somewhat grotesque depiction of the mother's passivity and disaffection (confirmed by the fact that, after her death, she is used by her family as a commodity for the achievement of material gains) should not deceive us. Whether or not Bellocchio intended to suggest this, her position of utter objectification and subordination evokes its opposite, the opening up of freedom itself, for it embodies the effect of the feminine act *qua* uncompromising overidentification with the fissure in the Big Other. The ultimate (unconscious) twist of the film lies in the realisation that, paradoxically, the mother *does* assume the position of the saint, for such a position implies what Lacan calls a symbolic suicide: an act of radical withdrawal from intersubjective space which, in Žižek's words, 'enables us to begin anew from the "zero point", from that point of absolute freedom called by Hegel "abstract negativity"' (Žižek, 2001b, p. 43).

4.3 *I CENTO PASSI*: RESUSCITATING OEDIPUS WITH MARCO TULLIO GIORDANA

In *La stanza del figlio*, Andrea epitomises the depoliticised postmodern adolescent whose knowledge of his own antagonistic potential remains utterly repressed, relegated to the abyss of an unconscious desire that can only manifest itself "underwater" – a metaphorical reference to the blissful primordial condition of maternal, uterine fullness. However, Moretti's "son" is innocent, because his unconscious desires have been unduly domesticated by his family's excessive attachment to the pleasure principle. The merit of the film is that it holds on to the explosive potential of the unconscious, in the sense that it does not gentrify its impact, but rather preserves it by relating it to trauma. With Bellocchio's *L'ora di religione* we witness an intriguing doubling of the son. The son is both Ernesto, the film's protagonist, and Leonardo, his own son. This doubling is reflected in the Italian title of the film: if *L'ora di religione* would seem to refer mainly to Leonardo, *Il sorriso di mia madre* calls into question Ernesto's side of the narrative. The subversive dimension, nonetheless, is inscribed in the characterisation of both sons. In the first scene Leonardo tries to free himself of God's control. Later, we learn that the question of his attendance to the religion hour causes a moral dilemma in his father, a dilemma that is exacerbated by the news of his dead mother's imminent beatification. If Leonardo can be regarded as a *flatus vocis* (a pretextual presence), Ernesto's complexity deserves attention, for his story unfolds as a meditation on the limits of self-consciousness: Ernesto thinks he knows, but he soon discovers that he does not know much at all, to the paradoxical extent that his rebellion eventually depends on the endorsement of a non-knowledge. It is here that the Oedipal dimension returns with a vengeance. The extraordinarily camouflaged twist of the film is that the dead mother indirectly shows her son the way out of his deadlock. How? By making visible to him the empty frame of the subject – an emptiness barely filled by the troubling enigma of her smile.

Meant as a reconstruction of a historically true event, Tullio Giordana's *I cento passi* chronicles the life of Giuseppe (Peppino) Impastato, the Sicilian anti-Mafia militant assassinated on 9 May 1978 – the same day in which the dead body of Christian Democrats President Aldo Moro, killed by the Red Brigades, was found in Rome. If in Moretti and Bellocchio's films we have sons who "do not know that they know" (i.e., their knowledge of the subversive potential they host is fully submitted to the unconscious), Giordana presents us with a son "who seems to know". Essentially, he knows that the king is naked: that the family unit, an appendix of the wider symbolic network (the Mafia), is a bad fiction that needs to be replaced with a better one. Crucial here is to see how this self-awareness develops. Peppino is not an outsider, he grows up within a family of *mafiosi*, his initial subject position is entirely determined by the Name of the Father, i.e. by the signifier Mafia. This implies that to young Peppino the Mafia is not *outside* the law, it *is* the law. However, a closer look tells us that the law is represented by two paternal figures, two fathers. Next to Peppino's real father Luigi (Luigi Maria Burruano) the director inserts a second paternal figure, whose role is much more ominous than that of the first one. I am referring to Peppino's uncle and Mafia boss Don Cesare Manzella (Pippo Montalbano), who in my view embodies a kind of Freudian primordial father, or a Lacanian father-*jouissance* – a gentrified version of the many "obscene paternal doubles" that we find in modern literature and cinema.[38] The detail not to overlook is that Cesare Manzella, unlike the biological father Luigi, introduces Peppino to a dimension of unrestrained enjoyment. The key sequence in this respect is the one where, after a family lunch, Don Cesare encourages Peppino, who is still a child, to sit on his knees and drive his modern powerful car. As Peppino enthusiastically accepts, the uncle whispers in his ear that if he wishes he can run over just about anybody, including all the colluded *mafiosi* who had taken part to the lunch. *This* is the decisive encounter that carves a traumatic split in Peppino's psychic balance. Lacanian psychoanalysis insists that life-changing encounters are at once contingent and necessary: although they could well have *not* happened at a specific time (Peppino might have not gone to that lunch) *they would have happened anyway in another context* – for "the letter always arrives at its destination", the traumatic *touché* awaits us all somewhere, sometime.

This preliminary sequence is therefore essential, as it tells us exactly why Peppino's awareness of the wickedness of the Mafia coincides with the death of Don Cesare Manzella (in the next sequence). The moment Don Cesare, boss of the bosses, is spectacularly blown up by the ambitious, up-and-coming *mafioso* Don Tano Badalamenti, young Peppino senses for the first time that there must be something wrong with his family and social milieu. At the obituary, the day of Don Cesare's funerals, he is sat in a huge upholstered armchair, deep in thought, observing the arrival on the scene of Tano Badalamenti, his future enemy. The parallel to draw here is with Freud's *Totem & Taboo*, where the primordial father, the "master of enjoyment", is killed by the sons, and his death results in the setting up of the totemic order. In our case the son who eliminates the primordial father is Tano Badalamenti who, however, does not incarnate another father-enjoyment for Peppino, but rather someone whose intervention is aimed at regulating the socio-symbolic order.[39] This is why Peppino does not see a substantial difference (only "a hundred steps", the distance from their respective homes) between Tano and his real father Luigi: they both function as classic paternal metaphors, totemic figures that interdict his access to the foretasted enjoyment.

The displaced narrative kernel of Giordana's film is therefore situated in the partly disavowed knowledge that Peppino's heroic anti-Mafia commitment (the film's driving emotional focus) is not simply triggered by his awareness that "the Mafia is bad", which would indeed confirm the most obvious critical view of the film as a pathetic, over-sentimental, and thus fundamentally hypocritical instance of moral interpellation; quite differently, Peppino's unremitting wrestling with the Mafia needs to be linked to the death of the mighty uncle, he who held the key to a universe of excessive enjoyment beyond the paternal injunction to abide by the law. Peppino's determination to fight the Mafia, all the way down to his own heroic sacrifice, is thus correlative to his unconscious perception that (the promise of his access to) enjoyment has been stolen. This knowledge manifests itself by subtraction, that is to say, through symbolic castration – through the sudden loss of the possibility of unrestrained enjoyment, a loss caused by the violent intervention of the Name of the Father (the letter of the law) which simultaneously allows the subject to enter (and transgress) the social order.

Basically, Don Cesare Manzella's assassination marks the split between the immediate availability of unreflected primordial enjoyment, and alienation in the symbolic order. By forcing Peppino into the symbolic order, this traumatic death simultaneously introduces him to a radically modified perception of enjoyment, as from now on he can only experience enjoyment as loss, i.e. as *jouissance*. Peppino's recital of Giacomo Lepoardi's famous poem *L'infinito* (Infinity, 1819), shortly before his uncle's death, works well as an intimation that he is about to leave the happy universe of untroubled enjoyment.[40] Ultimately, the hidden twist of the film rests on the recognition that Peppino's ethical drive stems from his confrontation with what we could call a "trace of lost enjoyment", a spectral appearance of the mythical freedom he might have enjoyed. Without this acknowlegment we would not be able fully to appreciate the ethical character of Peppino's choice. Giordana's film secretly indicates that a truly ethical stance depends on the subject's endorsement of the excessive libidinal remainder (*jouissance*) that accompanies, and problematises, his or her entrance in the symbolic order.

I cento passi

Assessed from the vantage point of the symbolic order, this predicament appears in an even clearer light: Peppino's "revolutionary élan" is triggered by his unconscious will to compensate for the loss of the kernel of his being, which inevitably ends up in a Real encounter with *jouissance*, i.e. with the masochistic primal fantasy that sustains the Freudian "going beyond the pleasure principle". Seeking compensation for loss of being does not imply, as we might be tempted to surmise, the potential acquisition of a condition of fullness, of blissful enjoyment. On the contrary, it leads us straight into the closed circuit of the death-drive. The film's second crucial Lacanian insight is that the subject's only way to truly compensate for loss of being depends on another, more radical loss: the loss of the very framework which feeds our reference to loss, the separation from "cosa nostra", the intimate core of our identity, the Thing inside anchoring us to our "unique sense of selfness". This theoretical reference to death-drive goes a long way to explain Peppino's "fanatic" resolve: in order to lose his loss of enjoyment, he has to assume a position of indifference towards his own symbolic network, his family *in primis*. Consequently, Peppino's passionate attachment to the cause brings him to trespass the very frontier of morality, encroaching upon that "religious suspension of the ethical" that we have designated as the central feature of Lacanian ethics. His Christ-like indifference to family ties cannot fail to appear cruel, and yet it is precisely this kind of cruelty that is required in authentic ethical acts. The key observation to make, however, is that the ultimate target of Peppino's mercilessly militant conduct is Peppino himself: whilst fighting an external evil, he is primarily struggling with his own inner substance, trying to break his own attachment to the symbolic network.

To use Pasolini's maxim, freedom affirms itself in the exercise of martyrdom, an act of self-directed violence aimed at detaching the subject from its own libidinally-sustained symbolic predicament. Peppino Impastato incarnates the (typically Pasolinian) self-destructiveness of drive (which also explains the subject-matter of Giordana's previous film, *Pasolini, un delitto italiano*, 1995):[41] what characterises Peppino's reckless behaviour is his unconscious knowledge that the fight for a different social order implies the passage through the Real of *jouissance*, through an unbearable encounter that collapses subjective resistances while concurrently demarcating the essence of the self.

Giordana's film may thus be viewed as an attempt to outline the profile of the true rebel. Despite its over-sentimental excesses, the film has the merit to show how moral interpellation is not enough, as the rebel must go *beyond the good*, assuming an estranged subject-position that cannot fail to appear cruel and unjust, as in the key sequence of Peppino's clash with his father. Having been informed of his son's scathing parodies of the Mafia, which are performed daily on his independent radio station ("Radio Aut"), Luigi punches Peppino in the stomach, pins him down to the floor and begs him, to the point of tears, to repeat after him the fourth commandment

('Honour thy father'). Nonetheless, Peppino resists the temptation to comply with his father's pitiable request and, whilst trying to wriggle out of his supine position, he shouts frenziedly in his face that he will not say it! The remarkable aspect of this highly distressing passage is that *it elicits sympathy for the father rather than for the son*, cunningly encouraging us to confront the fact that to be normal means, quite simply, to be cowards and hypocrites: the majority of us (the "moral majority") do not have the courage to disturb the relatively peaceful symbolic microcosm that we inhabit, regardless of weather we consider this microcosm to be morally justifiable or not. While we sense that Peppino's repudiation of his father borders on madness, we are simultaneously exposed to our own impotence, for the antagonistic act is here successfully configured as an exceptional intervention aimed, first and foremost, at ripping apart the agent's own mantle of comforting symbolic self-assurance. If Peppino initially might seem to be selfishly playing the hero, his obdurate attachment to an increasingly tragic position eventually expresses the very opposite of selfishness: love. As Žižek puts it apropos of Christ's crucifixion:

> The point here is not stupid masochism, humble acceptance of one's humiliation, but the endeavour to *interrupt the circular logic of the re-established balance of justice.* Along the same lines, Christ's sacrifice [...] suspends the logic of sin and punishment, or legal or ethical retribution, of "settling accounts", by bringing it to the point of self-relating. The only way to achieve this suspension, to break the chain of crime and punishment/retribution, is to assume an utter readiness for self-erasure. And *love*, at its most elementary, is nothing but such a paradoxical gesture of breaking the chain of retribution (Žižek, 2001c, pp. 49–50).

The enigma of Peppino's act can also be eviscerated through the classic Lacanian analysis of the 'peculiar statement' "freedom or death!": 'Curiously enough, in the conditions in which someone says to you, *freedom or death!*, the only proof of freedom that you can have in the conditions laid out before you is precisely to choose death, for there, you show you have freedom of choice' (Lacan, 1998b, p. 213). This logic is successfully rendered in the sequence of Badalamenti's encounter with Peppino after Luigi's death. Tano admonishes Peppino that now he has lost all protections, adding that whatever he will perceive as his personal freedom (for example, the freedom to carry on protesting against the Mafia) will be nothing but a kind concession from Tano himself. He is alive and free only insofar as Tano allows him to be. Cornered by such a warning, Peppino realises that his only way to salvage freedom is by choosing death. In a way, the letter used by the police as false evidence for Peppino's suicide – where Peppino, in a moment of juvenile romantic spleen, had written 'I want to abandon life and politics' – gets back to us the true message about the hero's assassination: despite the fact that Peppino Impastato was killed by the Mafia (the programmatic thesis of the film), his death should still be seen as an endorsement of the radical freedom at stake in the death-drive.

Nearly forty years before *I cento passi*, the Taviani brothers, assisted by Valentino Orsini, directed their debut feature *Un uomo da bruciare* (A Man for Burning, 1962), which anticipates the psychological tension at work in Giordana's film. Salvatore (Gian Maria Volontè), the protagonist, returns to Sicily after two years spent "on the continent" (in Rome), determined to take an active role in the organisation of the peasants' struggles against the Mafia-connected landowners. Often operating beyond the limits of legality, he manages to achieve a position of leadership in the local trade unions, and even pulls off an important success against the Mafia. However, he is soon isolated, as his methods are considered too risky and authoritarian. Disappointed and out of work, he accepts to work as a foreman for the Mafia. On his first day of work he conducts himself as inflexibly as he had done as a union activist. Then, later in the evening, he walks to the central piazza and starts shouting abuse against the Mafia. Unsurprisingly, the following day he is killed by an "accidental" explosion at work. The similarities between *Un uomo da bruciare* and *I cento passi* are indeed striking in terms of narrative/thematic development, setting and characterisation. From our methodological angle, the main parallel hinges on the way in which the respective main characters' "commitment to the Sicilian cause" eventually overlaps, reaching its climax, with their endorsement of the death-drive. Salvatore's loyalty to the anti-Mafia struggle is, like Peppino's, invested with an extraordinary quota of libidinal attachment. His ultimate strategy is also one of open and reckless provocation, propelled by a *plus-de-jouir*, a disturbing surplus of enjoyment which finds its ultimate accomplishment in the masochistic drive.

Peppino and Salvatore's parallel "vocation" to martyrdom can be expanded upon by looking at what is perhaps the single most paradigmatic example of the function of death-drive in Italian film, i.e. the mystery surrounding the death of anti-Fascist hero Athos Magnani in Bertolucci's labyrinthine *La strategia del ragno* (The Spider's Stratagem, 1970) – the film with which I have started this book. Bertolucci here follows the opposite narrative course with respect to Giordana and the Tavianis, in that his martyr is the starting point for a long and insidious enquiry into the meaning of heroism: the son is called upon to search for the truth about his father's assassination in the oneiric town of Tara, where his father is considered a hero (statues, street-names, cultural centres are dedicated to his memory). The further Athos Jr penetrates the secrets of his father's life, the more the murder mystery intensifies, while the identities of father and son become progressively intertwined, until their boundaries are practically indistinguishable. What counts here, against what seems to be Bertolucci's main thesis that every mythology thrives on lies (and also against his ambivalent insistence on the identification between father and son),[42] is the fact that (the effect of) heroism is derived from a *staged performance*: having betrayed his comrades' plot to assassinate Mussolini, Magnani Sr. had then demanded to be killed in an opera house, but in such a way that the blame would be laid on the Fascists. As with the two films previously discussed, the moral ambiguity of the hero is crucial, as his act eventually appears in a domain "beyond (what we normally regard as) the good". The nub of the question is that Magnani Sr.'s betrayal was functional to the *politicisation of his death-drive*, for he knew that his self-sacrifice would instigate a wave of genuine anti-Fascist hatred ('I will die so that the people can continue to hate, hate, hate Fascism').

The film's trust in the possibility of representing the unconscious, therefore, needs to be related to the narrative's own dislodged core: if Bertolucci conceives of the spectral town of Tara (actually Sabbioneta, near Mantua) as the ideal architectural equivalent of the unfathomable drives hosted by the narrative, such a powerful and indeed mesmerising visual reference (anticipated by the scattered images of paintings by Ligabue in the credits sequence) functions as a sumptuous disguise for the film's own partially disavowed libidinal core – that is, Athos Magnani's "will to die". To Bertolucci's credit, the film is successful in preserving an enigmatic aura around its hero's resolution, refraining from explicitly answering the key question: "why has he betrayed"? This reiterated reticence, which transpires particularly in the final part of the film, manages to pinpoint for us the symptomatic knot that structures the whole scenario, simultaneously inviting its denouement: *Athos has betrayed so that he can stage his own death*. And the point is that the son's discovery of the father's stratagem (his final bewildering realisation that the father was not the innocent martyr of Fascist repression) coincides with the film's disavowed acknowledgment that death-drive is the primary ingredient of any revolutionary act. Put differently, the establishment of a new positive order of believers (the community of Tara) incarnated in the master-signifier (Athos) necessarily ensues from a negative act of self-obliteration – which, incidentally, is exactly the same logic developed in *I cento passi*, with its final sequence of Peppino's funerals suggesting a future of collective anti-Mafia solidarity.

I cento passi

There is of course another crucial question that needs considering when assessing the correlation between Oedipus and death-drive: the question of woman. The films mentioned in this section entertain a thoroughly ambivalent relation to womankind. Peppino and Salvatore are almost ascetic in their deliberate avoidance of sentimental relationships; simultaneously, however, they are locked into an Oedipal relationship with their mothers, whose role is to allow them to devote all their energies to the political cause, for the incestuous desire for the mother is repressed and displaced onto political militancy. In other words, the destructive/liberating potential of drive is linked to the pathological attachment to the mother (in such a way that, again, we are reminded of Pasolini's personal predicament).[43] With Bertolucci's film, femininity appears in a much more ambiguous light. To start with, the mother is replaced by the father's mistress, whose name Draifa (Alida Valli), a feminine version of Dreyfus, is clearly symbolic of moral ambiguity. Moreover, the striking detail about Tara is the near absolute absence of women, and the consequent privilege accorded to the masculine signifier (the very name Athos is reminiscent of the famous Greek monastery from which territory all women are strictly banned).

The fairly obvious conclusion to this reading is that Magnani Sr.'s demise, similarly to Peppino and Salvatore's, finds its proper fulfilment in the Christian narrative of "rebirth through radical self-contraction" as elucidated by Hegel: Christ's sacrifice is a gesture of sublation (*Aufhebung*), whereby the divine, as it were, "traverses its own fantasy" (identifies with its own lack) for the birth of a new subject: the new community bound together by the Holy Spirit. Rather than breeding disenchantment, cynicism and resignation, the knowledge that the king is naked, that God/Athos is always-already dead (radically inconsistent), works as an exhortation to reconfigure the status of a given social totality. In his *Lectures on the Philosophy of Religion*, Hegel defines Christ as 'the God-Man' whose 'absolute finitude' is reflected in the fact that he died 'the aggravated death of the evil-doer', which implies that 'in Him humanity was carried to its furthest point'. The "divine finitude" that Hegel reads into the death of Christ, however, implies that the latter be intended 'in its polemical attitude towards outward things', rather than as a celebration of religion *per se*:

Not only is the act [Christ's death] whereby the natural will yields itself up here represented in a sensible form, but all that is peculiar to the individual, all those interests and personal ends with which the natural will can occupy itself, all that is great and counted in the world, is at the same time buried in the grave of the Spirit. This is the revolutionary element by means of which the world is given a totally new form. And yet in this yielding up of the natural will, the finite, the Other-Being or otherness, is at the same time transfigured (Hegel, 1962, p. 89).

The passage is highly significant in suggesting how radical transformations depend on the 'yielding up of the natural will', insofar as this intrinsically divine "passage through the zero (or lowest) point of humanity" is 'the revolutionary element' that gives the world 'a totally new form'. The self-effacement performed by the "contingent divine", in other words, is the fundamental condition for its return in the form of a new symbolic configuration:

Now, however, a further determination comes into play – God has died, God is dead – this is the most frightful of all thoughts, that all that is eternal, all that is true is not, that negation itself is found in God; [...] The course of thought does not, however, stop short here; on the contrary, thought begins to retrace its steps: God, that is to say, maintains Himself in this process, and the latter is only the death of death. God comes to life again, and thus things are reversed (Hegel, 1962, p. 91).

Hegel asserts the shameful death of the God-Man as a moment of absolute negativity through which Spirit enacts its conversion, its movement from "negation" to "negation of negation". The fictional sons (or father-sons) I have referred to all carry the divine weight of Hegelian negativity, for they meet their deepest selves in the death-drive – thus fostering change.

NOTES
1. Deleuze and Guattari emphasised how late capitalism's universal regime of profiteering relies on the constant disassembling of fixed identities and dislodging of traditional connections. In short, 'what they deterritorialize with one hand, they reterritorialize with the other' (Deleuze and Guattari, 1983, p. 257).
2. For a Lacanian analysis of Benigni's film in relation to the problematic question of the representation of the Holocaust through comedy see Žižek, 2001c, pp. 68–73.
3. The English title corresponds to the translation of the Italian subtitle (*Il sorriso di mia madre*).
4. The standard critical argument against Moretti's cinema is inevitably built around the question of his obsessive self-referentiality. Enrico Ghezzi, for example, lamented Moretti's stylistic mediocrity on the grounds that 'the only fundamental form, in itself remarkable, of Nanni Moretti's films, is Nanni Moretti's presence, which allows him to construct a long documentary about himself' (in P. Di Stefano, 1995, p. 23). Along the same lines, Moretti's arch-critic Goffredo Fofi claimed more recently that even *La stanza del figlio* is dominated by a sterile self-referential drift (see Fofi, 2001a and 2001b).
5. Cinema aside, Moretti has also recently taken on the role of a leading "girotondista", a neologism indicating his direct intervention in the public arena aimed at creating the conditions for a credible and effective leftist opposition to Silvio Berlusconi's government.
6. What we do not have in *La stanza del figlio*, in other words, is precisely the implicitly false critical posture of the Beautiful Soul – of the subject who laments the shortcomings of the world around him and, at the same time, keeps at a safe distance from it through an ironic, relativistic gaze that inhibits active participation.
7. As well as in the form of neurotic self-victimisation, Moretti's narcissism occasionally takes the form of proud and explicit self-praising, as in the "splendido quarantenne" (splendid 40-year-old man) monologue in *Caro diario*.

8. Roberti has emphasised the similarity with the narrative structure of Pasolini's *Teorema* (quoted in De Bernardinis, 2001, p. 194).

9. Incidentally, the narrative is ridden with images of open doors (also evoked by one of Giovanni's patients – the hypochondriac played by Silvio Orlando who indirectly determines Andrea's death – as he describes a dream) whose function is to corroborate the theme of the journey to the unconscious.

10. One of the clearest metaphors for *extimité* prior to *La stanza del figlio* is perhaps the elusive body itch in the third part of *Caro Diario*, eventually diagnosed as Hodgkin's disease (a condition truly experienced by Moretti). We find another interesting rendering of this concept in Mimmo Calopresti's debut feature *La seconda volta* (The Second Time, 1995), which focuses on the psychological legacy of the "leaden years" of political terrorism in Italy. Nanni Moretti plays Turin professor Alberto Sajevo, who was shot by political terrorist Lisa Venturi (Valeria Bruni Tedeschi) and suffers blackouts from the bullet still lodged in his head. It is the ambiguous relation to this bullet, as well as to the terrorist whom he meets for the second time twelve years after the incident, that functions as a metaphorical image of *extimité*. Much more than what the film is prepared to acknowledge, the Moretti character is fascinated by the over-proximity of the foreign "body" (the bullet, the terrorist).

11. In his controversial essay *Welcome to the Desert of the Real!*, Žižek contends that otherness as *extimate* is precisely what is at stake in the commonly shared representation of terrorism after the attacks on the Twin Towers of September 11, 2001: 'Whenever we encounter such a purely evil Outside, we should summon up the courage to endorse the Hegelian lesson: in this pure Outside, we should recognize the distilled version of our own essence. For the last five centuries, the (relative) prosperity and peace of the "civilized" West has been bought at the price of ruthless violence and destruction of the "barbarian" Outside: a long story, from the conquest of America to the slaughter in Congo' (Žižek, 2002b, p. 233).

12. Counter-transference can be defined as a disturbance of the analyst's normal work caused by his or her own neurotic excesses, normally as a reaction to the analysand's emotional responses. As is well known, Lacan placed great importance on counter-transference, whereas Freud tended to consider it as a danger to be avoided.

13. In *Seminar XI*, Lacan states that '[a]s soon as the subject who is supposed to know exists somewhere – I have abbreviated it for you today at the top of the blackboard as S.s.S. (*sujet supposé savoir*) there is transference' (Lacan, 1998a, p. 232).

14. 'As he is falling asleep, the father sees rise up before him the image of the son, who says to him, *Father, can't you see I'm burning?* In fact, the son really is burning, in the next room' (Lacan, 1998a, p. 34). Lacan refers here to the famous passage in Freud's *The Interpretation of Dreams* regarding a father's dream about his son's death. 'What is he burning with, if not with that which we see emerging at other points designated by the Freudian topology, namely, the weight of the sins of the father [...]. The father, the Name-of-the-Father, sustains the structure of desire with the structure of the law – but the inheritance of the father is that which Kierkegaard designates for us, namely, his sin' (Lacan, 1998a, p. 34).

15. In the opening scene of Kieslowski's *Film Blue*, for example, the car crash where Patrice and his five-year-old daughter die is ominously preceded by a close up on drops of oil leaking from the car's engine, as well as on a nearby boy who suddenly succeeds in a game of ball and cup. In more general terms, the entire narrative structure of *La stanza del figlio* is reminiscent of *Film Blue*, where the unexpected death of Patrice, a renowned music composer, kick-starts a process of radical self-discovery for his wife Julie (who eventually realises how her apparently idyllic conjugal life with Patrice was already "shattered" by her husband's secret affair with another woman).

16. To put it differently, Andrea's guilt originates in his full acceptance of the symbolic role rather than in its betrayal. As Žižek comments, 'the guilt materialized in the pressure exerted on the subject by the superego is not as straightforward as it may seem: it is not the guilt caused by the failed emulation of the ego ideal, but the more fundamental guilt of accepting the ego ideal (the socially determined symbolic role) as the ideal to be followed in the first place' (Žižek, 2000a, p. 268).

17. The sea that swallows Andrea seems to assume the classic metaphorical significance of the maternal, pre-symbolic substance where desires both originate and find their termination (a similar significance, incidentally, is given to the element of water in Moretti's *Palombella rossa*). The sea occupies the centre of the frame throughout the whole film, looming in the background of Giovanni's jogging sessions; or, more emphatically and ominously, framing his figure in the phone-box after the Sunday callout to his hypochondriac patient; or even more significantly at the very end of the film, when the family struggles to regroup by the French border.

18. Perhaps the purest formulation of 'abstract negativity' can be found, as Žižek suggests, in the early Hegelian notion of 'night of the world', first conceived in the *Jenaer Realphilosophie* manuscripts but developed in the later

Phenomenology of Spirit (see Hegel, 1977, pp. 18–9). Incidentally, I would be tempted to claim that contrary to the standard critical approach, this ahistorical "night of the world" is what Bellocchio's controversial *Buongiorno, notte* (Good morning, Night, 2003) really is about. As Umberto Curi has stressed, Bellocchio's film on the kidnapping and assassination of DC President Aldo Moro (one of the most traumatic events in recent Italian history) develops on a different plane with respect to history (see Curi, 2003). By proposing a visionary and thus radically alternative ending to the Moro affair (one of the terrorists dreams that Moro leaves the flat where he is kept unscathed), Bellocchio seems to focus on what Walter Benjamin called the splinters of Messianic time, i.e., the potential breaks in the course of history out of which a different historical outcome transpires. It is the dark and insidious undecidability of the event that *Buongiorno, notte* emphasises, the very fact that history is ultimately rooted in a radically ambiguous dimension where conscious decisions overlap with dreams. No wonder the narrative is punctuated by dreams relating to key historical events (the Russian revolution, the Resistance fight against Nazi-Fascism, etc.)! In short, with *Buongiorno, notte* Bellocchio develops a reflection on the relationship between history and its ahistorical (unconscious) kernel – a reflection he had also convincingly articulated in *Enrico IV* (Henry IV, 1984) and, particularly, *Il principe di Homburg* (The Prince of Homburg, 1997).

19. It is this insistence on the figure of the "saintly excremental remainder" that brought Pasolini to praise *Francesco, giullare di Dio* so unreservedly (see Pasolini, 1996, p. 21).

20. Flavio De Bernardinis sees in Andrea nothing less than the figure of the 'new man' (Andrós = man) whose role is to subvert bourgeois ideology (see De Bernardinis, 2001, p. 154).

21. Whether Moretti's "girotondismo" and general political views represent a step towards this new vision, however, is something I have strong doubts about.

22. This is therefore another "letter that arrives at its destination", since its final destination is not Andrea but his family, who through it have a chance to access the repressed truth about their son (his burning desire).

23. Significantly Giovanni lingers on the most revealing of these photos, with Andrea squatting beneath the frame of his desk, smiling. This picture can be related to the film title itself, and more extensively to cinema: a frame filled with fantasmatic content.

24. In Žižek's words, this implies that the worst danger, particularly in today's late capitalist constellation, 'consists precisely in our unwillingness to confront the abyss of the subject, i.e., in our unquestioned acceptance of some self-posited ground authorizing us to exert power' (Žižek, 2001b, p. 186).

25. This definition can be found in an interview with Bellocchio on the Italian DVD of the film.

26. Žižek contends that 'the bulk of what is written on *film noir* consists of cliché-ridden variations on its visual style (the influence of German expressionism [...]); on its narrative procedures (flashback, voiceover, etc.); on its social background (the corruption of the American megalopolis; the social impact of the Second World War; the emancipation of women [...]); on the *noir* existential vision (inexorable fate and its paradoxical interconnections with freedom, e.g.); etc.' (Žižek, 2001b, p. 149).

27. For Lacan's notion of *point de capiton* see Žižek (1992, pp. 87–8 and 100–04).

28. The name is, again, very revealing, as Baldracchi is a cognate of "baldracca", which in Italian means prostitute.

29. Given the narrative context, it does not seem far-fetched to read Ernesto's struggle as an attempt to free himself from the constraints of the symbolic order as a socially constructed fantasy. In Lacanian theory, fantasy has precisely such a "quilting", appeasing function, as it intervenes to fill the gaps opened up by symbolisation, securing by so doing the closure and ultimate efficiency of the symbolic field itself. One of Bellocchio's main concerns has always been that of exposing the fantasmatic dimension of power relations. In *L'ora di religione*, the representation of Catholic hegemony relies precisely on the fantasmatic support invested by Ernesto's family in the beatification of the mother: sainthood is presented as the fantasy that prevents the symbolic from collapsing.

30. This notion has obvious political repercussions, since it rehabilitates Georg Lukács' infamous theory, developed in *History and Class Consciousness*, that true knowledge is approachable only from a partial perspective (the revolutionary standpoint of the proletariat). Such a theory works against both the traditional reliance on scientific objectivity and the postmodern relativist wisdom on the necessity to replace objective truth with the endless shift of subjective positions.

31. Such predicament can be explained through Bruce Fink's paraphrases of Lacan's translation of Freud's *Wo Es war, soll Ich werden*: 'where the Other pulls the strings (acting as my cause), I must come into being as my own cause' (Fink, 1997, p. xiii). This is exactly the dilemma faced by Ernesto Picciafuoco.

32. See interview with Bellocchio on the Italian DVD.

33. On *objet petit a*'s role as mediator between signification and non-signification, see Richard Boothby (2003).

34. We could say that his new life starts from his son Leonardo, who in the last shot of the film is linked, however allusively, with the European flag, as if to suggest that the route to follow, at least on a geo-political level, necessarily passes through Europe.

35. This reference to madness is central to Bellocchio's belief in the liberating potential of what we normally perceive as "unconscious irrationality", an aspect of his poetics that comes to the fore in most of his films, and with emphatic resonance in his film-documentary *Matti da slegare* (Fit to be Untied, 1975).

36. The ambiguous episode of Ernesto's duel with count Bulla (Toni Bertorelli) could also be perceived as a figuration of drive, of Ernesto's will to engage in some kind of self-defeating struggle. Ernesto meets count Bulla at a party. After inadvertently making a mockery of the count's pompous declarations of monarchic faith and nostalgia, he is challenged by the latter to an old-fashioned sword duel. The fact that the duel proves to be a purely symbolic affair, as Ernesto's manifest inferiority prevents it from developing into a proper confrontation, would seem to confirm the fact that the object of drive is always a virtual object.

37. Incidentally, the sequence of the mother's rapturous death is reminiscent of the famous "Ecstasy of St. Teresa", the 17th century sculpture by Gian Lorenzo Bernini referred to by Lacan as an example of feminine *jouissance* (see Lacan, 1998b, p. 76).

38. Žižek (2001b, pp. 158–59) observes that, in literature, this figure of the "second father" was introduced by Joseph Conrad (Freud's contemporary), whose *Lord Jim* (1900) and *Heart of Darkness* (1902) rely on powerful, "all-enjoying" paternal metaphors such as, respectively, Mister Brown and Kurtz. In cinema, apart from Francis Ford Coppola's adaptation of *Heart of Darkness* (*Apocalypse Now*, 1979), the classic reference for the licentious father who has a crucial insight into enjoyment is, of course, Mr Ed from David Lynch's *Lost Highway* (1997).

39. In historical terms, this passage can also be seen in terms of the change from the old, traditional Mafia, to the new, much more cynical and profit-driven Mafia.

40. One of Leopardi's recurrent romantic themes, fully developed in *L'infinito*, is that the mind takes pleasure from situations where it comes up against sensory or intellectual limitations, because it is then able to enjoy wandering beyond them, imagining what might lie there. In *L'infinito*, the poet's view of the landscape is blocked by a small hill, so he is free to fabricate infinite spaces beyond. This "imagined immensity" allows for the mind's 'dolce naufragare' (sweet shipwreck), an essentially masochistic effect that ties in well with Peppino's own predicament.

41. Giordana's account of Peppino's death functions as a faithful reprise of Pasolini's own death as already reconstructed in his 1995 film: the victim is forced out of his car at night, in an isolated place, and beaten to a pulp by his killers. The shot of Peppino's blood-ridden face cannot but remind us of the well-publicised photographs of Pasolini's dead body, a parallel iconography that reveals the nauseating viscosity of the bodily Real. In *I cento passi*, this Real is productively opposed to the hedonistic theme of sexual liberation: when the "Northern hippies" descend on Sicily to preach their drugs-cum-sex anti-bourgeois strategy ('we must regain the right to enjoy the body'), Peppino is far from impressed. Indeed, their harmless "wild buttocks" demonstration (the decision to take a swim stark naked) is characterised by Giordana as the epitome of the false act.

42. The film ends with Magnani Jr.'s claim that 'a man is the sum of all men', which, if on the one hand brings to mind Marx's notion of *Gattunswesen* (species-being), whereby a particular individual is equated to the sum total of individuals, on the other hand it also foreshadows the political relativism implicit in the director's Buddhist conversion.

43. This is made explicit when Peppino reads to his mother Pasolini's poem 'A mia madre' (To My Mother), a poignant confession of his Oedipal attachment to her.

WORKS CITED

Adorno, T. W. (1984). *Aesthetic Theory*. London: Routledge & Kegan Paul.

Adorno, T. W. (2000). *Negative Dialectics*. London and New York: Routledge.

Adorno, T. W. (1997). *Dialectic of Enlightenment*. London and New York: Verso.

Adorno, T. W. (2001). 'Transparencies on Film'. In *The Culture Industry. Selected Essays on Mass Culture*. London and New York: Routledge, pp. 178–86.

Agamben, Giorgio (2000) *Means Without Ends. Notes on Politics*. Minneapolis: University of Minnesota Press.

Antonioni, M. (1970). *Zabriskie Point*. Bologna: Cappelli.

Antonioni, M. (2001). *Fare un film è per me vivere. Scritti sul cinema*. Venezia: Marsilio.

Aristarco, G. (1961). *Cinema italiano 1960*. Milan: Il saggiatore.

Bachmann, G. (1975). 'Pasolini on de Sade'. *Film Quarterly*, 29(2), Winter 1975–76, pp. 39–45.

Bakhtin, M. M. (1968). *Rabelais and His World*. Cambridge (MA): MIT Press

Barthes et al (1969). *L'analisi del racconto. Le strutture della narratività nella prospettiva semiologica che riprende le classiche ricerche di Propp*. Milano: Bompiani.

Barthes, R. (1970). *S/Z*. Paris: Seuil.

Barthes, R. (1988). *Cher Antonioni: 1988–1989*. Rome: Ente Autonomo Gestione Cinema.

Bataille, G. (1986) *Erotism: death and sensuality*. San Francisco: City Light Books.

Bataille, G. (1988) *The Inner Experience*. Albany: State University of New York Press.

Benjamin, W. (1968). *Illuminations*. New York: Schocken Books.

Benjamin, W. (1989). *Reflections. Essays, Aphorisms. Autobiographical Writings*. New York: Schocken Books.

Benjamin, W. (1989). *Walters Benjamin selected writings: volume 1. 1913–1926*. Cambridge, Mass.; London: Belknapp Press of Harvard University Press.

Bernardi, S. (2000), 'Rossellini's Landscapes: Nature, Myth, History' in Forgacs, D. Lutton, S. and Nowell-Smith, G. (eds), *Roberto Rossellini: Magician of the Real*, London, British Film Institute.

Bernardi, S. (2002). *Il paesaggio nel cinema italiano*. Venezia: Marsilio.

Betti, L. (ed.) (1978) *Pasolini. Cronaca giudiziaria, persecuzione, morte*. Milan: Garzanti.

Biarese C. and Tassone A. (1985). *I film di Michelangelo Antonioni*. Roma: Bulzoni.

Bonsaver, G. (2002). 'Three Colours Italian: an interview with Nanni Moretti'. *Sight and Sound*, January 2002, pp. 28–30.

Braudy, L. (1978). 'Rossellini: from "Open City" to "General della Rovere"', in *Great Film Directors: A Critical Anthology*, edited by Leo Braudy and Morris Dickstein. New York: Oxford University Press.

Brunette, P. (1996), *Roberto Rosellini*, Berkeley, Los Angeles and London, University of California Press.

Brunette, P. (1998). *The Films of Michelangelo Antonioni*. Cambridge: Cambridge University Press.

Bruno, E. (1979), *R.R.: Roberto Rossellini*, Roma, Bulzoni.

Butler, J. Laclau, E. and Žižek, S. (2000). *Contingency, Hegemony, Universality. Contemporary Dialogues on the Left*. London: Verso.

Chatman, S. (1985). *Antonioni, or, the Surface of the World*. Berkeley, Los Angeles, London: University of California Press.

Chatman and Fink, eds. (1989). *L'Avventura. Michelangelo Antonioni, director*. New Brunswick-London: Rutgers University Press.

Copjec, J. (1994). *Read My Desire: Lacan against the Historicists*. Cambridge, Mass. and London: MIT Press.

Copjec, J. (2002). *Imagine there's no woman: ethics and sublimation*. Cambridge-London: MIT.

Cuccu, L. (1988), ed. *Michelangelo Antonioni 1966/1984*. Rome: Ente Autonomo di Gestione per il Cinema.

Curi, U. (2003). 'La tragedia Moro, alla lettera'. Micromega, ottobre 2003, pp. 187–92.

De Bernardinis, F. (2001). *Nanni Moretti*. Milano: Il Castoro.

Debord, G. (1992). *Society of Spectacle*. London: Rebel Press.

De Gaetano, R. (2002). *La sincope dell'identità. Il cinema di Nanni Moretti*. Turin: Lindau.

Deleuze, G. (1986), *Cinema 1. The Movement-Image*, London, The Athlone Press.

Deleuze, G. (1989), *Cinema 2. The Time-Image*, London, The Athlone Press.

Deleuze, G. (1991). *Masochism*. New York: Zone Books.

Deleuze G. and Guattari F. (1983). *Anti-Oedipus. Capitalism and Schizophrenia*, Minneapolis: University of Minnesota Press.

Di Stefano, P. (1995). *Insopportabile Moretti*, 'Corriere della Sera', 7 August 1995, p. 23.

Duflot, J. (1993). *Il sogno del centauro*. Roma: Editori Riuniti.

Eagleton, T. (2003). *Figures of Dissent*. London: Verso.

Eco, U. (1968). *La struttura assente*. Milan: Bompiani.

Eisenstein, S. (1988). *Selected Works: Volume 1: Writings, 1922–34*. London: BFI; Bloomington and Indianapolis: Indiana University Press.

Fagioli, M. (1972). *Istinto di morte e conoscenza*. Rome: Nuove Edizioni Romane.

Feher Gurevich, J. ed. (1997). *Hysteria from Freud to Lacan: The Splendid Child of Psychoanalysis*. New York: The Other Press.

Fink, B. (1997), *The Lacanian Subject. Between Language and Jouissance*, Princeton, Princeton University Press.

Fofi, G. (2001a). 'Ma il suo minimalismo è irritante', *Il Messaggero*, 8 March 2001, p. 22.

Fofi. G. (2001b). 'Ecco perché Nanni Moretti non dice niente "di sinistra"', *Il Messaggero*, 24 May 2001, p. 21.

Foucault, M. (1977) *Discipline and Punish*. New York: Pantheon.

Foucault, M. (2003). *The Order of Things*. London and New York: Routledge.

Freud, S. (1961). *The Ego and the Id and other works, The Standard Edition 19*. London: Hogarth Press.

Freud, S. (1964). *Moses and Monotheism, The Standard Edition 23*. London: Hogarth Press.

Freud, S. (1973). *Notes on a case of obsessional neurosis. The Standard Edition 10*. London: Hogarth Press.

Freud, S. (1974). *The Ego and the Id*. London: The Hogarth Press.

Freud, S. (1997). *The Interpretation of Dreams*. Ware: Wordsworth Editions Ltd.

Garboli, C. (1969). *La stanza separata*. Milano, Mondadori.

Garroni, E. (1968). *Semiotica ed estetica*. Bari: Laterza.

Goldin, M. (1971). "Bertolucci on the *Conformist*". *Sight and Sound*, 40 (2).

Gordon, R. C. S. (2005). 'Real tanks and toy tanks: playing games with history in Roberto Benigni's La vita è bella/Life is Beautiful'. *Studies in European Cinema*, 2 (1).

Greene, N. (1994). *Pier Paolo Pasolini: Cinema as Heresy*. Princeton: Princeton University Press.

Heath, S. (1973). 'Film/Cinetext/Text'. *Screen*, 14 (1–2), pp. 102–27.

Heath, S. (1999). Cinema and Psychoanalysis: Parallel Histories. In Bergstrom, J. (ed), *Endless Night*. Berkeley, Los Angeles, London: University of California Press, 1999, pp. 25–56.

Hegel, G. W. F. (1962) *Lecturers on the Philosophy of Religion — together with a work on the proofs of the existence of God*. London: Routledge & Kegan Paul.

Hegel, G. W. F. (1977) *Phenomenology of Spirit*. Oxford: Clarendon Press.

Indiana, G. (2000). *Salò, or the 120 Days of Sodom*. London: BFI.

Jameson, F. (1990). *Late Marxism: Adorno, or, The Persistence of the Dialectic*. London & New York: Verso.

Jameson, F. (1992). *Signitures of the Visible*. New York & London: Routledge.

Jay, M. (1993). *Downcast Eyes: Denigration of Vision in Twentieth Century French Thought*. Berkeley: University of California Press.

Jefferson Kline, T. (1987). *Bertolucci's Dream Loom. A Psychoanalytic Study of Cinema*. Amherst: The University of Massachussetts Press).

Kant, I. (1914). *Critique of Judgement*. London: Macmillan.

Kant, I. (1996). *Critique of Pure Reason*. Indianapolis and Cambridge: Hackett Publishing Company.

Kant, I. (2003). *Kant on Swedenborg: Dreams of a Spirit-Seer*. West Chester, PA: The Swedenborg Foundation.

Kierkegaard, S. (1972). *Either/Or*. Princeton: Princeton University Press.

Kierkegaard, S. (2003). *Fear and Trembling*. London: Penguin Books.

Koch, G. (1993). 'Mimesis and Bilderverbot', *Screen* 34 (3), pp. 211–22.

Lacan, J. (1966). *Écrits*. Paris: Éditions du Seuil.

Lacan, J. (1975). 'R.S.I.'. *Ornicar?*, vol. 4, pp. 91–106.

Lacan, J. (1984) 'Comptes rendus d'enseignement 1964–1968', *Ornicar?*, vol. 29, pp. 7–25.

Lacan, J. (1988). *The Seminar. Book II. The Ego in Freud's Theory and in the Technique of Psychoanalysis, 1954–55*. New York: Norton; Cambridge: Cambridge University Press.

Lacan, J. (1989). *Écrits. A Selection*. London and New York: Routledge.

Lacan, J. (1991). *Le Séminaire. Livre XVII. L'envers de la psychanalyse, 1969–70*. Paris: Seuil.

Lacan, J. (1993). *The Seminar. Book III. The Psychoses, 1955–56*. London: Routledge.

Lacan, J. (1998a). *The Seminar. Book XI. The Four Fundamental Concepts of Psychoanalysis*. New York, London: W. W. Norton.

Lacan, J. (1998b). *The Seminar. Book XX. On Feminine Sexuality. The Limits of Love and Knowledge*. New York, London: W. W. Norton.

Lacan, J. (1999). *The Seminar. Book VII. The Ethics of Psychoanalysis*. London: Routledge.

Lacan, J. (2000). *The Seminar. Book III. The Psychoses*. London: Routledge.

Lacan, J. (2001a). *Le Séminaire. Livre VIII. Le transfert, 1960–61*. Paris: Seuil.

Lacan, J. (2001b). *Autres Écrits*. Paris: Seuil.

Laplanche, J. (1998). *Essays on Otherness*. Routledge: London.

Magrelli, E. (1977) *Con Pier Paolo Pasolini*. Roma: Bulzoni.

Marx, K. (1970). *Capital*, vol I. London: Lawrence and Wishart.

Metz, C. (1977). *The Imaginary Signifier. Psychoanalysis and the Cinema*. Bloomington: Indiana University Press.

Michelone, G. (1996). *Invito al cinema di Roberto Rossellini*. Milan: Mursia.

Miccichè, L. (1980). 'Antonioni visto da Antonioni', interview for RAI television.

Miller, J.-A. (1977). Suture (Elements of the Logic of the Signifier). *Screen*, vol. 18, n. 4.

Miller, J.-A. (2000). "On Semblances in the Relation Between the Sexes", in *Sexuation*, ed. Renata Salecl. Durham and London: Duke University Press. 3, pp. 13–27.

Moravia, Alberto (1961) 'Immagini al posto d'onore'. *L'Espresso*: 1 October 1961.

Muller and Richardson (eds.). 1988. *The Purloined Letter*. Baltimore and London: John Hopkins University Press.

Nietzsche, F. (1995). *Unfashionable Observations*. Stanford: Stanford University Press.

Nowell-Smith, G. (1961–2). 'La Notte'. *Sight &Sound* 31, pp. 28–31.

Nowell-Smith, G. (1963–4). 'Shape Around a Black Point'. *Sight & Sound* 33, pp. 16–20.

Nowell-Smith, G. (2000), 'North and South, East and West: Rossellini and Politics' in Forgacs, D. and S. Lutton, G. Nowell-Smith (eds), *Roberto Rossellini: Magician of the Real*, London, British Film Institute.

Oudart, J.-P. (2003). Cinema and Suture. In Žižek, S. (ed) *Jacques Lacan, Critical Evaluations in Cultural Theory*, vol. IV. London and New York: Routledge, pp. 10–22.

Pasolini, P. P. (1958). 'Il metodo di lavoro'. *Città aperta*: April-May 1958; reprinted in the appendix to the 1979 edition of the novel *Ragazzi di vita* (Einaudi: Torino, pp. 209–13).

Pasolini, P. P. (1960). 'Un pizzico di irrazionalità'. *Il Mondo Nuovo*, 18 December 1960

Pasolini, P. P. (1967). 'Ora tutto è chiaro, voluto, non imposto dal destino'. *Cineforum* 68, pp. 609–10.

Pasolini, P. P. (1968). *Teorema*. Milan: Garzanti.

Pasolini, Pier Paolo (1976). *Lettere luterane*. Turin: Einaudi.

Pasolini, P. P. (1984) *Selected poems* (translated from the Italian by Norman MacAfee and Luciano Martinengo; with a foreword by Enzo Siciliano). London: Calder.

Pasolini, P. P. (1987). *Lutheran Letters*. New York: Carcanet Press.

Pasolini, P.P. (1990). *Scritti corsari*. Milan: Garzanti.

Pasolini, P. P. (1993). *Bestemmia. Tutte le poesie*, Milan: Garzanti.

Pasolini, P. P. (1995). *Empirismo eretico*. Milan: Garzanti.

Pasolini, P.P. (1996). *Il film degli altri*. Parma: Guanda.

Pasolini, P. P. (1998) *Romanzi e racconti*. Milan: Mondadori (2 vols).

Pasolini, P. P. (2001) *Pasolini per il cinema*. Milan: Mondadori (2 vols).

Ragusa, O. (1976). *Narrative and Drama: essays in modern Italian literature from Verga to Pasolini*. The Hague: Mouton.

Ragland-Sullivan, E. and Bracher, M., eds. (1991). *Lacan and the Subject of Language*. New York and London: Routledge.

Rinaldi, R. (1982). *Pier Paolo Pasolini*. Milan: Mursia.

Rocchio, V. (1999). *Cinema of Anxiety: a Psychoanalysis of Italian Neorealism*. Austin. University of Texas Press.

Rondolino, G. (1981). *Luchino Visconti*. Turin: UTET.

Socci, S. (2003). *Bernardo Bertolucci*. Milano: Il Castoro Cinema.

Stack, O. (1969). *Pasolini on Pasolini*. London: Thames and Hudson.

Stavrakakis, Y. (1999). *Lacan and the Political*. London: Routledge.

Tinazzi, G. (1976). *Michelangelo Antonioni*. Firenze: La Nuova Italia.

Ungari, E. (1982). *Scene madri di Bernardo Bertolucci*. Milano: Ubulibri.

Viano, M. (1993). *A Certain Realism. Making use of Pasolini's film and practice*. Berkeley / Los Angeles / London: University of California Press.

Willemen, P. (1997). *Pier Paolo Pasolini*. London: BFI.

Žižek, S. (1992) *The Sublime Object of Ideology*. London: Verso.

Žižek, S. (1993). *Tarrying with the Negative*. Durham: Duke University Press.

Žižek, S. (1994). *The Metastases Of Enjoyment: Six Essays on Woman and Causality*. London: Verso.

Žižek, S. (1997). *The Plague of Fantasies*. London: Verso.

Žižek, S. (1998) 'Kant and Sade: The Ideal Couple' *Lacanian ink* 13, pp. 12–25.

Žižek, S. (2000a). *The Ticklish Subject*. London and New York: Verso.

Žižek, S. (2000b). *The Fragile Absolute*. London and New York: Verso.

Žižek, S. (2001a). *The Fright of Real Tears*. London: BFI.

Žižek, S. (2001b). *Enjoy Your Symptom*. London and New York: Routledge.

Žižek, S. (2001c). *Did Somebody Say Totalitarianism?* London and New York: Verso.

Žižek, S. (2001d). *On Belief*. London and New York: Routledge.

Žižek, S. (2002a). *Welcome to the Desert of the Real!*, London and New York, Verso.

Žižek, S. (2002b). *Revolution at the Gates*. London and New York: Verso.

Žižek, S. (2002c). *For They Know Not What They Do*. London and New York: Verso.

Žižek, S. (2003). *The Puppet and the Dwarf: The Perverse Core of Christianity*. Cambridge: Massachusetts; London: England.

Žižek, S. (2004a). *Organs Without Bodies: Deleuze and Consequences*. London: Routledge.

Žižek, S. (2004b). *Iraq: the Borrowed Kettle*. London and New York: Verso.

Zupančič, A. (2000). *Ethics of the Real*. London and New York: Verso.

INDEX OF NAMES